INDONESIA'S NEW ORDER

INDONESIA'S NEW ORDER

The Dynamics of Socio-economic Transformation

Edited by Hal Hill

UNIVERSITY OF HAWAII PRESS
Honolulu

Published in North America by
University of Hawaii Press
2840 Kolowalu Street,
Honolulu, Hawaii 96822

Published in Australia by
Allen & Unwin Pty Ltd
9 Atchison Street, St Leonards, NSW 2065

Printed in Malaysia by SRM Production Services Sdn Bhd

Library of Congress Cataloging-in-Publication Data:

Indonesia's new order: the dynamics of socio-economic transformation
  /Hal Hill, editor.
  p. cm.
  Includes bibliographical references and index.
  ISBN 0–8248–1660–9
  1. Indonesia—Politics and government—1966– 2. Indonesia—
  Economic conditions—1945– 3. Indonesia—Social conditions.
I. Hill, Hal, 1948– .
DS644.4.053 1994   94–7506
959.803—dc20   CIP

Contents

Contents

Tables

Tables

Figures

Notes on contributors

Patrick Guinness is Senior Lecturer in the Department of Sociology, La Trobe University, Melbourne. His research interests in Indonesia have included the social and cultural impact of industrialisation and urbanisation, and the implementation and impact of the *transmigrasi* program. His principal publications are *Harmony and Hierarchy in a Javanese Kampung* (Oxford University Press, Singapore, 1986) and *On the Margin of Capitalism: People and Development in Mukim Plentong, Johor Malaysia* (Oxford University Press, Singapore, 1992).

Joan Hardjono has a PhD in Geography from the University of New England, Armidale (Australia), and teaches at Padjadjaran State University, Bandung, West Java. She has lived in Indonesia since the late 1950s and has carried out extensive research in rural areas. She has written on a range of topics that include transmigration, education, rural development and environmental change in Indonesia. Her major publications include *Transmigration in Indonesia* (Oxford University Press, Singapore, 1977) and *Land, Labour and Livelihood in a West Java Village* (Gadjah Mada University Press, Yogyakarta, 1987).

Barbara Hatley is Senior Lecturer in the Department of Asian Languages and Studies at Monash University, where she teaches Indonesian literature and culture. Her major research interests are Indonesian theatre, traditional and modern, and gender issues in Indonesian literature and performing arts. Recent publications include 'Theatrical Imagery and Gender Ideology in Java' in J. Atkinson and S. Errington (eds), *Power and Difference: Gender in Island Southeast Asia* (Stanford University Press, Stanford, 1990), 'Contemporary Indonesian Theatre as Cultural Resistance' in A. Budiman (ed.), *State and Civil Society in Indonesia* (Monash Centre of Southeast Asian Studies, Monash University, 1991), and introduction and translation of the play 'Time Bomb' in N. Riantiarno, *Time Bomb and Cockroach Opera* (edited by John McGlynn) (Lontar Press, Jakarta, 1992).

Hal Hill is Senior Fellow in Economics, Research School of Pacific Studies, Australian National University (ANU). He is also head of the ANU's Indonesia Project, and editor of the *Bulletin of Indonesian Economic Studies*. His books include *Export-Oriented Industrialisation: The ASEAN Experience* (Allen & Unwin, Sydney, 1985; jointly with Mohamed Ariff), *Foreign Investment and Industrialisation in Indonesia* (Allen & Unwin, Sydney, 1988), and *Unity and Diversity: Regional Economic Development in Indonesia since 1970* (Oxford University Press, Singapore, 1989; editor and contributor). He has worked as a consultant for the Australian government, the Indonesian government, the World Bank, the Asian Development Bank, and several UN agencies.

Terence H. Hull is Senior Research Fellow in the Demography Program, Research School of Social Sciences, Australian National University. He has spent many years living and working in Indonesia. His research on fertility and family planning in Indonesia has included field work in villages of Yogyakarta, clinical studies in cities throughout the archipelago, statistical analysis of the family planning program, and investigation of the historical underpinnings of contemporary fertility decline. The results of this research have led him increasingly to examine the political context of demographic change, first in Indonesia, and, since 1983, in China, Vietnam and the Philippines.

Gavin W. Jones is Professor and Coordinator of the Demography Program, Research School of Social Sciences, Australian National University. He has spent five years working in Indonesia and for two decades has conducted research on marriage and fertility, urbanisation, labour force and education in Indonesia. He is co-author of *The Demographic Dimension in Indonesian Development* (Oxford University Press, Singapore, 1987). Other articles include 'Links between Urbanization and Sectoral Shifts in Employment in Java' (*Bulletin of Indonesian Economic Studies* 20(3), 1984), and (with Chris Manning) 'Labour Force and Employment during the 1980s' in Anne Booth (ed.), *The Oil Boom and After: Indonesian Economic Policy and Performance in the Soeharto Era* (Oxford University Press, Singapore, 1992).

Andrew MacIntyre is Senior Lecturer and Deputy Dean in the Faculty of Asian and International Studies at Griffith University in Brisbane. His current research interests are in the areas of comparative and international political economy, with a focus on Indonesia. His two major publications are *Business and Politics in Indonesia* (Allen & Unwin, Sydney, 1991) and a co-edited volume, *The Dynamics of Economic Policy Reform in Southeast Asia and the Southwest Pacific* (Oxford University Press, Singapore, 1992).

Jamie Mackie is Emeritus Professor in the Research School of Pacific Studies, Australian National University. His previous appointments include Foundation Professor in the Department of Political and Social Change, Research School of Pacific Studies, 1978–89, Research Director at the Centre for Southeast Asian Studies, Monash University, 1968–78, and Head of the Department of Indonesia Studies, University of Melbourne, 1958–67. He worked in the State Planning Bureau, Jakarta, 1956–58. His publications include *Konfrontasi: The Indonesia–Malaysia Dispute 1963–66* (Oxford University Press, Kuala Lumpur, 1973), and *The Chinese in Indonesia: Five Essays* (Nelson, Melbourne, 1976; editor and contributor).

Glossary

(Note: $ refers to US dollars.)

abangan: nominal Muslim

ABRI (Angkatan Bersenjata Republik Indonesia): armed forces

adat: custom, tradition

ADO (Alokasi Devisa Otomatis): Automatic Foreign Exchange Allocation, a scheme which linked provincial government receipts to regional exports

alang-alang (Imperata cyclindrica): grass which renders abandoned cleared land useless

aliran: grouping, school of thought

Aluk to dolo: the traditional religion of the Toraja of South Sulawesi

arisan: rotating credit organisations

ASEAN: the Association of Southeast Asian Nations

awig-awig: regulations

azas tunggal: unifying principle

Bakorstanas (Badan Koordinasi Stabilitas Nasional): the National Stability Coordinating Board; replaced Kopkamtib in September 1988, with a broader emphasis on the economic sphere

banjar: an ethnic group located mainly in coastal Kalimantan; in Bali the term refers to a community organisation

bapak: father, sir

Bapak Pembangunan: 'Father of Development', a title frequently attached to President Soeharto

Bapedal (Badan Pengendalian Dampak Lingkungan): Environmental Impact Management Agency

Glossary

Bappeda (*Badan Perencanaan Pembangunan Daerah*): Regional Planning Agency

Bappenas (*Badan Perencanaan Pembangunan Nasional*): National Planning Agency

becak: pedicab, tricycle

beras: milled rice

Bhinneka Tunggal Ika: Indonesia's motto, 'Unity in Diversity'

Bimas (*Bimbingan Massal*): the government's former agricultural extension package

BKKBN (*Badan Koordinasi Keluarga Berencana Nasional*): National Family Planning Coordinating Board

BPS (*Biro Pusat Statistik*): Central Bureau of Statistics

Bulog (*Badan Urusan Logistik*): the government's food procurement agency

cukong: Chinese businessmen, often in partnership with senior military officers or bureaucrats

daerah: region

desa: village

Dharma Wanita: an official association of wives of civil servants

DPR (*Dewan Perwakilan Rakyat*): parliament

Dulog: regional offices of Bulog

dusun: village far from urban areas

dwifungsi: dual function, of the armed forces

eka dasa rudra: rituals modelled on pre-colonial royal rituals

ENSO: *El Niño* Southern Oscillation

FAO: Food and Agricultural Organisation

gaplek: dried cassava chips

GBHN (*Garis-garis Besar Haluan Negara*): broad outline of national policy

Gestapu (*Gerakan Tigapuluh September*): 30 September Movement, associated with the attempted 1965 coup

gotong royong: mutual assistance

hak guna usaha: usage rights

Hari Korban: 'Day of Sacrifice'

Hari Raya Idul Fitri: the end of the Muslim fasting month

HTI (*Hutan Tanaman Industri*): commercial forestry

HYV: high-yielding varieties (of food crops)

IAIN (*Institut Agama Islam Negeri*): Islamic educational institution

IGGI: Inter-Governmental Group on Indonesia, the club of aid donors, formally disbanded in March 1992

Inpres (*Instruksi Presiden*): Presidential Instruction, a program of special grants from the central government

Inpres Penghijauan: Presidential Instructions on Regreening

Intam (*Intensifikasi Tambak*): program to raise shrimp production

IPPA: Indonesian Planned Parenthood Association

IPPF: International Planned Parenthood Federation
kabupaten: regency, administrative unit below the province
kampung: urban community or neighbourhood
kebatinan: (mystical) Javanese religious practices
kecamatan: subdistrict, administrative unit below the *kabupaten*
kedokan: sharecropping
kejawen: mysticism associated with the Javanese view of the world
KB (*keluarga berencana*): family planning
kelurahan: village administrative unit below the *kecamatan*
kepala desa: village head
keterbukaan: openness, referring mainly to the political sphere
kethoprak: professional troupe performing regional popular theatre
Kopkamtib (*Komando Pemulihan Keamanan dan Ketertiban*): Law and
    Order Restoration Command
Koran Masuk Desa: campaigns for newspapers to reach villages
Korpri (*Korps Pegawai Republik Indonesia*): civil servants' professional
    body
kromo: high Javanese speech used to denote respect towards one's elders,
    those of noble birth or of official standing
lenong: local Jakarta folk theatre
LKBN (*Lembaga Keluarga Berencana Nasional*): Family Planning Institute,
    formed in 1968
LKMD: advisory council of village elite
ludruk: professional troupe performing regional popular theatre
lurah: village head
Majelis Perwakilan Rakyat: Supreme Advisory Council
marga: district
mdundang binnia: fertility ritual only held after a series of crop failures
MPR (*Majelis Perwakilan Rakyat*): Supreme Advisory Council, meets every
    five years to elect the president and vice-president
Muhammadiyah: a Muslim educational movement
musyawarah: discussion, deliberation among all household heads before
    community decisions are made
Nahdatul Ulama (*NU*): Muslim organisation
negeri: state
NGO: non-government organisation
NIE: newly industrialising economy
NODR: non-oil domestic revenue
NRR: net reproduction rate
NTB: non-tariff barrier
OPM (*Organisasi Papua Merdeka*): Free Papua Movement
Panca Wali Krama: island-wide rituals modelled on pre-colonial royal rituals
    that legitimised, even created, the power of the ruler

Pamong Praja: local civil service

palawija: secondary food crops, including dry rice, maize, sweet potatoes, soybeans, peanuts and mung beans

Pancasila: five political philosophical principles that constitute the official national ideology

pasang-surut: tidal rice growing

pasar: market

pasirah: village chief

pembangunan: development

pemerataan: equity

pesantren: education involving both Islamic and secular subjects

Petisi 50: Petition of 50, a group of retired senior ABRI officers critical of the government

PDI (Partai Demokrasi Indonesia): Indonesian Democratic Party, an amalgam of nationalist and Christian parties

penghijauan: regreening

peranakan: ethnic Chinese who are more integrated into Indonesian society

Pertamina: the state-owned oil company

PIR (Perusahaan Inti Rakyat): Nucleus Estate Scheme, a program to assist smallholder cash-crop farmers

PKI (Partai Komunis Indonesia): Indonesian Communist Party

PKK (Pembinaan Kesejahteraan Keluarga): Family Welfare Movement

PNI (Partai Nasional Indonesia): Indonesian Nationalist Party

PPP (Partai Persatuan Pembangunan): Muslim-based political party

pribumi: indigenous Indonesian

priyayi: aristocratic or senior Javanese official

Prokasih (Program Kali Bersih): Clean River Program for urban rivers

PRPTE (Peremajaan Rehabilitasi dan Perluasan Tanaman Ekspor): Program for Rejuvenation, Rehabilitation and Expansion of Export Crops

pungli (pungutan liar): illegal payments, bribes

pusako: matrilineally inherited land

rantu: journey outside or overseas

Reboisasi: program of reforestation

Repelita (Rencana Pembangunan Lima Tahun): Five-Year Development Plan

rukun: harmony

Rukun Kampung: mutual assistance association in the village

Rukun Warga: local neighbourhood group

Sakernas (Survei Angkatan Kerja Nasional): National Labour Force Survey

santri: devout Muslims

sarak opat: the four elements which identified the political and territorial entity of the village community

sawah: wet rice

stabilitas: stability

suku terasing: shifting cultivators
sumbangan: exchange system, where exchange partners contribute cash and food at rites of passage
Susenas (*Survei Sosio-Ekonomi Nasional*): National Socio-Economic Survey
swasta: private enterprise
tambak: brackish-water ponds
tanah kritis: land undergoing erosion, in a 'critical' state
tanah negara: land not privately owned or classed as state forest
tayuban: traditional dance
Teater Remaja: yearly festivals of youth theatre
tennosei: (emperor) system in Meiji Japan
TIM (Taman Ismail Marzuki): arts complex in Jakarta
TFR: total fertility rate
TOTOK: ethnic Chinese less integrated in Indonesian society, in contrast to *peranakan*
TPI (Tebangan Pilihan Indonesia): selective cutting policy for forestry based on a thirty-five-year cycle
TRI (Tebu Rakyat Intensifikasi): smallholder cane intensification program
tumpangsari: system of intercropping
UNDP: United Nations Development Program
USAID: United States Agency for International Development
wereng: a brown plant-hopper pest (*Nilaparvans lugens*)
WNI (Warga Negara Indonesia): Indonesian citizen, but applied only to Chinese and certain others of 'foreign' origin
yayasan: foundation

Preface

The last quarter-century has been a period of extraordinarily rapid change in Indonesia. The Indonesia of the early 1990s is virtually unrecognisable from that of the mid-1960s. Since 1966 its economy has expanded by almost 500 per cent and its population by about 75 per cent. Its people are better fed, educated, and clothed than ever before. The incidence of poverty has declined significantly. For each 1000 live births, the number of babies who die before their first birthday has approximately halved. The nation is now able to feed itself. It is set to join the ranks of Asia's 'dragon economies', and industrial output now exceeds that of agriculture. The country is an economic entity for the first time in its history, as the revolution in transport and communications has unified previously disparate and isolated regions. In the mid-1960s Indonesia had begun to disengage from the international community. Now it is deeply enmeshed in global and regional politics and commerce.

Yet, notwithstanding these successes, the country faces daunting challenges in the 1990s and beyond. The record of poverty alleviation has been good, but the official poverty line is an extremely modest one, and there is a perception that the benefits of growth have been unevenly distributed. Fertility has declined substantially, but so too has mortality, with the result that population growth has yet to slow appreciably, and each year there are some 2.5 million new work force entrants. Education enrolment ratios have risen sharply and near universal primary school attendance has been achieved. But there is a great challenge to improve quality and to intensify efforts at the tertiary and vocational levels. There are moves towards openness, but the country still has a heavily-managed political system. The government has emphasised a unified strategy of national development in which the reach of the Jakarta government extends to the most distant and isolated areas, but there remain regions of disaffection. Indonesia's modes of artistic expression are fascinating and diverse, modern and traditional; yet the artistic community still chafes under restriction and censorship. Environmental challenges are immense, both in the areas of natural resource management and in the quality of urban amenities.

The purpose of this book is to provide an overview and analysis of Indonesia over the past quarter-century, covering all major facets of contemporary society, economy and politics. The lament of the past that the English-language literature on the country is superficial and thin clearly no longer applies. Over the past decade, for example, major volumes have been published on Indonesia's economy, ecology and demography, together with many specialist books. However, surprising as it may seem, there has not been a general book on the country since Ruth McVey's edited collection (*Indonesia*, HRAF Press, New Haven) published in 1963.

This volume has attempted to fill this gap. We have sought moreover to write in a style which is not excessively technical. In the process, we hope this book will be accessible and of interest to a wide audience. The first group we have in mind are Indonesian and Southeast Asian specialists who wish to have a 'compendium' at their fingertips, especially one which covers disciplines other than their own. Second, and related to the first, we hope that the book will be relevant as a text for courses in Indonesian and Southeast Asian studies. Another group for whom we have attempted to write is other area specialists who seek such a volume for the purposes of comparative analysis. Finally, there is a general readership which may find this volume of interest, including journalists, diplomats, business people and others who wish to obtain a general acquaintance with Indonesia.

The ultimate test of this volume will be its reception in Indonesia. Each of us has had long contact with the country. We have all been enriched immensely by that contact, both personally and professionally. If Indonesians regard this book positively, as a scholarly yet sympathetic analysis of their country's development since the mid-1960s, we will be well satisfied. Unfortunately, English-language publications do not enjoy wide circulation in the country, for reasons of both price and limited foreign-language reading skills. To remedy this shortcoming, it is our intention to produce a local *bahasa* Indonesia version of this book as soon as possible.

This book originated from a week-long conference entitled 'Indonesia's New Order: Past, Present and Future', which was held at the Australian National University in December 1989. Some forty academics and officials, mainly from Indonesia and Australia, presented papers to the conference, which was organised into panels. The major chapters of this book reflect

Preface

this organisation. The convenors of the conference then set about writing this volume, drawing on the conference presentations to some extent, but essentially writing independent essays assessing the past 25 years from their own perspective.

A project of this size has incurred many debts, and it is a pleasure to thank the people and institutions whose good work made the final product possible.

The conference was generously supported by the following bodies, which facilitated an exceptionally strong Indonesian presence in Canberra: the Ford Foundation, the Australia Indonesia Institute, the Australian Department of Foreign Affairs and Trade (through its grant to the Indonesia Project of the Australian National University), the Australian International Development Assistance Bureau (through its International Seminar Support Scheme), and the Research School of Pacific Studies at the Australian National University.

Many people contributed to the organisation of the conference. We wish to thank, in particular, Alex Bellis, Liz Drysdale and Lynn Parker for their exceptional efforts. We also wish to thank two of the session convenors who could not ultimately contribute to this volume, James J. Fox and Virginia Hooker.

Preparation of individual chapters benefited from the comments of many people, and we acknowledge their assistance in the relevant chapters. In addition, we owe a collective debt to the international panel of referees who assessed and commented most constructively on final drafts prior to publication: R. William Liddle, Ohio State University (politics); Bruce Glassburner, University of California, Davis (economics); Geoff McNicoll, Australian National University (demography); H.G. Brookfield, Australian National University (ecology and environment); R. Anderson Sutton, University of Wisconsin, Madison (culture and arts); and Greg Acciaioli, University of Western Australia (village social change).

The task of producing a final edited manuscript was rendered infinitely more enjoyable thanks to the enthusiasm and professionalism of Gary Anson, who assumed major responsibility for editorial production, and of Carolyn Dalton, who undertook the arduous task of converting sometimes messy, edited drafts into the final polished manuscript. John Maxwell kindly prepared the index.

Hal Hill
Canberra
March 1993

Introduction

Hal Hill and Jamie Mackie

Few governments have aroused as much controversy or such conflicting assessments in recent years as President Soeharto's 'New Order' regime in Indonesia. Economists have praised its achievements in transforming the chaos of 1965–66 into steady socio-economic growth, resulting in a broadly-based rise in living standards by the 1980s. Others have been impressed by the regime's outstandingly successful family planning program, by the rapid spread of basic education, and by Indonesia's contribution to regional stability through its key role in ASEAN. Yet observers of the political system have generally been far more ambivalent, acknowledging the benefits brought to the country by a strong and stable government, backed ultimately by the armed forces (ABRI), but linking these with the various repressive and authoritarian aspects of the regime, including its poor record on civil liberties.

Whereas economists, demographers and agriculturalists have mostly depicted the New Order's record in a favourable light, writings by other social scientists have taken a more negative view, a few of them offering extremely harsh and hostile assessments. The regime has been characterised as a 'showcase state' propped up by foreign capital, and its record described as the 'Indonesian tragedy'. Much of the criticism focuses on the infringement of civil liberties of former communist party (PKI) opponents of the regime. The birth of the New Order in 1965–66 saw one of the most terrible bloodbaths in the second half of the twentieth century, with several hundred thousand people losing their lives. The incorporation of East Timor in 1975 and continuing unrest there, culminating in the Dili massacre of late 1991, have badly tarnished Indonesia's international reputation. The heavy-handedness of the military, restrictions on freedom of association, and tight controls over press and free speech continue to attract criticism.

More generally, the pattern of socio-economic development pursued by the Soeharto regime has aroused antipathy in many quarters, both within Indonesia as well as overseas. The country has become unambiguously more capitalist, more integrated into the international economy, allowing markets to operate more freely, and has generated the accumulation of private wealth on an ever grander scale.

The contributors to this volume view these developments through a diverse array of analytical prisms. The approaches taken have been shaped by the subject matter and by each author's disciplinary background. Thus the chapter on culture and the arts (chapter 5) reflects the dismay felt by Indonesian writers and artists at the restrictions on literary expression. Conversely, the economics chapter (chapter 2) is coloured by the optimism engendered by the country's rapid economic growth, and especially by the dramatic expansion of manufactured exports since the mid-1980s. There has been no attempt in this book to create a consensus or deliberately strike a balance in our views or approaches to Indonesia, although we have tried to ensure that both sides of the picture have been presented. Each author has attempted to give a scholarly and dispassionate account, raising different questions and employing different analytical constructs. It is in the nature of intellectual enquiry, and of the various yardsticks of 'development' used by different disciplines and schools of thought, that there be such diversity of opinion, and so it is in the pages that follow.

Nevertheless, there are common themes running through virtually all the chapters, and it is useful to highlight these at the outset. At the risk of oversimplification, four themes seem to be particularly important:

1 'the setting'—the chaotic situation in 1965 and gradual consolidation of a social order which is now generally accepted;
2 rapid changes since then in all spheres—social, cultural, economic, and even political;
3 the constant theme of 'unity and diversity'—trends towards national integration, alongside continuing regional diversity and the conflicting pulls of regional and national identity; and
4 the New Order as a distinctive institution—the patterns and processes of institutional development, especially in its political and cultural dimensions.

The setting

All chapters draw a sharp distinction between the situations in the mid-1960s and of 25 years later. The Indonesia of the early 1990s is in many respects almost unrecognisable from that of the mid-1960s. At that time, the country's political structure was deeply fissured and under intense strain. The economy was in chaos, with inflation headed towards 1000 per cent, while its central government was unable to maintain even the most minimal standard of administrative services. Indonesia was widely regarded as an economic 'basket case', poorer even than other South Asian countries. There had been little private sector investment since the 1930s, and the process of industrialisation had barely commenced. The central government's authority over the main islands, which produced the bulk of Indonesia's export earnings, was disintegrating as they increasingly flouted Jakarta's unenforceable and unrealistic regulatory controls. Transport and communications systems were breaking down.

Under Sukarno Indonesia's relations with its neighbours were tense and uneasy as he drew the country into 'konfrontasi' with Malaysia in 1963–65, antagonism towards Britain and the United States, closer association with China, and withdrawal from the United Nations. The steady progress in education and health improvement during the early years of independence was reversed by the economic decline of the 1960s. Nutritional standards were at best constant, but in many regions declining; the people were exhorted to eat maize in the face of growing rice shortages. The political and cultural tolerance and efflorescence of the 1950s had given way to an environment of increasing control, politicisation, and suspicion of political enemies.

Ecological issues were rarely the subject of critical attention. But Java was frequently portrayed in neo-Malthusian terms, as 'asphyxiating for want of land', as a case study in gloomy 'economic arithmetic', and most commonly, as experiencing 'agricultural involution'. Socio-economic stagnation had its counterpart in demographic trends for levels of both fertility and mortality were high. Sukarno's disapproval of family planning ensured the maintenance of high fertility, while the decline in food supplies and the deterioration of the public health system resulted in high death rates.

Rapid change: mid-1960s to the early 1990s

The change in regime in 1966 marked a watershed in Indonesian history by almost any measure. Such a dramatic reversal in the course of national development has had few parallels among newly-independent societies in this century. Intense political instability, bordering on civil war, has given way to an almost bland uniformity and monotony. The drama and flamboyance of the Sukarno era has been replaced by the low-key and pragmatic Soeharto administration. The economy has been transformed by effective economic management and the ability to take advantage of a benign international environment. The size of the economy (that is, real gross domestic product) has expanded by over 450 per cent. Indonesia has experienced its first period of sustained economic growth, which, while it may not have matched the very high growth rates of the Asian 'tigers', has been one of the best of all third world countries.

The pace of socio-economic change is revealed by a few basic statistics. Rice yields have almost doubled, and Indonesia has been broadly self-sufficient in rice since 1985. Production of most food crops has increased substantially, but structural change in the economy has meant that agriculture's share of GDP has fallen from 50 per cent to 19 per cent. By 1991, the value of manufacturing output exceeded that of agriculture for the first time, indicating that Indonesia had crossed a key threshold in the path to industrialisation. Over this period manufactures rose from a negligible proportion of merchandise exports to over 40 per cent in 1991, with most of the increase occurring in 1984–91. A 'transport revolution' occurred in the 1970s as the ubiquitous 'colts' (light commercial vehicles) came into use throughout the country. The number of registered motorcycles, buses and commercial vehicles has risen twentyfold since the 1960s.

Socially, the break with the past has been equally dramatic. A sizeable urban middle class, numbering perhaps fifteen million people, has emerged for the first time in the nation's history. Urban Indonesia is becoming a mass consumption society. The chronic shortages and the traditional *pasar* (markets) of earlier times are giving way in the major towns to proliferating shopping malls full of a vast array of merchandise (often far beyond the reach of most Indonesians). Yet while the poor have also become undeniably better off, wealth is now displayed ostentatiously at the very top income levels to an unparalleled extent. Private capital has been accumulated as never before. During the 1980s vast private commercial conglomerates emerged, many owned by Sino-Indonesians, all possessing high-level political connections. The international connections of these enterprises have undoubtedly tipped the balance of power between the state apparatus and these private actors in the latter's favour. Whereas they had been crucially dependent on state largesse and patronage for commercial success in the 1970s, by the late 1980s the private sector had achieved very considerable autonomy.

Socio-economic change in rural areas has been equally striking. Technological change in the food crop sector has been particularly rapid, principally in the adoption of high-yielding varieties, and the commercialisation of agriculture generally. The number of landless villagers has certainly risen, and a new class of 'middle-sized farmers' has emerged, exercising considerable control over the most desirable village land and other resources (such as access to credit). On the other hand, minuscule land holdings still exist and the gloomy prognostications of the earlier literature on the green revolution, which predicted increasing polarisation and immiseration, have not eventuated. On Java, at least, increased off-farm rural employment opportunities have contributed significantly to rising living standards. Circular migration, commuting to fringe-urban employment, permanent relocation off Java, and declining birth rates have also assisted in averting the Malthusian scenario.

Commercialisation in other agricultural sectors has also proceeded rapidly, although in some instances the benefits to national welfare are debatable. The most remarkable transformation has occurred in the timber industry, where concessions have conferred immense fortunes on a favoured few. As a corollary, however, environmental management and fiscal supervision have been lax. In the past decade, large-scale private capital has begun to flow into the cash crop sector for the first time since the 1930s. Large agri-business enterprises are now found throughout the archipelago, even in the hitherto neglected eastern provinces.

The communications revolution and a rising middle class have also transformed the cultural life of Indonesia's cities. The bookshops and sidewalk stalls now teem with a proliferation of glossy, high-quality magazines. Titles like *Femina, Eksekutif, Prospek, Warta Ekonomi*, together with the well-established and best-known, *Tempo*, convey the flavour of both their contents and their clientele. The state television monopoly has been broken by more lively 'private sector' competitors (if that is the appropriate term for its privileged licence holders). Nor are these developments confined to the major cities. The new commercial culture has penetrated the countryside (*masuk desa*) thanks to satellites, rural electrification and improved distribution networks. While the state television network offers a bland diet of programs with a strong emphasis on 'national development', and artistic endeavours are still heavily controlled, the censor's black ink is no match for a fax machine; and yesterday's struggling artists have sometimes become the adopted favourites of the modern new rich. Moreover, increasing national wealth has often created new markets for traditional art forms rather than precipitated their demise. For example, the government now has the resources to sponsor traditional dance troupes, which are also becoming a popular tourist attraction.

The demographic transformation has been equally far-reaching. Indonesia has advanced quickly along the path of worldwide demographic transition from high to low levels of mortality and fertility. There is concern that the country's population growth rate has not yet fallen appreciably, but the absence of such a decline reflects fundamentally the sharp fall in mortality levels since the 1960s. Family planning has unquestionably been one of the regime's greatest success stories, initially in Central and East Java, Bali and North Sulawesi, but now virtually throughout the country. The short-term effects may appear unspectacular. But if we compare the population of 180 million in 1990 with the high or even medium projections computed twenty to thirty years ago we see that there are now perhaps fifty million fewer Indonesians than might have been the case in the absence of rapid socio-economic development and a vigorous family planning program. It is now possible to foresee what a generation ago would have been unthinkable: that Indonesia will probably achieve zero population growth in the next sixty to eighty years. Meanwhile, labour force growth is also slowing down, although with delayed effect, so that by the end of this decade the issue of employment generation will become one of quality much more than simply quantity.

Regional diversity

Indonesia is an extraordinarily diverse country in its ecology, economy, demography, social structures and culture. All contributors to this volume highlight this diversity, while also emphasising the changing nature of regional identities and relations with the centre. Some of the powerful centralising and integrating factors have already been mentioned. From the late 1960s until the mid-1980s the Jakarta government had hitherto undreamt-of financial resources at its disposal, as aid funds and oil revenues flowed in. With these resources, and facilitated by the revolution in communications and light commercial transport, the central government embarked on a massive infrastructure program which was able to integrate the country as never before.

Signs of national integration are observable everywhere. Buses ply the roads of Java advertising far-off destinations such as Banda Aceh, on the northern tip of Sumatra. It is now possible to reach any provincial capital by air from Jakarta within hours. Shipping services have expanded, even to the remote eastern regions. Incredible as it may seem, fishermen throughout the archipelago now use facsimile services in the course of their business. National television services penetrate distant and inaccessible villages.

These developments are having a profound impact on national and regional identities. Goods and people are flowing ever more quickly across provincial boundaries. The factories around Jakarta and Surabaya now target the national market, supplying everything from cooking oil to jeans to villages thousands of kilometres away, pushing aside smaller regional enterprises in the process. Regional disparities in prices and real wages—though perhaps not income levels—are almost certainly declining as a result. Distinctive regional cultures are also being threatened by these developments, although in some cases they are displaying surprising resilience. Indeed, national forms of cultural expression are increasingly taking on hybrid forms, incorporating various regional components.

If there is still a pronounced regional divide, it is now more between the country's east and west than the older dichotomy of Java and the outer islands. Allegations of 'Javanese imperialism' are still heard in some quarters, although less than before. They were heard frequently in the years after Jakarta crushed the regional rebellions in 1957–58, and later, at the height of the oil boom, when four provinces outside Java generated almost 75 per cent of the country's export earnings. But the stereotype is now becoming flawed, if indeed it ever was accurate. As the manufacturing boom gathers momentum, Java is regaining the position it held in the colonial era of being the country's pre-eminent foreign exchange earner. Moreover, Java's factories are providing the major increment to employment expansion, and its cities are the location of newly-emerging high value-added service activities. If one includes Bali in the equation, 'inner Indonesia' is also generating most of the revenue from the country's other major new export growth industry, tourism.

The most serious and widely discussed regional division is now between the increasingly prosperous and dynamic western part of the country (mainly Java, Bali and Sumatra, but including parts of Kalimantan) and the lagging east. Incomes in the latter region have traditionally been lower, and the society more heavily agrarian. During the 1970s the east–west divide was less pronounced because the central government had the resources to promote economic development throughout the country. As a result, the government sector loomed large in the poorer eastern economies. But with the end of the oil boom, government largesse dried up, and it was Java in particular which displayed a capacity for autonomous growth following the major policy reforms of the 1980s. If in the 1960s researchers found despair and poverty in parts of Central and East Java, in the 1990s they are more likely to find it in Timor, Flores or rural Irian Jaya.

The 'institutionalisation' of the New Order

Symbols, institutions and 'order' have been an important part of the New Order's 'nation-building' process. Five-year plans have dominated bureaucratic horizons and work schedules. Major presidential addresses, such as those on the eve of 17 August to commemorate independence and in early January for the budget, are important fixtures in the nation's political and bureaucratic life. For civil servants, a variety of seemingly ritualistic behaviour has become firmly entrenched: Monday morning parades, the wearing of Korpri (*Korps Pegawai Republik Indonesia*, the Indonesian Civil Service) uniforms, and the requirement that wives of senior officials participate in *Dharma Wanita* social activities. The civil service stretches throughout the country, from national to provincial levels and to the sub-tiers of governance.

The electoral process has also taken on a somewhat ritualistic character. The processes of election and appointment which lead up to the sitting of the People's Consultative Assembly (*Majelis Perwakilan Rakyat*) once every five years, to elect the president and vice-president, provide one example. The parliamentary elections are heavily managed and largely predictable in their outcome; only during the one month of election campaigning is vigorous political proselytising allowed, and only within officially sanctioned bounds. The president and his entourage make almost daily appearances in the nation's print and electronic media. Such occasions are always an opportunity to reinforce the government's rhetorical commitment to its trilogy of development (*pembangunan*), equity (*pemerataan*) and stability (*stabilitas*).

All this is far removed from the political ferment of the Sukarno era, especially in the later years. As economic decline accelerated, there was constant uncertainty about the direction of government. The style of the two presidents could hardly be more different—one volatile, unpredictable, charismatic; the other calm, pragmatic and reassuring, with an almost bland public image, and with a much more impressive record of development achievements. In the late Sukarno period, public administration all but collapsed, and only the army possessed a truly effective and nationwide command structure. But during the Soeharto era an effective and powerful civilian bureaucracy has evolved, not just at the national level but also among the lower tiers. Provinces and *kabupaten* (regencies) have their five-year plan documents and their sectoral and program targets. Although heavily 'top-down' in nature, the country's administrative system is slowly moving towards a measure of devolution and decentralisation.

Are these institutional patterns durable? Will they survive into the post-Soeharto era? Only time will tell. But most of the authors of this volume are inclined to believe that these institutions are likely to survive the most ardent attempts at reform.

While these differences in institutional structures and forms from the Old Order stand out, it is important not to lose sight of the continuities. For all the emphasis on smoothly functioning and effective administrative systems, the law and legal institutions are not yet strongly entrenched as a source of protection for the rights of ordinary people. The judiciary has not yet evolved into an independent and vigorous authority. Individuals are still subject to arbitrary incursions by the bureaucracy and the military. The legal system is brittle and unpredictable, and legal codification has proceeded little since the colonial era. Corruption, both petty and extravagant, is still rampant, in spite of the efforts to curb it by many honest public officials, and the vigilance of the press. For all the talk of *keterbukaan*, the Indonesian equivalent of *glasnost*, progress towards an open society and a transparent and accountable government is slow and erratic. While notions of an 'army-controlled regime' are grossly oversimplified, and civilian control at all levels of government is steadily expanding, the notion of the armed forces' *dwifungsi* (dual function) is tacitly accepted by all influential forces in society. There may be uncertainty about the nature of a post-Soeharto Indonesia, but there is no doubt that the army will have a large say in shaping that outcome.

These, then, are some of the key themes which run through the chapters that follow.

In their chapter on the politics of the New Order (Chapter 1), Jamie Mackie and Andrew McIntyre note the far-reaching and profound ramifications of the tragic events of 1965–66: 'Many of the best and worst features of the New Order political system can be traced back to the traumatic and bloody upheavals of those years'. In their discussion of political and administrative developments, two interrelated themes are dominant. These are the growing strength of the state, immeasurably more powerful than that of the pre-1965 period, and the immense personal authority of President Soeharto. In nearly all important respects his word is decisive. Yet he remains an enigma. His recent autobiography and various writings about him have done little to lift the veil.

After a brief survey of the various approaches adopted in the analysis of the New Order, Mackie and McIntyre provide a narrative account of the evolution of the New Order's power structure through three principal phases. Its early years, 1966–74, were a time of considerable fluidity. Following the abortive coup, the political balance was precarious and political freedom flourished (except for communists and their sympathisers). However, as Soeharto gradually exerted his authority, and *Golkar* emerged as an effective mechanism for winning the 1971 General Elections, political control tightened. A second period, 1974–82, described as a 'narrowing of the political base', was ushered in by the political protests of early 1974. Political parties were emasculated and press and campus freedom restricted.

The power of the state was immensely strengthened by the greatly increased oil revenues that became available in the second half of the 1970s, but President Soeharto's personal authority remained shaky for other reasons for several years. However, by the early 1980s he and his regime had successfully weathered these challenges and in the third phase, from 1984 onwards, Soeharto is seen as being in 'supreme control'. He even began to distance himself a little from the armed forces, courted Islamic and populist support, and implemented the economic reforms which enabled the economy to recover quickly from the precipitous decline in oil prices in the mid-1980s.

In Chapter 2, Hal Hill assesses the economic record as a 'qualified success story'. He contrasts the sense of despair, even desperation, in the mid-1960s with the recovery that soon followed. In 1965–66 inflation was out of control, production was declining and social indicators were deteriorating. Over the next two decades, Indonesia achieved remarkable improvements in rice production, macroeconomic stabilisation, family planning, poverty alleviation and structural adjustment. For the first time in the nation's history, Indonesia has experienced a quarter-century of sustained economic growth, resulting in a trebling of per capita GDP. Structural change has been equally rapid over this period, with the share of agriculture now less than 40 per cent of that in 1965 and manufacturing's share rising some 250 per cent. By 1991 Indonesia had passed two significant 'turning points' in the long sweep of economic development: manufacturing output exceeded that of agriculture, and manufacturing products (broadly defined) accounted for more than half of merchandise exports.

Notwithstanding this very creditable record, Indonesia still faces many daunting economic problems, and it is easy to point to instances where policy outcomes could have been better. The regime has been expert, first and foremost, at 'crisis management'—during the most difficult periods of 1965–66 (facing economic collapse and runaway inflation), 1975–76 (the Pertamina debacle), and 1985–86 (the halving of oil prices), the policy response has been swift and effective; in the first and last periods the government's action has been especially noteworthy. However, during periods of economic success, notably the oil boom period of 1973–83, the political will to enact tough reforms has been a lot weaker.

Hill identifies four principal episodes in economic policy and development. The first, between 1966 and 1970, centred on rehabilitation and recovery, and was characterised by macroeconomic stabilisation and the resumption of economic growth. This was followed by a period of rapid growth, between 1971 and 1981, dominated by the massive windfall revenue gains from oil. Next came the period of adjustment to lower oil prices, in 1982–86, when the economic policy environment lacked coherence. Macroeconomic and exchange rate management was generally tight and effective, but in the microeconomic domain there was a continuation of the trend towards costly intervention and regulation. This pattern was decisively reversed only in the final period, from 1986, when a number of bold reforms ushered in rapid growth, for the first time led by non-oil exports and the private sector.

In the first part of Chapter 3, Terence Hull relates Indonesia's tremendous geographic, cultural and ethnic diversity to population and fertility patterns. He contrasts Sukarno's extravagant assertion in the early 1960s that Indonesia could support double or treble its population (ironically, of course, a prediction which will certainly eventuate), with firm commitment of the Soeharto regime to fertility control. This policy has proved successful, with Indonesia's total fertility rate being almost halved through the New Order period, featuring especially marked declines in Java, Bali and North Sumatra.

Hull looks for an explanation of this transformation in terms of policies, certain individuals, changing community attitudes, and the role of external donors. As regards implementation, he points to the National Family Planning Coordinating Board (BKKBN) which, in spite of a certain amount of bureaucratic jealousy and jostling, has developed imaginative and comprehensive programs. Yet because mortality rates are also falling—another of the regime's important achievements—population growth has not yet slackened appreciably. But lower fertility is having a major impact: Indonesia's population at the turn of the century may be as 'little' as 208 million people, compared to projections in 1961, which assumed no fertility decline, of 280 million.

The labour force and education situation, analysed in the second part of Chapter 3 by Gavin Jones, is intimately related to these demographic developments. The labour force has changed significantly during the 1970s and 1980s, approximately doubling in size, and becoming less Java-centric, less concentrated in primary industries, less rural, less masculine, and much better educated. The 1980s was the last decade when the aggregate population was relatively unaffected by falling fertility; the rate of labour force expansion will slow markedly in the 1990s and beyond: 'By the first decade of the next century, growth of the working age population will cease to be a major problem in itself'.

Equally profound changes are observed in the case of education. There is now virtually universal primary school attendance, soon to be expanded to junior high school level. The New Order's concentration on primary level education has had important and positive distributional consequences. It is also socially beneficial, in that the social rates of return are generally high from public sector investment at this level. In addition, there has been a catch-up in terms of female enrolment and achievement, as well as a general 'evening' in performance differentials across regions. Nevertheless, daunting problems remain in terms of educational quality and content.

In Chapter 4, Joan Hardjono describes Indonesia's natural resource base and provides an assessment of environmental policies since the 1970s. Because Indonesia has long been regarded as a resource-rich country, with its vast forested areas, low population densities in central and eastern regions (especially Kalimantan and Irian Jaya), and significant petroleum and gas reserves, environmental issues have received little attention until recent years. Yet the problems are daunting: rapid resource depletion, the links between population growth, industrialisation and the environment, and the steady deterioration of the land resource base in many parts of the country. Moreover, there are powerful vested interests in all sectors, especially forestry, opposed to reform, with the result that 'enforcement is virtually impossible' for many environmental laws.

Within Java and Bali (Inner Indonesia), three principal environmental components are identified: the uplands area, lowland and coastal zones, and the cities. Each faces critical problems, but the uplands most of all. Intensive and ever-expanding cultivation of vegetables and other annual crops is placing tremendous pressure on Java's ecological base. These activities are both labour intensive and lucrative, yet they exacerbate erosion problems, deplete soil cover, and reduce soil fertility over time. Where such cropping is accompanied by tree-felling, Java's already inadequate forest cover is further reduced. Land disputes are increasingly common. Upland denudation also contributes to serious river sedimentation downstream and the pressure to occupy increasingly flood-prone land areas.

Some of these environmental problems are evident outside Java, but the Outer Islands also have to deal with a number of additional issues. Shifting cultivation has long since been practised in many parts of Indonesia, and these cultivators have been blamed—often unfairly—for ecological deterioration. The practice is now posing particular problems for governments, as questions of land use, access and ownership have never been adequately clarified. The transmigration program, involving the movement of large numbers of people from Java and Bali to more lightly settled regions, has brought these problems into sharp relief, although in recent years the scheme has been cut back considerably.

In Chapter 5, Barbara Hatley assesses major cultural developments in the New Order, embracing such diverse aspects as traditional modes of creative expression and popular music, the highly sophisticated dance forms of Central Java, and Jakarta's aggressive, brash mass media. This chapter reflects the ambivalence of the country's artistic community at all levels toward many political and social developments over the past 25 years. The electronics and media revolution now have the potential to obliterate traditional cultural forms, yet they also bring in vast new audiences and massive commercial opportunities. Government intervention is viewed with suspicion by some for its political motives, yet in other respects it has undoubtedly contributed to creative endeavour and the preservation of non-commercial but culturally important forms of artistic expression. The dramatic spread of modern communications has been crucial in the formation of a 'national' culture, yet regional cultures have continued to thrive in many areas. Hatley identifies two main phases of cultural development since 1965–66. The period 1966–76 was one of cultural efflorescence and rejuvenation for all except leftist artists. Artistic freedom expanded, previously taboo subjects were opened up, and economic growth created new opportunities and markets. However, a turning point occurred in the late 1970s when, especially following the campus protests of 1977–78, tighter controls were imposed: some press licences were revoked, arts sponsorship and censorship were tightened, and several key individuals were detained. Nevertheless, there was a continuing ebb and flow through the 1980s also, including an increase in commercial support for various artistic endeavours, carrying with it some potential for renewed cultural autonomy.

In the evolution of a national culture, much of the initial impetus came from two key institutions, both Jakarta-based: the literary magazine *Horison*, and the *Taman Ismail Marzuki* (TIM) arts complex. In this sense, the *pusat*, the national capital, shaped the nation's cultural agenda over this period, both in form and content. But other forces were also important. Regional cultures, mainly Java-based, maintained their importance, and several major figures emerged. There was an explosive growth in the mass media, where both general and specialist magazines proliferated, the film industry mushroomed, and the electronic media—television, radio and cassettes—spread throughout the country. Some traditional forms languished, however, such as the *wayang orang* dance drama.

In Chapter 6, Patrick Guinness surveys Indonesia's kaleidoscope of ethnic groups and cultures. Despite powerful integrating and centralising forces operating since Independence, ethnic identity continues to be a potent force in Indonesia. Moreover, ethnic differences do not conform to the nation's administrative boundaries. Frequently, there are distinct sub-provincial patterns, particularly outside Java–Bali. Several issues are highlighted by Guinness. The first is local identity and the impact of external (that is, external to the ethnic group) pressures for change. As the previous chapter also emphasises, there is a powerful elite sentiment in favour of developing a national culture and unifying symbols, born out of a fear that social fragmentation could threaten the country's hard-won independence. Nationwide rituals have become immensely important.

Related to this question of local ethnic identity is the development of a national system of law and administration. There have been concerted attempts to replace traditional laws and customs (*adat*) with a 'modern' legal code. Similarly, village administration has been brought firmly within the national government's bureaucratic apparatus following the introduction of the new Village Law of 1979, and its gradual implementation since then.

Drawing on much anthropological research, the author expresses scepticism about the beneficial effects of rapid agricultural and industrial growth, in contrast to the more positive assessment economists generally offer. Agricultural output may have increased but sharper social polarisation in the rural areas is seen as an outcome. Similarly, it is argued that rapid industrialisation has led to the demise of much small-scale enterprise and petty trading. This disruptive nature of low-wage manufacturing employment is stressed.

Guinness also reviews the place of major world religions in the New Order. While the government's policy has been tolerant towards recognised religions, it has been less so towards 'traditional religions which fail to meet certain criteria'. The government's ambivalent relationship with the Muslim community is analysed. There is, on the one hand, official concern that fundamentalism could seriously challenge the New Order and threaten the country's social stability. Efforts are being made, on the other hand, to appease adherents to Islam through funding the construction of mosques. Recently, the President has completed the pilgrimage to Mecca, and a Muslim intellectual association has been established.

1
Politics

Jamie Mackie and Andrew MacIntyre

In any country, the circumstances in which a major regime change occurs will usually exert a pervasive influence upon the character and subsequent development of the new one. That is especially likely to be the case where an authoritarian government assumes power in a national crisis, as occurred when the military-backed New Order regime under General Soeharto overthrew former President Sukarno and his leftist Old Order in 1965–66 after the abortive *Gestapu* coup attempt.[1] 'In our beginnings are our ends', it has been said. Many of the best and the worst features of the New Order political system as it exists today can be traced back to the traumatic and bloody upheavals of those years—the rejection of Sukarno's impassioned ideological adventurism in favour of the cautious, low-key policies espoused by Soeharto that soon led to sustained economic development, and the tacit acceptance of repression and covert political violence that have become almost institutionalised as mechanisms of social control. Despite the many benefits that the New Order has brought the country since 1965, the violence of those earliest months has deeply scarred the political record of the Soeharto regime, the Dili massacre of November 1991 being a horrific reminder of that aspect of its record.

President Soeharto's government has succeeded spectacularly, against most initial expectations, in transforming the poor and stagnant country it took over in 1966 into a dynamic and steadily developing one, fast becoming much less poor in the 1980s. Soeharto will go down in history as the man primarily responsible for that remarkable feat, no matter what else may be said of him. How he has done it is a more controversial issue, however, and one that is not as easy to address on the political as on the economic side. It is generally agreed that the power and competence of the state apparatus has been strengthened enormously, in terms of its administrative capabilities, the tax revenues available to it and its coercive muscle, but highly conflicting interpretations have been put forward about how or why that has come about, and whether it could have been done differently.[2] Might not the same results have been achieved at a lesser cost in terms of the huge numbers of people killed or imprisoned in the 1960s, or the suppression of left-wing and radical forces ever since, or the systematic denial of civil rights and liberties to dissidents of all kinds? These are controversial questions, some of them almost unanswerable. So too is the issue of whether the above might not have been achievable without the glaring social inequalities and elite opulence that have accompanied rapid economic growth. Tacit acceptance of the argument that violence and repression were unavoidable, or defensible in the circumstances, is ranged against severe condemnation of the regime and all that it stands for because of its disregard for basic human rights.

As we look back over the events of 1965–90, particularly at the political and socio-economic situation of the recent period, we are inclined in retrospect to focus on what the New Order has grown into rather than what it has grown from. The pluses loom more prominently in view than the minuses, as the great outburst of violence in 1965–66 recedes into the background. Conversely, to tell the story in chronological order is to produce almost the opposite effect, thrusting into the foreground the killings and jailings of communists (and others) in the early years of the New Order, to the point of overshadowing the political stability and economic development achieved later. A chronological approach makes it hard to avoid entanglement in the arguments that still persist about that darker side of the New Order's political record, or the many unresolved questions about what really happened on 1 October 1965, and in the months of violence that followed. Yet both perspectives must be taken into account if we are to produce a balanced assessment.

The character of the Indonesian political system has changed profoundly since the mid-1960s. A strong state has emerged out of what then seemed an incurably weak one—not just because the military took over in 1965–66 but also because the machinery of government and state–society relations have since been transformed fundamentally. The chaotic bureaucracy of Sukarno's final years has gradually been reformed since the 1970s as a result of the vastly greater budget revenues available from the oil boom as well as tighter fiscal discipline. The all-pervasive étatist, quasi-socialist ideology of the earlier years of independent Indonesia has been radically modified (although by no means abandoned) by the Soeharto government's utilisation of markets rather than controls, of private enterprise as well as

2

state corporations and of a far-reaching deregulation strategy in the late 1980s.

The sharp ideological turn-about that has occurred since 1965 is manifest not only in the political swing from left to right, but in many other forms also. It is apparent in more deferential, conformist patterns of behaviour and the abandonment of the former egalitarianism generated by the revolutionary struggle for independence, in the rejection even of the term 'revolution' in favour of blander phrases to describe that struggle, in the shift towards status-oriented modes of address, and in conservative, expensive dress styles and grossly opulent forms of housing for the rich.[3] At a more fundamental level, it is manifest also in the development of an increasingly capitalist, acquisitive and consumption-oriented society, just like other capitalist countries; in the emergence of a more substantial urban middle class and an embryonic capital-owning bourgeoisie; and in monopoly power and economic privilege for a few favoured cronies in or close to the presidential circle of family and friends. It is reflected above all in the widening gap between the very rich and ordinary Indonesians, the middle class, urban poor and peasantry, in terms of their income levels, assets and control over crucial resources.

In contrast to the revolutionary ferment of the Sukarno years, almost no popular protest movements or radical organisations (or even significant reformist ones) have raised their voices in public since the 1960s—far fewer than in South Korea or Taiwan. Occasional expressions of dissatisfaction among students or Islamic militants have often been portrayed, though not convincingly, as manifestations of widespread unrest by critics of the regime. The old supporters of the PKI (*Partai Komunis Indonesia*, Indonesian Communist Party) have been cowed into silence since 1965 by repressive and discriminatory measures against them. Predictions that 'the people' would soon rise up in revolutionary fervour against their rulers as they did in 1945, or smite them from revulsion at the high living, corruption and nepotism of the nation's leaders, or because of intolerable discontent among the poor, have simply not come about. Such views fail to recognise the extent to which incomes have risen at almost all levels, and the regime has won acceptance owing to the improvement in conditions for nearly everyone. Moreover, the New Order has effectively coopted key elements of Indonesian society into the power structure at every level by controlling access to the benefits which it can offer its supporters, and withhold from its opponents. The socio-political system that has emerged provides rewards to those who conform or at least do not rock the boat, but penalises dissidents or critics heavily. Hence the costs for any individual of opposing the system openly are high.

Two main themes stand out in the political story of how the New Order has developed since 1965. One is the strengthening of state power and its corollary, the steady weakening of political parties and other society-based forces, such as pressure groups, social classes, voluntary organisations such as NGOs (non-government organisations), independent interest groups and trade associations or other potential clusters of power—and even of Islam as a political force—or their subordination to the numerous quasi-corporatist institutions controlled by the state. This represents a quite remarkable development when contrasted with the extreme weakness of the state apparatus in the early years of Indonesia's independence, at a time when social and political movements were too vigorous to be constrained effectively (Table 1.1). By gradually excluding left-wing and other radical elements from participation in political life, then other dissidents also, Soeharto has brought about a transformation that eluded Sukarno, even in the years of his autocratic 'Guided Democracy'.

The second theme relates to the remarkable degree of personal authority that President Soeharto had managed to achieve by the late 1980s, even over the armed forces (hereafter ABRI, *Angkatan Bersenjata Republik Indonesia*), which initially provided his principal source of power during the years of transition and turmoil after 1965. Soeharto had become so much the paramount figure in the political system by the 1980s that the ABRI leadership was unable to impose its wishes on him in 1988–89 over various controversial issues relating to the vice-presidency and the business interests of the Soeharto family.[4] Previously he could not ignore the possibility of challenges from others of his generation if he made serious errors or misjudgements. But during the 1970s he managed to eliminate that danger by sidelining potential rivals and concentrating more and more power into his own hands. Soeharto has since imposed the stamp of his personality and political style upon the New Order so strongly (as did his predecessor, Sukarno, upon the 'Guided Democracy' years, 1959–65) that we simply cannot disregard the personal factor in any analysis of the political, social or structural dynamics of the regime.

This chapter consists of three parts. The first is a summary of various interpretations and explanations of the New Order political system that have influenced perceptions of it significantly. Then comes a brief chronological survey of the three main phases of political development since 1965. Finally, we look more closely at the way the political system works in terms of the main institutions of governance, particularly the armed forces, the role of ideology, Islam, and the nation-building process.

Theories, models and explanations of the political system

While most writers on the New Order political system tend to agree about its most striking features—its strongly authoritarian cast, the suppression of left-wing forces, the prominent role of the military, the great personal

Table 1.1 Society and state in Indonesia, 1945–90

	Old Order			New Order	
	1945–59	1959–65	1965–74	1974–84	1984–90
Society	Highly participatory mobilisation system; parties and mass organisations vigorous.	Parties increasingly constrained, but still used by Sukarno as counterweight to army.	Highly participatory at first, but less so after 1971 elections.	Popular participation in politics and policy-making much reduced.	Exclusionary regime; little popular participation in politics.
State	Constrained by lack of funds and constant need to ensure popular support; weak governments, with low levels of autonomy.	State autonomy much greater, but still severely limited by lack of funds and regional smuggling.	Government weak at first, but becoming stronger as economic growth increases revenues and control over resources.	Strong state, with oil revenues abundant; increasingly autonomous.	Strong state, highly autonomous despite declining oil revenues.

authority of President Soeharto, and so on—they differ widely in the interpretations, models or implicit theoretical assumptions they rely on to explain its underlying socio-political dynamics. Supporters of the regime put greater stress on policy outcomes or on the increasing effectiveness of the machinery of government rather than on how the policies are made, or in whose interests, while glossing over the more authoritarian aspects of the system and the human rights violations. Critics have been inclined to concentrate on the latter and to play down the former, attributing the economic successes of the early years, and the benefits, largely to foreign aid or investment—'borrowed power', in Feith's apt phrase (Feith 1980)—or in the later years to the links established between domestic capitalists and the multinationals. Their emphasis on external pressures was due partly to the fact that the state was not generally regarded as autonomous and self-directed in the early years of the regime, while the policies being pursued were clearly not attributable solely to pressures from particular classes or societal groups. Hence foreign capital was assumed to be the hidden power behind the scenes.

The earliest accounts of the New Order stressed its militaristic or authoritarian aspects, linking them frequently with the dependency theories which were then in vogue, as if the state were little more than a puppet manipulated by foreign capital (Mortimer 1973). Later accounts have put more emphasis on the increasing autonomy of the state, although with differing interpretations of the ways in which this has worked. The New Order was appropriately characterised as a *beamtenstaat*, a state run by and for its officials, by Ruth McVey (1982), and as a 'bureaucratic polity' by Jackson (1978a, 1978b), King (1982) and others, along the Weberian lines suggested by Riggs (1966).[5] Insofar as these terms imply that political activity, decision making and participation in policy formulation are confined mainly to members of the state apparatus, both civilian and military, they are illuminating about one major aspect of the political system. But they do not tell the whole story, for elements outside the state structure have at times been able to play roles of some importance in the political system and it has never been quite as monolithic as the notion of a bureaucratic polity suggests. Terms like 'bureaucratic pluralism' and 'corporatism' have also been used to reflect this aspect of the system and bring the society back in (Emmerson 1978, 1983; King 1982).

The term which we think best characterises one of the key features of the New Order polity is 'patrimonialism' (Crouch 1979), for it highlights the extent to which control over key financial resources, licences and essential facilities needed by business enterprises derive from the president and his immediate circle of lieutenants at the apex of the power structure. This feature of the political system derives from his greatly enhanced ability since the 1970s oil boom to dispense or withhold financial patronage and

opportunities of enrichment. These vertically structured patron–client relationships have proved since then to be at least as pervasive as the older
ethnic or *aliran* ties—literally, 'streams' or 'solidarity groups of great
intensity' (Soedjatmoko 1967)—which used to be regarded as the key
determinants of political alignments in Indonesia.[6]

While these interpretations focus mainly on the intra-bureaucratic
dimension of decision making and resource allocation, others have tried to
argue that relations between state and society have been structurally related
along more or less Marxist or dependency-theory lines under the New Order.
Robison (1978, 1986, 1989) has given a class analysis of political alignments and then, rejecting the crudely instrumentalist theory that state
policies reflected class interests, developed a more complex theory that the
New Order state is engaged in creating the necessary conditions for a
capitalist society and economy to develop. But he rejected the notion of
state autonomy advanced persuasively by Anderson (1983) to explain why
the support of society-based forces was no longer essential to the maintenance of the Soeharto regime. Others have tried to apply to Indonesia
concepts of corporatism and 'bureaucratic authoritarianism' used in the Latin
American development literature, some of them applicable in part (for instance,
the corporatist structures being created by the New Order state to exert control
over labour unions and private business firms), but not in their entirety.[7]

In the account that follows, we will be utilising elements from all these
interpretations eclectically, where they are relevant, without committing
ourselves exclusively to any one 'model' or theory by which the political
processes of the New Order are to be explained. The changing state–society
relationship will be central to our analysis of how state power has been
gradually enhanced and the strength of society-based groups steadily curtailed since 1966–67, as shown in Table 1.1. But the processes responsible
for those changes are best revealed by telling the story in narrative terms,
rather than by reference to a few structural characteristics of the society,
which have themselves been gradually evolving.

The evolution of the New Order power structure

The evolution of the New Order power structure can be traced through three
distinct phases since Sukarno's overthrow in 1965–67 (Table 1.2). The main
actors have been ABRI, the bureaucracy and President Soeharto himself. In
the first phase, 1965–74, ABRI was the key factor in the power configuration, although General (later President) Soeharto gradually became a major
player in his own right. He held office by virtue of ABRI's support for him,
yet his control over ABRI was at first severely circumscribed. The bureaucracy was in a very weak position at that time, having been discredited by
the economic and administrative chaos of the mid-1960s. It was also deeply

divided by factional and ideological rifts, distrusted by the military leaders because many supporters of Sukarno or the nationalist party (PNI) still held influential positions (until they were purged), and in general badly demoralised by its loss of status during the years of 'Guided Democracy'. Various other political forces were also important in the fluid politics of 1966–68—particularly the student action fronts, several of the old political parties, some Islamic groups and even the former pro-Sukarno constituencies—until they could be neutralised.[8] Soeharto and the ABRI leadership had to manipulate all these groups in the struggle to win out, irrevocably, over the Old Order, since they did not have them under the tight control that they later achieved.

In the second phase, 1974–83, the bureaucracy and state enterprises became much more effective instruments of government, some elements even emerging as wealthy power centres in their own right, such as the state oil corporation, Pertamina, or the food logistics agency, *Badan Urusan Logistik* (Bulog). Ultimately, however, ABRI was still the decisive force. President Soeharto himself was in a curiously vulnerable position in the mid-1970s, because of the Pertamina crisis (discussed below), although he regained the ascendancy dramatically soon after 1978.

In the third phase, from 1983 to the present, Soeharto has become by far the most powerful actor on the national stage, having built up immense personal authority as head of state quite independently of his close association with ABRI. Conversely, the influence of ABRI on the national stage has declined considerably, although at local levels ABRI officers still wield great power. Meanwhile, some sections of the bureaucracy, key economic ministries in particular, have gained in influence with the president, the ultimate decision maker, because of their technical expertise in a society and economy that is growing ever more complex.

Other elements and factors in the power configuration have also exerted influence to a lesser degree or in limited spheres from time to time, but as secondary rather than primary participants in the political drama. Subordinate elements of this kind include the political parties and Golkar, Islam as a semi-organised but always potentially significant political force, as well as the students and intellectuals (including parts of the press and media) who were a key element behind the overthrow of Sukarno and still see themselves as the 'conscience' of the New Order. The middle class in general could also be mentioned as generally supportive of the regime in a more passive but crucially important way, having benefited materially from the changes it has wrought; so also could the *swasta* (private) enterprises and big business groups, predominantly Chinese (discussed below), and various elements within rural society which have prospered under the New Order.[9]

Table 1.2 The New Order power structure: three phases of its evolution

	1965–74	1974–83	1983–90
Main features	Political consolidation and economic recovery. Broad anti-communist alliance.	Steady growth, boosted by oil boom. Increasingly patrimonialist state structure with high concentration of political control. 'New Order coalition' disintegrating.	Falling oil prices: strong deregulation thrust in economic policies. Political status quo unchallengeable. Presidential authority highly personalised.
Principal power relationships	Army dominant. President's authority not yet unchallengeable. Bureaucracy weak and ineffective, under severe purge of leftists. Technocrats' influence considerable.	Army still the dominant force. President's position vulnerable 1974–78, but then becomes stronger as economy improves. Bureaucracy gaining in influence and effectiveness. Technocrats' influence in eclipse.	President's personal authority at peak. Decline in ABRI political influence. Technocrats exert strong influence over deregulation policies.
Subsidiary elements in power structure	Political parties very active 1966–71; then constrained by 1972 reduction to two composite parties. 'Floating mass' doctrine limits its activities in rural areas. Golkar contests 1971 election with strong government backing. Private business groups weak (but *cukong* gain personalistic influence); some state enterprises amass wealth and local power. Islam a potent force backing New Order regime against PKI	Parties reduced to minor role in DPR/MPR. Golkar makes gains locally at their expense, although lacks political clout in Jakarta. A transitional phase: some private businesses and state corporations grow rapidly in boom conditions, others fall behind. Political influence of capital still limited. Islam and PPP assuming more oppositionist stance.	Parties at nadir. Civilian leaders within Golkar gain influence 1984–88, broaden local membership: ABRI reasserts control in 1988–89. Large conglomerates proliferate, some increasingly influential. State enterprises under attack for unprofitability. Islam weakened as political force; turns more to religious–social sphere
Political climate	Open, competitive, highly participatory atmosphere, relatively free expression of opinions, except for left. Blatant arbitrary repression of ex-PKI members and sympathisers.	Increasing constraints on political activity, press and public statements. But NGOs still hope for more open, institutionalised legal and administrative structures.	Tighter social control, with ideological conformity ensured by P4 indoctrination and *azas tunggal*. Strict limits on NGOs.

The origins of the New Order: 1965–74

Political tensions and social instability had been mounting almost to fever pitch during the final years of Sukarno's Old Order before the coup attempt of 30 September 1965 sparked the explosion that shattered his fragile regime. A group of radical-nationalist middle-ranking officers of the army and air force led by Lieutenant Colonel Untung made a strangely amateurish attempt to seize power, killing six senior army officers in the process, but failing in their attempt on General Nasution, the senior armed forces officer.[10] The coup attempt was quickly foiled by the adroit actions of General Soeharto, the Strategic Reserve commander, who assumed command of the army and quickly restored control in Jakarta, then in Central Java, the only other place where the conspirators took significant action. Soeharto occupied centre stage in the political drama from then on as the man in charge of the army, even though Sukarno remained titular president for more than two years before he was finally stripped of formal authority.

The New Order's official mythology about the coup portrays it as having been masterminded by the PKI, using Untung and his associates as cats' paws.[11] The truth is murkier but less sinister, for the theory that the coup leaders were basically a bunch of pro-Sukarno radical-nationalist colonels is probably much closer to the truth. Nevertheless, evidence from the later trials of the conspirators indicates that Untung was almost certainly being indoctrinated by PKI elements and urged on by them to take 'revolutionary' action on behalf of the suffering people, against the high-living, right-wing generals. It seems probable, too, that there was a split within the PKI Central Committee, with at least some members aware of the coup plans, although others were not; the PKI gave only half-hearted support to the coup attempt, but enough to implicate it fatally in the army's eyes.[12]

A backlash of nationwide hostility to the PKI soon followed, as its former adversaries seized the opportunity to settle old scores, particularly in Central and East Java and Bali, while regional army commanders imposed bans on the PKI or arrested its leaders, despite orders to the contrary from Sukarno. By December the PKI had been destroyed as a political force. The number of people killed at that time is unknowable, with estimates ranging between about 150 000 and 500 000 (the most generally accepted figures being close to 250 000), mainly in rural areas where land-reform conflicts had occurred in the previous years (Cribb 1991).

Sukarno manoeuvred desperately to hold on to power over the next few months as the economy drifted towards collapse, with inflation spiralling out of control. But he now had little left except revolutionary rhetoric to rally his dwindling supporters, consisting mainly of members of the old left-wing forces and the former nationalist party (PNI) who feared the prospects of life under an army-led regime backed by Muslim militants. The latter had been actively involved in the violence against the PKI, lest it become their turn next. Sukarno made a last-ditch effort to reassert his authority in early 1966 by mobilising mass support among radical groups against the increasingly militant New Order coalition of student action groups, Muslim organisations and middle-class intellectuals opposed to the Old Order. His tactics eventually provoked street rioting in Jakarta on such a scale that the army leadership finally stepped in on 11 March to restore order at Soeharto's instructions. Sukarno fled from the capital, but was later induced by a group of senior army officers to transfer executive responsibility to Soeharto for the restoration of law and order throughout the country. This letter of authority, later known as *Supersemar,* was to serve thenceforth as the legal basis for Soeharto's gradual assumption of full executive power.[13] In a strict sense, the establishment of the New Order regime dates from 11 March 1966.

Over the next two years, Soeharto moved cautiously to edge Sukarno out of power—too cautiously for the taste of some New Order activists who were pressing for a more drastic purge of former PKI and Sukarnoist elements—for the country hovered on the brink of civil war until well into 1967. Pockets of support for Sukarno and all he stood for were still deeply entrenched in many parts of Central and East Java, and even within the army itself. Soeharto chose to rely on meetings of the (provisional) MPR (*Majelis Permusyawaratan Rakyat,* Peoples' Consultative Assembly) to endorse his authority and a new economic strategy. He then reconstituted the cabinet to replace former supporters of Sukarno with his own men, and gradually rooted out old Sukarnoists from key positions in the bureaucracy and ABRI.[14] He resisted calls for more radical measures, preferring to rely on compromise and manipulation of support for his government in the MPR and parliament so as to highlight the difference between Sukarno's 'deviations' from constitutional proprieties and his own emphasis on formal legal procedures. In March 1967 Soeharto was proclaimed acting president by the MPR, and a year later president. Sukarno was thereafter kept under virtual house arrest until his death in 1970.

Meanwhile, the economic strategy of the New Order was marked by a dismantling of the numerous government regulations of the Sukarno era and a greater reliance on market forces to stimulate trade and production; policies devised by a group of University of Indonesia 'technocrats' with the assistance of IMF and World Bank experts. The results were dramatic. By 1968 production was increasing rapidly and the rate of inflation had fallen sharply, even though the tight money policies adopted were at first painful and highly unpopular. The new inflow of foreign aid from the United States, Japan and an IGGI (Inter-Governmental Group on Indonesia) consortium[15] was crucial at that time in helping the new government to survive until the economy started to pick up momentum in the early 1970s, with a sharp increase in foreign investment and rising oil production yielding higher foreign exchange earnings and government revenues than Indonesia had ever experienced (see chapter 2).

The years between 1966 and 1974 were characterised by remarkable political ferment and free expression of ideas (except for former communists), after the constraints and fears of the late Sukarno era. It was a time of great optimism and rejuvenation of Indonesia's social, cultural and educational life (see chapter 6). The press, book publishing and the arts flourished with unprecedented vigour, as did political debates about the socio-economic objectives the New Order regime should be pursuing. The basic political problem facing the New Order leaders and their supporters in those early years was how to institutionalise their power base and gain enough popular support to win the general elections Soeharto had promised soon after he took over.[16] It could not be assumed that they would outnumber the supporters of the Old Order in a fair vote. And the new government's leaders were not prepared to rely on any of the old anti-Sukarno parties as their main standard-bearer in the elections, or on a coalition of them.

The answer that gradually emerged was to build up a small anti-communist grouping of 'functional groups', loosely joined under 'Sekber Golkar' (the Functional Groups Joint Secretariat) into a semi-official party representing the New Order and to encourage supporters of the government, particularly ABRI and the regional bureaucracy, to join it or vote for it in the elections.[17] In the election campaign, both regional bureaucrats and the military applied heavy pressure on rural villagers to vote for Golkar, which won an unexpectedly high 62 per cent of the vote (Table 1.3). The Old Order parties polled very poorly and faded into political insignificance from then on. Only the Muslim parties showed much capacity to retain their traditional supporters in the face of pro-Golkar pressures.

The outcome of the 1971 elections set the basic pattern of political life in Indonesia, a pattern which has persisted in essentials ever since. Golkar was to become the government's vote-winning organisation and nominal institutional link with society. It received strong backing from civil servants, who came under heavy pressure thenceforth to join their professional body,

Table 1.3   Election results, 1971–92 (% of votes cast)

	Golkar	PPP ('Muslim')	PDI ('Democratic')
1971[a]	62.8	27.1	10.1
1977	62.1	29.3	8.6
1982	64.2	28.0	7.9
1987	73.2	16.0	10.9
1992	68.1	17.0	14.9

Note: [a] 1971 figures for PPP and PDI are based on the combined votes of parties which were merged in 1972–73 into these two groupings (although not strictly comparable *in toto*).

Source: Suryadinata (1989:137–9), and 1992 press reports.

Korpri (*Korps Pegawai Republik Indonesia*) (one of the key component groups in Golkar), and to dissociate from other political parties in the name of 'monoloyalty'. In accordance with a new doctrine of 'the floating mass', political parties were banned from organisational activities in rural areas except at election time. The nine parties were compelled to regroup in 1972–73, under the rubric of 'party simplification', into two large groupings—the PPP (*Partai Persatuan Pembangunan*), made up of the various Muslim parties, and the PDI (*Partai Demokrasi Indonesia*), an amalgam of nationalist and Christian parties. The government was thereby able to reduce them to a condition of such disunity and weakness that they have been unable to mount any effective challenge to Golkar at subsequent elections.

Political tensions between the government and its former supporters were sharpened by these and other developments during the two years that followed the elections. The new economic policies involving an open door to foreign investment became a matter of intense controversy as Japanese and US factories sprang up in and around Jakarta, usually on a joint-venture basis with Chinese Indonesian partners, creating severe competition for indigenous businessmen. Many of the latter were from the former Muslim small-business class, who were also affronted by President Soeharto's close financial dealings with Chinese businessmen (the so-called *cukong*), most notably with his old associate, Liem Sioe Liong, and also several military officers in the palace circle. A marriage law proposed to the parliament in 1973 was regarded by Muslims as in conflict with Islamic law and had to be withdrawn by the government after a storm of protest erupted. The political atmosphere was tense and volatile by the end of 1973 and exploded soon after in the incident known as Malari (*Malapetaka 16 Januari*) (disaster of 16 January) in early 1974.

The Malari affair was sparked by a state visit by the Japanese prime minister, Tanaka, which gave rise to student demonstrations in the streets of Jakarta against 'Japanese neocolonialism'. These soon developed into anti-Chinese rioting (and anti-'new rich' demonstrations more generally), the burning of the Toyota showroom, and a march on the presidential palace, halted only by the personal mediation of General Sumitro, head of the security organisation, Kopkamtib (*Komando Pemulihan Keamanan dan Ketertiban*, Law and Order Restoration Command).[18] In itself it was a relatively minor affray, but it had far-reaching consequences for two reasons.

The first was that Malari brought into the open a simmering power struggle between two of the president's principal lieutenants vying for influence as his right-hand man, General Sumitro, the man responsible for internal security affairs, and Lieutenant General Ali Murtopo, an influential 'troubleshooter' who handled most of the government's politically sensitive problems. The latter held no significant military position but had made himself influential as an adviser on broad politico-economic strategy. By accusing Sumitro (quite wrongly, it later emerged) of plotting with the dissident students to mount a challenge to President Soeharto, Ali Murtopo's faction succeeded in having him ousted and in the imposition of a strict crackdown on student dissent (Jenkins 1984). Many of the student leaders and their alleged mentors were arrested, including some of the country's most independent figures involved in the earlier anti-Sukarno struggle, such as Bujung Nasution, Mochtar Lubis and others.

The second effect of Malari was to highlight the danger to the regime of factional splits within the top leadership, if it entailed any risk of appeals to outside groups and the politics of the street. That was the gravamen of the accusations launched at Sumitro in the eyes of his critics. Intra-elite politics was henceforth to be quarantined from the masses. In that sense, Malari marked a decisive shift from the relatively open, pluralistic phase of political life under the New Order towards one in which society-based forces were to be largely excluded and rendered almost powerless to influence state policies or the distribution of power at the top.

Narrowing of the political base: 1974–82

The Malari affair can be seen in retrospect as a watershed in the develop-ment of the New Order political system. During the next decade, the political base of the regime narrowed sharply, as more and more of its former supporters became antagonised by its increasing reliance on exclusion, coercion and repression (Anderson 1978). The student activists were the first to be alienated, then the Muslims, later many among the intellectuals and professional middle classes, and finally even a number of retired senior ABRI officers who had been prominent in the founding of the New Order. At the same time, the power wielded by the state was greatly increased after the 1973–74 oil boom, which brought vastly greater revenues into the government's coffers than ever before. This made the political system increasingly patrimonial in character, for it now had unprecedented scope to bestow patronage upon its supporters, or threaten to deny access to lucrative financial resources, contracts or licences to its opponents or critics (Crouch 1979).

Paradoxically, Soeharto's personal authority and self-confidence was severely shaken for some time after the events of 1973–74. Even the improved economic situation brought about by the oil price rises was clouded for several years by a $10 billion debt crisis that gradually unfolded within the state oil company, Pertamina, in 1974–75, which the government had to bail out.[19] Its debts resulted from the profligate financial policies pursued by its head, Lieutenant General Ibnu Sutowo, a close associate of the president, who was reluctant to dismiss him. Many other things went wrong over the next few years, giving rise to widespread speculation that the ABRI leadership might move to replace Soeharto at the end of his current term. The armed takeover of East Timor in 1975–76 proved to be a military fiasco and a diplomatic embarrassment. The initial successes of the Green Revolution, the New Order's prime achievement up till then, came under threat from pest infestations, which seriously reduced rice production for several years, making expensive imports necessary.[20]

More seriously, the alienation of the Muslim community posed a risk that the PPP might be able to make serious inroads into the Golkar vote in the 1977 elections, which would have been regarded as a major setback to Soeharto's prospects of being nominated for a third term in 1978. So the regional military authorities as well as the bureaucracy were called upon to apply heavy pressure on voters before and during the campaign through intimidation, coercion and ultimately also vote-rigging, in order to ensure a big vote for Golkar. Such malpractices were more blatant in the 1977 elections than in 1971 or any later elections, yet the total PPP vote was above that of the various Muslim parties in 1971 while Golkar's was slightly down (see Table 1.3). Golkar also suffered humiliating defeats in Jakarta (where opponents of the regime rallied to PPP) and in the strongly Muslim province of Aceh. Between the elections and the meeting in March 1978 of the MPR, there was lively debate over the direction in which the country was moving, angry student demonstrations calling for Soeharto's replacement and bans on newspapers at one stage, all of which created a very tense political atmosphere in the weeks before the MPR met. Despite rumours that the ABRI leadership was divided over whether or not to nominate him again, it finally did so, although the MPR meeting which formally elected him took place in an atmosphere of great tension and rancour, with the Muslims bitterly antagonistic (McDonald 1980:240–9). That period can be seen in retrospect as the nadir of Soeharto's political fortunes.

Having survived that difficult phase, however, Soeharto took firm measures in 1978–79 to ensure that there would be no repetition of such opposition. His hard-line Minister of Education imposed stringent curbs on student protests within university campuses. A *Pancasila* indoctrination program known as P4 (*Pedoman Penghayatan dan Pengamalan Pancasila*)[21] was instituted to create ideological conformity around the official state philosophy (at a time when there were fears that the Khomeini revolution in Iran might give a boost to Islamic fundamentalism). The president pushed strongly in 1982–83 to have Pancasila proclaimed the sole philosophical basis (*azas tunggal*) of political parties and all other socio-political organisations, as well as of the state as a whole. This was a bitter pill for the PPP to swallow, but it could no longer resist effectively. The requirement of ideological conformity has since been a powerful weapon for curbing dissentient views of all kinds.

Soeharto had earlier brushed aside with almost contemptuous ease various efforts in 1979–80 by a strongly critical group of retired but senior and widely respected ABRI officers who formed the so-called *Petisi 50* (Petition of 50) and other organisations to demand political reforms and a reconsideration of the role the military had played in the 1977 elections (Jenkins 1984). His success in dismissing that challenge left him more securely in the saddle than ever by 1981–82, when the economy was booming and his critics in disarray. Over the next two years he brought about the transition from the last of the old '1945 Generation' officers at the top of the various armed forces to the first of the new generation of officers trained at the Magelang military academy, whose personal loyalty to him was unquestioning.[22]

In the 1982 elections, Golkar scored an easy victory at the expense of PPP, more than regaining the ground it had lost in 1977, without having to resort to much fraud or intimidation. The president was re-elected for a fourth term by the MPR without demur in 1983 and the personal ascendancy he had by then established was to prove quite unassailable thereafter. It was a far cry from the situation of uncertainty he had faced only five years earlier.

The great concentration of power in the president's hands between Malari and 1982–83 was a major change in the New Order political system, but is not easily reducible to any simple explanation. It cannot be attributed solely to the increase in oil revenues, although that was certainly a major factor, for he had run into troubles in 1978 at a time when the economy was already improving rapidly. His political skills in isolating or marginalising his potential rivals are an important part of the explanation, but not the whole of it. More fundamental, it seems, was the gradual depoliticisation of Indonesian life in the 1970s, as well as the changes taking place more broadly within the society at large and also within the state apparatus, tilting the balance between state and society increasingly in favour of the former (see Table 1.2).

The sharp separation between state and society became more clearly evident in the late 1970s than previously, for the government was by then less dependent on its capacity to extract tax revenues and political cooperation from below, its patrimonialist character greatly enhanced, for it was in a much stronger position to demand loyalty and obedience in return for the various forms of patronage it could bestow. The bureaucracy had become more competent and self-confident in the course of the 1970s, even vis-a-vis the military, while the state enterprises were performing better in some cases than before. So, with the students muzzled and the press cowed by threats to publication licences, with the two political parties rendered unable to rival Golkar, and with only a small and politically insignificant capitalist class to deal with, the state carried all before it, brooking no political opposition or obstruction from society-based groups or movements. Yet fears of Islam as a political force persisted through the years of worldwide Islamic resurgence after the overthrow of the Shah of Iran in 1979, and were constantly invoked to justify calls for vigilance and strict security measures, although Ayatollah Khomeini's fundamentalist doctrines exerted little appeal in Indonesia except among a few small fringe groups.

Soeharto in supreme control: 1982–92

The years after 1982–83 turned out to be very different in political character from the preceding decade in several respects, above all in being much blander and less turbulent than previously. The major change was due to basic structural shifts in the economic sphere, resulting from declining oil prices, at first quite gradual and easily manageable in 1982–83, but suddenly very sharp in 1985–86, producing a severe revenue crisis for the government. This necessitated a shift in economic policies towards progressive deregulation of the economy and much greater reliance on the private sector, which in turn had some significant political consequences. 'Bad times produce good policies', it is often said—and vice versa. The government's deregulation strategy proved remarkably successful in coping with the decline in oil revenues, promoting a dramatic increase in non-oil exports by 1988–89, especially of manufactured goods, so that there was only a minor setback to the country's momentum of growth. In fact, boom conditions prevailed in 1989–90 after the deregulation of the banking sector (Mackie and Sjahrir 1989).

Another important change was the marked increase in the personal authority of President Soeharto after his re-election for a fourth term in 1983. This altered the character of the political system greatly, for power became far more concentrated at the apex of the political pyramid than ever before. By the mid-1980s Soeharto was much more than just the commander-in-chief of the armed forces, and president by virtue of that fact. Soeharto's opponents had no realistic chance in the 1980s of displacing him, or of compelling him to change the structure or style of governance.

A corollary to the increasing power of the president was a decline in the political and administrative power of the military, not only in relation to him but also vis-a-vis the bureaucracy generally, as its competence and the technical complexity of governmental activities increased. With the old '1945 Generation' of military officers being replaced at the highest levels by the 'Magelang Generation' in the mid-1980s, top ABRI officers were better educated than their predecessors but less experienced politically. The president took care to ensure that the men at the top were personally loyal to him and unlikely to pose any challenge to his authority, as several senior officers had been inclined to do in earlier years. His pre-eminence was due partly to the fact that he had prevented the emergence of any credible rivals for his job, partly through his age, achievements and 'performance legitimacy'. For lack of any obvious candidate to succeed him or any alternative set of policies, ABRI became less and less capable of functioning as an independent political force than it had been previously, despite increasing strains in its relations with the president.

In the early 1980s it had seemed that the New Order was becoming so effectively institutionalised that when the time came for President Soeharto to be replaced, the ABRI leadership would have no great difficulty in ensuring a smooth transition to another man, almost certainly a senior military officer (Liddle 1985). But as the presidency became increasingly personalised after 1982, with the succession issue growing more prominent and Soeharto showing no sign of preparing either to step down or to groom a possible replacement, no one could be confident that the transition, whenever it might occur, would be smooth or easily manageable by the ABRI leaders (Crouch 1988). By 1987–88, as the rapidly expanding business activities of the Soeharto children became increasingly a matter of public controversy, the interests of the president and the ABRI leadership began to diverge on several key issues, and came to a head at the 1988 MPR session.

Another important feature of the 1980s was the relatively minor political role played by Muslim organisations, apart from a few minor outbursts of violence by small fundamentalist sectarians, which prompted stern government action but did not really threaten it seriously. The major change was the withdrawal of the *Nahdatul Ulama* (NU) from the PPP in 1984 and the latter's reluctant acceptance of the *azas tunggal*, with its implication that *Pancasila* took priority over Islam as its philosophical basis. This was followed by a shift of support to Golkar by several prominent Muslim leaders and a sharp fall in the PPP vote in the 1987 elections. Even the Muslims, it seems, had come to the conclusion that there was no future in being excluded from access to power and were looking for ways to come to terms with the authorities. By 1990–91 Soeharto himself was making conciliatory gestures towards the NU leaders with an eye towards the 1992 elections, and some of them were falling over themselves in their eagerness to seize the honour of nominating him. The wheel had turned almost full circle.

Finally, a development of potentially great significance in the late 1980s was the growing complexity and incipient pluralism of Indonesian society, especially of its patterns of property ownership and private-sector business structures, resulting from twenty years of rapid economic growth. Several rudimentary attempts by private business firms to influence government policies reflected this trend. Although it may seem to run counter to the tendencies noted above, towards centralisation of power in the hands of the president, the two processes operate on different levels, the latter within the state sphere, the former in the societal realm.

The deregulation policies which have dominated the economic strategy of the government through the 1980s have been accompanied by the emergence of well over forty huge private-sector conglomerates, which have spearheaded the transformation of the modern-sector economy, although they do not yet wield much political clout (Robison 1986; Mackie 1990c). The impulse toward those policies came essentially from the state, that is, from the president himself and the officials advising him, not from the business sector. It could be argued, in fact, that his unassailable control over the political system was a necessary condition of the (at times unpopular) deregulation strategy. While it seems inevitable that the business sector will in due course exert greater political influence on government policies, that day is still far distant. Yet it is something of a puzzle that it has done so to such a limited extent hitherto.

Major institutions and problems

The institutions of governance

Under the 1945 Constitution, Indonesia has a presidential system of government more similar to the US congressional system than the Westminster model—but without comparable 'checks and balances'—in which the legislature, the DPR (*Dewan Perwakilan Rakyat*, People's Representative Council, commonly called the parliament) and the MPR are far weaker in practice than the executive branch and have little capacity to constrain the president, the bureaucracy or the military.[23] As in the US congressional system, the presidency is the pivotal institution in the political structure. All key political appointments are made by the president, with cabinet ministers, senior military and civilian officials and top members of the judiciary all owing their positions to him. The cabinet has no more than an advisory role, as in the United States. The president can disregard his ministers, if he chooses, and he has ultimate power to override all official decisions and policy making.

According to the constitution, the supreme political authority is the MPR, which is convened every five years to elect a president and vice-president and to lay down the broad guidelines for state policy over the next five-year period.[24] While Soeharto has generally respected the letter of the constitution in convening the MPR regularly to carry out these functions, he has in practice let it exercise little independent authority. Because he is authorised to appoint over half the members of the MPR (with a large portion of the remainder being members of Golkar), there is little prospect of any serious challenge to him there. Since 1966 Soeharto has been elected and re-elected unopposed six times by the MPR.

The basic source of Soeharto's power, however, is not the constitutional authority of the presidency, but his ability to command the loyalty of the armed forces. Their support for the president is the most crucial factor in the New Order political system, although it is an exaggeration to describe the regime simply as a military dictatorship. The power structure is too diffuse for that. But Soeharto's ability to centralise decision-making authority, to maintain political stability and to implement a wide range of important policy measures have all depended in the last resort on the fact that he has been able to rely on the capacity to impose his will by coercive measures if necessary.

With the backing of the military, President Soeharto has been able to thoroughly dominate the MPR and the DPR and to manage the electoral process to ensure majority support there. Constitutionally, the DPR is empowered to monitor government actions and initiate legislation itself; in practice, however, it has been a feeble institution for most of the New Order period. Underlying its weakness is the fact that, as shown above, the government has effectively crippled the political parties by overt and covert forms of intervention in their affairs, ensuring that only party leaders acceptable to the authorities gain office.

Of the 500 seats in the parliament, 100 are reserved for military appointees; Golkar holds the great majority of the remaining 400. This means, of course, that the parliament is overwhelmingly made up of pro-government members. Its members are further weakened by the proportional representation electoral system—candidates are elected from large party lists for each province instead of being individually chosen by smaller electorates. Hence they have little direct relationship with the people who elected them and are highly vulnerable to manipulation by party leaders.

Virtually all key policy decisions are referred to the president. But because it is not humanly possible for him to become involved in more than the most important issues, a good deal of executive authority is inevitably devolved to ministers and the upper echelons of the bureaucracy. The influence and scope for initiatives left to these officials tend to be directly proportionate to the degree of trust placed in them by Soeharto.

The locus of power and influence in the political system is confined to the upper echelons of the civilian and military bureaucracies, with little effective leverage being exerted by political parties or Golkar, or by other pressure groups, hence the appropriateness of the term 'bureaucratic polity'. The term is made even more relevant by the all-pervasive dominance of the *pamong praja* at the provincial and lower levels of administration, combined with the very large group of inefficient, cumbrous state enterprises. Neither the president nor the various layers of civilian and military officials beneath him are greatly constrained by institutions representing societal interests. The two principal structures nominally responsible for representing such interests, trade or industry organisations and labour unions, have been kept under much tighter control during the New Order than in Sukarno's time.

20

As noted earlier, this is a system in which orders flow down from the top, but there is little scope for institutionalised input of pressures, requests or ideas from the bottom upwards.

Just as the government secured a very tight grip on the political parties in the 1970s, so it also moved to limit the scope for interest organisations to develop significant political capabilities. Government strategists adopted what amounted to a corporatist system for the containment of interest groups, under which steps were gradually taken to create, sponsor or designate particular organisations as the official bodies to represent the interests of almost all segments of the social and economic spectrum. Many of these organisations were gathered under the umbrella of Golkar, which ostensibly served to aggregate societal demands. The government maintained a close watch on the largest such organisations (for example, the peak trade union and business bodies, the teachers' association and the civil servants' organisation) and was able to ensure that those who rose to leadership positions within them were amenable to 'guidance'. What emerged over time was a pattern in which officially-sanctioned interest organisations tended to become formalistic and docile, and to play little role at all in terms of feeding membership demands into the policy process (Reeve 1985; MacIntyre 1990). Only in the late 1980s did any signs emerge that some minor changes might be occurring in this respect.

When Soeharto assumed power in 1966, the civil service was notoriously unwieldy, inefficient, corrupt and torpid. Parts of the bureaucracy had been almost a law unto themselves. Since then the civil service has been gradually transformed from an arena in which semi-autonomous bureaucratic fiefdoms did battle, into a more capable, professional and streamlined instrument of government.[25] Officials suspected of having communist sympathies were removed and military officers were placed in strategic positions within most government departments or agencies to monitor the behaviour of civilian officials. What emerged (albeit slowly and far from adequately) was a much more disciplined bureaucracy in which at least the key departments like finance, home affairs and industry have acquired some capacity to execute policies of increasing technical complexity.

Despite these improvements, corruption has remained an endemic problem, too deeply rooted to be eliminated from some parts of the bureaucratic structure.[26] In his most sweeping attempt at reform, the president simply removed the functions of the notoriously corrupt customs service in April 1985 and transferred them to a Swiss inspection agency. Corruption is a common phenomenon, of course, in most developing countries (and others). Yet Indonesia is often branded as the most corruption-ridden country in the region, because of the great size and scope of the bureaucracy and state enterprises, plus the fact that official salaries have lagged far behind the cost of living (so that in 1990, for example, they provided for barely one-third of an official's household needs). Despite periodic attempts to tackle the problem, few of them have been very successful. Another longstanding factor contributing to official corruption, however, has been the need for the president to secure the support and cooperation of key figures within the military and civilian bureaucracies through allowing them to derive additional income by exploiting their offices (Crouch 1979). Also, because so many state instrumentalities are involved in a vast array of commercial and allocational tasks (the latter increased greatly by the 1970s oil bonanza), numerous opportunities have arisen for 'cream-skimming' from official budgets for personal enrichment (Mackie 1970). But, above all, the involvement of Soeharto family members in money-making activities and the blurring of any line between private and public wealth has set a bad example to subordinates and hobbled the various anti-corruption drives that have been undertaken from time to time.

Paralleling the overhaul of the central bureaucracy has been transformation of regional government. Jakarta's control over the 27 provincial and numerous 'second level' municipal and *kabupaten* governments has increased to a degree that would have been barely imaginable in Sukarno's time.[27] Indonesia's archipelagic character and diversity create huge problems of central control and uniform administrative procedures, although complex unifying processes have been binding the major islands together in various ways for roughly a century (Mackie 1980; Drake 1989). But the central government's greatly increased capacity to exert control over ever-present regionalist inclinations has come about not so much through changes to the formal structure of the provincial government system (inherited from the Dutch colonial regime) as by binding them to it with financial subsidies. One crucial consequence of the oil booms of the 1970s was that they made possible vastly increased revenue transfers from the central government to regional authorities. The price the latter paid for a steady flow of funds to pay local officials and to finance local development projects was a compliant relationship with the central government. Regional councils are formalistic bodies with little autonomy, basically subordinate to local officials (often military officers) appointed by the central government. Known collectively as the *pamong praja*, this is a unique bureaucratic structure under the Ministry for Home Affairs, inherited from the colonial government, which has broadly-defined power to coordinate and supervise the work of other departments at all levels. It reaches down through the provincial and district levels all the way to the village, and since the late 1960s has enormously strengthened the central government's capacity to exercise social and political control throughout the rural areas (Schiller 1986).

The legal and judicial system is another of the formal institutions of government that must be mentioned. Based on the Napoleonic Code, the legal system has changed little since the Dutch colonial period. The judiciary in Indonesia has traditionally functioned more as an arm of the government than as an independent entity. The doctrine of the separation of powers of government is specifically rejected. The already low level of judicial autonomy has been aggravated by the fact that most senior posts in the Justice Ministry and the High Court have been filled since 1966 by graduates of the military law academy. The relatively minor changes to the legal system that have taken place under the New Order have greatly reinforced earlier tendencies for the judiciary to serve mainly as an instrument of the government. This has disappointed civilian lawyers, who were hopeful in the early New Order years that legal reforms and some progress towards the rule of law as a fountainhead of justice might emerge (Lev 1979). Some steps towards modernisation of the laws and legal system were begun in the 1980s, but little progress had been made by 1990.

The military as a political force

The armed forces, ABRI, have been the main pillar of the New Order political system from its earliest days, for they constitute the most cohesive, tightly disciplined organisation in Indonesia, as well as the most wide-ranging and truly 'national' in scope. Yet ABRI has always had to share power with civilian elements, working with political parties and mass movements in the early struggles to overthrow Sukarno, and later with the ministerial technocrats, the bureaucracy and Golkar as they became more important. Even the relationship between ABRI and the president was becoming a complex political and conceptual problem for both by the late 1980s.

Long before 1965, ABRI had interpreted its role as extending into the civil administration, in the provinces as well as nationally, by virtue of its contribution to the struggle for independence in 1945–49. Thereafter it justified this in terms of the part ABRI had played in 'saving the nation from the communist threat' in 1965. ABRI has always seen itself as the guardian of national security, which is defined to include not only external threats but also internal subversion of various kinds, and as the principal defender of the 1945 Constitution and *Pancasila*. The education and experience of ABRI officers, which stress discipline, fitness and toughness, mental as well as physical, sets them apart, almost as a special praetorian caste, from the civilian politicians and bureaucrats whom they regard as deficient in these qualities.

ABRI's civil as well as military role (*dwifungsi*, or 'dual function') is manifest in the fact that it is allocated one-fifth of the seats in the DPR, while senior officers hold key posts in the bureaucracy and regional administrative service, plus senior ambassadorial posts and top jobs in state enterprises (see McDougall 1982). Roughly one-third of the cabinet ministers in the 1980s were either senior military officers or former officers (not quite as many as earlier, however), with key ministries like home affairs, justice and the state secretaryship always retained in their hands. All but a small number of the provincial governors were ex-ABRI men in the 1970s, as were many lower-level administrators, although the proportion has declined since then. The supervisory reach of the military has also been extended right down to the village through a parallel hierarchy of local military commanders at almost every level of administration. It is no longer as intrusive a force in day-to-day administration of the country as in the 1960s, but ABRI officers still exercise wide powers of supervision and control over local officials and societal organisations throughout rural society.

Fear is a weapon ABRI has learnt to use with great effect to ensure it gets its way. The full extent of the army's role in the killings and arrests of Communists in 1965–66, or later in the cold-blooded 'mysterious killings' of criminal elements in 1982–83, has been hidden from public scrutiny, but in both cases terror was a powerful weapon and authorisation for its use came from the highest levels in ABRI.[28] Fear also undergirds the wide powers of the agency with primary responsibility for security and order, Kopkamtib, renamed Bakorstanas in 1988, a body responsible directly to the President, which exercises broad and loosely defined 'security', intelligence and interrogation functions.[29] Its security role puts it virtually beyond the scope of normal legal safeguards for ordinary citizens. ABRI units have been engaged in low-level anti-insurgency operations throughout Indonesia almost constantly since 1966.[30] These have been cited as the main security threats that constitute ABRI's *raison d'être*, although many of today's officers and troops have in fact had little or no field experience of combat, except in East Timor.

Soeharto imposed sweeping organisational changes on ABRI in the late 1960s, which transformed the previously unruly, semi-autonomous regional units and their commanders by greatly tightening the control of army headquarters over them. These reforms eroded the old loyalties of troops to their former regional divisions—which had previously been a source of serious military factionalism—by intermixing them, and enhancing their training and professionalism. In the process he greatly strengthened his own personal authority over the entire armed forces structure. No regional commanders have since been able to act as local warlords, as several did in the 1950s, or to ignore orders from the ABRI central command.[31]

The size of the armed forces has simultaneously been reduced very substantially, from over 340 000 in 1965 to 278 000 in 1989, while the proportion of the national budget allocated to ABRI has been reduced.[32] The army is now leaner, better trained and better equipped than in the 1960s, although it is still seriously lacking in many essentials; the navy and air force having been kept particularly small and weak because of early suspicions about their political loyalties. ABRI is neither large nor powerfully armed by international standards, especially in proportion to the vast territory it must cover. But its political influence is greater than that of any other body in the country.

Soeharto's relations with the ABRI top brass have not always been plain sailing. He antagonised General Nasution, his former superior officer, by shunting him into political insignificance in 1966–67, along with other senior divisional commanders, the 'New Order hawks', who opposed him over matters of political strategy in the late 1960s.[33] He has at times appointed to key command positions men whom he could trust to pose no challenges to him, passing over more senior or capable officers. He had his critics among the senior officers during the 1970s because of his reliance on a handful of personal advisers, notably Major Generals Ali Murtopo and Soedjono Humardhani, whose business interests and political activities alienated the more strictly professional field soldiers. The dissatisfaction peaked in 1978–80 in the form of various discussion groups of retired senior officers (and a few civilians), most notably the 'Petition of 50' group, which protested that the president was abusing the *dwifungsi* doctrine and putting the professional standing of ABRI at risk by engaging in excessively strong-arm tactics on Golkar's behalf in the 1977 elections (Jenkins 1984).

Soeharto swiftly outmanoeuvred his critics and punished the more intractable of them by withdrawing the usual 'facilities' normally made available to senior officers in the form of credits, business licences and the like. But in the process he made bitter enemies of several of the New Order's most capable and widely-respected generals, particularly Ali Sadikin, Dharsono, Sarwo Edhie and (for a time) Jasin. Some years later he also antagonised General Benny Moerdani, formerly one of his most loyal and trusted officers, who was bypassed in the selection of a new vice-president in 1988 and simultaneously removed from his position as armed forces chief-of-staff.[34] Since then many signs have emerged of a widening discrepancy between the political interests of ABRI as a continuing institution and the president's own short-term political strategies regarding the 1992–93 elections and the 'succession issue' more generally.

As a former general and army chief, President Soeharto has always identified himself closely with ABRI. In the last resort he depends upon it, although he has also made its leaders dependent on him for their positions. So long as that mutual dependency and loyalty persists, the future of his regime remains assured, but if it were to crumble—no longer as inconceivable a scenario after the Dili massacre as it seemed a few years earlier—the consequences could be unpredictable.

Ideology, social control and human rights

Ideological indoctrination has been a powerful instrument of social control under the New Order, both in persuading people to accept its policies, ensuring a high degree of outward conformity towards the wishes of the authorities and reducing their need to rely solely on the battery of severely repressive controls at their disposal. The mechanisms of indoctrination and repression are so intertwined that it is often difficult to discern where each begins and ends. Critics and opponents of the regime know they must resort to self-censorship on 'sensitive' issues in order to keep well inside the limits of what is pèrmissible. The terms of the Anti-Subversion Law, which has been used to prosecute those who overstep those limits, are 'so broadly worded as to provide no meaningful guidance' (Asia Watch 1990:136).

The press has had to tread a fine line in any critical comment because overt censorship, bans on the reporting of 'security-related' issues, often broadly or capriciously defined, and the ultimate sanction of suffering unexplained withdrawal of publication licences, makes the risks of printing certain types of stories too great to incur. Yet despite the restrictions on freedom of expression and the self-censorship it engenders, commentators can get away with the use of generally recognised code words for the discussion of sensitive issues, on which some degree of public debate is possible (see chapter 6). Several editors have learned how to approach the limits of the permissible with admirable skill and courage, publishing critical reports and comment indirectly or obliquely, so that some parts of the press, at least, remain lively and vital despite the restrictions, although many unfortunately do not.[35]

Great emphasis has been put on the centrality of *Pancasila* as the ideological basis of Indonesian nationhood, with any 'deviation' to the left or the right, either towards communism, 'laissez-faire capitalism', or Islamic extremism, being deemed a potential threat to national unity. The five pillars of *Pancasila* (belief in God, nationalism, humanity, sovereignty of the people, and social justice) are more frequently defined negatively in terms of what they rule out rather than in positive terms about the kind of society they ideally foreshadow.[36] It can be argued that in such a culturally heterogeneous society as Indonesia, divided socially as well as ideologically since 1945 between advocates of an Islamic society, a socialist or communist one, and some variant of capitalism, this kind of second-best formula has at least served to rule extremist options out of court by upholding a vaguely middle-of-the-road consensus. In the *Pancasila* indoctrination courses of 1979–80 great emphasis was put on the unacceptability of appeals to religious and ethnic solidarity as a basis for political organisation, against which *Pancasila* enjoined religious tolerance and social equality. Despite the gap between ideal and reality, or the intellectual shortcomings of the social philosophy underpinning *Pancasila*, it can be said that it seems to have become widely accepted as the national ideology—and the alternatives to it are certainly regarded as socially and politically divisive. But while the content of that ideology may be unexceptionable, its intellectual hegemony has had disturbing consequences.

One strange aspect of that hegemony, incidentally, is the great emphasis President Soeharto has put on the notion that Indonesia is not and should not be a 'capitalist' society, despite abundant evidence that his policies are steadily making it so, particularly at the uppermost income levels. The great emphasis he gives in his rhetoric to 'the cooperative principle' and Article 33 of the constitution which enjoins it cannot disguise the basic contradiction and cognitive dissonance involved here.

The invocation of *Pancasila* has served to maintain social control in various ways. Not only has it undercut the legitimacy of alternative ideologies, which had earlier been the source of intense party conflict during the Sukarno era, but it has had the effect of constraining the public expression of dissentient ideas and opinions within the limits of what is safe and uncontroversial. It has thereby induced a strong inclination towards conformity and self-censorship in public utterance because of the risks involved in straying beyond the limits, intentionally or otherwise. The use of *Pancasila* as a unifying ideology for a modernising Indonesia has in all these respects had much in common with the use made of the *tennosei* (emperor system) by the rulers of Meiji Japan, as described by Gluck (1985), to achieve a modicum of consensus in lieu of the fierce ideological debates that had been raging between traditionalists, reformers and radicals.[37] Even if they did not really believe in it, people were prepared to pay lip service to it and avoid challenging it.

Indoctrination occurs in many forms, the most focused being the P4 courses that are obligatory for all civil servants—and many other groups in the society. All state officials are also required to be members of *Korpri*, which constantly reinforces their adherence to *Pancasila* and their 'monoloyalty'. The wives of civil servants in all government bodies have to join *Dharma Wanita*, the official womens' organisation, headed always by the wife of the senior official, which inculcates an ethos of unquestioning obedience and acceptance of hierarchy and discourages independent thinking on political or social issues.[38] At the grassroots level, the traditional principle of *gotong royong* (mutual cooperation) is reinforced and manipulated by state officials as an extension of *Pancasila* in order to maintain social solidarity and minimise social disruption (Sullivan 1991:16).

Social control has also been exercised through the deployment of more directly coercive mechanisms. Former communists were excluded almost completely from employment in the bureaucracy or state enterprises in the early years of the New Order, while suspected communists were kept in line by the requirement that they obtain a certificate indicating 'non-involvement in *Gestapu*', without which all sorts of facilities became unobtainable. This highly flexible and arbitrary rule was further extended in the late 1980s by a regulation discriminating also against the children of parents who had been or might have been influenced by Marxist thinking (Asia Watch 1990:39–41). The sweepingly vague provisions of the Anti-Subversion Law, enacted in Sukarno's time, and the death penalty imposed under it, have been used frequently against supposed enemies or critics of the government. Overt dissent has been virtually silenced in the 1980s, not only by the government's broad powers of detention and its use of legal weapons to silence critics who overstepped the bounds of what was permissible, but also through the fear of being blacklisted, or the denial of rights to travel abroad, or exclusion from access to 'facilities' at the top end of the social spectrum.

Much more could be said for and against the poor human rights record of the New Order, but only some brief comments in its defence will be added here.[39] First, there is no strong tradition of legal or civil rights in Indonesia's indigenous cultures, and few close analogues to western liberal ideas of individual liberty. The major value systems of most ethnic groups in Indonesia tend to subordinate the rights and wishes of individuals to those of the family and the community (Reeve 1985:25). Individualism is commonly equated with selfishness. Open criticism of the ruler or the authorities, or dissent from official doctrine, is a source of acute psychic discomfort to many Indonesians. There is endless debate about how to adapt the modern laws and institutions of the country to traditional values and mores, or to those of Islam, which themselves differ greatly from one part of the country to another. In that regard, the nation-building process still has a long way to go. So it is premature to expect Indonesian officials and military officers to uphold modern western legal concepts or doctrines of human rights that they regard as alien.[40]

Second, it should be borne in mind that many courageous and enlightened Indonesians in the law, the media, the NGOs and the intellectual community more generally are not satisfied with the status quo in this respect and have been pushing for changes more in line with modern international norms in law, in court procedures and in rights to free speech. But they are doing so in their own idiom, not those of the west. The Legal Aid Bureau has figured prominently in this struggle, which has waxed and waned since 1965, sometimes gaining ground, but too often losing out (Lev 1987). Values and perceptions of individual rights are changing throughout Indonesian society, although slowly and with few clear guidelines for the future.

Third, it is probably true to say that private expression of criticism and dissenting opinions still occurs more uninhibitedly in Indonesia than in, for example, Singapore, despite press controls and a plethora of intelligence agencies. While Soeharto's regime is authoritarian and repressive in many respects, there is sufficient leeway that relatively few of its citizens would regard it as a police state—apart from its victims, who are in most cases out of sight and mind.

Nation building and national unity

One of the major achievements of the Soeharto regime has been to solidify considerably the sense of national unity of Indonesia. This is in sharp contrast to the situation before 1965, with threats of regional secession, bitter and ingrained tensions between Java and the outer islands, the deep-seated ideological and social conflicts of the 1960s and the fervid rhetoric of that time about what kind of 'national personality' was appropriate for the new Indonesia. These problems have not entirely disappeared, but the tension has largely gone out of them. Regionalism is not a major issue, except in Aceh, Irian Jaya and East Timor, all quite special cases.[41]

The task of welding a unified nation out of Indonesia's many islands, ethnic groups, cultures and religions has constantly been a major concern for all governments since 1945. The various regional rebellions of the 1950s underlined the precariousness of Indonesia's national unity. Complaints about exploitation, neglect and domination by the Jakarta authorities that fuelled regional resentments at that time have been largely mitigated by the flow of funds and development projects now provided by the central government. While it would be absurd to imply that the problems of nation-building, regionalism and decentralisation have yet been resolved, there did seem to be a more general inclination in the 1980s to accept the national framework of institutional and political arrangements that bind the 27 provinces of Indonesia together than there was before 1965.

Crucially important in the process of welding the nation together has been the state-run education system and the 'national' outlook, ideology and values it inculcates, as well as other institutions like ABRI and the bureaucracy. These have all created strong centripetal pulls towards unity by virtue of their strongly national rather than regional orientations. So also has the national radio and television network and, to a lesser extent, some parts of the press. Over a longer time span, the trading networks, banking and credit system and almost universal dependence on Jakarta for capital and know-how have had the same effect, especially in the boom conditions since 1979 (Mackie 1980; Drake 1989). Regional secession is now simply not an attractive option for most parts of the country, apart from a few provinces with large resources of oil or timber (Hill 1989).

Pride in being an Indonesian and in partaking of a distinctive national identity, while at the same time retaining a regional or ethnic identity as a Balinese, Batak or Javanese, has been another key element in the nation-building process. The geographical and cultural diversities constantly depicted on national television, usually in the form of regional costumes, dances and music, and in the press, seem to have become accepted as integral parts of the colourful amalgam that is generally regarded as the national culture. Whereas ethnic and regional identities once seemed potentially dangerous sources of separatist sentiment and conflict, cultural and religious diversity is officially extolled as an intrinsic part of 'being an Indonesian'. Indonesians of most ethnic backgrounds have learnt to live fairly comfortably with multiple identities since the 1960s, in particular the educated middle classes, who have benefited most from the achievements of the New Order.

This does not mean, of course, that all the problems of national integration have been solved, or that there are no divisive ethnic or social tensions to be resolved. Serious disagreements about national goals and strategies persist on many fronts: the place of Islam in national life; dislike of the increasing 'Javanisation' of political and socio-cultural arrangements; and the widening gap between the wealthy or well-connected and the poorer salary earners, between farmers, rural workers and city dwellers, and so on. Basic value conflicts persist between traditional and modern lifestyles, especially in the big, cosmopolitan cities.

It is the middle classes, above all, who participate most fully in the benefits of the 'national metropolitan superculture' (H. Geertz 1963) and whose education, jobs and life experiences make them especially conscious of their identity as Indonesians rather than just as members of the various ethnic groups. Their geographical and socio-economic mobility has expanded the range of their ideas and personal contacts, as well as their consciousness of the nation as a multi-ethnic unit, due in large part to the economic and communications developments of the last twenty years that have bound the country together in an increasingly dense network of commercial interchange.

The nation-building process occurs through a combination of coercive and persuasive measures in virtually all developing countries. Certain courses of action are closed off to its citizens, while others are opened up, or made more attractive. In Indonesia, the political extremes of right and left have been excluded from the mainstream of the ideological consensus the New Order has been building upon, very much as in Meiji Japan. There has been general support for this across a broad middle band of the ideological spectrum. People do not want to return to the ideological conflicts of the past, just as in China few want to return to the excesses of the Cultural Revolution. Fears of a relapse into the social turmoil of 1965–66 are still strong in the memories of many who lived through that period.

Indonesia's heterogeneity still poses massive problems of nation building that will probably take decades or even generations to resolve fully. Yet steady progress is being made. Solutions are likely to be worked out within a framework of general acceptance of the New Order structures and institutions by the regions (or at least of their main features), rather than of demands for their fundamental reshaping, as before 1965.

Islam and politics under the New Order

The strongly Islamic (*santri*) part of the Indonesian population has had mixed fortunes under the New Order.[42] Muslim groups were among the most militantly anti-communist within the early New Order coalition, deeply involved in mass attacks on the PKI in several regions in 1965–66. So they expected to be rewarded with office and political power after the overthrow of Sukarno. They were angered by their terse exclusion from positions of real political power by Soeharto—who was a known exponent of Javanese *kebatinan* (mystical) religious practices, which were anathema to them—as they gradually found themselves marginalised politically. The Muslim political parties were compelled by the government to combine against their wishes into the PPP in 1973, then gradually pushed into a position of open hostility to the Soeharto regime during the 1970s over various issues of great concern to them.

Relations between the government and the Muslims were at their worst in the mid-1970s. The Muslims resented the process of fusion into one party, the PPP, under great pressure from the civil authorities, and were angered by the introduction into the DPR of a national Marriage Law in 1973 which disregarded key principles of long-accepted Islamic law on the subject. Government interference in later PPP leadership struggles to ensure the election of pliable leaders added to their rancour (see Nasir Tamara 1990:18–19). So, too, did its heavy-handed coercion and vote-rigging in the 1977 elections, when the PPP believed it would make big gains at the expense of Golkar, since it was by then widely acknowledged to be the only effective 'opposition' force in the political system.

Soeharto's insistence on pushing at the 1978 MPR session for acceptance of *kebatinan* as a 'belief' officially recognised by the Department of Religion further alienated the Muslims, aggravating the polarisation within society more deeply. And the 1982–84 drive to have the *Pancasila* accepted by all organisations as the *azas tunggal* (unifying principle of the state) was objectionable to them on theological grounds, although they were ultimately forced to acquiesce. Relations with the government were badly strained, too, by its heavy-handed crackdown on minor Islamic fundamentalist groups after the Iranian revolution and the Tanjung Priok incident of 1984, followed by other outbreaks of violence, mostly quite minor and capricious, for which Islamic extremists were blamed.[43]

In the mid-1980s, a new and younger leadership group headed by Abdurrahman Wahid in the old NU, the major religious organisation within the PPP, urged that it adopt a new strategy of abjuring political activities and dissociating from the PPP in order to concentrate on more purely

31

religious and social welfare activities (Nasir Tamara 1990). That strategy has been largely adopted, despite some opposition within both organisations. In the 1987 elections the PPP did not campaign on directly Islamic issues and the NU permitted its members to vote for any party, with the result that the PPP vote fell sharply. More significantly, President Soeharto himself began courting Muslim support for Golkar in the 1992 elections, a major turn-about in political alignments.

In the long term, however, the most significant feature of the changing status of Islam since 1966 has been the impressive spread of its educational institutions funded from the state budget—including the new IAIN (*Institut Agama Islam Negeri*) at the tertiary level—which are now sending substantial numbers of their graduates into various offices within the bureaucracy, both secular and Islamic. At the local level, Islamic organisations feel they are making real progress in the spread of the faith (Hefner 1987a). The visible manifestations of Islamic belief, such as participation in the Friday mosque service, in daily prayers and the use of verses from the Koran in opening public meetings, are far more prominent than in the 1960s. The old *santri–abangan* cleavage has not entirely disappeared, but it is much more blurred and less significant politically and socially than it used to be.

At the regional levels, in particular, the authorities have learnt to come to terms with the more strongly Muslim groups in society, and in many cases have been quite successful in winning their cooperation or acquiescence through policies of cooptation, and provision of financial support for their social and educational activities. The most striking feature of Islam under the New Order is that despite all the efforts of the state apparatus to control or tame the Muslims as a political force or a potential source of opposition to the regime, their solidarity and mass backing has remained remarkably intact. Islam remains a potentially powerful force, the mosques and their Friday sermons not easy to control under the New Order's ideological dragnet. On the purely religious plane, moreover, Islam has been growing stronger across almost the entire archipelago than at any previous time in its centuries-long history of gradual proselytisation there.

The Chinese minority: political and economic aspects

Because of the great economic strength of Indonesia's ethnic Chinese minority, numbering between four and five million in 1990, and their almost complete exclusion from significant positions of formal political power under the New Order, their status is problematic.[44] The very rich tycoons, such as Liem Sioe Liong, exert considerable indirect influence on certain types of economic decisions, mostly on particular contracts or credit allocations rather than on more general economic strategy, through their personal and financial connections with government officials, much as the Southeast Asian Chinese have always done. Little is known publicly about such dealings, however, or the full extent of their impact on economic policy-making or policy implementation. Less wealthy ethnic Chinese businessmen have to resort to bribes and pay-offs of many kinds at lower levels in order to clear away the bureaucratic obstructions placed in the way of their business operations (often deliberately). Yet political vulnerability as members of an unpopular minority leaves them in a precarious position which constrains their ability to alter this situation much.

Chinese Indonesian businessmen are now unquestionably the wealthiest in the land, the foremost pioneers in the development of the increasingly capitalist economic structure that is emerging in Indonesia; but they are not allowed to parlay their economic power into political influence except through personalistic connections with the authorities.[45] Nor can they act collectively as an ethnic group, or as the core element within Indonesia's newly-emerging middle class, or propertied bourgeoisie, to play a more active part in shaping the key institutions, policies or ideology of the nation.[46] Yet the economic position of virtually all Chinese Indonesians has improved considerably under the New Order, at all levels of society, probably more than that of all but the wealthiest *pribumi*. Thus these political constraints are not a heavy price to pay for their prosperity, although the discrimination rankles.

They are more readily accepted today as Indonesians than they were in the 1960s (although still not totally) and are becoming more like their neighbours in the middle-class suburbs to which many thousands have been moving, where they face the same headaches as other Indonesians about public transport, access to schooling and disturbing juvenile delinquency. The level of overt hostility to them is far below that which boiled over into violence in 1965–66, although there is still a lot of covert discrimination against ethnic Chinese, regardless of the fact that nearly all of them are now Indonesian nationals.[47] In fact, the Soeharto government's handling of 'the Chinese problem' ranks as one of its less recognised success stories, despite its inadequacies. Although several outbreaks of anti-Chinese violence have occurred, the authorities have moved firmly to contain it in each case before it got out of hand and spread, unlike the various episodes in the 1960s.

Yet as they are members of an unpopular minority subject to constant discrimination and extortion because they are regarded as something like 'second-class citizens', even the wealthy Chinese businessmen feel vulnerable and insecure. The ugly term 'pariah capitalists', applied by Riggs to the Chinese in Thailand and the Philippines in the 1960s, is still appropriate to the Chinese Indonesians.[48] And it suits the ruling elite, unfortunately, to keep it that way, and not to remedy the civic and social inequalities implicit in the notion.

Steady progress towards acculturation and ultimate assimilation has occurred since 1966 and long-term changes in the character of the Chinese minority are slowly advancing that process, although Indonesia lags far behind Thailand in blurring the ethnic boundary lines. There is no longer such a significant distinction as before between the alien, China-oriented *totok* newcomers among the Chinese and the partially acculturated *peranakan* families, long resident in Indonesia and who were in most cases Indonesian citizens. All but a handful of ethnic Chinese have become Indonesian citizens, nearly all speak some Indonesian, at least, and most now attend Indonesian schools, including children of *totok* families, the former Chinese-language schools and newspapers having been closed.

Because relations between Indonesia and China became badly strained during the two years of mutual suspicion and tension after *Gestapu* and in 1967 were 'frozen' (that is, not formally broken, although in effect so until normalised again in 1990), for over twenty years, both alien Chinese and Chinese Indonesians came to realise they could no longer rely on support from Chinese embassy officials in the event of difficulties. They had no choice but to come to terms with Indonesian authorities as best they could and rely on Indonesian citizenship to ensure them equal rights, at least formally (Coppel 1983; Tan 1991).

A dozen or so wealthy Chinese businessmen became notorious in the early years of the new regime as *cukong* (financiers and intermediaries), who provided badly-needed funds and supplies to the ABRI leadership in return for political protection and favours. The best known was Liem Sioe Liong, who had been associated with President Soeharto during his days as military commander in Central Java long before 1965 and is still closely associated in extensive business ventures with him and members of his family. Liem has become by far the richest person in Indonesia, one of the three foremost billionaires in all Southeast Asia, controlling a huge conglomerate enterprise estimated to be worth more than $3.5 billion in the late 1980s. By then at least fifty other large conglomerates had acquired assets of over Rp200 billion (approximately $100 million), 80 per cent of them Sino-Indonesian in ownership, many of them closely connected with members of the Soeharto family, and all having personal connections with governmental authorities to a greater or lesser degree.[49] Inevitably, their prominence gave rise to a great deal of resentment against the Chinese generally, as well as against 'conglomerates' and big business, while the term itself became a code word alluding also to the business interests of the Soeharto family.

The politics of economic policy

One of the defining features of the New Order has been its starkly different approach to economic policy in comparison with the Sukarno period. This was an inevitable response to the economic chaos facing Indonesia in

1965–66. With the country close to bankruptcy and the economy clogged up by overregulation, one of Soeharto's first steps was to summon a group of US-trained economists at the University of Indonesia to advise him on how best to reverse the decline. This step was crucial, for the market-oriented, outward-looking approach of the economists has characterised Soeharto's overall strategy ever since.[50]

The immediate priority of the new team of 'technocrats', as they came to be known, was to curb inflation, stabilise the rapidly-depreciating rupiah, negotiate debt rescheduling and obtain foreign aid and private investment to restore productive capacity. These liberalising reforms reflected both the orientation of the technocrats themselves and, equally, the conditions demanded by their western creditors in return for the rescheduling of the country's heavy debts and the negotiation of new loans. Foreign investment laws were liberalised in order to entice foreign capital back into Indonesia. The trade regime was overhauled, enabling raw materials and capital goods to again flow into the country. More generally, there was a reduced emphasis on state-led attempts at industrialisation, with preferential treatment to state enterprises now reduced and priority given to encouragement of private sector investment in industry.

This free-market strategy lost some of its momentum in the early 1970s. Two developments led the government to return to a reassertion of the previously prevalent nationalist and interventionist economic themes. One was the popular backlash that emerged from both right and left in response to the liberalisation of economic policy, especially against the active encouragement of foreign investment, which was criticised strongly as 'selling out' to foreign capital. A sharp resurgence in nationalist sentiment culminated in the January 1974 Malari incident. The government responded by tightening up on the terms of foreign investment and introducing measures to assist domestic businessmen. The second development, even more crucial, was the oil boom of 1973–74. The resulting surge in revenue removed the most severe policy constraint upon the government's development plans. With the worst of the economic chaos left by Sukarno now behind it, the government felt able to deviate a little from the initial purity of its free-market doctrines.

As in all other spheres of policy-making, President Soeharto's position has been pivotal here. But struggles between contending factions competing for the president's ear have characterised economic policy-making increasingly since the mid-1970s. Three groupings in economic policy debates can be broadly delineated: old-style economic nationalists, interventionists and free marketeers. Old-style economic nationalism is still an influential school of thought, expressing constant reservation about the free-market ideology and a profound distrust of foreign capital, although it has not been strongly represented at the ministerial level. This ideological tradition finds supporters in the press, some sections of the military and in university circles. While welcoming the economic achievements of the New Order, old-school economic nationalists reiterate the collectivist economic principles enshrined in Article 33 of the constitution and recall Sukarno's determination to stand up to western economic interests, even at the cost of telling the United States in 1964 to 'go to hell' with its aid.

Of much greater direct influence on economic policy has been the second grouping, the interventionists. This is a diverse cluster of powerful figures within the government who, together with their private-sector counterparts, have pressed for active government intervention in and regulation of market behaviour. Key figures in this cluster, such as Minister for Research and Technology, Habibie, former Pertamina head, Ibnu Sutowo, and several Ministers of Industry, have been committed to building up indigenous industrial capabilities by protecting target industries or providing them with massive financial subsidies. The principal institutions involved have been the Department of Research and Technology, the Department of Industry, the Investment Board, the food procurement agency, Bulog, and, in the 1970s, the state oil company Pertamina. While this grouping is philosophically close to the old-style nationalists, its leading members accept many of the views of the technocrats on deregulation. But they have also come into conflict with the latter over their involvement in extravagant rent-taking projects, over which there has been a constant tug of war.

The technocrats and other market-oriented bureaucrats have been the most cohesive of the three policy groupings, being concentrated in the Ministry of Finance, the Planning Agency, Bappenas, and Bank Indonesia. The cohesiveness of the groups stems largely from the fact that they are the ideological 'radicals', the bearers of a set of ideas which carry the promise of major economic and political change but diverge from the old ideological orthodoxy represented by Article 33 of the constitution. Like their counterparts in other countries, developing and developed, they are more strongly committed to markets and competition rather than government intervention in production and investment decisions. Yet their ideas are quite alien to the mainstream of Indonesian political thinking. This sets Indonesia apart from other ASEAN countries, not to mention Taiwan or South Korea. Notions of unrestrained capitalist competition and the supremacy of markets have not yet achieved ideological legitimacy in Indonesia. Hence advocates of liberalisation (a term the technocrats avoid using in public discourse) have had to move very cautiously in seeking to promote their agenda for economic reform.[51]

To a large extent economic policy under the New Order has been characterised by a see-sawing between the arguments of the interventionists (supported, generally, by the old-style nationalists) and those of the technocrats. The influence of the latter has been greatest in periods of inclement economic conditions, principally the immediate post-Sukarno years (already mentioned) and the period from 1983 to the present. During the intervening years their influence was heavily circumscribed. The resurgence in nationalist and interventionist ideas in the early 1970s manifested itself in a number of ways. Foreign investment regulations were once again tightened. Trade and industry policy was redirected as the country set off on a state-led drive for import substituting industrialisation. Armed with the revenue from oil taxes, the government began investing heavily in state enterprises and basic infrastructure in a bid to develop an integrated industrial base. Notable here were the activities of the giant state oil corporation, Pertamina, and its counterpart, Krakatau Steel. Pertamina was of particular importance due to the fact that it was also the point of collection for oil taxes. As oil revenues continued to grow, so did the state's capacity to involve itself directly in the economy and lead the way in industrial development by sponsoring large-scale investment projects in key industries. Importantly, however, there was no active bias against private entrepreneurs, as had been the case under Sukarno. Indeed, a number of politically favoured business groups received highly preferential treatment in terms of access to credit, licences and so on, and were able to expand rapidly.

As the government became increasingly awash with funds from the oil sector, so the interventionists continued to gain policy ascendancy over the liberal technocrats. The influence of the liberals tended to be confined to macroeconomic policy issues, with the nationalists controlling most aspects of trade and industry policy. This trend continued throughout the 1970s, except for a brief interruption following the staggering discovery that Pertamina was, in effect, bankrupt and unable to sustain the debt burden it had acquired through mismanagement and rampant corruption. The massive financial rescue operation mounted to save Pertamina did not, however, lead to any fundamental changes in the overall economic orientation. Indeed, the current favouring economic interventionism and nationalism was soon running even faster following the second oil boom in 1979. In a period of plenty, the market-oriented policy prescriptions of the liberal technocrats found few supporters.

Commencing in the mid-1980s, this picture began to change, as the policy pendulum moved back in the direction of the economic liberals. This ushered in what has been the longest sustained period in which market-oriented ideas have held sway in economic policy debates. Although a number of factors were involved in this gradual reorientation of economic policy, the key variable was the marked economic downturn beginning in the early 1980s. Having enjoyed a sustained and unparalleled period of high growth rates during the 1970s and into the early 1980s, the Indonesian economy was subject between 1984 and 1986 to extreme buffeting as a result of the collapse in oil and other primary commodity prices, the recession in the global economy and an unfavourable realignment of the major currencies. Coming together, these various factors combined to induce severe contraction in the Indonesian economy and rapidly rising current account deficits.

The effect of these adverse developments was to create an opening for the liberal technocrats to expand their influence. Put simply, the economic crisis of the mid-1980s created a situation in which continued reliance on interventionist and inward-looking economic policies had become increasingly untenable. In a pattern similar to that in the economically uncertain early years of the New Order, Soeharto turned increasingly to the liberal technocrats. This enabled them to mount a sustained policy reform drive aimed at deregulating the economy and encouraging the development of export industries.

To begin with, the pace and extent of reform was moderate, and, indeed, at times ambiguous, for the resistance of groups within the government opposing fundamental reorientation remained strong. This was scarcely surprising given the long tradition of state interventionism. As a result, the initial policy adjustments were confined mostly to those areas where the liberal technocrats had greatest influence—macroeconomic policy and the financial services sector. As the balance of payments worsened, the political pendulum in economic policy debates began to swing further away from the interventionists, and the liberal economists within the government were able to push for more far-reaching reforms. This was particularly so following the sharp drop in oil prices in early 1986. Since then, there has been a steady series of policy reform packages to deregulate financial markets, reform the taxation system, and liberalise the trade and investment regimes. The reforms have brought about far-reaching changes, stimulating a gradual shift away from reliance on primary production with the expansion of the manufacturing sector and in particular setting the economy moving in a more export-oriented direction.

The policy reforms brought about by the economic liberals have won Indonesia applause from foreign investors as well as from institutions such as the World Bank and the IMF. But the very success of the liberals has also given rise to conditions which may serve to undermine their dominant position in policy debates. The bouts of rapid growth brought about by their reforms have resulted in very rapid expansion of big business, which in turn has led to growing concern about economic inequality. In addition, their steady drive to extend deregulation is bringing them into increasing conflict with the interests of politically well-connected business people (including members of the president's family), who operate as *rentiers* and generate great wealth on the basis of selective government interventions in the market. These factors, together with the evident determination of key figures such as Minister Habibie, may lead to a partial resurgence of the interventionists in economic policy-making.

The status of big business

Two decades of rapid economic growth have had numerous consequences. One of the most conspicuous has been the emergence of a sizeable local business class, and in particular a limited number of very large family-owned conglomerates. Predictably, these large combines have been overwhelmingly controlled by Chinese Indonesians, the most notable exceptions being the rapidly-expanding business empires of President Soeharto's children. Coinciding with the accelerating pace of liberal economic policy reforms in the late 1980s and early 1990s, there has been a marked increase in the level of public criticism of the big conglomerates.

Anti-Chinese sentiments and broad-based resentment at economic concentration is of course nothing new in Indonesia. What makes this most recent wave of criticism remarkable is the way in which it has focused on the very largest conglomerates and drawn critical connections between their extraordinary prosperity and the government's economic policies. There has been much public commentary arguing that rather than leading to improved economic circumstances for the great majority of Indonesians, the government's shift towards more market-oriented policies during the 1980s has served principally to make the very wealthy even wealthier still. Resentment has been sharpened by the perception that many of the most successful of the conglomerates have prospered primarily because of cronyism.

The key to the sudden upsurge of critical attention directed towards the conglomerates in 1989–90 appears to have been the reinvigoration of the Jakarta Stock Exchange and the simultaneous deregulation of the private banks. A series of regulatory reforms since late 1987 has transformed the Jakarta Stock Exchange from being an inconsequential institution to a potentially significant component of Indonesia's capital market. A rapid surge in the number of firms wanting to go public, together with the entry of several international securities firms, saw the exchange transformed from its previous torpor into a rapidly-expanding capital market. Coinciding as it did with the rapid expansion of private banks, this seemed to indicate (briefly, and prematurely) that the private sector was awash with funds.

These developments in the late 1980s were an important factor behind the wave of critical attention towards the conglomerates for two reasons. First, they drew attention to the size and prosperity of some of the leading business conglomerates; second, the other big corporations were seen as benefiting disproportionately from the deregulation of capital markets. In order to list their shares, companies have had to disclose certain information about their assets and performance. While the auditing and reporting standards adopted by firms wishing to go public have unquestionably been dubious in many cases, the fact remains that they have had to publish much more detailed financial profiles than ever before. This was an important development as many of the leading firms had previously been deliberately tight-lipped about their financial circumstances. One result has been that the public could see for the first time just how well they are in fact doing. And their financial statements have attracted widespread media attention. Thus, the disclosure requirements of the stock exchange have catapulted corporate wealth into the public eye.

On top of this is the fact that firms going public did extraordinarily well on a booming stock market in 1989–90 (although it slumped later). With most new issues of shares being heavily oversubscribed (partly because of interest from international investors), a number of firms saw their listed stocks skyrocket in value. Not surprisingly, this fuelled popular perceptions that it is big business which is benefiting most from the deregulation of the financial sector—and, indeed, from economic liberalisation more generally.

The rapid growth of the stock exchange together with parallel developments such as the deregulation of the banking sector (and subsequent mushrooming of private banks) have stimulated critical interest in the affairs of big business and served to bring latent social resentments back to the boil. In response to the heating up of debate on the conglomerates, President Soeharto summoned 27 of the country's leading business figures to his ranch at Tapos (near Jakarta) for a meeting, at which he delivered a homily on the need for business leaders to act in a socially responsible manner and to consider the well-being of the wider community rather than simply their own. In what was a well-publicised media exercise, Soeharto reiterated and re-emphasised a call made early in 1990 for leading companies to transfer 25 per cent of their shareholdings to designated cooperatives. It appears that the president's actions were designed principally to defuse mounting public resentment by attempting to create the impression that the government would force big business to behave in a more altruistic fashion. In practice, the government has not taken any firm measures against the conglomerates. Ultimately, a greatly watered-down arrangement was introduced which imposed only very slight costs on the conglomerates.

The surge in resentment towards the big conglomerates has not led to any marked shifts in economic policy. Despite intensified government rhetoric concerning the plight of the poor, the government remains committed to its market-oriented rapid-growth strategies. But if the upswing of criticism of big business does not have immediate policy implications, it is nonetheless of long-term significance for it marks a gradual strengthening in the class dimension in Indonesian political life.

Political implications of an expanding bourgeoisie

That there is a sizeable business class in Indonesia is no longer in any doubt. The high-rise office buildings which now crowd Jakarta's boulevards are a stark testimony to its existence. Significantly, these buildings are inhabited not only by foreign companies: local firms feature prominently. Indeed, by comparison with other Southeast Asian countries, foreign investment has played a relatively small part in Indonesia's economic development. But if there is no longer debate about the emergence of an Indonesian bourgeoisie, there is still great uncertainty about the political importance of the fledgling business class. What has been the impact, if any, of the local business community upon policy?

In the past, business in Indonesia has been seen by most analysts as having surprisingly little political clout. While certainly not suppressed actively in the way the labour movement has been, business organisations have generally been weak and thoroughly coopted by the government. The prevailing pattern of interaction between business and the state has been 'clientelistic' links between individual business people seeking particular favours from senior officials in return for kickbacks of various sorts. This is regarded as especially typical of Chinese Indonesian business people, who have been unwilling to contemplate open and collective political action, relying instead on cultivating personal connections to influential patrons within the government. While clientelistic links have plainly helped some business firms become enormously wealthy through favoured access to government licences and contracts, cheap credit and the like, they have not generally translated into a capacity to influence wider policy decisions.

In sum, for most of the New Order period, the state has been widely seen as relatively unconstrained by business pressure in the shaping of policy decisions. Indonesia's business class has frequently been described, in the terms applied to Thailand by Riggs (1966), as a 'bureaucratic polity' and its business class as impotent 'pariah entrepreneurs'. There have indeed been strong grounds for this view. In most cases the fastest growing large business groups have been heavily dependent upon preferential political treatment, which, inevitably, brings into question the degree of autonomy or potential for independent political action the leaders of Indonesia's business class in fact enjoy. Second, notwithstanding the growth of indigenously-controlled firms, it remains inescapably the case that the great majority of firms are in the hands of Chinese Indonesians, who remain politically vulnerable and thus ultimately beholden to the government for protection.

In spite of the continuing force of the 'statist' orthodoxy, this feature of Indonesia's political economy is no longer as clearly defined as it once was. There have been signs in recent years that this picture is beginning to change as some sections of the private sector have begun to organise themselves more effectively for collective political action. In a growing number of industries, business associations have become more assertive and effective. Some of the more conspicuous cases have emerged in the export sector or in industries in which one politically favoured individual or clique has been granted monopoly privileges to the detriment of other producers. More broadly, however, it can also be seen that the private sector is now emerging as the driving force in the Indonesian economy as the level of direct state involvement in the economy declines. The private sector now plays a far larger role in the economy, and we should not be surprised to see industry groups becoming more forceful political players. This means that, in addition to the established pattern of clientelistic or crony bonds, we are likely to see some sections of business develop a greater capacity to promote collective interests and secure a more effective voice in the policy process.

Foreign relations and the East Timor problem

If a dramatic reversal of economic policy was one of the first and most striking moves of the New Order regime, a complete reorientation of foreign policy was another. Under Sukarno, Indonesia's foreign policy had become increasingly radical. Since independence a lodestone of Indonesian foreign policy thinking has been the belief that it should maintain a non-aligned stance in world affairs, avoiding military alliances and resisting pressures to take sides in the cold war hostilities between the superpowers and their respective teams of supporters. During the 1960s, however, Sukarno's non-aligned stance took on an increasingly anti-western flavour as he moved towards ever closer relations with China. As part of his international crusade against all manifestations of colonialism and imperialism, Sukarno also entered into a melodramatic quasi-military conflict or 'confrontation' against the new, neighbouring state of Malaysia, declaring it a stooge of the imperialist forces.

After the overthrow of Sukarno, Indonesian foreign policy began to swing rapidly to the right. His flirtation with Beijing was ended abruptly by the New Order's military leaders, amidst accusations that China had been secretly aiding the Communist Party in Indonesia. Diplomatic relations with China were 'frozen' in 1967, remaining so until 1990. The conflict with Malaysia was quickly brought to an end, despite Sukarno's opposition. But the reorientation of Indonesia's foreign policy was not simply due to the conservative ideological disposition of the military. It was also implicitly part of the price that had to be paid by the new government if it was to secure the goodwill—and thus the financial support—of the major western powers. The immediate concern of the New Order leaders in 1966–67 above all else was economic stabilisation, which required western aid through the IGGI consortium, including the World Bank and the IMF.[52]

While the rapid reorientation of Indonesia's foreign policy did indeed please the major western powers—the result being that aid and foreign investment soon began to flow into Indonesia again—the switch attracted considerable criticism within Indonesia. The about-face in foreign and economic policy gave rise to objections that the government was selling out to western capitalism and that Indonesia would become trapped in the dependency syndrome. These concerns reached their climax in early 1974 with the Malari riots, although they gradually abated as the oil boom enhanced the country's financial independence.

Once the initial swing from left to right had occurred, foreign policy matters became less crucial. The two main concerns of the foreign ministry were to maintain the country's standing as one of the leading members of the Non-Aligned Movement by demonstrating that Indonesia was not just tied to the coat-tails of US foreign policy, and to build up more cordial relations with its neighbours by co-sponsoring the formation of ASEAN. Because the New Order has been preoccupied with maintaining political stability and promoting economic growth, foreign policy issues have had comparatively low priority. The Foreign Ministry has not been a powerful part of the state structure. Successive Foreign Ministers have had to contend with interference by the armed forces leadership in various international issues deemed to have security implications, particularly the Vietnam conflict. The weakness of the Foreign Ministry is further underlined by the fact that one of Indonesia's most important international relationships—its links with the CGI/IGGI consortium—is managed primarily by the economic ministries within the bureaucracy.

In substantive terms, the New Order's principal foreign policy priority has been to stabilise and institutionalise closer working relations with Indonesia's Southeast Asian neighbours. Not only did Jakarta take an active role in sponsoring the creation of ASEAN in 1967 in order to promote greater trust and cooperation with the region, it has also provided a site for the ASEAN secretariat and was host to the 1976 Bali summit meeting at which the ASEAN partners endeavoured to strengthen the fledgling organisation in the face of the communist victories in Indochina. In practice, this was only really achieved when the organisation was confronted with a serious external threat by the Vietnamese invasion of Cambodia in 1979.

During the 1980s Indonesia sought both to maintain ASEAN solidarity and to play a leading part in promoting a resolution to the Indochina conflict. In this it was constrained by the fact that its sympathy for the Vietnamese position in the stalemate was sometimes at odds with Thai and Singapore policies. For the sake of maintaining ASEAN unity, Indonesia was forced to accept compromises with the latter, although in the final stages of the negotiations which led to a solution of the Kampuchea conflict, Indonesia played a leading role in finding an acceptable solution.

The most troublesome issue in Indonesian foreign policy since 1975 has been the East Timor problem, which has been a source of minor but constant embarrassment, mainly in its dealings with major aid donors, the UN and the Non-Aligned Movement. After the collapse of Portuguese colonial rule in East Timor in 1974–75, Indonesia became increasingly involved in the civil conflict that developed between rival factions there, largely out of fear of a left-wing takeover and 'a Cuba on its doorstep' (at a time when the communist victories in Indochina were creating fears of international instability in the region). This led to Indonesian troops invading the terrritory, at first covertly, then openly, in late 1975, ostensibly in response to requests for support from the pro-Jakarta faction—the grounds used for the formal incorporation of the territory as part of Indonesia in 1976. But the process of annexation by military force was crudely and clumsily handled, arousing widespread international condemnation in the UN and elsewhere, which only partially abated in the 1980s.[53]

Indonesia's legal and moral status in East Timor is weakened by the fact that it could not advance the anticolonialist principle—which was successfully used in its earlier struggle to gain control of West Irian—that it had a valid legal and historical title as the successor state to the former Netherlands Indies. Instead, Indonesia has in turn been accused by its critics of colonial annexation, even within the Non-Aligned Movement for several years. Although the Soeharto government has allocated far greater development funds to the region and brought about major improvements in educational facilities and infrastructure, military dominance of the region and the heavy-handed suppression of pro-independence forces has been a source of constant protests against Indonesian control.

Recognition on a de jure basis has been withheld by the UN and most of the major powers, pending a satisfactory form of plebiscite, although several governments, including Indonesia's ASEAN partners and Australia, have eventually accepted the fait accompli. Indonesia chose in the 1980s to tough out the criticism and embarrassment it had incurred in the hope that the issue would gradually recede into the background, since the scope for compromise solutions is limited. But East Timor remained a running sore, for a handful of Fretilin guerrillas continued to hold out in the hills, and the heavy-handed measures taken by the military authorities in dealing with all opponents or critics there have simply kept the resistance alive. The killing of large numbers of demonstrators by the military in November 1991 has brought the issue to the forefront of international attention again, and could have quite unpredictable consequences for both domestic and foreign policy.

Conclusion: Soeharto and his regime

What conclusions can we draw about the character and durability of the New Order regime after its first quarter-century? The answers we might have given in 1989–90, when the economy was booming and President Soeharto's position at the helm seemed unassailable, would have been much more confident and positive than the ones that seem appropriate in the aftermath of the Dili massacre of November 1991. The massacre has brought to the surface a lot of questions about the fragility or brittleness of the regime (words preferable to 'stability'—a question-begging term) that were previously concealed.

At the end of the 1980s, two features of the evolution of the New Order political system over the previous quarter-century stood out. One was the predominance of President Soeharto himself and the high degree of personal control he had acquired over an increasingly concentrated power structure. The other was the extent to which the regime in general had become a self-perpetuating patronage system from top to bottom, rewarding those who have a place in it and penalising all who are excluded. This will make it extremely difficult for any reformist movement or coalition to bring about major changes from within the system, or open it up in more democratic or pluralist directions, because so many people have a vested interest in its maintenance. At most, some minor concessions may be allowed to advocates of reform, but not radical restructuring.

The part played by President Soeharto in bringing about this state of affairs has been so crucial that something must be said in conclusion about the man himself and his impact on the course of Indonesian history. Soeharto's own political and administrative style and his Central Javanese background have strongly influenced the highly-centralised processes of government that have evolved since 1966. His personality is reflected in the sensibly pragmatic planning mechanisms and economic strategies adopted, as well as in the blatant corruption and repression of opposition or dissent that he has tolerated or encouraged. His hand can be seen, too, in the form taken by the nebulous ideology of *Pancasila* and the concept of '*Pancasila* democracy', now invoked so commonly as the epitome of Indonesia's distinctiveness and traditional values (something Sukarno tried to conjure up as the 'national personality' with far less success). In both its achievements and its shortcomings, the New Order has been shaped by Soeharto's personal qualities as much as the Old Order was by Sukarno's.

Yet the inner man remains curiously unknown, almost cryptic and elusive, even to his closest associates. He generally presents himself as calm, dignified, restrained, soft-spoken, almost avuncular—'the Smiling General'.[54] Unlike Sukarno, whose entire life, even down to his love affairs, seemed to be conducted on a public stage, Soeharto has remained an intensely private man, devoted to his family, and his cattle farm. Indonesians refer to him as *tertutup* (reserved, shut off)—a quality respected by Javanese and utterly unlike the extrovert Sukarno. 'No one knows what that man thinks . . . That is the secret of his power', commented one senior politician who had watched him closely for years. Only occasionally does Soeharto lose his cool, or reveal much of his inner feelings and thinking.[55]

As the controlling figure at the apex of the political system, he has had great power to bestow delegated authority or material benefits upon loyal supporters, in the form of licences, credits or contracts, or access to funds held in semi-official foundations, and to deny them to opponents or critics. This patrimonialist aspect of his power conforms with his political style, paternalistic character and self-image as father to his people, rewarding and punishing his children, as in a family. Yet the obverse side of that coin has been his extraordinary blind spot about the harm being done to the people's trust in the regime by his children's avaricious business activities. The concentration of political, military and economic power in what now looks increasingly like an embryonic family dynasty has become very worrying to many Indonesians. It has also thwarted earlier hopes that the New Order would become sufficiently institutionalised that the succession issue would pose no great problems.

Because of all the uncertainties about the succession issue, no final or confident judgement on either Soeharto or his regime can yet be made. All that can be offered is at best a provisional assessment. If the transition to Indonesia's third president is managed smoothly, whenever it occurs, and if economic progress continues, Soeharto will go down in history as a great leader who lifted Indonesia out of the chaos of the Sukarno years. If not, if elite unity is badly fractured or ABRI factionalism gives rise to open political brawling, with contending groups bidding for popular support among diverse societal groups, future judgements may be very different, particularly if serious violence ensues (Crouch 1988).

At this stage, we can do little more than list the major strengths and weaknesses of the man and his regime, leaving the value judgements on these to the reader and to history. On the positive side, the New Order has succeeded in restoring political stability to a country that was plagued by instability and imminent social conflict. It has created political conditions favourable to steady economic development and managed the country's growth strategies with an impressive degree of success. It has greatly increased the effectiveness of an almost crippled bureaucratic apparatus, enabling critically important policies to succeed, such as the rice intensification program, the family planning program, the great expansion of the higher education system and the switch to manufactured exports.

There is now far greater predictability in government policies than before (although less than might be wished) and some degree of responsiveness to pressures from below. Soeharto's pragmatism, shrewdness and realism in adapting the government's policies to the circumstances of the times have served the country far better than did Sukarno's doctrinaire ideology. Soeharto has in general shown good judgement in his choice of high-calibre ministers and senior officials, both civil and military, with surprisingly few failures and many notable successes. His foreign policy

46

aims of restoring confidence in Indonesia among its Southeast Asian neighbours have been cautious and sensible, except in the case of East Timor.

On the negative side of the ledger, however, must be counted the high cost in lives and loss of freedoms involved in the destruction of the PKI, the poor record on human rights ever since then, most notably in the exclusion of former PKI members or their families or sympathisers from public employment or office, and the continuing reliance on coercion, repression and undercover violence as instruments of social control. The rule of law and the autonomy of legal institutions have been weakened rather than strengthened, while arbitrary abuses of power at all levels have been widespread. Above all, the president has set a bad example to the bureaucracy through his tolerance of dubious business and financial practices among those immediately around him. He has shown little concern about the importance of drawing a clear line between private and public money. That might have been more justifiable if his sole aim had been to create a strong indigenous capitalist class at any cost, but Indonesia's frail new group of embryonic business leaders, apart from the palace circle, has probably been weakened in relative terms during the 1980s.

While it may be inappropriate to assess the New Order by the standards of more industrialised western countries, it is reasonable to compare its performance with those of other ASEAN nations. In that company, Indonesia scores quite well in terms of economic progress and policies (even though its rates of economic growth have been lower than those of all the others except the Philippines), for it was a much poorer country in 1966. But it scores badly in terms of corruption and financial malpractice. As for governmental responsiveness to pressures from within the society (a less question-begging term than 'democracy'), New Order Indonesia ranks far behind Malaysia and Thailand, and even behind 'buttoned-down' Singapore. State power is vastly more overbearing there than in the other ASEAN countries (apart from Singapore, perhaps), while the earlier vigour of independent society-based forces has given way to flaccidity. The kind of progress towards more democratic institutions and procedures being demanded successfully by the middle classes of countries such as South Korea and Taiwan since 1985 has barely started in Indonesia.

Much will now depend upon what happens when Soeharto goes—and what form his departure will take (Crouch 1988). Will the ruling elite be cohesive enough to guard against dangerous splits after his guiding hand is no longer on the helm? Have the processes of political institutionalisation and elite consolidation gone far enough to ensure that the transition will be a smooth one? Can it be expected that a post-Soeharto regime will move in a more democratic and participatory direction (however defined, and no matter how slowly), rather than a more authoritarian one?

If the answers to these questions prove to be 'yes', then the verdict of history on the Soeharto regime will almost certainly be a favourable one. If not, especially if another period of troubles and political instability like the mid-1960s occurs (an unlikely prospect, one might expect, provided the economy remains buoyant), the shortcomings of the Soeharto regime are more likely to bulk as large in the history books dealing with the New Order as its achievements.

Notes

1   *Gestapu*, an acronym derived from *Gerakan Tigapuluh September* (30 September Movement), is described below. The terms Old Order and New Order came into use during the power struggle of early 1966 as a means of distinguishing supporters and opponents of President Sukarno. Soeharto was actually a major general on 1 October 1965, becoming a lieutenant general four months later and a full general in July 1966. Since his retirement from the army in 1976 he has generally been referred to as President Soeharto.

2   For generally favourable interpretations of the New Order, see Liddle (1985, 1991) and Emmerson (1983). Strongly critical accounts portraying it as a 'military dictatorship' backed by international capital can be found in Mortimer (1973), Caldwell (1975) and Southward and Flanagan (1983); more reasoned and illuminating interpretations of a critical nature are Anderson (1978, 1983), Robison (1986) and Budiman (1990). Two of the most balanced and informative accounts of the New Order are Crouch (1978) and McDonald (1980). A wide range of views (none by Indonesians, unfortunately) can be found in Anderson and Kahin (1982).

3   A minor but revealing illustration of the way things have changed is the almost complete abandonment of the old revolutionary-era word *saudara* (brother) for 'you' and its replacement by *bapak* (father, sir), which has much stronger status implications. The advertisements in *Tempo* and other up-market publications provide a revealing glimpse into the lifestyles of the new rich.

4   Soeharto was at first little more than the most senior of many army generals such as Adjie, Dharsono, Kemal Idris, Panggabean, Sumitro, Jusuf, Jasin, Surono and others. (General Nasution, previously commander-in-chief of the armed forces, was quickly manoeuvred into obscurity and deprived of opportunities to speak in public because of his critical views.) By the 1980s, all potential challengers to Soeharto's authority had been sidelined and the most senior officers were men whom he had brought to the top. See Jenkins (1984).

5   Significant differences are discernible between Riggs' concept of the 'bureaucratic polity' as he applied the term to Thailand in the 1950s and the looser meanings attached to it by Jackson and King. The comparison by Girling (1981) of the Thai and Indonesian version of the bureaucratic polity is illuminating on the differing political dynamics of two systems.

6   The categorisation of Javanese society in terms of the three *aliran*—i.e., *santri* (devout Muslim*s), abangan* ('statistical Muslims' of a more syncretic, mystical outlook, usually lower class) and *priyayi* (aristocratic, official or upper-class variants of *abangan* beliefs, usually inclined towards Javanese mystical beliefs

48

rather than strict Muslim doctrines)—derives from various works by Geertz (1956, 1960) and proved more useful than class analysis in explaining Old Order political alignments. These categories have become less relevant to party alignments, although by no means entirely so under the New Order, and are becoming blurred by socio-cultural changes affecting the position of Islam in Indonesian society.

7   King (1982) provides the fullest discussion of the applicability of corporatist theories to Indonesia; see also MacIntyre (1990:10–14). For attempts at class analysis of the New Order, see Mortimer (1973) and Caldwell (1975).

8   The pro-Sukarno forces at that time consisted mainly of the *abangan* and *priyayi* elements in society (see note 6), who had provided the main base of support for the PKI and PNI up until 1965 and had come into conflict with the more militantly Islamic groups, particularly in East and Central Java. Land reform disputes had developed both an economic and a socio-political aspect in these regions, and lay behind the violence of 1965–66. See Cribb (1991:75–7).

9   See Young (1990) on the complex issues of who constitute the rural counterparts to the urban 'middle classes' and how they have become the primary benficiaries of the economic policies of the New Order. Since there is no clearly definable class of 'landlords' or dominant peasants, it is these groups which constitute the regime's main basis of support throughout rural Indonesia.

10 The fact that Nasution was not captured or killed was not a major factor in the failure of the coup attempt; Soeharto promptly took control and exercised the initiatives on both military and political fronts, from the morning of 1 October (see *Indonesia*, no. 1, for his official report on the events of that day). For the fullest and most impartial account of the coup and its background, see Crouch (1978) and the references cited therein.

11 Nugroho and Ismail (1968) provide the nearest thing to an 'official' ABRI version of the *Gestapu* episode, using evidence from the special military tribunal trials of suspected participants to refute the argument advanced in the 1966 'Cornell paper' on the episode—republished later as Anderson and McVey (1971)—that the PKI was not responsible for the coup attempt and had only been minimally involved.

12 While the 'Cornell paper' (see note 11) on the origins of the coup probably overstates the case for minimal or nil involvement by the PKI, it most likely comes closer to the truth about what actually happened than the official mythology that has developed since then. See Crouch (1978:97–135) for the most judicious summary of the conflicting interpretations and the relevant evidence.

13 *Supersemar* (*Surat Perintah Sebelas Maret*, The Letter of Command of 11 March) came to acquire almost talismanic status as the legal and moral authority legitimating Soeharto's rule in the early years of the New Order.

14 Feith (1968) provides an excellent on-the-spot assessment of the complex politics of 1966–68 prior to Soeharto's elevation to the Presidency, when he was under pressure from the militantly anti-communist and anti-Sukarno 'New Order radicals' and their supporters in the army, notably Lieutenant Generals Dharsono and Kemal Idris, who wanted him to move further and faster towards

a more participatory regime than his cautious, almost conciliatory tactics towards the Old Order forces allowed. Yet the hard line towards PKI elements was set fast by this stage.

15 IGGI (Inter-Governmental Group on Indonesia), an aid consortium of twelve nations, was headed initially by the United States, Japan, the Netherlands and Australia.

16 Although the PKI had been shattered and hundreds of thousands of its former members killed, arrested or browbeaten into silence, millions of its former supporters were still free to vote; so too were even larger numbers of old PNI voters. The methods of political exclusion and social marginalisation of ex-PKI members (and their close relatives), principally through their need to have a *surat tidak terlibat* (certificate of non-involvement in *Gestapu*), issued by the local authorities, for all sorts of jobs and career moves, are spelled out more fully in Caldwell (1975) and Amnesty International (1985).

17 The best accounts of Golkar's origins and rationale are in Reeve (1985) and Ward (1974); Suryadinata (1988) provides a useful picture of its structure after the 1984 changes in leadership.

18 Toyota was accused of links with Madam Soeharto through its joint-venture partner, Astra International, whose offices were attacked by demonstrators on 13 January.

19 See McCawley (1978), Glassburner (1976) and Howell and Morrow (1974) for further details on Pertamina and its 1974–76 financial crisis.

20 The government's heavy-handed treatment of the trivial 'Sawito affair' in 1976 was symptomatic of its nervousness about any challenges to the president's good name. See Bourchier (1984) for a thorough analysis of the political significance of the 'Sawito affair' and the reasons for the regime's intense nervousness about its political dangers.

21 The five principles of *Pancasila*, nebulous though they are as the basis for a social or political philosophy, have generally served the purpose of providing a unifying national ideology, except in the more intransigent Muslim circles.

22 Apart from Lieutenant General Moerdani, the youngest of the '1945 Generation', there have been no outstanding leaders among the senior officers of the 1980s; and Moerdani, being a Catholic, could only hope to be the future king-maker, not the king. His close association with and loyalty to the president used to be legendary, but has come under strain since 1988. On generational changes affecting the ABRI leadership in the mid-1980s, see the various surveys in *Indonesia* entitled 'Current Data on the Military Elite' between 1983 and 1988.

23 The functions of the DPR are broadly analogous to those of the US Congress. The MPR, designated in the constitution as 'the supreme embodiment of popular sovereignty', normally meets only once every five years to elect the president and vice-president.

24 The *Garis-garis Besar Haluan Negara* (GBHN) (Main Lines of National Policy) has considerable symbolic significance as a general statement of the government's strategy, including its five-year plan, over the years immediately ahead; but its formal legal and political status is shadowy.

25 Emmerson (1978:90) observes: 'Compared to what it was during the first two

decades of independence, the bureaucracy today is less inflationary in size, less dispersed in its loyalties, and more able to act. For the context of public administration in Indonesia, 1965 was a watershed.'

26 A good official statement on the nature and extent of corruption in the early New Order years is the report of the 'Commission of Four on Corruption', appointed by President Soeharto in 1970 in response to press revelations of financial scandals in government bodies and around the presidential circle (Mackie 1970); the issues were substantially the same as they remained in the late 1980s, although the scale had increased dramatically by then.

27 On regional government, the basic structure has changed little except in detail since the authoritative and very readable account of its working by Legge (1961); see also MacAndrews (1986) and Schiller (1986).

28 The killing without trial of more than 5000 suspected criminals, usually by 'mysterious gunmen' in the dark of the night, was the security forces' response to a mild wave of low-level crime in several rural areas of East and Central Java in 1982–83, authorised by the highest levels of ABRI (see Bourchier 1990).

29 Kopkamtib was established in March 1966. Bakorstanas (*Badan Koordinasi Stabilitas Nasional*, National Stability Coordinating Board) replaced it in September 1988, with a broader emphasis on the economic sphere, but still with wide, vaguely-defined powers.

30 Since the 1965–67 anti-PKI 'clean-up' operations in East and Central Java, the army has been most actively involved in combat against ex-PKI and SCO (Sarawak Communist Organisation) elements in West Kalimantan for several years; later in various Irian Jaya operations; in the occupation of East Timor in 1975–76, followed by constant pacification campaigns there; and latterly against the GPK (*Gerakan Pengacau Keamanan*) (troublemaker) rebels in Aceh in the 1980s and, most notoriously, in the Dili massacre of November 1991.

31 Further organisational changes occurred in the 1980s, most notably the historic generational transfer of senior command positions from the last of the old '1945 Generation' officers to the much younger group of initial graduates from the National Military Academy.

32 In 1990, ABRI had a total of 278 000 men (cf 340 000 in 1968), of whom 212 000 were in the army (cf 275 000), 40 000 (cf 42 000) in the navy, and 25 000 (cf 24 000) in the air force (IISI 1992).

33 The foremost of the 'hawks' in 1967–69 were Dharsono, Kemal Idris and Sarwo Edhie; later also there were Ali Sadikin, Moh Jasin and others. General Nasution, in virtual political exile, was rather separate from both groups.

34 Moerdani was removed from his post as ABRI commander-in-chief and replaced by Tri Sutrisno in February 1988, only a few days before the MPR meeting, and later appointed to the essentially ceremonial post of Minister of Defence. It is hard to avoid the conclusion that Soeharto made those changes in order to ensure that Moerdani did not have direct control over troops.

35 On the press, see Rogers (1982) and D. Hill (1992). Despite the occasional examples of courageously independent reporting, much of the press is quite uncritical, its ill-paid journalists being easily corrupted by the blandishments

of 'envelope reporting' (bundles of money presented to them by their subjects to avoid adverse comments in their stories).

36 A critical but illuminating account of the use made of *Pancasila* and the P4 (*Pedoman Penghayatan dan Pengamalan Pancasila*) indoctrination program of 1979–80 is given by Morfitt (1981); analyses of the content and ideology and various aspects of the use made of *Pancasila* under the New Order are given by Reeve (1985) and Sullivan (1991).

37 Even though few Japanese were strongly enthusiastic in Meiji times about the conservative and intellectually diffuse *tennosei* ideology (as could also be said of *Pancasila*), 'few wished wholly to secede from society as it was then constituted' (Gluck 1985:278). By successfully persuading others of the validity of its world view, Japan's oligarchs had less need to rely on force. Much the same has been true of Soeharto's Indonesia.

38 On *Dharma Wanita*, see Zumrotin (1989) and Suryakusuma (1991), who employs the notion of 'State Ibuism' (*ibu* being the Indonesian word for mother) as an ideology promoted actively by state authorities, a concept based on Djajadiningrat (1987).

39 A summary of the situation by Asia Watch (1990:1) puts it bluntly: 'Tight control is maintained over thought and speech. "Justice" continues to be up for sale. Over a hundred political trials conducted in 1989 and 1990 . . . are evidence of . . . the continuing intolerance of dissent, whether from students, intellectuals, Muslim teachers or ethnic nationalists. Books, both Indonesian and foreign, which portray Soeharto or his government in an unfavorable light . . . are banned. The poison of an anti-communist witch-hunt continues to affect millions of people, including children one or two generations removed [from the PKI] . . . Prisoners linked to a coup attempt in 1965 are being executed, twenty-five years after their arrest. Subversion charges, which can carry the death penalty, are imposed in so cavalier and arbitrary a fashion that the very threat of being branded a subversive can be enough to silence protest.'

40 The more cosmopolitan Indonesians accept the notion (although many others would not) that their country should accept human rights as expressed in the UN Charter because they are universally valid and binding, having been accepted by many other developing as well as developed countries as part of an emerging international consensus. Indonesia has subscribed to the 1948 Universal Charter on Human Rights, but not to the 1968 Covenant on Political and Legal Rights and Duties.

41 The problems of regional discontent in Irian Jaya and East Timor stem from the circumstances in which they were incorporated into Indonesia's national territory long after 1950, which have left a continuing sense of distinctness and antagonism; see May (1986) and Taylor (1991). The reasons behind Aceh's small but troublesome 'Independent Aceh' movement, active since 1978 on a minor but potentially troublesome scale, have complex historical roots in that province's early relations with the Jakarta government between 1945 and 1962. See Nazaruddin (1985).

42 For the meaning of *santri*, see note 6. On Islam under the New Order, see 'The Long Ramadhan: Islamic Politics under the New Order' in *Prisma*, no. 49, June 1990.

43 The Tanjung Priok riots arose out of an incident in which a Muslim prayer-house was allegedly violated by two military officers attempting to remove inflammatory posters; at a protest demonstration two days later, troops fired on the crowd, killing at least thirty, possibly over 100 people; see Asia Watch (1988:92–5).

44 The term 'Indonesian Chinese'—preferably 'Chinese Indonesians', which implies that they are Indonesian nationals—is used here in the crudely racial sense to refer to the entire minority of Chinese ethnic origin, both Indonesian citizens and aliens; the latter have diminished in number to less than ten per cent of the total since the acquisition of citizenship was made easier in 1979, after nearly two decades of wrangling over the issue. The old Chinese term *hoa chiau*, meaning 'sojourners', formerly used for all overseas Chinese, is dropping out of circulation in favour of the more neutral term, *hua ren*, meaning Chinese residing abroad; see Suryadinata (1989:2). On the position of the Chinese minority more generally under the New Order, see Coppel (1983), Suryadinata (1986) and Tan (1991).

45 For lists of the large Chinese conglomerates, see Robison (1986:278–88) and Mackie (1990c, 1992).

46 Many have played prominent public roles of various kinds as individuals, but not as Chinese and not as capitalists. A list of these would include Chinese Indonesians such as the respected lawyer Yap Thiam Hien, film director Teguh Karya, badminton champion Verawarti Fadjrin, dramatist Riantiarno and many others. See Tan (1991) and Lev (1991).

47 On the anti-Chinese violence of the 1960s, see Mackie (1976a) and Coppel (1983); on later developments, see Tan (1991).

48 Riggs' 'pariah entrepreneurs' have been well described by McVey (1992:16) as 'political outsiders . . . who depended on bureaucrats for political protection and who were in turn parasitised economically by the officials'.

49 The sources for these estimates of the number and wealth of the conglomerates are presented in Mackie (1992).

50 On the politics behind economic policy since 1966, see Crouch (1978:317–30), Robison (1986:132–47), Glassburner (1978), and Hill, chapter 2 this volume.

51 See Wardhana (1989), Soesastro (1989) and MacIntyre (1990).

52 For an account of foreign policy under the New Order, see Leifer (1983).

53 The most comprehensive surveys of the East Timor story, written from a strongly anti-Indonesian viewpoint, are Dunn (1983) and Taylor (1991); for the best account providing an Indonesian perspective, see McDonald (1980).

54 See Roeder (1969) for the only biography in English of any substance so far. Liddle (1985, 1991) offers some useful analytical ideas, but does not attempt to probe behind the mask Soeharto has cultivated so effectively to conceal the inner man.

55 On the other hand, what are we to say of the strange matter of his 'autobiography' (Soeharto 1989), which was almost boastful in its denial of credit for the New Order's achievements to any of his lieutenants and in its claims that they were due solely to him?

2

The economy

Hal Hill

If the central purpose of economics is to understand why and how growth rates vary across countries and over time, Indonesia surely provides one of the best 'laboratories' for such a study. By the mid-1960s many informed observers despaired of any prospect of significant economic advance. Benjamin Higgins, the author of one of the most influential books on development economics at that time, characterised Indonesia as the 'chronic dropout' (Higgins 1968). Gunnar Myrdal, in his monumental work, *Asian Drama*, offered an equally sober assessment: 'As things look at the beginning of 1966, there seems to be little prospect of rapid economic growth in Indonesia' (Myrdal 1968:489). Other social scientists were equally pessimistic, with the demographer Nathan Keyfitz fearing that population pressure on Java was becoming so intense that the island was '. . . asphyxiating for want of land' (Keyfitz 1965:503).

Yet little more than a decade later Indonesia was being hailed as one of Asia's success stories. Economists cite Indonesia from 1966 to 1968 as one of the most swift and effective instances of inflation control in the twentieth century. By the late 1980s Indonesia was being classified among the select group of developing countries destined shortly to become newly-industrialised economies, following the successful path of Asia's outward-looking industrial economies. President Soeharto has received international awards in recognition of the country's success in food production and family planning. Once the world's largest importer of rice, Indonesia

For helpful comments on earlier drafts, I am indebted to Heinz Arndt, Colin Barlow, Bruce Glassburner, Benjamin Higgins, Jamie Mackie, Chris Manning and Thee Kian Wie.

achieved self-sufficiency in this crop in the mid-1980s. The country was held up as a model among the OPEC group in investing its oil revenue gains effectively and in adjusting quickly to declining oil prices in the early 1980s. Later in the decade, the country attracted international attention for its continuing success in poverty alleviation, even during the period of painful macroeconomic stabilisation occasioned by a halving of world oil prices. In the mid-1960s Indonesia had left the United Nations and was in the process of disengaging from the world economy. Yet after 1966 it enjoyed one of the closest relationships with international development agencies and the donor community.

How did this transformation occur? Apart from the oil boom of 1973–81, the international economic environment was no more supportive of economic development after 1966 than before, so the changes must have been principally domestic in nature. And, of course, they were. A new, orthodox and pragmatic regime of economic management signalled a decisive reorientation. The government provided a stable economic and political environment, property rights were respected, Indonesia reentered the international community, prices (especially the exchange rate) reflected conditions of demand and supply, and the provision of public goods such as physical and social infrastructure began to increase substantially. It is easy to document all manner of mistakes, scandals and inappropriate interventions, and to point to other countries—though not many—that have done better. But public administration and economic management of a poor, ethnically diverse archipelagic state such as Indonesia is a daunting task, and the essential recipe is one in which the government has got its policies 'right' more often than it has not, and has displayed political will to take tough and unpopular decisions when necessary.

Indonesia—then and now

A brief comparison of economic conditions and indicators at the outset of the New Order period and some 25 years later is a useful reminder of the magnitude of Indonesia's economic transformation. The following quotation, by one of the key figures of the New Order, captures the flavour of the seemingly hopeless situation in 1965:

> Any person who entertains the idea that Indonesian society is experiencing a favourable economic situation is guilty of lack of intensive study . . . If we fulfil all our [foreign debt] obligations, we have no foreign exchange left to spend for our routine needs . . . In 1965 prices in general rose by more than 500 per cent . . . In the 1950s the state budget sustained deficits of 10 to 30 per cent of receipts and in the 1960s it soared to more than 100 per cent. In 1965 it even reached 300 per cent. (Sultan Hamengkubuwono IX, quoted in Panglaykim and Arndt 1966:3, 19)

According to virtually every indicator, the improvements between 1965 and 1990 have been striking (Table 2.1). Real per capita GDP has trebled in just a generation, and the economic decline of the first half of the 1960s has given way to strong positive growth for almost the entire period of 1966–90. Virtually all sectors of the economy have performed impressively. Rice yields have risen quickly, almost doubling on Java. Indonesia's modern industrial sector was tiny in 1965. Subsequently, industrial output rose tenfold or more in a range of sectors. Even the per capita output of a 'basic good' such as textiles has risen by more than 600 per cent. The transport infrastructure has experienced a virtual revolution in terms of road and air capacity and the passenger fleet, with large increases in all sectors except rail. Underpinning these changes have been macroeconomic stability (reflected in reduced inflation), sustainable external borrowings, and a sharp rise in the investment ratio, the latter peaking at over 30 per cent during the oil boom period. High growth has been accompanied by equally rapid structural change: agriculture's share of GDP has more than halved, while industry—and within it, manufacturing—has doubled. Manufacturing once consisted primarily of food and rubber processing, but by 1986 these sectors had shrunk to just one-fifth of their former share. Moreover, although social developments have lagged in some respects, there have been impressive declines in poverty incidence and infant mortality, while educational opportunities have spread rapidly.

Viewed from a 1965 perspective Indonesia's performance has been better than most observers would have dared to hope for. But the record provides no grounds for complacency. Conditions were so disastrous in 1965 that any return to normalcy would have resulted in significant improvements. And although domestic policies have been the critical ingredient, the international environment has generally been supportive. Indonesia experienced a huge increase in its terms of trade from the early 1970s, which was so large that even after the decline in oil prices in 1985–86 the ratio remained well above the 1970 figure. The country has had continued access to foreign aid, particularly when it needed it, in the second half of the 1960s and the mid-1980s. Exogenous technical change in the form of the new rice varieties assisted in transforming Indonesia's once gloomy agricultural prospects. In any case, in the political arena the revolution of rising expectations heavily discounts these achievements. For a new generation of Indonesians entering the work force, the universities and the political process, a comparison with the 1960s is irrelevant. Their future options are defined by what is on offer in the booming East Asian economies, not the stagnation which was present in Indonesia before 1966 and is evident in so many parts of the Third World. Thus, while economic circumstances are no longer as desperate as they were in the 1960s, the challenges to policy-makers in the 1990s are in many respects just as formidable.

Table 2.1   Indicators of Indonesian economic development, 1965–90

Indicators	Mid-1960s	c.1990
1 Real GDP per capita:	1960–65	1988–90
Growth (%)	–0.4	±5
1990 $	190 (1965)	570 (1990)
2 Shares of GDP (%):		
Agriculture	50	22
Industry	13	40
Manufacturing	8	20
3 Industry: % of food and rubber		
products in total manufacturing	60 (1963)	12 (1986)
4 Industrial production per capita:		
Textiles (metres)	4.1	28.0
Electricity (kWh)	17.7	194.5
Fertiliser (kg)	1.1	39.1
5 Agriculture:		
Rice consumption/capital (kg/year)	92	155
Rice yields (Java only, tons/ha)	1.7	3.2
6 Investment:		
Gross domestic investment as % of GDP	8	36
7 Inflation (% increase)	>500	8–10
8 Debt:		
Total ($ billion)	2.4	68
% of exports	524	229
9 Transport/infrastructure:		
Domestic air travel (million departures)	0.4	9.0
% of roads in 'good' condition	5	31
Registered motor vehicles ('000)		
Buses and 'colts'	20	469
Trucks	93	1,024
Motorcycles	308	6,083
10 Poverty:		
Java % very poor	61	10
% 'sufficient'	8	36
Outside Java % very poor	52	7
% 'sufficient'	10	47

A comparative assessment

Indonesia has performed well compared to other Asian developing nations and the OPEC group (Table 2.2). Its per capita GNP is less than that of all those in the sample except the two Asian giants and Nigeria. But from 1965 to 1990 it grew faster than all except China, another country which enacted major reforms during this period. Agriculture played a key role in this superior record, with Indonesia among the top performers both in the growth of output and food production. The contrast here with the two OPEC states is particularly stark, and only China (in the 1980s) is clearly ahead. Despite this rapid growth, Indonesia experienced the largest decline in the share of

Table 2.2 Comparative indicators of economic and social development

	Other ASEAN			Large Asian countries		Other OPEC		Lower middle income countries
	Indonesia	Philippines	Thailand	China	India	Mexico	Nigeria	
1 Economic indicators								
GNP per capita—$, 1990	570	730	1420	370	350	2490	290	1530
growth, 1965–90 (%)	4.5	1.3	4.4	5.8	1.9	2.8	0.1	1.5
Inflation (%)								
1965–80	36	11	6	0	8	13	15	24
1980–90	8	15	3	6	8	70	18	65
Agricultural growth (%)								
1965–80	4.3	3.9	4.6	2.8	2.5	3.2	1.7	3.6
1980–90	3.2	1.0	4.1	6.1	3.1	0.4	3.3	2.5
Agriculture's share								
in GDP—1990 (%)	22	22	12	27	31	9	36	17
% decline 1965–90	57	15	63	29	30	36	35	23
Index of food production per capita 1988–90 (1969–71 = 100)	145	103	136	154	122	109	97	107
Gross domestic investment								
(% of GDP)—1965	8	21	20	24	17	20	15	19
—1990	36	22	37	39	23	20	15	23
Central govt expenditure								
(% of GNP)—1972	15	14	17	na	11	11	9	17
—1990	20	20	15	na	18	18	na	15
Exports as % of GDP—1990	26	28	38	18	8	16	39	28
Terms of trade, 1990 (1970 = 100)	236	43	49	na	61	74	147	na
Net ODA as % of GNP—1990	1.6	2.9	1.0	0.6	0.6	0.1	0.7	1.6
Debt service as % of exports—1990	31	21	17	10	29	28	20	20

2 Social indicators

Life expectancy (years), 1990	62	64	66	70	59	70	52	65
Adult illiteracy (%), 1990	23	10	7	27	52	13	49	25
Infant mortality (per 1000)								
1988	68	44	30	31	97	46	103	57
% decline 1965–88	47	39	66	66	35	44	42	47
Daily calorie supply (per capita)								
1989	2750	2375	2316	2639	2229	3052	2312	2768
% increase 1965–89	54	27	8	37	10	19	6	15

Notes: na: not available. In some cases data refer to one year earlier than that stated.

Source: World Bank, *World Development Report*, various issues.

agriculture. The expanding oil sector explains part of the decline; another factor was the underdeveloped state of manufacturing and services in 1965 and their dynamism thereafter.

Other macroeconomic and trade indicators are illuminating. Indonesia's record on inflation is moderately good, although inferior to most Asian countries in the sample. Investment levels have risen sharply since the mid-1960s, and Indonesia's record is comparable to most of the others, especially since 1990 marked the end of a half-decade of Jakarta's fiscal austerity. Similarly, government expenditure is in the mid-range of the comparisons. For a large country, Indonesia has quite high exposure to international trade, although the terms of this engagement are shifting from commodity exports to manufactures. That Indonesia has profited unambiguously from its reintegration into the international economy is illustrated by its terms of trade and foreign aid receipts. Its terms of trade in 1990 were more than double the figure of 1970, even after the sharp fall in oil prices in the mid-1980s; this presents a marked contrast with the declining figures recorded for all other countries except Nigeria. Aid to Indonesia remains significant, at well over double the share of GNP found in the Asian giants and the OPEC states. However, its debt service, while manageable, is a good deal more onerous than some of the other countries.

Indonesia's social achievements are satisfactory, but not as impressive as the economic indicators in international perspective. Its life expectancy exceeds only that found in India and Nigeria, while in adult illiteracy and infant mortality (and its rate of decline), Indonesia assumes an intermediate position, generally behind its East Asian neighbours. Reflecting the strong agricultural performance, daily per capita calorie supplies are adequate, *on average*, and have risen the most quickly.

Much of the detailed comparative research on Indonesia has been with reference to the OPEC group, where, faced with a common exogenous shock, it is possible to trace government responses to the windfall oil revenue. Gelb and Associates (1988) provide the most comprehensive assessment in their six-country study over the period 1974–84. The Indonesian record compares very favourably with the other five. The windfall gains accruing to Indonesia were, relatively, the smallest of the six (about 17 per cent of GDP compared to a group average of 23 per cent). It had easily the most impressive economic—and particularly agricultural—performance, and it directed the highest proportion of its development spending to rural areas. Gelb concluded that Indonesia was '. . . the only country in the sample to implement a determined policy of expenditure reduction and exchange rate realignment before the fading of the second oil boom' (p.91). Moreover, 'only Indonesia and possibly Ecuador managed to strengthen and diversify the non-hydrocarbon traded sectors during the windfall decade' (p.136).[1]

The economy

An overview of economic development, 1965–91

Rapid growth

The economy recovered surprisingly quickly from the dislocation of the first half of the 1960s, recording double-digit growth for the first time in 1968.[2] Thereafter, rapid growth, of at least 5 per cent annually, was maintained until 1982, when softening international oil markets induced a sharp slowdown (Figure 2.1). This subdued expansion continued until 1986 (except for 1984, as massive oil and gas investments came onstream, boosting industrial expansion to 10 per cent), when policy reforms which commenced in the mid-1980s began to take effect. By the late 1980s, the economy had recovered to over 7 per cent growth, the highest figure since 1980.

The broad sectoral aggregates mirror this record, with some exceptions. Industrial expansion has been the most uneven, with spectacular increases recorded in some years prior to 1980. The seven cases of super (double-digit) growth all occurred in the period 1968–77. They reflect a combination of factors: dramatic increases in manufacturing capacity as the backlog in consumer demand was overcome, a more effective exploitation of mineral resources, and the impact of the construction boom. Conversely, industrial growth has been slow in some years, especially in the late 1970s and early 1980s when Indonesia adhered to OPEC production quotas; manufacturing growth was very sluggish in 1982 and 1983. Thus until the recent period of broad-based, export-oriented growth, the industrial sector has swung between periods of boom and bust.

Agricultural expansion has, not surprisingly, been slower and less erratic. Growth has exceeded the historically high figure of 5 per cent on only a few occasions, most especially over the period 1978–81, which laid the foundations of the much-vaunted achievement of rice self-sufficiency in 1985. This was in marked contrast to the sluggish performance around 1970, and especially the lean harvest of 1972. The latter coincided with poor harvests in other major producing nations, and precipitated the rice crisis of that year. Of all major sectors, services has most closely followed the economy's growth rate. Rebounding quickly from the mid-1960s stagnation, services grew by at least 8 per cent in most years between 1968 and 1981. The rate of expansion then slowed down, as did the economy as a whole, before picking up in the late 1980s.

Episodes in economic policy and development

At the risk of oversimplification, it is useful to demarcate a number of subperiods since 1966, each identifiable in terms of the major economic trends and policy emphases. First, there was the *rehabilitation and recovery* of 1966–70. Over this period, the government was concerned above all else

61

Figure 2.1   Economic growth, 1965–91 (%)

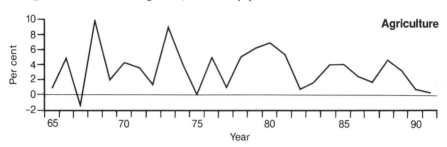

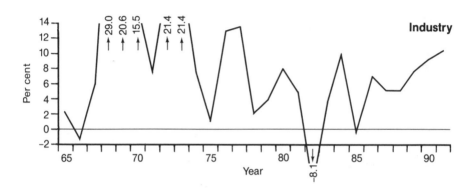

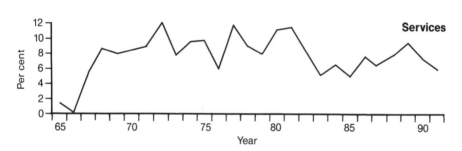

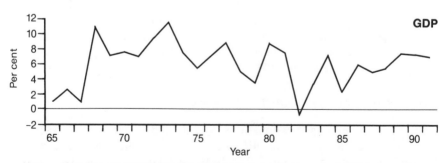

Note: 1991 data are preliminary; data are based on a spliced constant 1983 prices series.
Source: BPS, *National Accounts*, various years.

to control inflation, to re-establish ties with the international donor community, and to rehabilitate physical infrastructure. The introduction of orthodox monetary and fiscal policies brought inflation down surprisingly quickly. The government's clear commitment to economic orthodoxy and its international re-engagement resulted in a strong investor response. The economy grew at an annual average rate of 6.6 per cent. In effect, 1968 marked the beginning of the strong recovery phase, with growth of 10.9 per cent.

The second subperiod was the *rapid growth* of 1971–81. Real GDP increased at an annual average rate of 7.7 per cent and in all years grew by at least 5 per cent. It was also a period of extraordinary economic and policy turbulence. There was the poor rice harvest and doubling of rice prices in late 1972. Then followed the quadrupling of international petroleum prices in the second half of 1973. In its wake there was the Pertamina debacle of 1975–76 and the resurgence of a nationalist economic agenda. Towards the end of the decade (November 1978) a large and ill-fated devaluation occurred, designed to restore the competitiveness of non-oil tradable sectors, and shortly afterwards the Iran–Iraq war precipitated another round of major price increases.

Next came *adjustment to lower oil prices* in 1982–86 when falling oil prices, rising external indebtedness and a sudden decline in economic growth in 1982 signalled an end to the period of oil-financed growth and abundance. The policy response was ambivalent. The macroeconomic adjustments—especially fiscal policy and devaluation—were generally prompt and effective. However, trade barriers proliferated, a trend arrested only in 1986, when oil prices fell very sharply. Owing partly to a good agricultural performance, the economy continued to grow over this period, at a respectable annual average rate of 4.6 per cent (but much lower in gross domestic income terms). External indebtedness rose sharply.

The final period has been one of *liberalisation and recovery* from 1987 in which continued fiscal austerity, effective exchange-rate management, and decisive microeconomic reform together resulted in a strong recovery beginning in 1987. Annual growth from 1987 to 1991 was 6.9 per cent, approaching the average for the period 1971–81, but on this occasion achieved without buoyant oil revenues. The two dominant trends were a pronounced shift to outward orientation, especially in manufactures, and the growing commercial strength and independence of the private sector.

Rapid structural change

Indonesia's structural transformation has been rapid. The declining relative importance of agriculture was particularly fast in the early 1970s, hastened by the oil boom and the indifferent agricultural performance of some of these years, while for much of the 1980s there was no significant change in its share. Correspondingly, most of the increase in industry's share occurred over the period 1967–77 and after 1988. There was no major change in the share of services. Excluding the oil and gas sector, agriculture's decline has been less pronounced, but it still almost halved over the period, while services have displayed a steadily increasing trend (Figure 2.2).

Interpreting the macroeconomic record

Several caveats need to be attached to this record, none of which, it needs to be emphasised, detracts fundamentally from the proposition that Indonesia's economic performance since 1966 has been good. First, while it is undeniable that rising oil prices contributed to high rates of economic growth in the 1970s, growth was rapid even after adjusting for the terms of trade effect. This has been illustrated by several authors who have compared growth in the conventionally-defined gross domestic product and gross domestic income, the latter incorporating the impact of movements in the terms of trade. As the economy continues to diversify quickly away from its heavy reliance on oil, the two series will increasingly converge.

The second caveat, that rapid growth has been purchased at the cost of

Figure 2.2   Structural change, 1966–91 (% of GDP)

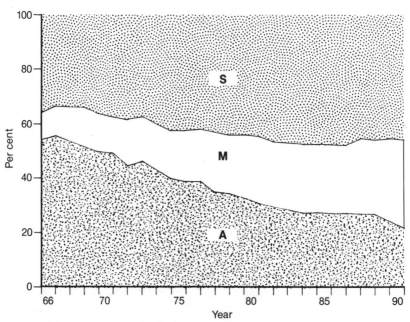

Note: Data exclude the mining sector. A, M and S refer to agriculture, industry (manufacturing, utilities, and construction) and services respectively.

Source: BPS, *National Accounts*, various years.

extensive exploitation of non-renewable natural resources, has been addressed by researchers using a 'natural resource accounting' framework. Particularly relevant here is the work of Repetto et al. (1989), who computed a 'resource adjusted' growth rate over the period 1971–84 of 4 per cent per annum, compared to 7.1 per cent for GDP. Valuable as this research is, the numbers are subject to a wide margin of error,[3] and in any case the conclusions become less relevant as the share of the natural resource sector shrinks. Other qualifications to Indonesia's growth record relate to the country's rising external debt and to distributional considerations. These issues are examined below.

Rapid technological change

Accompanying these high rates of economic growth and structural change has been equally rapid technological change. In the mid-1960s Indonesia's technological base was extremely weak. The liberal environment after 1966 and rapidly-rising investment rates had a profound effect on the pace of technological development. Extremely labour-intensive technologies in agriculture, industry and services, whose use had been prolonged by the chaotic business environment of the late 1950s and early 1960s, now began to disappear very quickly.

Numerous studies have documented far-reaching technological changes, including Timmer (1973) and Sadli (1973) on rice-milling,[4] Sinaga (1978) on agricultural mechanisation, Collier et al. (1973) on rice harvesting, Dick (1981) on urban public transport, Hill (1983) on weaving, and Nelson (1986) on cassava processing.

The social implications of these changes have been profound and the source of much critical comment. Technological innovation is, inherently, a disruptive process. Many of the groups and individuals adversely affected are also the most vulnerable, particularly since social support networks tend to weaken as the forces of commercialisation become more powerful. Nevertheless, the process of rapid technological change was inevitable, and an essential prerequisite for broad-based increases in living standards. Consumers wanted cheaper textiles, rice and public transport. Indonesian firms have to compete in international markets.

Investment and efficiency

High rates of investment have facilitated rapid technological change and provided the base for sustained economic growth. Investment picked up quickly during the rehabilitation phase of the late 1960s. Gross domestic investment as a share of GDP almost doubled in 1966–67 (4.5 per cent to 8 per cent) and again between 1967 and 1971 (8 per cent to 15.8 per cent). The share continued to rise higher, to historically unprecedented levels, under the impetus of the oil boom and the government's massive public investment programs, reaching 25 per cent in the early 1980s. A surprising feature of the 1980s is that, notwithstanding the cuts to the government's development budget, investment levels held up strongly.

How productively have these funds been invested? The incremental capital output ratio (ICOR), a crude indicator of efficiency, was extremely low (between one and two) during the rehabilitation phase, when investment opportunities were plentiful and quick-yielding. The ICORs then began to rise to 2.5–3 in the mid-1970s as the government embarked on many ambitious, capital-intensive projects. Slower economic growth but continuing high investment resulted in a further rise to over six during the early 1980s. Indonesia's high ICOR over this period became a matter of concern among economists, and was one of the factors triggering debate over the 'high-cost economy' in the mid-1980s. However, the resumption of rapid growth in the late 1980s, more efficient and labour-intensive than before, saw the ICOR fall back to less than four and approximate internationally accepted norms.

Planning and ideology

It is a mistake to view the change in regime in 1966 as a switch from a 'socialist' to a 'capitalist' or 'free-market' regime. There remains a deep-seated mistrust of market forces, economic liberalism, and private (especially Chinese) ownership in many influential quarters in Indonesia. Such sentiment has been subdued during the most decisive periods of liberal economic reform—1967–72 and after 1985. But since 1966 the policy pendulum has swung back and forth, between periods of more or less economic intervention. Indonesia in the mid-1960s may have been 'the most laissez faire socialist economy in the world', a remark attributed to a former prominent economist and businessman, Dr J. Panglaykim. But as Sadli et al. (1988) observed, in perhaps the best and frankest exposition of New Order economic ideology, the embrace of a liberal economic order after 1966 has been half-hearted and ambivalent.[5] This ambivalence is exemplified by former Vice-President Hatta's advocacy of cooperatives as a desirable form of ownership and organisation (see Higgins 1958), and by the continuing debate concerning interpretation of the 1945 Constitution.[6]

Despite the change of regime in 1966, it is not easy to identify a coherent philosophy, much less a precise set of economic and social objectives, over the last quarter-century. The *Garis-Garis Besar Haluan Negara* (Broad Outline of Government Policy) and the five-year development plans (*Repelita, Rencana Pembangunan Lima Tahun*) enunciate economic objectives at the broadest level. These include economic growth, economic stability (that is, low inflation), reduced dependence on foreign aid (and by implication a 'manageable' foreign debt), and equity (between individuals, regions, but most of all ethnic groups) and poverty alleviation. There are then what may be termed a second tier of more specific objectives, some of which are an elaboration of the main goals. These include the maintenance of environmental quality, the development of technological capacity, the enhanced role of women, the promotion of indigenous (especially *pribumi*) enterprise, employment generation, and food self-sufficiency.

The objectives are generally couched in a vague and all-embracing manner. In their interpretation, three fundamental considerations need to be emphasised. Firstly, there is much less discussion in official documents of options and trade-offs: between growth and environmental quality, between laissez faire and positive discrimination in favour of *pribumi* entrepreneurs, and so on. Secondly, the emphasis accorded to these objectives has fluctuated considerably since 1966. In the late 1960s stabilisation and rehabilitation of basic infrastructure understandably received the highest priority, and all other social and equity objectives were subordinated to the overriding imperatives of economic recovery. The economic successes of these early years, combined with the massive windfall oil revenues after 1973, transformed key parameters. Economic nationalism re-emerged as a potent political force, and a range of economic policies became more restrictive. Subsequently, the difficult circumstances of the 1980s forced another major reappraisal, and a shift towards liberalism. A final feature warranting emphasis is that, as in most countries, the regime rarely speaks with one voice on matters of detail. On industrial policy, for example, there has been a long-running debate between those advocating a 'guided' industrial policy and groups proposing a less-interventionist strategy.

For all the discussion of 'planning' in Indonesia—the five-year plans, the 25-year long-term plans, the pivotal role of the National Planning Agency (*Bappenas*) and the regional planning boards (*Bappeda*), and the prominent position of the Planning Agencies (*Biro Perencanaan*) in many government departments—there is surprisingly little detailed planning effort. The *Repelita* indicate the government's broad priorities in the coming five years; they contain estimates of trends in a wide range of macroeconomic, sectoral, demographic and social indicators, and they attempt to place these estimates within a consistent macroeconomic analytical framework. The plans also attempt to inject financial content into these projections by indicating likely trends in the magnitude and structure of public sector investments. But economic forecasting, developed on the basis of macroeconomic models, is an inherently uncertain exercise subject to wide margins of error. This was especially the case for Indonesia during the period 1972–85. One price—oil—so dominated the economy's fortunes that even the most carefully constructed forecast could prove to be quite unreliable. Indeed, a number of *Repelita* became dated and virtually irrelevant shortly after their publication for this reason alone.

The swing of the pendulum between liberalism and *dirigisme* is nowhere better illustrated than in the government's foreign investment and trade policies, and in the role of the state enterprise sector. The new regime, in urgent need of foreign capital and technology, but inheriting a tarnished reputation among foreign investors, had little choice but to institute a radical change in foreign investment policy. Its 1967 law, and similar changes in the separately administered petroleum sector, ushered in an era of unprecedented foreign investor interest in Indonesia, and sharply increased investment flows. This very open posture continued for about six years. By about 1973 the government began to introduce restrictions on foreign investment. These restrictions were intensified in early 1974 in response to the so-called Malari disturbances accompanying the visit of the Japanese prime minister. A local partner was henceforth required in all cases, regulations relating to employment of expatriate personnel were tightened, and more sectors were closed to new joint ventures. For most of the oil boom decade, entry procedures for foreign firms remained opaque, complex, time consuming and costly, with the second oil boom period further accentuating the resurgence in economic nationalism.

During the 1980s, however, the policy pendulum swung back towards a more liberal regime, as economic growth and investor interest declined. Intent on diversification away from the oil sector, the government saw the need to provide a more attractive investment environment. Some administrative simplifications were introduced in April 1985, while in the following year the 'May 6 package' extended this process considerably. In 1988 the introduction of the 'Negative List' (*Daftar Negatif*) clarified regulatory provisions still further. Finally, in April 1992, 100 per cent foreign ownership was again permitted (with conditions), resulting in a policy as open as that first introduced a quarter-century earlier.

In important respects the government's policy towards state enterprises has been a mirror image of its foreign investment regime, again reflecting the interplay of ideology and fiscal restraints. The new government began to reform the large, ramshackle state enterprise sector quite quickly.[7] In 1967 a number of enterprises were handed back to their former (foreign) owners, and a measure of commercial autonomy was granted to those firms remaining in state hands. A major reorganisation occurred in 1969, when most state enterprises were established as limited liability corporations, subject to the commercial law in the same manner as private corporations.

However, the first oil boom pushed reform—and certainly privatisation—off the public agenda. There was now scope for the government to shape the pattern of industrial development by investing directly in such priority areas as steel, fertiliser, aluminium, petroleum refining, and cement. Consequently, government equity investment in state enterprises rose sharply, with a lag, by almost tenfold in nominal terms over the period

1972–76. This process of expansion came to a sudden halt in 1975–76 at the time of the Pertamina scandal, when it was revealed that the state oil company's external debts exceeded $10 billion, equivalent to almost 30 per cent of Indonesia's GDP at that time.[8] Nevertheless, the general repercussions of the Pertamina debacle for the state enterprise sector were surprisingly limited. There was no major overhaul of administrative procedures, nor a re-evaluation of these enterprises' role in the economy. Investment levels remained buoyant through the first half of the 1980s, as the government embarked on a second round of ambitious 'industrial deepening' projects. It was only in late 1986 that a change in direction was evident when the president instructed the Coordinating Economics Minister to undertake a comprehensive review of the state enterprise sector. In addition, owing to the government's limited fiscal resources in the second half of the 1980s, these firms grew slowly.

Despite the many public statements regarding the importance of improved efficiency in the state sector, the reform process has moved much more slowly than in the case of foreign investment or trade policy. State enterprises have been the Achilles heel of the regime. They occupy a prominent position in the economy, much larger than that in most developing countries. The winds of privatisation have not been felt very strongly in Indonesia. By the late 1980s government entities contributed about 30 per cent of GDP, and almost 40 per cent of non-agricultural GDP (Hill 1990c:55). Yet almost every detailed study of these enterprises has pointed to their poor commercial performance.[9]

A major reason for the slow progress in state enterprise reform, apart from bureaucratic resistance, is the continuing non-*pribumi* (mainly ethnic Chinese) commercial dominance. As the previous chapter emphasises, the role of the Chinese community in Indonesia is a subject of great sensitivity. Although less than 3 per cent of the population, this group controls much of the modern commercial–industrial sector, especially the newly-emerging business conglomerates. The notion that indigenous economic control needs to be extended strikes a responsive chord throughout Indonesia, as of course it does in Malaysia too. According to such a view, a large but poorly-performing state enterprise sector, the dramatically expanding business empires of the presidential family, an inefficient cooperatives sector and, until recently, subsidised credit programs with large arrears can all be tolerated because at least they provide a *pribumi* counterweight to this non-*pribumi* commercial power.

Just as the late 1960s represented one of the high points of economic liberalism with respect to foreign investment and state enterprises, so too was this the case with trade policy.[10] But import bans began to reappear in the early 1970s, and the trend towards regulation gathered pace in 1974, in the wake of the Malari protests and in response to demands for protection of 'national' firms and industries. As the inter-sectoral implications of the oil boom became increasingly evident, these pressures intensified: the November 1978 devaluation was motivated more by a desire to protect non-oil tradeable activities than by conventional balance of payments considerations. The second round of oil price increases provided a further fillip to a rapidly increasing array of trade restrictions. While the government continued to maintain an open international capital account and freely convertible currency, there were three dominant features of the trade regime during the first half of the 1980s. Firstly, there was increased resort to non-tariff barriers (NTBs), and the nature of these NTBs became increasingly complex.[11] Secondly, trade policy became a much more explicit instrument of industrial policy over this period—large projects, such as those in the Krakatau Steel complex, were granted not just import protection but complete authority over their industry's imports. Finally, the granting of trade protection became an intensely politicised process, as it was increasingly obvious that powerful political business interests were the prime beneficiaries of these measures.[12]

The counterattack, to arrest and reverse the drift towards regulation, began in 1985 as oil prices continued to decline. Economists at the University of Indonesia and elsewhere attempted to shape the political agenda by initiating the debate on the 'high-cost' economy. In April of that year, sweeping reforms were introduced into the corrupt customs service, with major responsibility handed over to the Swiss surveying company SGS. The next major step was the introduction of effective import liberalisation measures for exporters in May 1986, under which firms were able, quickly and cleanly, either to import duty free or seek reimbursement for such duties. The dismantling of quantitative restrictions and the shift to tariffs commenced effectively in October 1986 when the first of the reform packages was introduced. Further trade packages were introduced in 1987 (January and December), 1988 (November), 1990 (May) and 1991 (June), in addition to the many other reforms enacted over this period.

There can be little doubt that the packages have transformed Indonesian industry from a protected, inward-looking sector to one which is increasingly outward-looking and internationally competitive. The very success of the packages added to the momentum for reform, and to 'winning over a new constituency for further reform'.[13] For the first time in the country's history an export lobby emerged in manufacturing industry, a group for which an internationally efficient economy was of equal if not more concern than the dispensation of licences and other bureaucratic largesse.

Finally in this section on government intervention, the discussion would be incomplete without reference to corruption, a perennial topic of debate and comment in Indonesia. Hardly a month passes without press reports of a new set of corruption allegations, or judicial proceedings at home or abroad which reveal illegal payments. Some of the major cases are referred to elsewhere in this chapter—the Pertamina affair of 1975–76, numerous scandals in the state banking sector (and, more recently, the stock exchange), the failure of the government to appropriate a reasonable portion of the rents from the forestry industry, and blatant corruption in the Customs Service until 1985. These and many other major revelations are of course just the tip of the iceberg. Illegal payments and exactions are an everyday occurrence for all manner of government services. The focus of discussion and public perceptions may have altered, but the importance of the topic has not diminished. In the 1970s concern centred on *komersialasi jabatan* (the 'commercialisation' of public sector offices). Later in the decade, the acronym *pungli* (*pungutan liar*: illegal payments) was used widely.

Since the mid-1980s the business dealings of politically prominent families, especially the sons and daughters of the president, have received much more attention. Several large business empires within the presidential family have been established in less than a decade. The reach of these new, politically-powerful conglomerates is extraordinarily wide, from trade monopolies, hotels and manufacturing, to commerce and even 'community services' such as television education. Some of the rent-seeking activity has been so brazen—as in the clove trade monopoly established in December 1990—as to anger even the regime's staunchest supporters. Undoubtedly, this new and virulent form of cronyism has soured the business environment for both foreign and (non-favoured) domestic investors alike.

Despite endless discussion of the topic, there have been very few careful studies of the incidence of corruption. It is a particularly serious problem in countries such as Indonesia that are characterised by an authoritarian political system, a controlled press, a poorly-paid civil service, and a complex commercial regulatory regime. Nevertheless, the problem needs to be assessed in proper perspective. It is certainly not just a phenomenon of post-1966 Indonesia.[14] Moreover, there have been some notable achievements, particularly in the 1980s. The blatantly corrupt Customs Service was tackled decisively in April 1985. The banking reforms of 1983 and 1988 removed most credit subsidies and reduced the incidence of 'command loans' (whereby banks were instructed to lend to favoured individuals without the usual commercial evaluation), both sources of significant corruption. Many NTBs were removed, and with them the revenues accruing to the licence-holder. The taxation system was overhauled, and tax regulations more vigorously enforced. The State Audit Office became more active, as did various parliamentary committees. Finally, it needs to be remembered that Indonesia's open international capital account and freely convertible currency have removed a source of corruption endemic in so many other developing countries.

Sectoral developments

Agriculture

The record of agricultural development since 1966 is a mixed one. The highlight has been the success of rice, especially over the period 1977–87. From its status as the world's largest rice importer in the late 1970s, the cherished and elusive goal of rice self-sufficiency was achieved in 1985 and has been maintained broadly since then. But the cost has been considerable. Inputs subsidies, especially fertiliser, have been very high. Moreover, non-food agricultural development has been much less impressive. With a few notable exceptions—most importantly palm oil—the cash-crop sector has not displayed the dynamism evident in some neighbouring countries. This is especially the case in the smallholder sector, where a combination of neglect, discrimination in favour of plantations, and inappropriate policies have resulted in slow output growth and virtually stagnant yields.

From 1966 to 1991 agricultural output growth averaged 3.8 per cent per annum. Food crops have always dominated the sector, generating consistently about 60 per cent of agricultural value added. The relative size of the other subsectors has also changed very little over this period—smallholders (about 13 per cent of total value added), plantations (2–3 per cent), livestock (a little over 10 per cent), fisheries (7–8 per cent), and forestry (about 5 per cent). Output growth has been more uneven among those sectors directly dependent on international markets and prices: compare, for example, the fluctuations in smallholder, plantations and fisheries output, all more export-oriented than food crops and livestock (Figure 2.3). The major subsector, food crops, has grown quite steadily since 1970. Dominated by rice, output has fallen in only two years—in 1972 when a particularly severe drought occurred, and in 1977 when pests caused major disruption. The strong output growth of 1978–81, which laid the base for self-sufficiency a few years later, is also evident. Most of the sharp increases in smallholder and estate production can be attributed to rising international prices; for example, coffee smallholder output in the late 1970s, and estate rubber production in the mid-1970s and mid-1980s. The extent of crop specialisation between smallholders and estates is illustrated by the fact that these sectors' output growth is not highly correlated. In the case of forestry, the subsector subject to the most intensive government regulation, the prohibition on the export of unprocessed timber and the removal of easily accessible stands both explain the sharp fall in production throughout most of the 1980s.

In terms of output growth, rice has been the success story, dominated by the growth of *sawah* (wet rice): *sawah* output rose by more than 250 per cent in 1966–91, while apparent per capita consumption jumped by almost 80 per cent. Yields more than doubled over this period, and contributed about 85 per cent of the increased production (Table 2.3). Rice

Figure 2.3　The growth of agricultural output, 1966–91 (%)

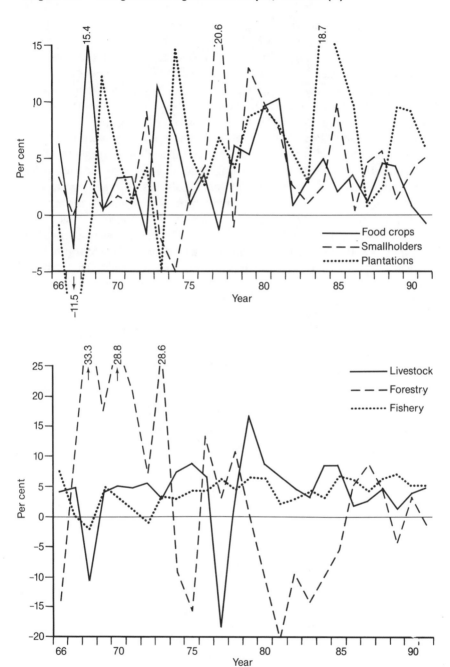

Note:　　1991 data are preliminary; data are based on a spliced constant 1983 prices series.
Source:　BPS, *National Accounts*, various years.

dominates the Indonesian diet, except in a few of the eastern provinces, and in the late 1960s had a weight of 31 per cent in the Jakarta 62 commodity CPI. It is therefore not surprising that rice became a major preoccupation of the government after the macroeconomic stabilisation phase of 1966–68 was completed: 'food policy *was* rice policy' during *Repelita I* according to Mears and Moeljono (1981:23), although a decade later the government began to place more emphasis on food-crop diversification.[15]

The first decade after 1966 saw mixed results in the government's rice campaign, and for much of the 1970s the record was indifferent. In 1972 a prolonged dry season resulted in falling output, and domestic rice prices doubled in the last four months of the year. Problems emerged again a few years later: arrears under the *Bimas* credit program escalated, there was a prolonged drought in 1976, and outbreaks of the *wereng* (brown plant hopper) pest, which first appeared in the 1974–75 season, were particularly serious in 1977. It appeared that Indonesia would never be able to achieve significant output increases, much less the goal of self-sufficiency. By the late 1970s it was importing up to one-third of the world's traded rice, becoming something of a price-maker on international markets.[16]

However, the mid-1970s was something of a watershed in rice policy, the effects of which were to become evident by the end of the decade. There

Table 2.3   Agricultural production and yields, 1966–90

Product		1966	1969	1974	1979	1984	1990
Food crops							
Rice (*sawah*)	P	15 517	21 474	27 871	24 732	36 017	42 825
	Y	1.92	3.28	3.80	3.22	2.66	4.57
Rice (*ladang*)	P	2443	2082	1844	1551	2119	2354
	Y	1.45	1.42	1.59	1.37	1.74	2.09
Maize	P	3717	2293	3240	3066	5288	6734
	Y	0.98	0.94	1.22	1.39	1.71	2.13
Cassava	P	11 233	10 917	13 775	13 751	14 167	15 830
	Y	7.42	7.40	9.10	9.60	10.50	12.10
Cash crops							
Estates:							
Rubber	P	209	223	249	275	314	310
	Y	0.44	0.46	0.57	0.62	0.64	0.62
Palm oil	P	174	189	351	600	1080	1809
	Y	1.57	1.55	2.14	2.62	2.83	2.43
Smallholders:							
Rubber	P	528	558	571	616	715	927
	Y	0.32	0.32	0.31	0.32	0.32	0.36
Coconuts	P	1130	1165	1356	1596	1738	2263
	Y	0.76	0.69	0.66	0.63	0.58	0.70

Notes: P—Production in 1000 ton.
Y—Yield in ton/ha.
na—Not available.

Source: BPS, *Statistik Indonesia*, various years.

was a concerted effort to accelerate the spread of high-yielding varieties (HYVs). Their share of rice-crop plantings over the decade 1970–80 more than doubled, from about 30 per cent to 68 per cent, rising still further to 85 per cent in 1985. Prices moved in favour of rice farmers in a number of respects: the government maintained domestic prices above international levels, and after 1977 the rice/fertiliser price began to rise in response to sharp increases in fertiliser (and pesticide) subsidies.[17] Consequently, rice production began to grow rapidly after 1978, aided by good rainfall and the absence of pest problems, but reflecting more fundamentally the measures discussed above. The country weathered the 1982–83 drought, the most serious in ten years, and output growth resumed quickly in 1984 and 1985. In November 1985 President Soeharto announced that rice self-sufficiency had been achieved, on the occasion of an invited address to the fortieth anniversary conference of the UN Food and Agriculture Organisation. Indonesia engaged in very little international trade from 1985 to 1990, until a prolonged dry season in 1991 hastened a shift away from the rigid and politically-motivated desire not to import rice.

The preoccupation with rice meant that the rest of the food sector was largely neglected, at least until the late 1970s. The government initiated some intensification programs for maize, peanuts and soybeans during *Repelita II*, concerned at the indifferent rice performance and the need to diversify diets. This nutritional diversification extended to wheat imports, then seen as a cheaper means of purchasing calories, and encouraged by its larger and less volatile international market. But over the period 1968-78 *palawija* (that is, non-rice food crops) output was largely static (Table 2.3).

It was only during *Repelita III* that *palawija* crops received anything like the same attention as rice. Maize yields proved quite responsive, and this crop experienced something of a technological revolution beginning in the late 1970s. Rising demand from the commercial livestock industry also induced greater output. Cassava, long regarded as an inferior good, registered much less yield improvement.[18]

The record in cash crops has been much less impressive. Except for the much-publicised success of palm oil, and a few minor crops such as cocoa, output growth has been slow and erratic. Most of the increased production has been achieved through area expansion, except for palm oil and larger plantations producing a few of the other crops. Smallholder yields have either declined or stagnated (Table 2.3). Since smallholder farmers dominate most cash crops, Indonesia's agricultural performance in this respect has been disappointing.

The history of the cash-crop sector therefore appears to be one of lost opportunities. After 1966 the sector might have been expected to grow more quickly, as a unified foreign exchange rate was adopted, big investments in infrastructure got underway, and the political situation became more secure.

International prices in the 1970s were also generally favourable, rubber in particular benefiting from the higher cost of synthetic rubber during the oil boom period. There were some improvements: in palm oil especially, increased yields for most crops produced by the plantations, and smallholder area expansion. But inefficient management of and costly subsidies for the state-owned plantations, insecure land access for some private estates, and ineffective promotional programs for smallholders have all retarded growth. The oil boom also hindered international competitiveness through the squeeze on non-oil tradeable activities. In the 1980s, falling oil prices produced the opposite outcome, via real effective depreciations of the rupiah. However, this competitive advantage was nullified somewhat by generally low international prices.

Indonesia's missed opportunities are nowhere better illustrated than in the case of natural rubber.[19] Three countries—Indonesia, Malaysia and Thailand—have dominated the industry since 1960, producing 75–80 per cent of world output (and a higher share still in earlier years). Malaysia has traditionally been the dominant producer, accounting for about 40 per cent of the total until about 1980. Malaysian output began to contract slowly during the 1980s, at which point Indonesia, long the second major producer, might have been expected to become the dominant supplier. However, Thailand, which produced about one-sixth of Indonesia's total in 1960 and one-third in 1970, is now moving into first place. Thai output grew rapidly, at an annual rate of 5.7 per cent in the 1970s and 10 per cent in the 1980s, compared to Indonesia's rate of 2–3 per cent over the two decades.

Among the other agricultural subsectors, forestry has expanded the most unevenly and been the source of the greatest controversy. Output and exports, mainly from Kalimantan, grew rapidly in the late 1960s in response to high world prices. Indonesia's forests had hitherto remained largely unexploited owing to poor infrastructure and cheaper supplies elsewhere. Most studies of the industry since 1970 report that forest management and conservation practices have been poor (see chapter 5). There have also been frequent allegations of corruption in the awarding of forest concessions, and criticisms of the industry's suboptimal fiscal practices.[20] In the early 1980s the government introduced a log export ban, to achieve conservation objectives and greater local processing. Forestry output in consequence fell during the first half of the 1980s and by 1985 was a little over half that of the late 1970s. This was accompanied by a boom in plywood exports, which through to 1986 generated about half of the country's total manufactured exports. However, the economic benefits of the prohibition have been questionable. Rents have been dissipated in the construction of inefficient plywood factories, a condition imposed on award of a concession.[21] In 1988 a similar ban was placed on rattan exports, accompanied by even more onerous regulations regarding the location of processing sites.

What of the future for Indonesian agriculture? Two of the factors which propelled agriculture and especially food crops in the 1970s—technological advance and subsidies from the oil boom—are unlikely to be significant. Expert opinion (see, for example, Ruttan 1990) holds that dramatic yield increases are not in prospect. Rather, incremental gains will be achieved by mixing inputs, adapting to climatic variations, and obtaining higher yields in upland areas; Java's per hectare yields are already very high by international comparison, and a repetition of the doubling which occurred in the period 1967–90 seems out of the question. The large subsidies over the period 1970–88—in pesticide, fertiliser, irrigation, credit, and research and extension services—are also a thing of the past.[22] Fiscal austerity since the mid-1980s has also starved many state agricultural enterprises of much needed capital injections.

Moreover, rapid economic growth and industrialisation may be causing fundamental shifts in the comparative advantage of Java–Bali away from food-crop production. Higher value-added activities—manufacturing, poultry, tourism and recreational services—not to mention the inexorable urban sprawl, are placing increasing pressure on agricultural land. These activities are also drawing labour out of agriculture, although there is no evidence yet of sustained increases in real agricultural wages. If food-crop production is to rise, most of the increase will therefore have to be generated off Java–Bali. However, yields in these regions are much lower. They average about two-thirds of the Java–Bali figure, while at the margin some Department of Agriculture estimates assume 3.5 hectares of land is required to replace the loss of one hectare of prime *sawah* on Java. Yields in the outer islands have been increasing more slowly (since 1966 by about 60 per cent, compared to the doubling on Java–Bali), reflecting both less-intensive promotional efforts and the increased cultivation of marginal rice lands.

There is, however, some room for optimism in assessing Indonesia's likely food equations. In the case of food crops, domestic demand can be expected to grow more slowly as both population growth and demand elasticities continue to decline.[23] (The exception is the demand for animal feedstuffs, a product of the increased commercialisation of the livestock industry.) In addition, the removal of input and credit subsidies in the late 1980s has not had the adverse effect on output that many had expected. In the case of cash crops (and livestock and fisheries also), there is considerable scope for expansion, and these are activities in which Indonesia might be expected to retain a comparative advantage for decades to come. The challenge for the 1990s will be to achieve the same successes registered in other non-oil exports, notably manufactures and tourism. Continuing tight exchange rate management, which has seen a sharp real effective depreciation of the *rupiah*, will provide a competitive spur. There is great scope also for increased efficiency: by improving smallholder yields in processing quality, by lowering marketing margins through improved physical infrastructure and better information flows, and by reform of the large but generally inefficient state agricultural enterprises.

For these gains to be realised, the agricultural sector needs less regulation and more promotion. The sweeping trade reforms of the 1980s hardly affected agriculture; sugar in particular continues to receive very high protection and is intensely regulated (Nelson and Panggabean 1991). It needs to be emphasised, however, that Indonesia has not yet embarked on the Northeast Asian road of high agricultural protectionism (see Anderson, Hayami and Associates 1986).[24] During the 1970s domestic prices were similar to those in international markets, with some smoothing out achieved by *Bulog*. As international prices declined in the 1980s, domestic prices for the first time began to consistently exceed international levels, by some 20–50 per cent. Effective protection was almost certainly higher, notwithstanding extensive protection for manufactures, owing to credit and input subsidies. There may indeed have been some justification for modest protection, as a means of overcoming information bottlenecks and quickly inducing farmers to adopt HYVs (Timmer 1989, 1991), and also as a crude but immediate means of recycling oil revenue into rural areas. But the arguments for protection for the food-crop sector are now much less persuasive. The most effective strategy for agricultural development would therefore seem to be a combination of promotional measures—increased agricultural extension and research, and large investments in rural infrastructure—and less intervention in output markets.

Manufacturing[25]

Manufacturing, the most dynamic sector of industry since the oil boom, has grown extremely quickly, at an annual rate of almost 12.5 per cent in the period 1965–91. This implies a doubling of real output about every six years, or a ninefold increase over the quarter-century. Since 1978 a separate non-oil manufacturing series has been published (see Figure 2.4). This series particularly highlights the strong performance of the non-oil segment since 1984, and also the contribution of state-financed oil and gas processing capacity to industrial growth in the peak years of 1980 and 1984. Part of the explanation for the rapid increase overall is the low base at the start of the period. Apart from some brief spurts in the 1930s and 1950s, Indonesia had barely begun to industrialise and in the 1960s was Asia's principal industrial laggard (Donges, Stecker and Wolter 1974; McCawley 1981; Soehoed 1967).

There have been at least four subphases within this era of high growth and rapid structural transformation, each one corresponding to differing policy emphases and shaped in part by international economic developments. They mirror largely the episodes identified above in the second section of

Figure 2.4   The growth of industrial output, 1966–91 (%)

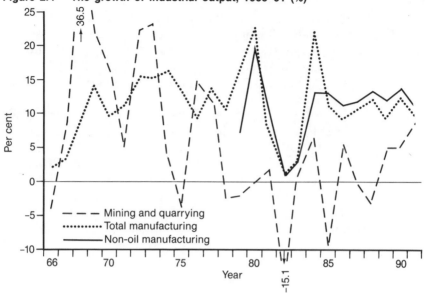

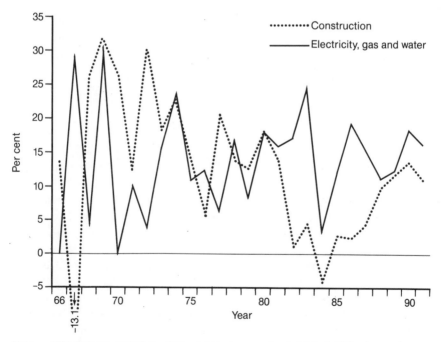

Note: 1991 data are preliminary; data are based on a spliced constant 1983 prices series.

Source: BSP, *National Accounts*, various years.

this chapter. The initial period of very rapid growth from 1967 to 1973 was driven mainly by liberalisation and the return to normal economic conditions. There was a large backlog in consumer demand, and consumer spending began to rise quickly under the impetus of high economic growth. There was, as noted, undoubtedly a shake-out of some traditional labour-intensive and cottage industry, but the broad-based expansion more than compensated for their demise.

The oil boom led to a fundamental reappraisal of industrial policy objectives. It ushered in a second phase, of state-directed industrialisation characterised by high but inefficient growth. Rising protection and state commercial investments ensured that the large increases in income over this period fed directly into demand for domestic manufactures. The decline in oil prices after 1981 triggered a third phase, of policy reappraisal. During 1982–85 the response was limited to prudent macroeconomic management and a large devaluation in 1983. Indeed some of the thrusts of the previous period remained in place. Huge state investments in oil and gas—planned in an era of abundance—were brought on stream, and the government resorted to increased use of non-tariff barriers. However, after 1985 there was an unambiguous change of direction, leading to the fourth and final phase featuring a range of bold deregulation packages, a larger role for the private sector, and an emphasis on exports.

Manufacturing expanded by more than 10 per cent in about two-thirds of the years between 1969 and 1991 (Figure 2.4). Virtually all sectors expanded quickly, although most consumer goods at a slower rate, and some capital goods industries were hit hard by the slump in the mid-1980s (Table 2.4). The growth of many industries was spectacular. During the 1970s much of this was due to the small initial levels of production, but high growth persisted in many cases during the 1980s, well after the early establishment phase and during the recession years.

Accompanying this high growth, there have been at least eight features of Indonesia's industrialisation which deserve comment. First, in addition to the expansion reported in Table 2.4, there has been a dramatic increase in the quality and range of products planned. Some of the 1960s manufactures were of such indifferent quality that they could almost be regarded as 'non-tradeables'. Very few capital and intermediate goods were produced in the mid-1960s.

A second feature has been the flood of new technologies from abroad since 1965. For two ten-year periods prior to the New Order (approximately 1940–50 and 1956–66) there was virtually no new manufacturing investment, and during the first half of the 1960s Indonesia increasingly cut itself off from international commerce. Consequently, the country had an extremely antiquated industrial stock by the late 1960s. Rapid technological modernisation hastened the demise of much of this extremely labour-inten-

Table 2.4   Output of selected industrial products, 1969–90^a

Product	Unit	1969	1979	1984	1990	Annual growth (%) 1979–90	1969–90
Consumer goods							
Cooking oil	'000 ton	263	452	267	490	0.7	3.0
Margarine	'000 ton	7.5	18.5	34.1	44.1	8.2	8.8
Kretek cigarettes	bil. sticks	19.0	41.5	79.7	139	11.6	9.9
White cigarettes	bil. sticks	11.0	28.6	26.9	34.8	1.8	5.6
Yarn	'000 bales	182	998	1782	3573	12.3	15.2
Textiles	mil. metres	450	1910	2402	5028	9.2	12.2
Garments	mil. dozen	na	na	26	58.6	na	na
Intermediate goods							
Plywood	'000 cub. m.	na	na	4249	8400	na	na
Paper	'000 ton	17	214	543	1400	18.6	23.4
Fertiliser (all types)	'000 ton	85	2089	4427	7012	11.6	23.4
Soap	'000 ton	133	203	160	223	0.9	2.5
Auto tyres	'000	366	2898	3944	8220	9.9	16.0
Cement	'000 ton	542	4705	8854	15 890	11.7	17.5
Glass sheets	'000 ton	na	67.3	152.1	354	16.3	na
Steel ingots	'000 ton	na	122	901	1988	28.9	na
Aluminium sheets	'000 ton	na	9.5	24.5	41	14.2	na
Engineering goods							
Dry batteries	mil.	54.0	462	772	1158	8.7	15.7
Motor vehicles	'000	5.0	103	154	271	9.2	20.9
Motorcycles	'000	21.4	222	272	410	5.7	15.1
TV sets	'000	4.5	660	773	1082	4.6	29.8

Notes: a Data refer to fiscal years; that is, 1969 to 1969–70, etc.
na—Not available.

Sources: Republic of Indonesia, *Nota Keuangan*, and *Lampiran Pidato Kenegaraan*, various years.

sive technology. Large-scale capital-intensive investments were a central feature of the government's state enterprise investments in the 1970s and 1980s—nowhere better illustrated than in the grandiose schemes of Minister Habibie—ranging from aircraft and shipbuilding to ammunition and electronics.[26]

A third and related feature has been the growing sophistication, scale and depth of the industrial sector. The average size of large and medium firms (defined as at least twenty employees) rose from 92 to 141 persons in 1974–88. The increase would almost certainly have been much greater if reliable data using consistent definitions were available for the mid-1960s. Real labour productivity in manufacturing has risen sharply, too: among large and medium firms it grew at about 9 per cent annually between 1975 and 1986. Another indicator relates to structural change, in particular the shift from simple consumer goods and resource-processing industries to more capital-intensive heavy industry. In 1963, for example, food (including beverages and tobacco) and rubber products generated about 60 per cent of manufacturing value added in large and medium firms; just 23 years later their share had fallen to 12 per cent. More generally, the share of consumer goods industries has fallen significantly over this period, reflecting both rapid structural change and a pronounced push into heavy industry.

Notwithstanding these transformations, a continuing feature of Indonesian industry from the colonial era of the 1930s to the chaos of the early 1960s and to the rapid growth of the late 1980s has been its extraordinary diversity. At one end of the spectrum are multimillion dollar industrial plants employing best-practice technology, often enclave in nature, with large foreign inputs and integrated within the international economy. These may coexist with small, seasonal household units that rarely employ wage labour and sell only within the immediate neighbourhood. Both are engaged in manufacturing, but they are as different as multinational banks and occasional rural moneylenders in the finance industry. It is clearly inaccurate to label this diversity as 'dualism', since the phenomenon is best seen as a continuum from large to small. But sharp differences will persist for many decades until labour markets begin to tighten, markets become better integrated, and low-wage cottage enterprises are driven out of business.

A fifth feature, not always appreciated by critics of Indonesia's development path, is that manufacturing employment growth has been respectable. Manufacturing employment grew at an annual rate of about 5.6 per cent for the whole sector and for large and medium firms from 1975 to 1986, and similar rates were probably achieved before and after this period. By implication, small industry (officially defined as five to nineteen employees) has held its position as has, presumably, cottage industry, the latter based on estimates of 'residual' employment figures.

There is, sixth, the spectacular increase in manufactured exports after 1985. Over the preceding fifteen years, Indonesia stood out as the only market-oriented developing East Asian economy which failed to register rapid and broad-based growth in manufactured exports. Export pessimism was widespread in some Indonesian government and community circles over this period, based on a belief that there were fundamental and inherent obstacles to the country ever becoming an internationally efficient supplier of manufactures. Yet the delayed emergence of Indonesia as a 'near NIE' (newly industrialising economy) can be explained quite easily by a combination of factors: a stifling bureaucratic and regulatory regime, the inter-sectoral effects of the oil boom, a strong (and captive) domestic market, and a dearth of commercial expertise following the dislocations of 1957–66. These impediments were pushed aside in the late 1980s and the resultant surge in manufactured exports constituted a strong vindication of orthodox economic policy prescriptions. Manufactured exports rose fourfold in 1980–85; they nearly doubled again in 1985–87 and 1987–89; and rose a further

50 per cent in 1989–91. During the period as a whole, real exports grew at an annual rate of 30 per cent. Much of the early growth was in plywood, following the log export ban of the early 1980s. But by the late 1980s the base had broadened considerably to include garments, textiles, footwear, furniture, fertiliser, paper and many other products. For much of this period, reflecting Indonesia's factor endowments, natural-resource-based products comprised a relatively large share of manufactured exports, at 40–50 per cent of the total. Although by 1991 this had declined to 30 per cent, such a figure set Indonesia apart from its dynamic East Asian neighbours.

A seventh feature of manufacturing, ownership patterns, reflects the interplay of 'policy' and 'industrial economics' factors. Foreign investors are prominent in industries where, if entry is permitted, they are able to exploit their advantages in technology (such as petro-chemicals, synthetic fibres, motorcycles, sheet glass, electronics), brand names (white cigarettes, pharmaceutics, breweries), and knowledge of international markets (footwear). There was a sudden rush of foreign investors into Indonesian manufacturing after 1967, and again after 1987, but in aggregate foreign ownership remains quite modest. The ownership data of course understate the extent of foreign involvement, owing to the presence of strong licensing tie-ups in activities closed to foreign equity (for example, in much of the automotive industry), and to the many other forms of commercial linkages. The large state enterprise sector reflects the government's strategic imperative after 1974, to guide the pattern of industrialisation in the 'commanding heights' of industry. The state is particularly prominent in oil refining, LNG, sugar refining, cement, fertiliser, aircraft, spinning and weaving, and machine goods. Domestic private firms, the third ownership group, are generally smaller, less capital-intensive and found more commonly in labour-intensive, consumer goods industries than the state or foreign groups. The differences, however, are narrowing over time, especially with the advent of large and diverse domestic conglomerates. Technology-intensive industries are no longer the preserve of foreign firms, since these indigenous operations now have the capacity and experience to acquire modern technology from abroad.

Finally, the spatial patterns of industrialisation deserve emphasis, especially the three major features of the factory industrial sector since the mid-1960s. First, Java's share of manufacturing output and employment has been declining steadily. This conclusion applies to non-oil manufacturing, but especially to the total manufacturing sector since most of the large oil and gas installations constructed since the mid-1970s are in Sumatra and East Kalimantan.[27] Parts of Sumatra and Kalimantan have absorbed most of Java's declining share. Secondly, there are marked regional patterns of industrial activity, reflecting resource endowments and the supply of key industrial inputs. In particular, with the exception of Bali, Batam Island and (to a lesser extent) Medan, almost all 'footloose' manufacturing activities are located on Java. Thirdly, within Java there is a pronounced west–east pattern evolving, with large industrial complexes evident around Jakarta, Surabaya and surrounding areas, and a much smaller base of medium and small enterprises found in the two central provinces. Manufacturing in Java is almost entirely a north-coast and north–central phenomenon.

The services sector

The services sector has played a crucial role in underpinning the growth of tradeable goods activities in agriculture and industry. It has generated employment opportunities and foreign exchange earnings (notably in the case of tourism), and provided an ever wider array of personal services as community incomes rise. The sector has consistently produced 35–40 per cent of GDP, and in most years over 45 per cent of non-oil GDP. Value added in services has always exceeded the combined total of value added in the more publicised food-crop and manufacturing sectors, in the early 1990s by a margin of some 30 per cent. Services output has grown rapidly throughout the period 1967–91, in all years at more than 4 per cent and for over half the period at more than double this rate (Figure 2.1). Its expansion has been more even than that of agriculture and industry, where international prices, climatic factors and changes in policy regimes have resulted in a more erratic growth path. In most years services have contributed more than 40 per cent of the increment of GDP, and more than 50 per cent to non-oil GDP, reflecting the historic sectoral shifts evident in all economies.

Within services, trade (including also hotels and restaurants) has always been a dominant subsector, producing on average about 40 per cent of sectoral value added. The government sector, essentially measured by public service salaries, is the next largest, with 15–20 per cent of the total. Transport and communication and financial services are sizeable, accounting for 13–14 per cent and 10–11 per cent of the total respectively, followed by the miscellaneous group, other services, at 8–9 per cent and accommodation at 6–7 per cent.

Growth among these subsectors has fluctuated considerably since the late 1960s (Figure 2.5). The transport and communication industry grew at a spectacular rate over the period 1971–83 as aid and then oil revenue was poured into long-neglected physical infrastructure. The revolution in light commercial road transport further hastened this growth. The public administration subsector also expanded quickly over this period, as civil service numbers and especially remuneration rose significantly.[28] The control of inflation induced a renewed confidence in the banking sector, which was ravaged by the events of the early and mid-1960s. Monetisation increased quickly, and much of the government's oil revenue was channelled through state banks over this period. Another episode of high growth commenced

Figure 2.5   The growth of services output, 1966–91 (%)

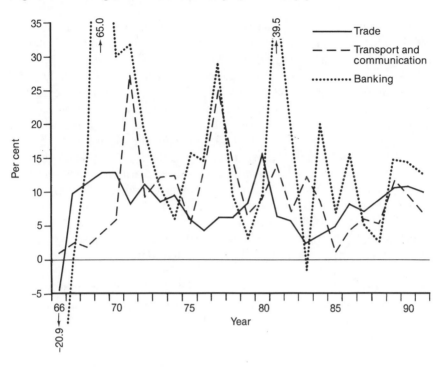

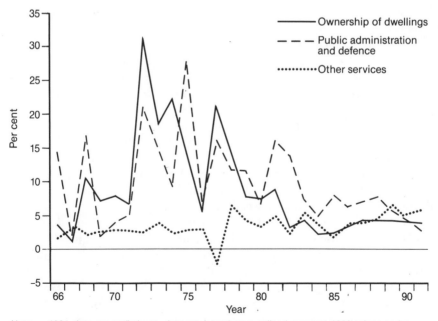

Note: 1991 data are preliminary; data are based on a spliced constant 1983 prices series.
Source: BPS, *National Accounts*, various years.

in 1989, in the wake of the banking deregulation of late 1988. Trade grew steadily in line with the expansion of commercial activity, without displaying the peaks and troughs of the other subsectors.

Two important features of the services sector are its extremely rapid transformation and pervasive regulation. The first factor has meant that many of the service activities of the early 1990s bear little relation to those which existed 25 years ago. The second factor has sometimes hampered the growth of these sectors, and resulted in the inefficient provision of services.

The expansion is nowhere better illustrated than in the case of physical infrastructure, transport and communication. Over the period 1966–90 there was an increase of 2200 per cent in the number of buses, 1900 per cent in domestic air freight, 900 per cent in the case of power generation and the number of trucks, 2600 per cent in cement output (though not domestic supplies), while international telephone calls increased some 400 times. Some of these increases reflect the low initial base figures, that is, the abysmal state of infrastructure in the 1960s. In other cases, notably tele-communications, the increases reflect technological breakthroughs and are part of a rapid global expansion. There have also been a few instances where expansion has been slow, such as in rail and ocean sea-transport. But on the whole the trend has been one of high growth, continuing from the catch-up phase of the late 1960s and 1970s right through the 1980s. Moreover, these aggregate figures do not provide a comprehensive picture of the improvement in the range and quality of transport and communication services.

Within the transport sector,[29] road transport has expanded the most rapidly, owing to the vast improvement in road conditions especially off-Java, the introduction of relatively inexpensive light commercial vehicles (known universally as 'colts'), and the growth of other four- and two-wheeled transport. The industry is responsive to consumer needs, providing services ranging from modern and well-equipped long-distance buses to colts servicing urban and short-distance inter-city networks. The 'transport revolution' is manifested in the fact that it is now possible to travel from the northern tip of Aceh to Sumbawa (east of Lombok) by road and vehicular ferry. Another manifestation of the revolution, disturbing to some, is the demise of *becak* (rickshaw) transport, and for that matter of bicycles. *Becak* have now become little more than providers of residual urban and fringe-urban transport, a trend hastened by urban authorities, who frequently regard them as incompatible with a modern transport system and as embarrassing reminders of Indonesia's 'backwardness'.

Despite these major improvements, some notable deficiencies remain in the transport networks. The underinvestment in public transport facilities on major urban arterial routes, in part owing to fare and zoning restrictions, is evident everywhere. In sectors dominated by state enterprises, notably rail and to a much lesser extent shipping, transport has expanded more slowly. However, regulatory reforms of 1985 and 1988 have greatly improved services.

Tourism has witnessed spectacular growth since the mid-1980s. The industry languished in the 1970s (the numbers barely doubling in 1974–83) for much the same reasons as other non-oil exports. The oil boom, operating through the exchange rate, made Indonesia a comparatively expensive country to visit; and the government's lack of interest was reflected in tight regulations pertaining to visas, aircraft landing rights, and investments in tourism facilities. Declining oil prices and the evident success of tourism elsewhere prompted a major policy rethink. Tourism began to grow rapidly from the mid-1980s, emerging as a major source of export growth alongside that of manufactures, and for similar reasons. Real effective devaluations conferred a competitive edge. Visa-free entry for many nationals was introduced, and points of entry for international airlines extended. A package of measures introduced in December 1987 simplified the previously complex procedures for investing in the industry.[30]

Developments in other service industries reflect this mix of growth and regulatory reform. In the area of financial services, despite the rapid expansion, government regulations and protection of the state sector stifled the emergence of an efficient industry through until the late 1980s. As noted below, state banks were little more than agencies for the central bank until 1983, with little incentive to compete and innovate. Similarly, the insurance industry was heavily regulated until 1988. No new licences for foreign non-life insurers were issued after 1975, the number of domestic non-life insurers was frozen from 1974 to 1982, and only three companies (two government-owned) were permitted to offer reinsurance services (Nehen 1989). The reforms of October 1988 quickly changed the structure of the industry, as new domestic private entrants, especially, began to out-compete the hitherto protected state firms.

Monetary and financial developments

The distinction between the Old and New Order is nowhere more pronounced than in monetary and financial developments. Mounting budget deficits resulted in accelerating inflation in the first half of the 1960s, and there was a total absence of political will to tackle the problem. The Soeharto government tackled inflation surprisingly quickly and effectively. Indeed, one of the hallmarks of the regime since 1966 has been its commitment to control inflation. There have been inflationary episodes, especially during the peak of the oil booms. There has also been a good deal of 'financial repression', and until recently monetary policy instruments have been blunt and underdeveloped. But the regime has established a credible reputation for basically sound macroeconomic management: each burst of inflation has been followed by corrective intervention. In the conduct and outcome of monetary policy and financial development since 1966 at least five important features stand out:

1   An open international capital account since 1970. In consequence, exogenous shocks such as the oil price fluctuations have been transmitted quickly to the domestic economy, posing particular challenges for the short-run management of the money supply. (In this respect, also, Indonesia has enacted its policy reforms in reverse order to that suggested in the [primarily Latin American] sequencing literature, with little adverse effect.)

2   A fixed exchange rate (with the US dollar, rather than a bundle of currencies) for lengthy periods, including the first five years of the oil boom period. Thus the government was without one of the standard economic policy levers, and adjustment to the large terms of trade increase over the period took other forms, principally rising inflation.

3   The 'balanced budget' principle. While introduced for commendable political reasons, it has in some respects hampered the government's fiscal flexibility.

4   In the conduct of monetary and financial policy there has been a continual tension: between regulation and direct controls, which broadly characterised the system in the 1970s, and indirect market-based interventions, which become increasingly important in the 1980s; and over the extent to which social and equity objectives (such as small-enterprise development) can be pursued alongside the usual macroeconomic objective of internal balance, principally the control of inflation.

5   The transformation of monetary and financial institutions has been quite dramatic. Monetary 'restocking' has occurred, initially in response to lower inflation and a renewed confidence in the currency, and later as additional financial securities were introduced. New financial institutions have evolved. However, fiscal and monetary instruments still remain quite underdeveloped. There is no real government bond market, and open-market monetary operations are still evolving.

Inflation and money supply

Figures 2.6 and 2.7 provide a summary picture of monetary developments over this period.[31] The government was able to control inflation much more quickly than was expected. The budget deficit, which prior to 1966 had been the direct and major cause of money supply growth, was quickly reduced. Inflation peaked at an annual rate of almost 1500 per cent in mid-1966, but fell sharply and was effectively under control by 1969, when the annual rate was just 15 per cent (Figure 2.6). The very low inflation of

Figure 2.6   Inflation and the growth of money supply, 1967–91 (%)

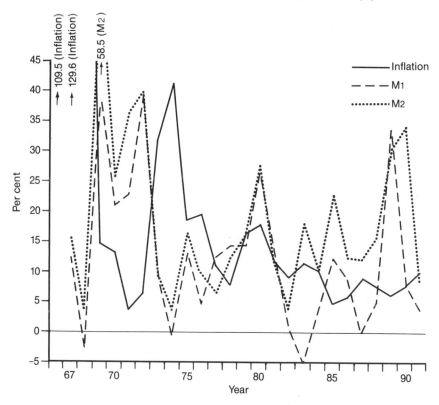

Note: M1 (narrow money) and M2 (broad money) growth rates have been deflated by the inflation rate; that is, they are real growth rates.

Source: IMF, *International Financial Statistics*, various issues.

1971 and 1972 was short-lived, however. Real money supply (that is, nominal money supply deflated by the inflation rate) continued to grow very rapidly through to 1972, at a rate far higher than that consistent with low inflation, even allowing for the monetary restocking which was still occurring. The 1972 rice crisis saw retail rice prices double over the period August–December, and was viewed by some as the proximate cause of the sharply rising inflation in 1973. However, an accommodating monetary policy and rising international inflation—combined with the fixed exchange rate—were the underlying causes.

Inflation accelerated further in 1973 in response to the quadrupling of oil prices, soaring to 40 per cent in 1974. Despite the tremendous political pressure to spend the windfall gains domestically, the government's macroeconomic response was reasonably prompt, if blunt. Unwilling to depart from its fixed exchange rate regime, the authorities chose to fight inflation by, in effect, running a budget surplus with the central bank, and by

Figure 2.7   **Money supply as a percentage of GDP, 1966–91 (%)**

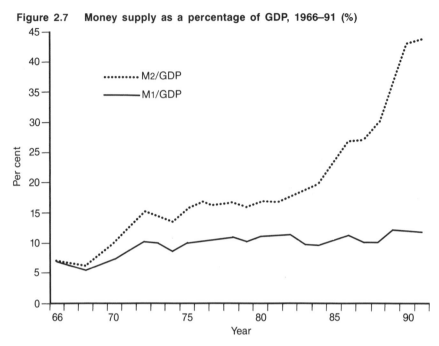

Note: M1 (narrow money) and M2 (broad money) growth rates have been deflated by the inflation rate; that is, they are real growth rates.

Source: IMF, *International Financial Statistics*, various issues.

introducing an anti-inflationary package in April 1974.[32] The Pertamina debacle in the following year ironically facilitated the process of monetary restraint, by draining large volumes of liquidity from the system. Both inflation and money supply growth slowed as these measures took effect, although for most of the second half of the 1970s inflation remained stubbornly high, hovering between 10 and 20 per cent.

Inflation rose again in 1979. In November 1978 the rupiah was devalued by 50 per cent against the US dollar, and a determined but largely ineffective program of domestic price controls was employed to make the devaluation 'stick'. However, less than a year later, oil prices began to rise steeply. Once more, the government had great difficulty sterilising the monetary impact of the oil boom. Money supply growth accelerated, even though the government again ran an effective surplus with the monetary authorities. Commercial credit and rising international reserves were the main sources of money supply growth over this period, and their impact far outweighed the government's fiscal contractionary efforts. In other respects, however, the experience of the first and second oil booms differed. The second oil boom was smaller (that is, in terms of the percentage oil price increases) and of shorter duration. By 1982 oil prices were tapering off. Moreover, the government had learned some lessons from the first boom, and it had its monetary control instruments (although clumsy) firmly in place.

The 1980s reforms

Developments after 1982 differed from those of the 1970s in three important respects. First, oil prices fell and remained low. Hence the previous trigger to inflation—the monetary impact of rising terms of trade—disappeared, and in some years exerted a negative impact. In 1982, 1983 and 1987 real M1 (but not M2) growth was either negative or close to zero. Second, the government slowly began to develop a more sophisticated approach to monetary policy management, in particular through increased resort to indirect intervention rather than direct regulatory controls. Third, in consequence especially of the first factor, inflation remained low, and for most of the 1980s was less than 10 per cent. This rate was achieved in spite of two large nominal devaluations (in 1983 and 1986), and virtually continuous 'crawling peg' depreciations in other years.

The first set of monetary and financial reforms was enacted in June 1983. The state banks were now permitted to set some deposit and lending rates, except in the case of the still extensive priority programs. Credit ceilings were partially removed. There was also the first shift to open market operations, with the development of new monetary policy instruments. Implementation of these reforms remained patchy and spasmodic, however, and the government still lacked the instruments to deal with the consequences of an open international capital market.[33]

The next major reforms, introduced in October 1988, proved to be the most decisive financial policy initiative of the decade.[34] These reforms had a dramatic impact. The long-dormant stock market suddenly sprang into life and for a short period registered the most spectacular increases in value and volume of turnover in the world. Indonesia for the first time experienced a genuine private banking sector boom, as these institutions began to compete aggressively for customers and market share. The state banks, long accustomed to operating as administrative arms of the central bank, were slow to adjust to these new commercial opportunities, and the decline in their market share accelerated. Private banks began to offer a wide selection of financial portfolios, including very attractive term deposit rates. The response in terms of money aggregates was that narrow money (M1) grew slowly over this period, but broad money (M2), which includes term deposits, began to grow very quickly (Figure 2.6).

It is important to emphasise that the impact of financial liberalisation was certainly not confined to major cities and urban areas. During the early 1980s it was recognised that the heavily subsidised and inefficient village operations of the major government bank, Bank Rakyat Indonesia, could no longer be sustained in the face of declining oil revenues. A range of innovatory rural credit schemes was therefore introduced, offering much higher interest rates but more flexible service. As Patten and Rosengard (1991) and Snodgrass and Patten (1991) demonstrate, most of these schemes have been very successful. The enthusiastic consumer response indicates that price is a less important consideration than flexibly designed packages in the implementation of rural credit schemes.

These reforms unleashed a more competitive private banking sector, but macroeconomic management faced new challenges. Higher money supply growth and the boom of the late 1980s renewed inflationary pressures, forcing Bank Indonesia to push interest rates still higher to cool the economy. Over this period, also, several financial scandals—seemingly a feature of each Indonesian economic and financial boom—diminished public and investor confidence in the efficiency of the reforms.[35] Also, throughout 1990 and 1991 mismanagement, manipulation and fraud began to tarnish the image of the Jakarta Stock Exchange. Foreign and domestic investors began to withdraw from the exchange, the pace of new listings slackened off, and most of the much-vaunted state enterprise offerings failed to materialise.

Fiscal policy[36]

There are two fundamental differences between fiscal policy in the pre-1966 and post-1966 eras in Indonesia. The first is, as noted, that the government ceased being a major and direct contributor to inflation through its mounting budget deficits. Early in the life of the New Order regime, the government adopted the 'balanced budget' principle. Although in a conventional economic sense the government has continued to run budget deficits, the balanced budget rule has been firmly adhered to ever since and is one of the basic tenets of the regime.

The second major difference concerns the size of government. As a share of GDP, government revenue and expenditure more than doubled over the period 1965–75. The increases have been essentially revenue-driven, as first aid and debt flows then rapidly rising oil prices swelled the government's coffers. In the second half of the 1980s, non-oil domestic revenues began to rise significantly. The size and funding of this expenditure has had two immediate and important political implications: the central government has had hitherto unimaginable resources at its disposal, thus reinforcing its political authority; and until the early 1980s most of the government's revenue was raised painlessly, financed by foreign taxpayers and oil consumers.

The size of the government sector

The size of the government sector has risen dramatically since the mid-1960s. Real government expenditure (that is, nominal expenditure deflated by the CPI) has risen approximately 21 times over the period 1966–90, from about Rp1.4 trillion to Rp30 trillion, measured in 1985 prices. The increase was particularly sharp during the rehabilitation phase and the first oil boom; real expenditures doubled in 1966–69 and more than doubled again from 1971 to 1975. A further sharp increase occurred around 1980, with real expenditures rising some 60 per cent in 1978–80. Expenditure levels then remained flat for much of the 1980s, with a succession of austere budgets in the wake of declining international oil prices, but a strong recovery occurred at the end of the decade. Through until 1980 government expenditure, as a share of GDP, rose substantially (Figure 2.8). The sharpest increase occurred during the first oil boom period, with the share rising from 14.9 per cent in 1971 to 21.6 per cent in 1975. It declined during the early 1980s, while there was little change during the period of vigorous growth in the late 1980s, the first genuine private sector boom in the nation's independent history.[37]

Trends in revenue and expenditure

In the case of revenue, the picture is dominated by the changing relative importance of the three main aggregates, oil and gas revenue, other domestic revenue—usually referred to as non-oil domestic revenue (NODR)—and foreign aid. In the late 1960s aid played a major role, providing 25–30 per cent of government revenue. Before their prices began to rise steeply, oil and gas contributed 10–20 per cent of the total, with the remainder, 50–60 per cent, coming from NODR (Figure 2.9). Increasing oil prices resulted in the share of oil almost doubling from 1971 (25 per cent of the total) to 1974 (48 per cent), rising still further to its peak share of 62 per cent in 1981. Over this period the share of aid fell to less than 20 per cent, and during the early 1980s it was as low as 12–13 per cent. However, just as the government could credibly point to a reduced dependence on foreign aid, declining oil prices produced another major change in revenue composition. By 1986, the low point in international prices, oil's share in revenue had fallen to 29 per cent, less than half that of its maximum in 1981. Even nominal oil revenues fell sharply, from Rp11.1 trillion in 1985 to just Rp6.3 trillion in 1986. The importance of the flexible and prompt international donor response was underlined during this difficult adjustment period. Aid revenues rose sharply, from Rp3.6 trillion in 1985 to Rp5.8 trillion in 1986 and Rp10 trillion in 1988. As a share of government revenue, the increases were sharper still, from 15.7 per cent to 30.3 per cent in 1985–88. By 1990 aid was as important to the Indonesian government as it was in 1972,

Figure 2.8   The government budget as a percentage of GDP, 1966–91 (%)

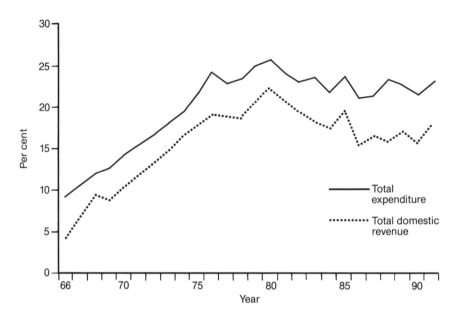

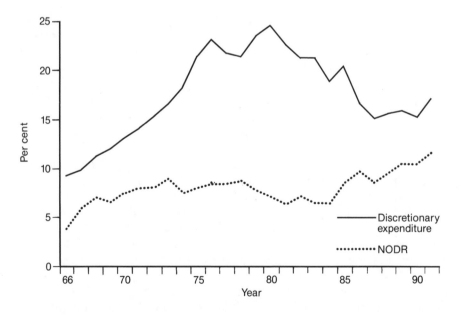

Note: Discretionary expenditure refers to total expenditure less payment of debt principal and interest.

Source: Republic of Indonesia, *Nota Keuangan*, various issues.

Figure 2.9   The composition of government revenue, 1967–91 (% of total)

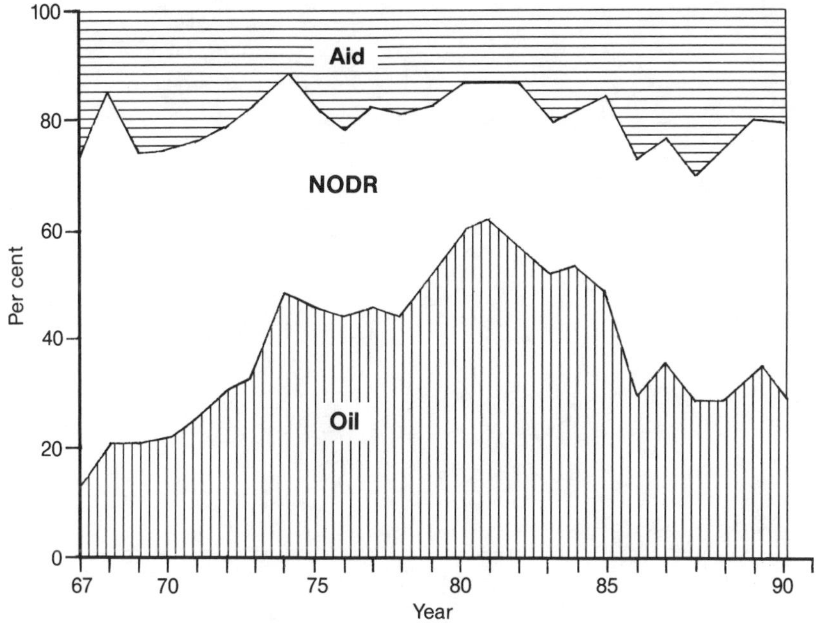

Source: Republic of Indonesia, *Nota Keuangan*, various issues.

immediately before the first oil boom. Despite the successful program of adjustment in the late 1980s, Indonesia has not yet achieved one of its major fiscal objectives, that of reduced dependence on foreign aid.

From the late 1960s until the mid-1980s the NODR category was overshadowed by oil and aid. Its share of total revenue halved over the period 1968–79 (from 64.9 per cent to 30.2 per cent), and fell still further during the second oil boom, to as low as 25.8 per cent in 1981. Despite the opportunities for rapid increases in NODR during the high growth of the 1970s, the oil boom induced a lazy fiscal regime. Consequently, real NODR rose quite slowly over this period, doubling from 1969 to 1975 and rising a further 60 per cent between 1975 and 1981.[38] The share of NODR then began to rise again, almost doubling in the years to 1991. Much of the initial increase was simply the result of declining oil revenues, as real NODR rose slowly over the period 1980–84, by just 12 per cent. However, the 1984 tax reforms (see below) and more vigorous collection efforts, both spurred on by declining oil revenues, produced the first really significant increases since the late 1960s. Real NODR jumped over 40 per cent in 1985, and more than doubled between 1984 and 1989.[39]

The trends in expenditures mirror those of the revenues in important respects. Real government expenditure rose very sharply in the 1970s, in direct response to the oil revenue and aid inflows. The government quickly

Figure 2.10   **Macroeconomic balances, 1969–91 (% of GDP)**

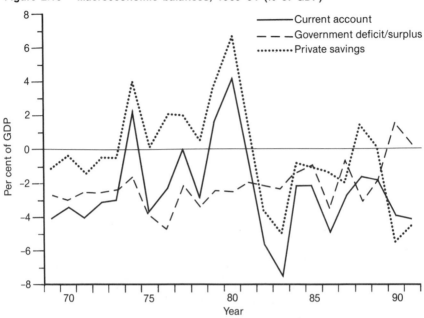

Source: IMF, *International Financial Statistics*, various issues; and author's estimates.

began to allocate an increasing proportion of its budget to 'development' expenditures, the latter's share rising from 20 per cent in 1969 to 56 per cent at the height of the oil boom in 1976. The seemingly inexorable growth in government expenditure came to a sudden halt in 1984, when for the first time in the regime's history real expenditure actually declined. Real expenditure declined further in 1986, when the government faced its most serious fiscal problems since 1966.

These difficulties were compounded by the fact that, just as the oil revenue began to decline, debt servicing (DS) obligations rose sharply. DS, which is classified as part of the routine budget, absorbed less than 10 per cent of expenditure throughout the 1970s, and in the mid-1970s was less than 5 per cent. However, it rose sharply in the 1980s, from 8.4 per cent in 1982 to 14.5 per cent in 1985 and 30.3 per cent in 1987. The government thus faced a 'scissor' problem, hemmed in by declining revenue and rising DS payments. Consequently, the government's 'discretionary expenditure' (that is, total expenditure less DS payments) fell more sharply still. Measured in 1985 prices, it peaked at Rp19.5 trillion in 1985, but fell by almost one-fifth to Rp15.9 trillion in 1986. It recovered in the late 1980s, but even by 1989 it was only 7 per cent higher than that of 1981, equivalent to a fall of about 10 per cent in per capita terms over the decade.[40] The adjustment process was facilitated by sharp reductions in a range of government subsidies, including rice, petroleum, fertiliser and pesticides.

No slogan has been more central in the New Order's economic philosophy than that of the balanced budget (BB). In an economic sense, of course, the BB is a fiction. The budget is 'balanced' only because the items financing the deficit (aid and external borrowings) are counted as revenue. If they were excluded, the budget would not be in balance and in most years the government would be revealed as running a deficit. However, the BB rule has proved to be a clever and effective political tactic to guard against a recurrence of the financial excesses of the early 1960s. By ensuring that expenditure is determined by revenue—the latter albeit elastically defined—the government has been able to control political pressures demanding economically unsustainable expenditure levels.

The budget's economic impact is far less clear. The government has consistently run a deficit, and an increasingly large one in the late 1980s, if the measure adopted is total domestic revenue (oil and non-oil) less all expenditure. Yet such a measure does not capture accurately the domestic economic impact of the budget, since there are large 'leakages' (abroad) on both sides of the ledger: almost all debt service payments are to creditors abroad; the import-intensive oil sector includes significant payments to factors abroad; and a substantial, though probably declining, proportion of the development budget consists of material and capital imports. A number of alternative estimates of the budgetary impact have been proposed. The most widely accepted are those prepared by the IMF. According to this definition, the government has consistently run a deficit, in the range 2–3 per cent of GDP, somewhat lower (less than 2 per cent) in 1974, 1982, 1984–85 and 1987, and considerably higher (above 3.5 per cent) in 1975, 1976 and 1986 (Figure 2.10). Prima facie, this series suggests that the government has not attempted to run a countercyclical fiscal policy, since small and large deficits have both been recorded in years of boom and recession.

Trade and balance of payments[41]

The balance of payments

By 1965 the government was unable to service its hard currency debt of some $2.5 billion. In December of that year, for the first time, the central bank was unable to honour letters of credit. For 1966 debt repayments were estimated to be about $530 million, exceeding the projected official foreign exchange earnings of $430 million. However, in response to the series of trade liberalisations enacted between 1966 and 1969, the progressive adoption of a unified exchange rate (completed in 1970), and the return of settled economic conditions, exports began to rise quickly from the late 1960s, quadrupling over the period 1969–72. The most dramatic increase then occurred in 1974, when the nominal value of net oil exports rose more than fourfold. These values held up in the next few years, followed by a further massive increase in 1978–80. Export values fell quickly from the 1980 peak, plateaued for three years from 1982 to 1984, then plunged precipitously in 1986 to less than one-quarter of the nominal value in 1980 and lower even than that of 1974.[42] The value of oil and gas exports recovered somewhat from the trough of 1986, but remained flat apart from a temporary increase in 1990 following the short-lived Middle East dispute. Throughout this period price variations have been the major factor determining the fluctuations in the value of oil exports (but not LNG exports, the volume of which has grown steadily); Indonesia usually observed OPEC output quotas, and expansion has been inhibited by financial factors—exploration has been less attractive during periods of low prices, while the fiscal regime deterred companies during the peak oil price periods. Table 2.5 provides a summary picture of the balance of payments over the period 1969–91.

The magnitude of these external shocks is illustrated clearly in Figure 2.11. Over the period 1971–75 the real international oil price almost quadrupled, followed by a 90 per cent rise in 1978–81. The slide was almost as severe, with the real price declining by over 25 per cent in 1981–84 and more than 100 per cent in 1986. Because oil has until recently dominated Indonesia's balance of payments, the terms of trade have mirrored these fluctuations closely. Non-oil commodity exports were significant prior to 1970 while manufactures grew rapidly after 1985. But over the period 1971–87 Indonesia was very much a petroleum-dependent economy, with all the potential for instability that this status implied.

The major autonomous movements in the current account, independent of oil price fluctuations, have been the growth of non-oil exports and rising interest payments on external debt during the 1980s. Although overshadowed by oil, non-oil exports grew quite strongly for some periods of the 1970s in response to favourable international commodity prices. However, most commodity prices remained depressed in the 1980s, with the result that the value of non-oil exports declined from 1979 to 1983. Growth, however, has been sustained and rapid since 1984 as the manufacturing export boom took hold. Interest payments on external debt became a significant factor in the increased service 'imports' recorded from the late 1970s.

Indonesia entered the first oil boom period with a comparatively high though sustainable current account deficit, which over the period 1969–72 was some 30–50 per cent of merchandise exports. This inherited feature, plus the surge in non-oil imports, explains why current account deficits continued to be recorded during the first oil boom. The sudden increase in oil prices in 1979, the devaluation of late 1978, and fiscal caution in the

Table 2.5 Summary balance of payments, 1969–91[a] ($ million, selected years)

	1969	1973	1974	1975	1978	1979	1980	1981	1982	1985	1986	1987	1990	1991
1 Net oil/LNG exports[b]	92	641	2638	3138	4010	6975	10 601	9761	7166	6123	2584	3760	6010	4723
2 Net non-oil/LNG exports	-593	-1397	-2776	-3992	-5165	-4777	-8470	-12 551	-14 205	-7955	-6635	-5467	-9751	-9556
Merchandise trade	-349	-708	-1789	-2606	-2753	-1879	-4974	-8825	-10 203	-3903	-2625	-1095	-4068	-2921
Services trade	-244	-689	-987	-1386	-2412	-2898	-3496	-3726	-4002	-4052	-4010	-4372	-5683	-6163
3 Current account (=1+2)	-501	-756	-138	-854	-1155	+2198	+2131	-2790	-7039	-1832	-4051	-1707	-3741	-4361
4 Official capital movements	371	643	660	1995	2208	+2690	+2684	+3521	5011	3432	5472	4575	5006	5262
5 Debt amortisation	-31	-81	-89	-77	-632	-692	-615	-809	-926	-1644	-2129	-3049	-4082	-4367
6 Other capital movements[c]	62	+549	-131	-1075	456	-1253	-299	1140	+1795	572	+1232	+1709	+5856	4447
7 Total (=3+4+5+6)	-99	+355	+302	-11	877	2943	+3901	+1,062	-1159	528	524	1528	3039	981
8 Errors and omissions	+56	+5	-311	-353	-169	-1253	-1165	-2050	-2121	-498	-1262	+57	+263	e
9 Monetary movements [=-(7+8)][d]	+43	-360	+9	+364	-708	-1690	-2736	+988	+3280	-30	+738	-1585	-3302	-981

Notes: a Refers to fiscal years (that is, 1969 refers to 1969–70, and as for following years).
b Includes services for oil and gas.
c Includes SDRs 1969, 1978–80.
d A negative amount refers to the accumulation of assets.
e Included in 'other capital movements' for 1991 only.

Source: Republic of Indonesia, *Nota Keuangan*, various issues.

99

**Figure 2.11   The terms of trade, oil prices, and 'competitiveness,' 1971–91
(indices, 1980 = 100)**

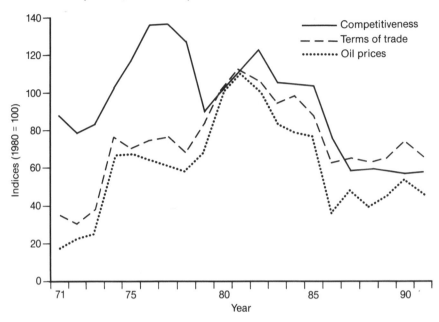

Note: Oil prices refer to nominal prices of Minas crude ($ per barrel), deflated by the wholesale
price index for industrial economies.

Sources: The oil price and terms of trade data are from Republic of Indonesia, *Nota Keuangan*,
various issues. The wholesale price data are from the IMF, *International Financial Statistics*,
various issues. The 'competitiveness' data are from the Morgan Guarantee real effective
exchange rate series, calculated as nominal effective exchange rates adjusted for inflation
rates.

wake of the Pertamina crisis of 1975–76, all combined to produce the
regime's first current account surpluses in 1979 and 1980. However, the
delayed effect of the import response to the second oil boom, together with
a sudden softening in international oil markets, resulted in an alarmingly
large current account deficit in 1982. The deficit was quickly reduced as
the government took prompt remedial action. However, it increased sharply
again in 1986 as oil prices collapsed. Once more, the deficit was brought
down quickly. The government's tight balance of payments management is
illustrated further in Figure 2.10.[43] As a percentage of GDP, the current
account deficit was comparatively large in 1969–71. A surplus was recorded
in 1974, and again in 1979–80. The sharp deterioration of 1982 and 1983
is clearly evident, the latter year registering the highest percentage deficit
of the entire period, greater even than the figure for 1986.

Because so much of the capital transactions have been in the government
sector, the capital account has generally responded to and accommodated

developments in the current account, rather than the reverse.[44] Official capital inflows reflect the very large aid receipts over the entire period. During the 1970s debt amortisation was relatively quite trivial. The debt from the Sukarno era was rescheduled, many of the new loans contained a significant grace period before repayment commenced, and the economy was growing so quickly that even rising absolute debt repayments were a shrinking percentage of GDP and exports. The first significant increase in debt amortisation occurred in 1977, but payments plateaued over the next four years. Repayment obligations began to rise quickly only after 1983, which coincided with declining oil prices. Indonesia, like other oil exporters, then faced its most severe problem of external indebtedness. As would be expected, other capital flows have fluctuated much more. At the beginning of the period, SDRs (special drawing rights) from the IMF were sizeable, being more than half the 'other' total in 1969. Thereafter, as Indonesia's balance of payments strengthened, SDRs became quite unimportant. Except for 1974, foreign direct investment was positive in all years and private sector flows became especially important in the late 1980s.

External debt

How did Indonesia manage to avoid the debt crisis which affected so many developing countries—particularly oil exporters—in the 1980s? Indonesia's debt was already sizeable at the peak of the second oil boom in 1980, at $21 billion, equivalent to 28 per cent of GDP. However, buoyant exports at this time resulted in a low debt-service ratio. Declining oil prices in the first half of the 1980s resulted in rapid debt growth. Both total debt and its proportion of GDP doubled between 1980 and 1986; the debt-service ratio increased faster still. As noted above, the maturity profile of the debt placed further strains on the balance of payments: while net resource flows continued to be large and positive, net transfers became negative.[45] Perhaps the most difficult period of debt management was 1986–87, when a large current account deficit, rapid appreciation of the yen (in which some 40 per cent of Indonesia's debt was denominated) following the G-7 Plaza Accord on realignment of major currencies, and negative net transfers resulted in a sharp escalation of debt, which peaked at 72 per cent of GDP in 1987.

If Indonesia was ever going to have to reschedule or default on its external debt it would have been at this time. Thereafter, debt management became a good deal more comfortable, although the total rose sharply again in 1990, owing largely to a substantial increase in private sector borrowing. An important factor facilitating adjustment over this period was the debt structure. The 'short-term' (less than one year maturity) component of the total official debt remained small throughout the 1980s, never exceeding 20 per cent. Indonesia was therefore less vulnerable to sudden swings in creditors' perceptions of the country's economic prospects. Of significance also was the concessional component of the debt, which remained in the range 25–30 per cent for most of the decade.

The key to Indonesia's successful adjustment over this period has been emphasised in the sections above. During the oil boom period, the government recycled a significant proportion of the windfall revenues into the agricultural sector, mainly food crops. After the mid-1970s, macroeconomic management was reasonably tight and effective. The government's response from the early 1980s was also prompt and far-reaching. Large government projects were cancelled or scaled down in 1983 (and again in 1991), while a regime of fiscal austerity was maintained continuously after 1983. Two large devaluations occurred in 1983 and 1986 and, combined with low inflation and a continuing downward 'float', exchange rates constituted an important spur to competitiveness. Trade policy reforms enabled exporters to compete without significant domestic cost handicaps. Finally, a more liberal foreign investment code, combined with the above reforms, attracted a flood of new investment.

The importance of these reforms is illustrated by trends in the exchange rate and foreign investments. The realignment and liberalisation of the exchange rate in the early years of the New Order regime was swift and effective. By 1970 all vestiges of the old multiple exchange rate system had been removed entirely and a market-approximating rate had been established. Following a further devaluation in August 1971 the rupiah was then pegged to the US dollar for over seven years, ushering in a period of unprecedented exchange rate stability.[46]

This was followed by the surprising and ill-fated 50 per cent devaluation of November 1978: surprising because of the strength of the balance of payments at the time of the devaluation; ill-fated because less than twelve months later the Iran–Iraq dispute led to a second round of very large oil price increases. However, in the post-oil boom period exchange rate management was particularly effective. There were large devaluations in March 1983 and September 1986, and a gradual nominal depreciation for much of the period since then. Both devaluations had little inflationary impact. They 'stuck' because money supply growth was very low, partly as a result of the sharp decline in oil prices. Fiscal policy was also austere over this period, including a freeze on civil service wages for three years from 1986 to 1988.[47]

Foreign investment also began to make a significant contribution to economic recovery and export growth in the second half of the 1980s. Absolute amounts rose rapidly after 1986, and for the first time foreign firms began to engage in efficient, export-oriented projects, mainly in the manufacturing sector but also in services. Over the whole New Order period, as noted earlier, foreign investment flows have fluctuated considerably in response to domestic economic conditions and the regulatory regime. These investments grew rapidly from the late 1960s in response to the new liberal fiscal and regulatory regime, the prospects of lucrative import-substitution projects, and rising oil prices. During the 1970s rapid economic growth made Indonesia an attractive destination for foreign firms, but they were deterred by an ever more restrictive regulatory regime. There was a jump in foreign investment in 1983, a year of low economic growth, as investors sought to take advantage of fiscal incentives which were withdrawn as part of the 1984 tax package; investor interest was subdued in 1984–86. In 1987 and 1988 sweeping changes to the investment regulatory regime were announced, which, combined with the other reform measures and accelerating economic growth, generated strong investor interest, for the first time primarily export-oriented in nature (Pangestu 1991b; Thee 1991).[48]

Structural adjustment and the export boom, 1985–

The 1980s manufacturing export boom generated by the policy changes surprised even the proponents of reform. Indonesia, for half a century the home of dualism, supply-side rigidities and export pessimism, began to

Figure 2.12   Commodity composition of exports, 1966–91 (% of total)

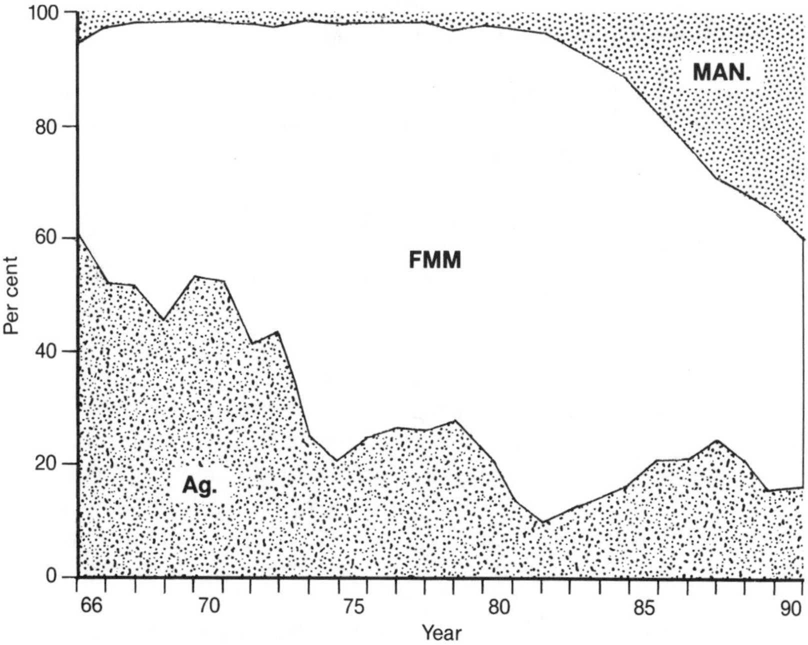

Note: The following definitions are used (SITC codes): agriculture—0, 1, 2 (excl. 27 and 28), 4;
         fuels, minerals, metals—27, 28, 3, 68; manufactures—5, 6 (excl. 68), 7, 8.

Source: BPS, *Eskpor*, various issues.

emulate the record of its outward-looking neighbours in its dramatic export success. This structural change is revealed in the rising share of manufactures in exports, from less than 3 per cent in 1980 and 6 per cent in 1983 to over 40 per cent in 1991 (Figure 2.12). By 1987 the value of the manufactured exports exceeded that of the once dominant agricultural commodities, and by 1991 manufactures (broadly defined) constituted over half of all merchandise exports. This percentage increase exaggerates the real economic significance of the export boom for a number of reasons. Part of the increase is explained by declining commodity prices, especially oil but also traditional cash crops such as rubber, in the 1980s. Enforced export substitution, notably the log export ban, accounted for much of the early increase, when plywood alone generated 40–50 per cent of the manufacturing total. Finally, domestic value added in most manufactured exports is a good deal less than that in the two other, resource-based, sectors. Nevertheless, the importance of the rise in manufactures should not be understated. The real value of these exports increased at an annual average rate of over 30 per cent during the period 1980–91, and there was a steady diversification away from the 'export substitution' exports and towards a wide range of labour-intensive manufactures for which 'genuine' comparative advantage factors were the crucial arbiter of commercial success.

Shifting regional patterns of international commerce

The final major feature of Indonesia's international economic relationship since 1966 has been the pronounced shift away from North America and Europe and towards the Western Pacific region, particularly Japan and the Asian NIEs. This reorientation is primarily the result of three factors. First there is the rapid growth of the East Asian region. The second is the ever stronger economic complementarities between a low-wage but resource-rich Indonesia alongside the resource-poor, high-wage economies of Japan and the NIEs. Third, political–institutional changes have gradually weakened old ties to Europe, in particular, in place of strongly-growing networks based on ASEAN and other regional initiatives. These changes are evident in Indonesia's trade patterns, and even more so in investment, aid and services transactions where proximity effects are particularly powerful.

In the case of trade, Japan and the developing economies of East Asia have been significant throughout the period 1966–90, with a share fluctuating in the range 40–60 per cent, well in excess of the combined US–EC total of 25–45 per cent. The Japan–East Asia group has been particularly important in Indonesia's exports, at the peak of the oil boom absorbing some 70 per cent of the total, while the EC share fell sharply over this period from around 20 per cent in the late 1960s to less than 5 per cent. The US share has fluctuated in the range 15–30 per cent, with no clear trend evident. In the case of imports, the changes are less pronounced, with Japan and developing East Asia each providing 20-30 per cent of the total, and the United States and European Community generally in the 15–20 per cent range.

As noted, the reorientation towards Japan and developing East Asia is more pronounced in the case of investment, aid and services. Japan has been the dominant investor in the sectors under the purview of the Investment Coordinating Board, BKPM (essentially all but oil, gas and finance), providing almost 60 per cent of the realised total for the period 1967–91. Recently, the Asian NIEs have become the major source of investment, as firms have shifted their labour-intensive industries into the newly competitive low-wage countries such as Indonesia (Thee 1991). Japan has also emerged as Indonesia's largest aid donor in the 1980s by a very large margin, eclipsing the once important US and EC donors. There are no reliable and comprehensive estimates of services trade by region, but here also the picture appears to be one of growing Western Pacific dominance. In tourism, for example, the three major sources have been Japan, Australia and Singapore, with other NIEs and ASEAN countries playing an increasingly important role.

Poverty

Equity (*pemerataan*), and social justice more generally, has been one of the central objectives of the New Order regime, as enunciated in the *Trilogi Pembangunan* (Development Trilogy). After the initial stabilisation phase, this objective has been emphasised strongly in each *Repelita* and in numerous presidential and other official statements. But in part because it has become almost a political slogan, 'equity' has rarely been given a great deal of empirical content. For different groups and over different periods of time, the concept—not to mention the measures—has varied. For academics, the statisticians at BPS, and increasingly the government, 'poverty' has been defined and analysed as persons below variously defined poverty lines, while 'distribution' has come to be measured by assorted indices of inequality.

Indonesia's record of poverty alleviation is regarded as an international success story. The country's progress has been praised by the World Bank,[49] confirming its apparent status as a member of the unique East Asian club of countries which have maintained good distributional outcomes in the presence of high growth. Precise quantification of the factors explaining the equity record is not possible. But three seem particularly relevant: favourable initial conditions, targeted government programs, and a labour-intensive growth trajectory in food crops and some manufacturing and service industries.

There appears to have been no significant change in equality for the whole country over the period 1965–90 (Table 2.6).[50] There is an increase—hardly significant—in 1978, at the height of the oil boom, followed by a steady decline and levelling off. For all but the first two years inequality is lower in rural areas, a common pattern owing to the concentration of high income earners and spenders in cities. The urban ratio shows very little change over the whole period, peaking in 1978. In rural areas the ratio displays a continuous decline after 1978, and was very low by 1990. As a corollary, the incidence of poverty has fallen sharply: the *percentage* of the population in poverty in both rural and urban areas in 1990 was well under half that of 1976. The *numbers* in poverty approximately halved, falling at a slower rate owing to population increase. In particular, rapid urbanisation explains why the urban poor were more or less equally numerous over this period, despite the sharp decline in percentage terms. Combining these figures with earlier poverty estimates—for example, as reported in Booth (1992:343)—Indonesia's record on poverty alleviation has been a resounding success.

This conclusion, of sharp declines in poverty rates, appears to be robust, as ever more sophisticated quantitative analyses all pointed in the same direction.[51] However, Indonesia's equity and poverty record continues to be the subject of vigorous domestic debate, and at least five qualifications are variously attached to these favourable conclusions.

First, the results depend crucially on one (increasingly politicised) data set. There is no independent verification of the data (although BPS is a highly professional and accessible statistical organisation); and there is obvious under-reporting in the expenditure data owing to the fluctuating but sizeable discrepancy between average expenditure from the income and expenditure surveys (*Susenas*) and per capita personal consumption expenditure from the national accounts. Secondly, some rural researchers, mainly anthropologists, continue to report case studies of immiseration (see chapter

Table 2.6   Trends in the Gini ratio, 1964–65 to 1990[a]

	Urban	Rural	Total
1964–65	0.34	0.35	0.35
1969–70	0.33	0.34	0.34
1976	0.35	0.31	0.34
1978	0.38	0.34	0.38
1980	0.36	0.31	0.34
1981	0.33	0.29	0.33
1984	0.32	0.28	0.33
1987	0.32	0.26	0.32
1990	0.34	0.25	0.32

Note: [a] Based on household expenditure data.

Sources: Unpublished BPS data for 1978–90, and Booth (1992:335) for 1964–65 to 1976, based on *Susenas* data.

7). Indeed, one of the puzzles of the record since 1970 is that the results of the macro (*Susenas*) and micro data sources diverge. Part of the explanation may lie in the difficulty for rural researchers of obtaining quantitative time series observations. And not all such research points in the same direction.[52] Third, the data refer only to interpersonal inequality, as measured by household expenditure. Other components of distribution are not considered. For example, there are no reliable estimates of the distribution of wealth in Indonesia, yet for non-agricultural sectors wealth would almost certainly be more unequally distributed. Finally, the incidence of poverty is obviously sensitive to the measure used. There is no consensus concerning the appropriate definition in Indonesia and elsewhere—on absolute or relative definitions, on rice-based or monetary measures, on 'objective' or 'subjective' concepts.[53] The most commonly used poverty lines in Indonesia are lower than many other countries (Booth 1993). Nevertheless, debate over the poverty lines does not invalidate the fundamental conclusion of a significant decline, whatever index is used.

The above analysis has focused primarily on monetary measures of poverty and equality. There is of course a range of other 'quality of life' indicators, including environmental quality (see chapter 5), education (chapter 4) and health (chapter 3). An additional variable sometimes used to measure changes in living standards is wage trends. In comparing the periods before and after 1966, Papanek (1980:82–120) points to the irony that the Old Order regime espoused workers' rights and generally fostered trade union development, but almost certainly presided over a period of declining real wages. By contrast, the regime since 1966 has kept workers' associations closely in check, but workers' conditions have generally improved.

A comprehensive survey of trends in real wages across sectors, occupations and regions in Indonesia has yet to be written. But several writers have identified major trends in some segments. The most complete and recent analysis is that of Jones and Manning (1992:379–83), who conclude that:

Unskilled wage rates, particularly in rice and construction, stagnated for much of the 1970s but began to rise—quite sharply in some sectors such as manufacturing and estate agriculture—towards the end of the decade and in the early 1980s. They appear to have levelled off again, and in some cases declined from around the mid 1980s. (p.379)

This conclusion is confirmed by Papanek (1980), who examined trends in the 1970s, and by two studies of agricultural wages—Jayasuriya and Manning (1990), and Naylor (1990). A feature of the latter study, analogous to the discussion above on poverty lines, is that conclusions regarding real wage trends depend to some extent on the selection of the deflator.

Regional development

The *daerah* (region) has always been a major preoccupation of Indonesian governments. Indonesia is an extraordinarily diverse country in its ecology, demography, economy and culture, and the colonial impact exacerbated these differences. Post-Independence governments have been grappling with the daunting challenges of establishing central authority throughout the archipelago and, more recently, of ensuring reasonably uniform development patterns for cosmopolitan urban dwellers and traditional, isolated shifting cultivators alike. It is perhaps no exaggeration to state that Indonesia has only become a national *economic* entity since 1970. Although political control had been firmly established in most regions by 1960 (Mackie 1980), regional economic integration was poor. Smuggling and the evasion of Jakarta's controls were rampant. Regional price variations were large, even for basic goods such as rice. Labour mobility was constrained by the poor state of physical infrastructure. Information flows were weak.[54]

Table 2.7 provides an overview of regional performance and structure since the 1970s. The data highlight both the country's regional diversity and the reasonably uniform pattern of development.[55] The prosperous provinces are found mostly in the central–west regions of the country (columns 1–3): Jakarta, with a per capita income always at least double the national average; the booming tourist economy of Bali; and the resource-rich economies of East and Central Kalimantan, Aceh and South Sumatra. The exclusion of mining from the three oil and gas provinces (Aceh, Riau and East Kalimantan) has some effect, although East Kalimantan is still the highest-income province outside Jakarta. The first and last of these provinces are comparatively lightly settled and have strong non-oil components in their economies. At the other extreme, most parts of Sulawesi, eastern Indonesia and Java consistently record incomes which are well below the national average. The Java provinces pose the least serious problems now—contrary to the gloomy scenarios which abounded in the 1960s—because they are not far below the national average and because their social and physical infrastructure is superior. The Sulawesi provinces have fallen steadily behind the rest of the country and lack a dynamic leading sector which can arrest this trend. Most serious of all are the three Nusa Tenggara provinces, where limited natural resources, distance and neglect have together resulted in serious problems of poverty and underdevelopment.

The poverty estimates broadly confirm these regional income variations (column 14). Poverty incidence in Java and Sumatra is generally low—less than 10 per cent in all of rural Sumatra, except for the special case of Lampung, to which Java's 'overpopulation' problem has apparently been transferred, and less than 20 per cent for all of rural Java. Poverty is rather high in East Kalimantan according to some estimates, perhaps reflecting the enclave nature of development in that province. It is above 20 per cent in all of Sulawesi, although somewhat lower in traditionally egalitarian North Sulawesi. The figures are high for the rest of eastern Indonesia—especially for Irian Jaya—although the Bali figure appears anomalous.

Economic growth has been spread reasonably evenly over Indonesia's provinces (column 3). Some of the mineral economies have grown slowly or experienced negative growth. But this has generally been so because of the size of the mining sector and slow growth in oil and gas production. In some cases—Aceh and Irian Jaya—the non-mining component has grown quickly.

Table 2.7 also highlights large interprovincial variations in economic structure. With the exception of Sulawesi and eastern Indonesia, agriculture now contributes less than 40 per cent of gross regional product in most instances. For the industrialising provinces of West and East Java that share is below 30 per cent; in both these provinces manufacturing accounts for over 20 per cent of output, and these shares are higher than those of any other province except Jakarta. On Java–Bali, too, the percentage decline in agricultural employment has been faster than in most other regions (columns 4–6). The comparatively high manufacturing shares for Kalimantan are somewhat misleading. Apart from the special case of East Kalimantan, much of the non-agricultural activity has been associated with the timber process-ing boom. There is virtually no footloose industry in the outer islands, as would be expected given their distance from major markets, supply-side deficiencies (especially skilled labour and support infrastructure), and the absence of any wage cost advantage. The Nusa Tenggara provinces remain the most agrarian of all, reflecting their poverty and lack of dynamism.

Regional export patterns illustrate further this interprovincial economic diversity (columns 9 and 10). At the height of the oil boom, in 1976, Riau and East Kalimantan generated 61 per cent of Indonesia's exports. Jakarta, with its better port facilities, mineral-rich South Sumatra and Irian Jaya, and the traditionally strong North Sumatra cash-crop economy produced another 27 per cent. No other province earned more than 2 per cent. The nine provinces of Sulawesi and eastern Indonesia contributed just 1.9 per cent. The most important change since the mid-1980s has been the re-emer-gence of Java as a significant source of exports, reflecting the spectacular growth of manufacturing exports and falling energy prices. In 1991, Riau, East Kalimantan and Aceh (where massive LNG investments came on stream) still produced 41 per cent of the total, but Java's share more than doubled from 15 per cent to 37 per cent. Jakarta's export share has always been inflated to the extent that exporters trans-ship through Tanjung Priok owing to its superior facilities and shipping networks (Azis 1989), but West Java's manufactured export boom also lifted this figure. A sharp rise is also evident in East Java.

Table 2.7 Indicators of regional structure and development

	GRP, 1990 Rp billion	GRP per capita, 1990 Rp'000	GRP per capita, real growth 1973–90 (%)	Manufacturing as % of GRP, 1990[a]	Agriculture as % of employment, 1990	Decline in agricultural employment share, 1971–90 (%)	Net exports as % of GRP,[c] 1989	Govt as % of GRP,[d] 1989	% of exports[e] 1976	% of exports[e] 1991	% of foreign investment,[f] 1967–91	Buses per 1000 persons,[g] 1990	Local revenue as % of GRP,[h] 1989–90	% of population in poverty, 1987
	(1)	(2)	(3)	(4)	(5)	(6)	(7)	(8)	(9)	(10)	(11)	(12)	(13)	(14)
Sumatra														
Aceh	8290	2448	12.5	11.1	66	16.5	66.8	5.0	0.2	10.7	2.3	0.6	0.72	12.50
excl. oil	2897	737	6.4											na
North Sumatra	10 833	1063	5.3	17.7	61	19.9	10.3	8.2	7.1	6.1	7.5	3.5	0.99	7.0
West Sumatra	3297	829	7.1	12.1	60	16.2	19.9	10.5	0.7	0.7	0.1	2.9	0.98	7.9
Riau	13 231	4493	-3.2		58	16.4	48.8	1.9	43.2	17.3	5.6	1.3	0.88	
excl. oil	2672	907	3.4	7.7										
Jambi	1414	709	3.3	17.0	70	11.4	20.0	9.8	0.8	0.9	0.1	2.2	0.94	6.5
South Sumatra	8268	1304	3.4	20.3	65	12.4	9.5	8.0	4.4	2.4	2.7	3.4	0.58	15.0
Bengkulu	795	684	7.2	3.0	71	18.9	-13.8	20.7	n	n	0.1	1.6	1.06	8.8
Lampung	3217	540	2.5	11.1	70	14.7	19.8	15.9	1.5	1.2	1.3	0.7	0.94	34.4
Java–Bali														
Jakarta	22 855	2481	5.9	26.4	1	72.2	71.2	6.6	11.2	26.1	24.1	20.5	2.29	na
West Java	31 358	917	5.5	23.2	37	39.8	18.8	9.7	1.8	0.9	29.3	1.4	0.86	23.0
Central Java	21 689	763	6.0	16.7	48	24.8	9.6	12.9	0.7	2.5	5.1	0.6	0.99	41.0
Yogyakarta	1901	654	4.2	10.3	46	19.8	-28.1	18.1	n	n	0.1	0.8	1.35	25.2
East Java	29 161	769	5.8	21.0	50	27.0	2.7	10.2	1.6	7.9	7.0	3.1	0.89	38.8
Bali	3018	1090	8.0	5.3	44	36.3	-1.1	12.1	0.1	0.6	3.9	0.9	1.80	40.0
Kalimantan														
West Kalimantan	2743	860	6.0	18.7	73	17.9	-5.6	9.9	1.2	1.9	0.3	0.7	0.73	27.6
Central Kalimantan	1376	998	5.8	10.2	62	25.4	-8.0	9.9	1.0	0.4	0.6	0.1	0.38	17.7
South Kalimantan	2326	887	4.5	17.2	54	24.2	32.0	9.0	1.1	2.1	0.5	0.4	0.83	15.4
East Kalimantan	10 770	5821	4.8		43	34.3	55.4	2.9	17.6	12.5	3.3	3.4	0.76	8.2
excl. oil	4410	2383	4.7	20.2										

110

Sulawesi

North Sulawesi	1507	593	4.8	5.7	56	18.3	-6.6	18.2	0.2	0.2	0.7	3.5	1.56	27.7
Central Sulawesi	982	581	4.7	5.8	68	14.5	9.2	14.1	0.2	0.1	0.1	1.0	0.89	29.8
South Sulawesi	4241	610	5.2	6.9	58	16.3	3.9	13.9	0.3	1.6	2.8	1.4	1.20	42.0
Southeast Sulawesi	821	616	5.0	2.3	68	20.2	4.7	20.5	0.4	0.2	0.1	0.5	0.66	55.8
Eastern Indonesia														
West Nusa Tenggara	1290	383	4.6	2.9	54	21.4	-5.8	15.3	n	n	0.1	0.4	1.10	47.1
East Nusa Tenggara	737	361	4.7	2.3	75	11.7	-16.5	18.9	0.1	n	0.1	1.1	1.53	53.0
East Timor	269	364	4.7b	1.7	74	14.4	-14.4	23.9	n	n	0	1.6	0.94	45.3
Maluku	1463	809	5.1	14.0	62	22.3	33.3	11.4	0.6	1.3	0.2	0.6	0.85	25.0
Irian Jaya	2047	1247	0.7		72	na	52.5	7.0	4.0	2.5	2.2	2.5	0.55	41.0
excl. mining	1217	742	6.3	4.3										
Indonesia	196 919	1098	3.6						100	100	100	2.6	1.11	
excl. mining	171 471	956	5.0	18.4	50	24.7								

Notes:
a Non-oil manufacturing as a percentage of non-oil GRP.
b 1983-90 only.
c Net exports of goods and services as a percentage of GRP.
d Government current expenditure as a percentage of GRP.
e Percentage of merchandise exports.
f Approved foreign investment, excluding oil and financial services.
g Includes minibuses (colts).
h Revenues raised by provincial and second-tier (kabupaten, municipalities) governments as a percentage of non-oil GRP.
n—Negligible (less than 1 per cent).
na—Not available.

Sources: BPS, *Pendapatan Regional Propinsi-Propinsi di Indonesia*, various issues; BPS, *Statistik Indonesia*, various issues; BPS, *Buletin Ringkas*, various issues; and other unpublished BPS statistics; Republic of Indonesia, *Nota Keuangan*, various issues; and Bank Indonesia, *Statistik Ekonomi-Keuangan Indonesia*, various issues.

Additional data in Table 2.7 highlight various other aspects of Indonesia's regional economic diversity. The large export surplus generated by the resource-rich provinces, and Jakarta owing to its port facilities, is illustrated in column 7, as is the 'deficit' in several poor regions. As a corollary, the government's economic presence is relatively much larger in the latter cases, where, in contrast to the western region, a dynamic private sector has yet to emerge (column 8). Local public sector revenue bases tend to be more strongly developed in regions such as Jakarta and Bali, where hotels and other activities generate funds for provincial governments (column 13). Western Indonesia has attracted much more foreign investment (excluding oil, gas and financial services) than the east (column 11); from 1967 to 1991, Jakarta and West Java alone absorbed over half the total, while Java–Bali received some 70 per cent. Finally, as one indicator of the west's superior physical infrastructure, column 12 shows there are relatively more buses in these provinces, especially as the higher Jakarta figure would include some trans-Java services.

This pattern of reasonably even regional development is corroborated by several studies which have calculated 'Williamson' indices of regional inequality. Esmara (1975), the first researcher to analyse the data systematically, estimated the index for Indonesia in 1972 to be about 0.95 (in the range 0–1). However, if the oil and gas sectors were excluded it fell to about 0.52, while the exclusion of three high-income provinces resulted in a halving, to 0.26. This placed Indonesia among the 'low regional inequality' countries for which data were available from the 1950s and 1960s. As the data base improved, empirical research extended in three directions: calculating trends in regional inequality, especially during and after the oil boom; examining the social dimensions of regional inequality, and comparing social and economic performance across provinces; and probing the sectoral dimensions of these outcomes.

Most studies agree that there was no significant increase in inequality during the decade from the mid-1970s.[56] The record of social progress across regions is equally impressive (Hill 1992b). Inequalities in education and health indicators are remarkably and consistently low, reflecting strong government attention to these areas and historical strengths in some poor regions. The inequality of poverty incidence, being less amenable to direct policy intervention, remains a good deal higher. However, the association between economic and social performance across provinces and over time is surprisingly weak. There are cases where economic and social indicators are both good (Jakarta being the prime example) or both poor (Lampung, the Nusa Tenggara provinces). However, there are many instances where the correlation is not strong—either good social indicators and lagging economies (for example, North Sulawesi and West Sumatra), or relatively high-income economies accompanied by indifferent social indicators (the West Java experience).[57]

What explains Indonesia's good record on regional development? Part of the answer is in the third strand of empirical regional research, in which the inequality indices have been calculated at a sectoral level. Booth (1986) undertook such an exercise, finding as would be expected a much lower index for agriculture. Thus the strong performance of agriculture—in particular food crops—has contributed indirectly to the good regional outcomes. More generally, for all its faults, the rigid, highly-centralised system of government administration has, in a suboptimal fashion, ensured reasonable uniformity in delivering government services. Programs in education, health and physical infrastructure on a national scale have been implemented. The government's fiscal equalisation measures, and its recycling of the windfall revenues from a few mining enclaves through routine and development budget expenditures, have ensured that all provinces have shared in the oil (and foreign aid) booms to some extent.[58]

The regional policy agenda has altered significantly during the course of the New Order. In the early years, provincial administrative capacity was in many cases so weak and the bottlenecks to regional economic integration so large that a strong centralised system was inevitable and probably necessary. By the 1990s this argument carried much less force: Indonesia is a national economic entity as never before, and regional administrative capacity is now much stronger. Moreover, unlike the case in the oil boom period, the government's fiscal position is tight.

One of the most pressing regional policy issues is regional finance. While the current system is still fiscally quite generous to the regions, provincial and subprovincial governments are placed in a straitjacket, having no authority to alter their fiscal mix, and no incentive to enhance efficiency of tax collections.[59] The challenge here is for the government to walk a tightrope between the contending claims of national unity and regional autonomy. A return to some form of the old ADO (*Alokasi Devisa Otomatis*, literally 'Automatic Foreign Exchange Allocation') system, which linked revenue to export earnings, would have serious inter-regional equity implications, and exacerbate the inequalities between east and west (or, more particularly, the mineral regions versus the rest of the nation). The solution will presumably lie in a package of measures comprising some revenue sharing, a limited devolution of revenue and expenditure responsibilities, and a stronger link between tax effort and revenue, while at the same time ensuring some nationally-devised social, economic and infrastructure goals are achieved.

There is also a strong case for greater emphasis on regional comparative advantage. The notion of self-sufficiency, especially in agriculture, is deeply entrenched in Indonesia, and it embraces not only national thinking but also aspirations at the *daerah*. Related to this is a Jakarta-based emphasis on nationally implemented programs, which does not always incorporate sufficient recognition of regional variations in ecology, agronomic conditions and institutions.

Conclusion

It is easy to point to flaws in Indonesia's economic policy record since 1965: the Pertamina fiasco, and seemingly chronic problems of corruption and nepotism; an adherence to rigid notions of self-sufficiency, in rice and even in some heavy industry; ineffective fiscal and environmental management of some of its natural resources, particularly the forests; the sharp rise in external indebtedness in the 1980s, particularly that arising from exchange rate fluctuations; and the slow pace of development of more sophisticated fiscal and monetary policy instruments.

But to concentrate on these issues is to ignore the fundamental fact that in conventional economic terms the Indonesian record over the past quarter-century has by and large been a resounding success. For example, of the 78 developing countries for which the World Bank, in its *World Development Report 1992*, was able to estimate real per capita growth of gross national product for 1965–90, only six countries recorded a higher figure than Indonesia's 4.5 per cent. Four of these are special cases in one way or another (Botswana, Lesotho, Oman and Paraguay). There are thus just two countries where the performance has been unambiguously superior; namely, the East Asian 'stars' of China (5.8 per cent) and South Korea (7.1 per cent). (Taiwan, not included in the World Bank's data, would also be in this category; Malaysia and Thailand are only a little behind.) Other indicators of economic and social progress from the control of inflation to the spread of education are also in the high range among developing countries.

Yet Indonesia is still a very poor country, and remains in the World Bank's 'low income' group. It will take many decades before the great majority of the population will be assured of a decent standard of living. High growth is the only sure route to a broad-based improvement in living standards. Other chapters in this book examine the social, political and environmental constraints to rapid development. Here it will be appropriate to conclude by drawing attention briefly to some of the key economic challenges.

First, some time in the reasonably near future—probably the first decade of the next century—Indonesia will cease to be a significant net energy exporter. It will continue to export coal and gas, but its oil export surplus will be exhausted. The experience of the 1980s provides some optimism for the belief that this transition can be handled effectively. The energy sector has shrunk rapidly in its contribution to export earnings and government revenues. Improved efficiency, tight economic management, and rapid export diversification enabled Indonesia to adjust quickly to the sharp fall in oil prices during the 1980s, and there is no reason why these trends cannot continue. Most of Indonesia's high-growth East Asian neighbours are of course resource-poor economies.

The second major challenge will be to entrench the culture of international orientation and export efficiency. The last five years have demonstrated that Indonesia has much to gain from rapid export-oriented growth of industry and services. It is only really during this period that Indonesia has begun to follow the East Asian path of labour-intensive, outward-looking growth. The country's basic demographic equation is such that, even with declining fertility, the labour force will continue to grow quickly for many years. Moreover, underemployment of labour, reflected in low and uncertain earnings, is still a major problem.

To sustain such a course of development, two requirements are of fundamental importance. The first is a conducive and liberal economic environment—low inflation, a predictable and transparent policy environment, an open economy (to goods, people and technologies), an effectively managed exchange rate, and an external debt whose servicing is financially sustainable. The second requirement is a human resource development strategy which ensures that the nation's work force is efficient, competitive and flexible. It will be many years before Indonesia's 'labour surplus' characteristics disappear and, as in the Asian NIEs during the 1980s, tightening labour markets result in sharply rising real earnings. In such conditions, rising skills and productivity are the key to improved real wages.

The third major challenge concerns equity, in all its dimensions. Rapid economic growth is an essentially disruptive process, and is sustainable in the long run only if there is a general community perception that the benefits are being fairly distributed. It is easy to point to spectacular instances of private wealth accumulation and ostentatious consumption in the Indonesia of the early 1990s. These sit uncomfortably alongside mass living standards, which are still very low. Most careful and rigorous analyses of social indicators in fact conclude that the benefits of rapid growth have been distributed reasonably fairly. However, Indonesia's equity picture is complicated by ethnic and regional dimensions. It is no exaggeration to state that the country's social integrity and cohesion will be threatened as long as there are sharp divisions between the *pribumi* and non-*pribumi* groups, and between the richer and poorer provinces. Thus, the particular challenge is to ameliorate these divisions while ensuring a continuation of overall rapid growth.

Notes

1 These differences were illuminated further in the case of Indonesia and Nigeria by Pinto (1987).

2 A note on Indonesian national accounts statistics is appropriate here. Although their quality has improved enormously since the mid-1960s, one continuing limitation is that the Central Bureau of Statistics (BPS) has never published a consistent, long-term (twenty years or more) series. The data employed in this section are based on spliced series, calculated backwards from the last estimate.

3 These relate to the 'prices' selected and the assumptions regarding physical reserves of natural resources; to the inclusion of forestry (which is, in principle at least, a renewable natural resource); and to the measurement of the extent of soil erosion on Java.

4 Timmer's paper triggered a spirited debate with a team of researchers: see Collier et al. (1974) and Timmer (1974) for a reply.

5 'When the New Order government came in it abolished the extensive price controls of the old regime because it wanted to rely on the price mechanism for the allocation of resources. Such is still the ruling policy, but old habits die hard. One of the economic doctrines of the New Order is that it is against "free fight competition", because the latter is too much identified with "capitalism", which even the New Order cannot embrace' (Sadli et al. 1988:364).

6 One illustration is the meaning of the word *menguasai* in Article 33 of the Constitution. Most economists interpret this as state 'control' over—in the sense of regulation of—major sectors of the economy, but some invoke the phrase as justification for state ownership. As Soesastro et al. (1988:33) point out, '[F]orty years after the adoption of the constitution different interpretations of Article 33 continue to exist'. See also Rice (1983:60ff.).

7 For good overviews of the state enterprises sector over the New Order period, see Habir (1990) and Pangestu and Habir (1989). McCawley (1971) provides a particularly detailed case study of a state enterprise in the 1960s—the state electricity company (PLN)—and cites other studies over this period.

8 For comprehensive analyses of the Pertamina episode, see Glassburner (1976), McCawley (1978), and several of the *BIES* Surveys over this period.

9 These studies include: Dick (1987), whose study of inter-island shipping included a section on the state shipping company, Pelni; Funkhouser and MacAvoy (1979), who undertook a comparison of 150 firms based on data from the early 1970s; Gillis (1982), who compared mining companies in Bolivia and Indonesia; Hill (1982), who examined state and private weaving companies; McCawley (1971,1978), who studied the state electricity company (PLN) and the state oil company (Pertamina) respectively; McKendrick (1989, 1992), who included a detailed study of the state aircraft company IPTN; and Soesastro et al. (1988), who assessed state enterprise performance as part of a broader study of fiscal policy.

10 Pitt (1991) provides a detailed account of developments over this period.

11 Pangestu and Boediono (1986:9–22), writing at the time when these devices were most commonly employed, identify some 22 separate instruments.

12 Though long the subject of informed, albeit discreet, comment in the Indonesian community and press, the first systematic exposé of the complex networks of political and business patronage over this period, extending to the president's family, was provided in a three-part *Asian Wall Street Journal* (*AWSJ*) series (24–26 November 1986). A more recent example is the report in the *Far Eastern Economic Review*, 30 April 1992. Muhaimin (1991), Robison (1986) and Yoshihara (1988) adopt a more scholarly and detached approach, though their material is generally less up-to-date.

13 The quote is from the former Coordinating Economics Minister, Professor Ali Wardhana, one of the driving forces behind the reforms, as cited in Soesastro (1989:84). Soesastro's article is the best general analysis of the reform process of the late 1980s. As an illustration of the effectiveness of the packages, according to unpublished World Bank estimates, between mid-1986 and mid-1991 the percentage of imports (by value) covered by import licensing fell by over half, from 43 per cent to 13 per cent; as a share of production values the decline was smaller but still very significant (41 per cent to 22 per cent). Barrichello and Flatters (1991) provide an illuminating account of this trade reform process, written from a political economy perspective.

14 As Mackie (1970:87–8) points out, corruption '. . . was becoming almost endemic under the Sukarno regime, when his disastrously inflationary budgets eroded civil service salaries to the point where people simply could not live on them and where financial accountability virtually collapsed because of administrative deterioration'.

15 Important studies of rice over the first decade of the New Order include Afiff et al. (1980), Birowo and Hansen (1981), Fox (1991), Mears and Moeljono (1981), and Timmer (1975). Booth (1988b) and Pearson et al. (1991) examine developments over a longer period, while Tabor (1992) focuses primarily on the 1980s. Timmer (1991) provides an excellent account of rice price policy over the period 1966–89.

16 Mears and Moeljono (1981:49) reflected authoritative thinking at the time, stating that '. . . it seems that the goal of self-sufficiency in rice by 1985 (or any reasonable time thereafter) will be very hard to achieve'.

17 The fertiliser subsidy rose from Rp32 billion in 1977 to Rp756 billion in 1988 before tapering off; the pesticide subsidy peaked at Rp175 billion in 1987 but has since been abolished. Moreover, as Tabor (1992) points out, the official fertiliser subsidy estimate understates the real economic subsidy owing to the concessional energy prices paid by fertiliser producers.

18 Two comprehensive volumes on *palawija* crops are Falcon et al. (1984) and Timmer (1987), which examine cassava and maize respectively.

19 I am indebted to Colin Barlow for supplying the data in this paragraph. See also Barlow (1991), Barlow and Jayasuriya (1984), Barlow and Muharminto (1982), Barlow and Tomich (1991) and Tomich (1991).

20 Ruzicka (1979), for example, concluded that public forestry revenues were between one-quarter and one-half of what could reasonably be expected from an efficient fiscal regime. The situation has apparently improved little since

then. Press reports in 1991 of research conducted by Rizal Ramli and colleagues indicated that the returns through the 1980s have been similarly low.

21 See Lindsay (1989) and references cited therein for a discussion of these issues. In June 1992 the ban was revoked, replaced by very high export taxes and leaving untouched the fundamental fiscal issues.

22 Morrisson and Thorbecke (1990) have recently provided a fresh perspective on these subsidies, by calculating the domestic agricultural surplus for Indonesia using a 1980 Social Accounting Matrix. Not surprisingly, though unusually for developing countries, they found that the surplus was negative, meaning that 'the nonagricultural sector provided a net excess of goods and factors to agriculture . . . of Rp74 billion' (p.1086). Significantly, they estimated the net positive public transfer from the government to agriculture to be some Rp175 billion.

23 Informed estimates (for example, Pearson et al. 1991, ch.7) suggest domestic demand for rice will grow by 2–2.5 per cent annually through the 1990s.

24 Anderson (1992, Table 8.3), citing data from Webb et al. (1990), reports Indonesia's agricultural producer subsidy equivalent over the period 1979–87 to be 11 per cent, higher than a number of developing countries (the figure for Thailand was –4 per cent), but well below that of Korea (61 per cent), the United States (30 per cent), and all other OECD countries except Australia. The same source (Table 8.4) cites estimates prepared by Barker, Herdt and Rose (1985) showing Indonesia's 'producer-to-border' price of rice to be very close to unity (0.98) over the period 1976–80, close to the median figure for Asian rice producers.

25 This section draws substantially on Hill (1990a, 1992a). See also Poot et al. (1990) for a detailed quantitative study of industrialisation up to the mid-1980s.

26 The rise of Minister Habibie, and his impact on industrial policy-making, is one of the most fascinating but poorly documented features of the New Order policy environment. McKendrick (1989, chs 2 and 3) contains the most detailed account. No accurate financial records have ever been published. The minister appears to be able to operate a personal fiefdom, immune to financial constraints and accountable only and directly to the president.

27 Whether Java has a 'disproportionate' share of industry depends on the treatment of oil and gas processing. In 1985, when its population was 60 per cent of the total, Java's manufacturing shares were 74 per cent and 52 per cent for non-oil and the total respectively, while the employment share was 78 per cent. There is, of course, nothing inherently desirable in the island's population and industry shares being similar.

28 However, contrary to the experience of many army-backed regimes, defence expenditure has been modest throughout the New Order period, rarely exceeding 2 per cent of GDP and less relatively than most Asian developing countries. Even allowing for substantial 'off-budget' activities, Indonesian defence expenditures would still be low.

29 Howard Dick has published extensively on various aspects of transportation in Indonesia. See Dick (1981, pts I and II) on urban public transport, Dick

(1987) on inter-island shipping, and Dick and Forbes (1992) for an overview of the period since the late 1960s.

30 For an overview of the industry's development, see Booth (1990). Jayasuriya and Nehen (1989) provided a more detailed analysis of tourism in Bali.

31 In addition to *BIES* Surveys, there are a number of detailed studies of monetary policy and performance over this period. Arndt (1971) studied the banking system during the peak inflation period and immediately thereafter. Grenville (1981) provides a detailed study up to the late 1970s, while Arndt (1979) focuses particularly on monetary policy instruments during the 1970s, and Nasution (1983) examines the development of financial institutions. Woo and Nasution (1989) provide a lengthy study of macroeconomic policy through to the early 1980s, in the context of external debt management. Cole and Slade (1992) trace financial developments over the whole period, while Binhadi and Meek (1992) provide a more technical discussion of monetary policy developments in the 1980s. Pangestu (1991c) assesses the 1980s record in an ASEAN context. Odano et al. (1988) survey financial development through to the mid-1980s, while Boediono and Kaneko (1988) investigate the factors affecting inflation over the same period. McLeod (1992) assesses the 1992 Banking Law.

32 Interest rates were increased, the banks' reserve requirements were raised to 30 per cent and ceilings were placed on commercial credit expansion. The latter in particular became one of the principal instruments for controlling money supply growth over the next few years.

33 For example, in September 1984, fears of a devaluation prompted massive capital flight and drained domestic liquidity to such an extent that overnight rates on the inter-bank market reached 90 per cent. Similar problems arose in the first half of 1987 and in early 1991, in both instances culminating in decisive though heavy-handed intervention by the Finance Minister, who ordered state enterprises to withdraw very large deposits from state banks and to purchase Bank Indonesia certificates.

34 Its major features were that all domestic banks, provided they were sound, were now free to open new offices, and new private banks were permitted; foreign banks were allowed to operate outside Jakarta subject to certain conditions; non-bank state enterprises were permitted to deposit up to 50 per cent of their funds with private (national) banks; reserve requirements for commercial banks were cut from 15 per cent to 2 per cent of their liabilities; a 15 per cent tax on bank deposits was introduced, primarily to stimulate the stock market; and monetary policy instruments and the swap on foreign borrowings were fine-tuned.

35 In September 1990 it was announced that Bank Duta, a large nominally private bank which possessed impeccable political connections, had incurred foreign exchange losses of $420 million. A rescue operation was quickly mounted and several business-connected foundations (*yayasan*) contributed large sums to the bank.

36 The general literature on fiscal policy in Indonesia is now substantial. Developments through to the late 1970s are analysed in detail by Booth and McCawley (1981a) and Glassburner (1979). Asher and Booth (1992) focus

primarily on the 1980s, as does Nasution (1989). Boediono (1990) provides a policy-maker's perspective on fiscal policy throughout the New Order period. Asher (1989) provides an overview in an ASEAN context. Informed studies of taxation policy include Gillis (1985, 1989), Kelly (1989, 1993), Lerche (1980) and Uppal (1986). There is also a substantial regional finance literature referred to later in this chapter.

37   These figures, of course, vastly understate the government's economic role in Indonesia: the state has a powerful regulatory presence in the economy, and it operates a large public enterprise sector. Moreover, a large though unknown amount of government activity occurs off-budget. The most famous example of this was the state oil company, Pertamina, in the early 1970s, but it is also the case with defence expenditure and some of the 'strategic industries'. Especially during the oil boom and before the financial reforms, the large government banking sector was the conduit for much of this off-budget expenditure.

38   From 1969 to 1981 real GDP rose some 2.4 times, while real NODR rose by a factor of 3.3. While the 'tax buoyancy' (the elasticity of increased NODR with respect to increased GDP) exceeded unity, it should have been much higher given the extremely low initial base.

39   Important compositional shifts within the NODR group have also occurred, most significantly the declining importance of trade taxes (down from 37 per cent of NODR in 1969 to less than 10 per cent after 1985), and a sharp jump in value-added (formerly sales) tax, the latter's share rising from 16 per cent in 1984 to 29 per cent in 1985 following the tax reforms. Major studies of the tax reforms and their aftermath include Gillis (1985, 1989) and Kelly (1989, 1993).

40   The government was, however, able to insulate the community—and particularly civil servants—from some of the austerity by focusing most of the cuts in the development budget, which fell from 54 per cent of the total in 1983 to 35 per cent in 1987, the latter identical to the share in 1969.

41   There is no comprehensive study of Indonesia's trade patterns and policies since the mid-1960s. Rosendale (1981), based on a doctoral dissertation completed in the late 1970s, provides a particularly detailed analysis of the balance of payments through to 1977. Warr (1992) focuses on the oil sector and adjustment issues, primarily in the 1980s, while Woo and Nasution (1989) examine debt, trade and macroeconomic adjustment issues through to the mid-1980s.

42   The decline would have been sharper still but for the commencement in 1977 of LNG exports, the value of which by 1990 equalled that of oil and oil products.

43   The data in Figure 2.10 are presented on a calendar year basis, whereas those in Table 2.5 refer to fiscal years. This explains the minor discrepancies between the two series.

44   Owing to its very open international capital account, estimates of private sector external indebtedness are necessarily very crude. However, for most of the period after 1966, public sector debt probably accounted for well over 80 per cent of the total. Rising private sector external debt did however become an

issue of heated public debate from around 1990, especially as some of it appeared to have been undertaken by politically powerful individuals with the possibility of state guarantees.

45 'Net resource flows' refer to capital disbursements (that is, drawings on loan commitments) less principal repayments. These are approximately equivalent to lines 4 + 6 less line 5 in Table 2.5, allowing for some differences in classifications and calendar–fiscal year presentations. 'Net transfers' are defined as net resource flows less interest payment (or disbursements less debt service payments). Interest payments are grouped within the somewhat mis-leading 'services trade' (line 2 of Table 2.5).

46 In fact, there was probably too much 'stability'. The massive inflows of funds from oil and aid for the first time in Indonesia's independent history trans-formed the balance of payments. If the rupiah had been allowed to float freely, it almost certainly would have appreciated, as most writers of this period emphasise. For extended commentaries, see several *BIES* Surveys over this period, in addition to McCawley (1980) and Rosendale (1976, 1981).

47 While the overall impact of exchange rate movements is clear enough, the precise magnitude of these changes is not. The issue here is whether the devaluations should be measured by means of a 'competitiveness' index—a 'real effective' rate, adjusting nominal exchange rate movements for relative inflation rates in Indonesia and its major trading partners—or by means of a relative price index of tradeables to non-tradeables. For discussion of these issues, see Arndt and Sundrum (1984) and Warr (1984, 1986, 1992).

48 Two additional observations are relevant concerning trends in foreign invest-ment. First, domestic approvals have exceeded those of foreign firms in all but four of the 23 years in the period 1968–91, and in every year after 1975. Moreover, the gap between the two has widened in the late 1980s as the domestic conglomerates became a real commercial force. The second obser-vation is that, despite Indonesia's openness to foreign investment since 1967, and especially in the period 1967–74 and after 1986, in *relative* terms Indo-nesia has not been a large recipient of foreign investment. Among the devel-oping market economies of East Asia, for example, only Korea and the Philippines have received less (again in relative terms), the former owing to a deliberately restrictive strategy, the latter the result of political uncertainty and slow growth. See the appendix charts in Hill (1990b).

49 See, for example, the *World Development Report 1990*, which reported that Indonesia experienced one of the sharpest reductions in poverty incidence among countries surveyed (see pp.41–3).

50 The Gini ratio is a measure of inequality (dispersion) which ranges from 0 (perfect equality) to 1 (perfect inequality). A ratio of 0.3 is regarded as 'low' by international standards, while that in excess of 0.5 is 'high'.

51 See, for example, Ravallion and Huppi (1991), Huppi and Ravallion (1991) and World Bank (1990b). Booth (1992, 1993) provides a synthesis and analysis of secondary data sources from the mid-1960s until 1990.

52 A notable exception is the resurvey by Singarimbun (1990) of the original village in Yogyakarta used in the Penny–Singarimbun research. He found that, over the period 1972–89, average income (in rice equivalent terms) had risen

by about 37 per cent (still well below the national rate of increase, however), and the percentage of the 'very poor' had declined by some 32 per cent.

53 On the latter, see Firdhausy and Tisdell (1992) for an application to Indonesia.

54 Several of the economic surveys of provinces in the outer islands published in the *Bulletin of Indonesian Economic Studies* in the late 1960s and early 1970s capture the flavour of this economic isolation. References to these surveys can be found in the relevant chapters of Hill (1989).

55 The 1971 data are included for illustrative purposes only, and should be regarded as very approximate. Greater confidence can be attached to the regional estimates only after 1974, and it was not until the late 1980s that the discrepancy between the sum of the regional totals and the national figure was removed.

56 See Azis (1990), Uppal and Budiono (1986), Kameo and Reitveld (1987), and Hill (1992b). Much depends on the treatment of the resource-rich provinces here: including them, the income (production) based index of inequality may be as high as 0.9. However, estimates which exclude mining altogether (and even a smaller number of exceptional provinces), or are based on personal expenditure data, are much lower, in the range 0.18–0.25. It is therefore accurate to portray Indonesia as a 'moderately low' regional inequality case.

57 Islam and Khan (1986) have pointed to another dimension of this pattern, by correlating poverty incidence and inequality (within each province) on the basis of 1976 data. Somewhat surprisingly, there was generally a linear correspondence between the two measures, with all but four provinces being in the low (poverty)–low (inequality), medium–medium or high–high categories.

58 This is not to argue that the regional expenditures have incorporated an explicit needs-based criterion—detailed case studies show they have not (Azis 1990; Ravallion 1988)—but at least these expenditures rose extremely rapidly after the mid-1970s, and their impact filtered through to the poorer provinces.

59 These issues are discussed extensively in Azis (1989), Booth (1986, 1988b), and Devas and Associates (1989). Earlier analyses, which focus on essentially similar issues, include van Leeuwen (1975) and Shaw (1980).

3

Demographic perspectives

Terence H. Hull and Gavin W. Jones

FERTILITY DECLINE IN THE NEW ORDER PERIOD:
THE EVOLUTION OF POPULATION POLICY 1965–90

Terence H. Hull

Underpinning the changes of President Soeharto's New Order government were a battery of social welfare policies aimed at providing universal, basic health and education services, designed to build the nation's 'human capital' and fulfil the socialist aspirations of equity and welfare contained in the 1945 Constitution. Among the welfare policies, the family planning program was the most innovative and problematic. It aimed at the combined goals of reducing population growth rates, reducing fertility (and particularly the number of high-risk pregnancies) and providing women with control over their reproduction.

These policies were extended and strengthened over the following three decades, and by 1990 had become integral elements of the New Order regime's identity. Achievements in providing health, education and reproductive rights to the population have become major parts of the regime's claims of success and legitimacy. This chapter examines the development, impact and implications of the fertility control policy to evaluate these claims.

Evaluating New Order fertility control policies

The fourth population census of independent Indonesia, conducted in October 1990, was a crucial test of the fertility control and health policies and programs of the New Order government of President Soeharto. Most importantly, it offered a definitive measure of the trend in population growth rate, the most straightforward quantitative objective of the policy. The preliminary results of the count, announced on the last day of 1990 by

President Soeharto, showed a decline in growth rates and confirmed the falling fertility rates observed through the 1970s and 1980s (Ananta and Arifin 1990).

Nationwide, 39 689 427 households were enumerated, and a total population of 179 194 223 listed, not including the homeless, seafaring and isolated peoples, who added an additional 127 418 (or 0.07 per cent) to the total. This implies an average household size of 4.5 persons, compared to 4.9 in the 1980 census. The total enumerated population was lower than had been projected prior to the census, with the result that many observers labelled the exercise as 'unsurprising'. The intercensal growth rate implied by this result was 1.96 per cent, down from the 2.33 per cent recorded for the 1971–80 intercensal period (Table 3.1). The 1990 results indicate a substantial decline in intercensal population growth rates nationally, and for many large provinces. Readers should be cautious in comparing these figures with either previous enumerations or other publications on the Indonesian census since the geographic coverage of the census has changed over the years (for instance, the inclusion of East Timor since 1975). Also, the definitions of 'resident or permanent population' and the formula used to calculate the growth rate vary from one publication to another. Nonetheless, such details have a minor impact on the pattern which emerges: generally declining growth rates nationally and in the most populous provinces, and increasing growth rates in Riau, the provinces of Kalimantan, Southeast Sulawesi and Irian Jaya.

Despite great speculation about the success or failure of family planning and transmigration programs, and growing questions about issues of spontaneous migration and the impact of census rules on place of enumeration, the preliminary results provided important clues about the components of demographic change. It is safe to assume that fertility is falling in most of Indonesia, and that substantial inmigration has been affecting the numbers of people in Riau, Bengkulu, Kalimantan, Southeast Sulawesi, and Irian Jaya, where growth of population still exceeds 3 per cent per annum, a rate that doubles the population every 23 years.

If it is clear that fertility is falling, the question arises as to how this could have happened in a nation where the founding president had been heard to proclaim that the nation could feed double the population, and that birth control would promote immorality. In the mid-1960s Indonesia had high fertility by world standards and there was little sign that this situation would change quickly. The government rejected the concept of population control, and it was technically illegal to import or distribute contraceptives. Indonesian women on average bore more than six children over the course of their reproductive lives. Twenty years later the scene had changed dramatically. The nation's total fertility rate (TFR) had fallen from six to an average of 3.3 children per woman in 1985. Over roughly the same

Table 3.1   Indonesia's population, 1971–90

Island/Province	Total population ('000)			Growth rate (%)	
	1971	1980	1990	1971/80	1980/90
Indonesia	119 232	147 383	179 322	2.33	1.96
Sumatra	20 812	27 980	36 555	3.25	2.67
Aceh	2009	2611	3416	2.88	2.69
North Sumatra	6623	8361	10 256	2.56	2.04
West Sumatra	2793	3407	3999	2.18	1.60
Riau	1642	2169	3306	3.06	4.21
Jambi	1006	1446	2016	3.99	3.32
South Sumatra	3444	4630	6377	3.25	3.20
Bengkulu	519	768	1179	4.31	4.29
Lampung	2777	4625	6006	5.61	2.61
Java	76 102	91 282	107 574	2.00	1.64
DKI Jakarta	4576	6503	8254	3.86	2.38
West Java	21 633	27 454	35 381	2.62	2.54
Central Java	21 877	25 373	28 522	1.63	1.17
Yogyakarta	2490	2751	2913	1.10	0.57
East Java	25 527	29 189	32 504	1.47	1.08
Kalimantan	5152	6721	9110	2.92	3.04
West Kalimantan	2020	2486	3239	2.28	2.65
Central Kalimantan	700	954	1396	3.40	3.81
South Kalimantan	1699	2065	2598	2.14	2.30
East Kalimantan	734	1218	1877	5.57	4.32
Sulawesi	8535	10 378	12 522	2.15	1.88
North Sulawesi	1718	2115	2479	2.28	1.59
Central Sulawesi	914	1290	1711	3.79	2.82
South Sulawesi	5189	6062	6982	1.71	1.41
Southeast Sulawesi	714	942	1350	3.05	3.60
Nusa Tenggara	6618	8469	10 165	2.71	1.83
Bali	2120	2470	2778	1.68	1.18
West Nusa Tenggara	2202	2725	3370	2.34	2.12
East Nusa Tenggara	2295	2737	3269	1.94	1.78
East Timor	na	555	748	na	2.98
Maluku	1089	1411	1856	2.85	2.74
Irian Jaya	923	1174	1641	2.64	3.35

Sources: BPS (1981a), (1981b), (1991a).

period the TFR for China fell from 5.8 to 2.6 (Poston and Gu 1987:531) and in what has been described as a 'Reproductive Revolution' Thailand's TFR declined from 6.6 to around 3.4. In these and other countries of Asia, such major changes in family-building behaviour coincided with numerous radical social, political and economic changes. The period was one of high and strengthening rates of economic growth, the attainment of universal primary education, and rapid improvement in health conditions, and especially increased infant and child survival. Most significant in demographic terms, the period was also one of unprecedented state assistance and intervention in the area of contraceptive services.

This chapter proposes an approach to understanding fertility decline by focusing on the evolution of institutional change in key areas of social and economic life which have resulted from, and have implications for, emerging world views, ideologies, policies and government structures of the New Order. The approach is useful in answering the questions: why did fertility decline precipitously in the 1970s and 1980s?; and why did fertility not decline much before 1970? The answers to these questions go to the heart of the changes wrought by the New Order. It is not merely a matter of 'the right policies firmly implemented' but rather a story of transformations in attitudes about family, community, and governmental responsibility, among both the elite and the mass of Indonesians. In this story, 'historical accident' and dynamic individuals have played roles in promoting change which were in many ways much more important than rigorous policy argumentation or voluminous data analysis.

Sources of fertility control policy

Prior to the 1950s fertility was high throughout Indonesia. By 1960 this situation had changed, and fertility in Java was below that of the other islands by a difference of about one child on average. Throughout the archipelago, fertility was traditionally restrained by prolonged breastfeeding, abstinence practices and abortion, and by marital disruption. After about 1930 the age at first marriage began to rise in Java, and the other islands soon followed this pattern. This had a slight dampening effect on fertility, but neither it, nor traditional practices, could be said to have put fertility 'within the calculus of choice' for parents (Hull 1983).

In the early 1950s a number of developing countries perceived the problems that high rates of population growth posed for development planning, and that high rates of fertility posed for maternal and child health. India and China established family planning programs with the goals of reducing fertility and growth rates, and gradually other countries followed suit. The effort was not without difficulty, and it was soon apparent that while some people were interested in controlling fertility, many others had either strong preferences for large families or strong distaste for contraceptive methods. Culture, religion and education shaped community responses to these issues, and leaders caught in early phases of nation building were often sensitive to any issues which might provoke divisions in their constituencies.

This was exemplified in Indonesia, where President Sukarno, with characteristic bravado, rejected community requests to institute a program of population control, declaring that Indonesia could support a population

126

double or treble the 97 million counted in the 1961 census. In more reflective moments, he admitted that the major problem of family planning was the probability that it would give offence to Muslims, and would fail to have an impact on the growth rates of a largely illiterate population (Soeharto 1984:204; Aidid 1987). One of Indonesia's most prominent economists also noted that a 'population control policy has an undertone of pessimism concerning the potential of the nation', which was a notion at odds with the nationalism of the time (Sadli 1963:22). This linking of population issues with a sense of despair was by no means limited to Indonesian leaders. A well-known Dutch commentator of the period wrote:

> Children are born far in excess of the means of subsistence and so they have to die by the millions. Even so far as there is birth control it is chiefly from a primitive individual feeling of factual impotence to extort from nature even a minimum existence for one self and for a child at the same time. (Boeke 1953:77)

Despite Sukarno's attitude and the laws inherited from the Dutch which restricted the import or sale of contraceptives, women's groups and doctors had quietly promoted birth control from the early 1950s, and in 1957 the Indonesian Planned Parenthood Association (IPPA or PKBI) was formed, and later associated with the International Planned Parenthood Federation (IPPF). The head of the new organisation was Sukarno's personal physician, Dr R. Soeharto, and the vice-head was Dr Hirustiati Subandrio, whose husband was the foreign minister and former ambassador to Britain. While posted in London the Subandrios had discussed issues of birth control with the IPPF and had helped to arrange for Indonesian medical specialists to travel abroad for training in maternal and child health, and family planning.

Over the tumultuous years from 1959 to 1965, the political balance shifted dramatically; democracy waxed and waned, authoritarian rule and violent reactions and revolts unsettled the people. Finally, a bloody attempted coup in September 1965 was resolved by the destruction of the communist party, and the murder of huge numbers of accused communist party members or sympathisers. Among those jailed was Subandrio, and his wife was forced out of many positions, including her role in the family planning movement.

This period of government transition marks the most crucial nexus in the politics of family planning in Indonesia. The history of the period written today reduces events to a simple series: President Soeharto signed the World Leaders' Declaration on Population (1967), he then formed the Family Planning Institute (LKBN) in 1968, and eventually in 1970 raised the status of the LKBN to that of a coordinating board (BKKBN) with a chairman directly responsible to the president (Soeharto 1970). His central role in the formation and unswerving support for the implementation of the family planning program was recognised in his receipt of the UN Population Award in 1989.

While there is no doubt that he has made an outstanding contribution to the program over the years, a more detailed investigation of the events surrounding the initiation of a government program is important for the insight it gives into Indonesian politics of the period, and the lesson it suggests to other nations concerning the importance of unorthodox initiatives in promoting sensitive issues like family planning.

Two actors in this period are particularly important: President Soeharto and governor of Jakarta, Ali Sadikin. Jakarta was a volatile centre of political activity, and the high rate of inflation, rapid urban growth and appalling housing and transport services were exacerbating people's frustrations at the Old Order. 'By late 1965', wrote Abeyasekere (1987:210), 'there was little to be proud of in Jakarta. Like the President's grandiose and ill-founded dreams, the skeletons of his unfinished monuments towered above slums and rotting refuse.' In April 1966 Sukarno appointed as governor Ali Sadikin, a marine whose previous responsibilities had been in the area of logistics and formulation of battle strategy. The city offered a substantial challenge, and he approached it with the zeal of a military campaigner, assembling his 'troops', setting his goals, and making frequent tours of the 'battlefield'. Unlike Soeharto, whose problems involved political jockeying and grand strategy, Sadikin was daily confronted with the practical problems of administering a city's needs. Population issues, though potentially relevant to both, had a very different meaning in the two settings.

In recalling the period, a former US ambassador was disappointed that his first meeting with Soeharto (in May 1966) was related to the latter's request for a $500 million grant for the problematic population resettlement (transmigration) program as a means of controlling Java's population growth rate. In turning down the request, the ambassador commented that movement of the increment of Java's population would require a daily departure of a ship far larger than the *Queen Mary*, and suggested that birth control might be a more efficient option (M. Green, personal communication, 1988). At that meeting, and over the next year, Soeharto indicated no interest in birth control, primarily because of concern over the potential rousing of religious sensitivities about the issue. In addition to the occasional suggestions of the US ambassador, there were numerous other people in Jakarta pressing for birth control, including US-trained planning officials (technocrats), Ford Foundation advisers, IPPA leaders, medical doctors, and visiting World Bank missions. The president was cautious in his consideration of these calls.

In contrast, the hard-driving governor of Jakarta was quickly learning the lessons of population in his attempts to renovate a city with poor housing, schooling, transport and basic services. The rapidly growing population meant that no matter how fast the new administration worked, the problem always seemed to grow at a faster rate. By mid-1966 Sadikin was regularly making speeches linking urban problems to rapid population growth, and towards the end of the year he issued a challenge to the IPPA to work up a project which would help to ease the rate of natural increase in the capital. The 'Jakarta Pilot Project' was inaugurated on 22 April 1967, and represented the first government-funded family planning program in Indonesia (IPPA 1969). The governor frequently assisted these activities by giving strong speeches of support at the opening of clinics and seminars, and by promoting the integration of family planning activities in the city's health department. Between 1966 and 1968 most official family planning initiatives were taken under the aegis of the Jakarta government, and later, as programs moved to other areas, the example of Jakarta was cited as proof that a strong, responsive leadership could overcome the problems of religious opposition and community intransigence.

Later Sadikin was to encounter serious opposition to his dynamic attempts to promote economic growth in Jakarta, and after his retirement in 1977 he suffered a major falling out with the regime, which has made him a virtual 'non-person' in the official histories of the period. In considering the politics of the initiation of a family planning program, it is important to see the crucial role he played in breaking through the imagined barriers which inhibited other policy-makers from taking up the cause of population control. His impassioned calls for reduced population growth rates stemming from the pragmatic demands of his position carried weight not only with other leaders, but also with the citizenry; and his conservative Muslim background gave him credibility when he declared that family planning would not be promoted in a way which could undermine the morals of the community. More dynamic than Soeharto, more respected than Sukarno, Sadikin played a unique role in the early days of family planning, and it is likely that the program would have encountered a very different reception had he not been the person to give it the imprimatur of government sponsorship.

Bureaucratic politics of family planning, 1968–88

Once the political decisions were made to initiate a family planning program, a whole new set of political issues came to the fore as the program established its place in the bureaucracy. Most obvious were the questions of budgets and staffing, but there were also important issues related to the exercise of authority, including the determination of who was to control clinics and outreach services, how research priorities were to be set, who would set the terms of evaluation, and who had the right to solicit and manage foreign assistance.[1]

In a purely formal sense the answers to these questions in Indonesia were contained in the description of the BKKBN as the agency charged with coordinating the activities of line departments. However, from the outset, the BKKBN was much more than a coordinating agency. In the early years foreign donors invested heavily in the board to build a strong bureaucracy capable of handling the logistic, training and promotional tasks they believed were beyond the capability of established departments (BKKBN 1973). As the BKKBN took on more implementational responsibilities, the 'coordination' became more directive, and assumed increasing characteristics of 'control', with a growing staff becoming involved in setting up and running research and action projects. The family planning fieldworkers were hired directly by the BKKBN rather than the Department of Health, and as time passed they pressed for permanency within the government structure. The growing establishment justified an expansion of BKKBN presence in provincial and regency-level government, and after a decade of growth, the board had become a quasi-departmental institution.

Understandably, the rapid growth of the BKKBN and the organisation's ready access to foreign assistance were causes of jealousy among the more established government departments, in particular the Department of Health and the Central Bureau of Statistics. From ministerial suites to district offices and clinics, complaints were voiced about the tendency of the BKKBN to push in to territory far beyond the needs of 'coordination'. On the other hand, the BKKBN was addressing a problem of great urgency—a population explosion—and justified its activism as a necessary expedient to circumvent complex and moribund bureaucracies. Foreign review teams regularly reinforced this argument, though over time it became clear that long-term development would require the program to be well-integrated into line departments, and strongly rooted in the community. By the end of the 1970s, the BKKBN made greater efforts to involve departments and community groups in the implementation of foreign-financed projects, and assisted in training their staff.

This has not eliminated the bases of conflict. A great deal of rivalry still exists between the BKKBN and the Central Bureau of Statistics concerning the methods and purposes of measuring fertility levels and contraceptive use. In the early 1980s the BKKBN presumed to be the central authority on all forms of population policy, but the establishment of a State Ministry of Population and Environment under the leadership of a feisty minister soon forced the BKKBN back to its more narrow mandate of coordinating efforts of fertility control. In some areas the BKKBN has consistently maintained superiority over implementing agencies. Nominally, research institutes have autonomy in the implementation of demographic research, but with 'coordinating' control over population funds, the BKKBN has been able to determine priorities for research, distribute funds to approved researchers, direct funds away from unfriendly critics or topics, and occasionally prevent the release of research results which present the program in an 'inaccurate' way or threaten to create sensitive issues.

The BKKBN achieved legitimation through the development of a large establishment, and the vertical and horizontal integration of its activities in the government structure. Over two decades it has become a ubiquitous feature of Indonesian society, with the blue BKKBN symbol adorning posters, houses and vehicles across the archipelago, and family planning slogans appear daily on television, radio, in traditional forms of theatre, among scouts, women's groups and school classes, and features regularly in presidential speeches. Often these messages are from the departments of Information, Education, Health or Women's Affairs, but it is a sign of the entrenchment of the BKKBN that, whatever the source, people identify them merely as *kah-bay* (KB, the acronym for Family Planning) and see them as a seamless fabric. But, far from seamless, the program has been often torn and stretched in the tussle of bureaucratic politics, though the BKKBN has been brilliant in quickly repairing damage and maintaining the illusion of perfect balance.

Expanding contraceptive availability

The BKKBN faced some formidable obstacles in 1970, not the least of which was the problem of setting priorities for work in a nation of thousands of islands, hundreds of mother tongues, and severely depressed economic conditions. It seemed natural that the program would have to concentrate first in Java and Bali, since these were the islands of most notable 'over-population'. They were also the areas most geographically and culturally accessible to the national capital of Jakarta. The first five-year development plan (*Repelita I*) specified that the urban areas of Java would be the initial focus of attention, and that rural areas would be covered gradually as clinics could be built and staff trained (Hugo et al. 1987:305). The rate of spread of services would be determined by the success of delivery at each stage. In the end an alternative view prevailed. The report of a 1969 World Bank mission to Indonesia, issued in early 1970, argued that family planning deserved higher priority than it had been given in the *Repelita I*, and this should be reflected in the establishment of a comprehensive presence of the program at all levels of government down to the village, and a crash program of training of paramedical and non-medical personnel to carry services to village areas where there were no clinics (Singarimbun 1970:103).

This approach saw the 'problem' as being essentially the high rate of growth in rural areas, and thus the program should serve these first using whatever resources were already at hand, relying heavily on mobile teams, special drives to get acceptors, and promotion of contraceptive methods which could be distributed by paramedical personnel. Because it was likely to be expensive, this approach would have to rely on heavy inputs of foreign assistance to provide contraceptives, vehicles and finance for buildings and equipment (Khoo 1982).

By the mid-1970s the basic strategy of the program had been set. Services were not to be limited to clinic settings, but would attempt to bring birth control directly to village homes. Total involvement of the bureaucracy, rather than narrow reliance on health personnel, would be fostered to ensure the smooth running of the program. Finally, the high priority given to population control by the national leadership prevented complacency at lower levels from inhibiting the work (Hull and Mantra 1981:268ff; McNicoll and Singarimbun 1983).

The experience of the first few years of program activities showed that the basic strategy produced different results in the various provinces and subprovincial units of government, depending on the availability of resources and the commitment of government officials. In East Java and Bali there were relatively large numbers of clinics per unit of population, and highly-committed officials, and the numbers of acceptors of services rose rapidly. In West Java clinic coverage was least effective, and there were numerous problems of leadership and local resistance to the program, which were reflected in lower rates of acceptance. Overall, though, the program developed an elaborate and effective set of procedures for delivering supplies to remote areas, and encouraging couples to try modern forms of contraception. In 1974 the program was expanded to ten of the most promising provinces in the other islands, and in 1977 the remainder of the country was officially brought into the program (see, for instance, Freedman, Khoo and Supraptilah 1981).

Five institutional characteristics were most important in expanding contraceptive services:

1   A total involvement of relevant vertical governmental structures, rather than a reliance on a single unit like the Department of Health. The key agency in family planning has coordinating functions, but also has sufficient funds and control over funds to ensure commitment by other units. At lower levels of government, leaders are judged according to the family planning performance of units under their control. The early and continuing commitment of President Soeharto has thus been systematically transferred to lower levels of leadership (Hull 1987; Saparin 1977).

2   The incorporation of the prime and quasi-governmental women's association in the program. The PKK or Family Welfare Movement is found in virtually every community, and enlisting the cooperation of this organisation in motivation and implementation efforts has been the main rationale behind government claims that the family planning program is based on 'community participation'. The fact that PKK membership

is not a genuinely voluntary association but a hierarchical organisation headed by the wife of the Minister of Home Affairs, with each descending level headed by the wife of the corresponding senior government official, makes it in fact another arm of the government bureaucracy, and belies the notion of true community participation. However, the recruitment of the PKK has lent increased legitimacy to the program both in Indonesia and abroad, and in locations where the PKK is active has led to higher levels of participation in the program than would have otherwise been achieved (Hull 1983, 1986).

3   Target orientation of planning and implementation. From the earliest days of the program there has been a tendency to set goals in terms of new acceptors, and these have been calculated and promoted down to the lowest levels of administration. Moreover, the process of target-setting has been taught and generalised to the extent that local government and clinic personnel often set their own targets to further encourage their staff and broaden coverage of the administrative procedures. This elaboration of targets has been at times accompanied by systems of incentives or disincentives. At the central level, very long-term goals (such as halving fertility between 1970 and 1990) are analysed in terms of implications for targets and services, and these form the basis for arguing for funds and materials for the program (Moebramsjah et al. 1982; Moebramsjah 1983; Sumbung 1989).

4   Frequent use of special drives concentrating resources and attention for short periods of time to achieve specific program objectives. In the early 1970s these drives were efforts to identify, motivate and serve potential clients in remote rural areas. Later drives were used to promote specific methods of contraception and motivate the clinic staff. In the 1980s 'safaris' were organised to mobilise local bureaucracies to support the program and to overcome pockets of inertia. These drives were generally preceded by weeks of preparation, accompanied by much ceremony and hospitality for high-status visitors, and recorded for later television reports by staff of the BKKBN and Department of Information (Hull, Hull and Singarimbun 1977; Hull 1987; Warwick 1986).

5   Promotion of a limited degree of local autonomy in planning and implementation within a frame of strong central guidance. Top BKKBN leaders point to the cultural and economic diversity of Indonesia and say that each region will need its own approach to family planning. At the same time, memories of regional revolts and fear of losing power mean that the central government is quick to discourage signs of real differences in policy-making, or setting priorities. Thus the local freedom to develop programs is bounded by the need to adhere to centrally-established patterns and budgets. It is thus common to find similar

programs in different provinces, each with a name drawn from the local language, and each displayed as 'innovative'. (Hull 1987)

Crucial to the development of the family planning program as an institution was its evolution within the framework of the Soeharto government (Parsons 1984). The New Order has achieved bureaucratic control both horizontally and vertically in ways which eluded both the Dutch and Sukarno, and it has done so during a time of substantial economic growth related to the oil boom and large receipts of foreign economic assistance.

Social and political changes

The political and social changes wrought in the transition from the Old to the New Order were far-reaching (Hull 1986). It might have been anticipated that they would affect family-building patterns, especially since the new regime called for reduction in the rate of population growth through family planning (Cantor 1982). At the time though, few observers thought that the government had much hope of significantly reducing fertility (see Freedman 1986). It was thought that large-family traditions were too entrenched, religions too conservative, and the government too disorganised to be successful at promoting small families and distributing contraceptives. However, by concentrating attention on the prospects of a family planning program in itself, they were ignoring some of the priority issues identified by the military and technocrats which were to have great impact on the development of family planning: reform of government administration; provision of mass schooling; opening the country to foreign aid, trade and investment; and expansion of the health services to rural areas. A review of Indonesian fertility trends during the twenty years after 1965 will show how far the experience of the New Order negated the pessimistic predictions concerning family planning in the early 1970s.

Fertility decline, 1960–90

Table 3.2 shows the basic pattern of fertility decline recorded from 1960 to 1987. For Indonesia as a whole the decline was over 40 per cent, and the pace of decline has apparently increased over time. The word 'apparently' should be stressed because the fertility measures available for provinces of Indonesia are subject to a wide range of errors related to sampling and problems of data collection and data processing. On the positive side, we should note that all the various fertility estimation techniques yield consistent results, and all indicate major fertility declines (see also Hull 1980; Hull and Hull 1984).

The recorded reduction in fertility nationwide is reflected in major declines in most regions, with similar percentage reductions showing up in

Demographic perspectives

Table 3.2   Total fertility rate estimates by province, late 1960s to late 1980s

Region	1967–70	1986–89
Indonesia	5.61	3.33
Sumatra	6.54	4.14
DI Aceh	6.27	4.37
North Sumatra	7.20	4.29
West Sumatra	6.18	3.89
Riau	5.94	4.09
Jambi	6.39	3.76
South Sumatra	6.33	4.22
Bengkulu	6.72	3.97
Lampung	6.36	4.05
Java	5.26	2.93
DKI Jakarta	5.18	2.33
West Java	5.94	3.47
Central Java	5.33	3.05
DI Yogyakarta	4.76	2.08
East Java	4.72	2.46
Nusa Tenggara	na	4.18
Bali	5.96	2.28
West Nusa Tenggara	6.66	4.98
East Nusa Tenggara	5.96	4.61
East Timor	na	5.73
Kalimantan	5.89	3.80
West Kalimantan	6.27	4.44
Central Kalimantan	6.83	4.03
South Kalimantan	5.43	3.24
East Kalimantan	5.41	3.28
Sulawesi	6.02	3.56
North Sulawesi	6.79	2.69
Central Sulawesi	6.53	3.85
South Sulawesi	5.71	3.54
Southeast Sulawesi	6.45	4.91
Maluku	6.89	4.59
Irian Jaya	(7.20)	4.70

Notes: na–Not available.
The figures for some provinces should be treated with caution due to problems of sample size and data quality. The rates for Irian Jaya seem particularly suspect. Irian Jaya figures for 1967–70 refer only to the urban area.

Sources: 1967–70 and 1986–89 rates calculated using the Own Children Method were reported in Mamas (1983:31–5) and Sukarndi (1992:33). Primary data sources are the population censuses of 1971 and 1990.

Sumatra, Java and Sulawesi, and quite low rates of reduction evident only in the poor and remote eastern islands of East and West Nusa Tenggara and Timor, and the relatively backward area of Southeast Sulawesi. West Kalimantan, with less than 30 per cent fertility decline, and Aceh and South Sumatra also have relatively slow performances, but have nonetheless registered fertility consistent with a 4–4.5 child family on average. By contrast the experience of North Sulawesi is remarkable, with a decline of

135

TFR from 6.8 to 2.7 children in a decade and a half, giving it one of the highest rates of fertility decline nationwide next to Bali. Since the province began receiving assistance from the national program only in 1974, the revolutionary social change which has taken place in this province makes it an ideal laboratory for demographic analysis (see Jones 1977; Jones 1989a). Similarly, Bali (Hull 1978; Streatfield 1986), Yogyakarta (Hull and Hull 1977) and East Java (Hull, Hull and Singarimbun 1977) have attained substantial reductions in fertility which have been related to their unique political and cultural settings.

Changing institution of marriage

The vast majority of births in Indonesia occurs within marital unions which have been ceremonially recognised by the community and/or legally recognised by the state. These forms of recognition do not necessarily occur at the same time, nor do they necessarily precede conception, and the relative timing of these events has been changing over recent years (Hull and Hull 1987). Despite such changes in timing of ceremonies, the age of marriage remains strongly related to the timing of the onset of sexual relations and childbearing. Table 3.3 shows how the singulate mean age at marriage has been rising in all provinces of Indonesia throughout the 1960s, 1970s and 1980s, to the point that nearly all provinces today have average ages over twenty, and in ten regions the average is over twenty-two.

The age at marriage has risen because the nature of the institution of marriage is evolving from traditional patterns where parents arranged matches for their young adolescent daughters to more modern forms of couples finding and courting their own partners. This new pattern meant that old customs of delaying cohabitation until the sexual maturity of the couple were no longer relevant, and these gave way to increasing proportions of young people beginning sexual relations before marriage. Schooling, literature and films appear to be the basic causes of the change in these patterns, though the consequences of early cases of change were traumatic for families and communities and must have played a strong role in making parents accept the demands of their younger children. These conflicts were not isolated, but related to a general rift developing between parents and their children over issues of autonomy, respect, and adherence to convention in an age and society craving modernity.

If the demands of children to choose their own friends and marriage partners created strains in their families of birth, it was a factor producing greater strength in their new families of reproduction. The couple tended to be closer in age, and with falling mortality rates this meant that joint survival as a couple increased. The romantic basis of the marriage, and the relatively mature ages at which they married, meant that one of the major traditional

Demographic perspectives

Table 3.3   Trends in the age at marriage of women in Indonesia, 1964–85

	Year of survey or census			
Region	**1964**	**1971**	**1980**	**1985**
Indonesia	na	19.3	20.0	21.1
Sumatra	19.9	19.9	20.6	21.7
Aceh	na	19.5	20.8	21.6
North Sumatra	na	20.8	21.7	22.6
West Sumatra	na	20.3	20.8	22.0
Riau	na	20.0	20.7	21.9
Jambi	na	18.4	19.2	20.8
South Sumatra	na	20.0	20.7	22.0
Bengkulu	na	19.7	19.6	20.8
Lampung	na	18.0	18.9	20.4
Java	18.1	18.7	19.5	20.7
Jakarta	20.0	20.2	21.7	23.4
West Java	17.4	17.8	18.5	19.8
Central Java	18.2	19.0	19.8	21.0
Yogyakarta	20.7	21.8	22.5	23.4
East Java	18.1	18.7	19.4	20.3
Nusa Tenggara	na	20.8	21.6	22.1
Bali	21.7	20.8	21.2	22.3
West Nusa Tenggara	21.0	19.2	20.3	20.2
East Nusa Tenggara	na	22.4	23.1	23.6
East Timor	na	na	na	22.4
Kalimantan	18.6	20.0	20.2	21.2
West Kalimantan	na	20.9	20.9	21.5
Central Kalimantan	na	19.7	19.8	20.5
South Kalimantan	na	19.2	19.6	20.9
East Kalimantan	na	19.6	20.5	21.2
Sulawesi	19.5	20.7	21.6	22.3
North Sulawesi	na	21.6	21.7	21.3
Central Sulawesi	na	20.6	20.7	21.8
South Sulawesi	na	20.5	21.8	22.9
Southeast Sulawesi	na	19.9	20.6	20.8
Maluku	na	22.0	21.6	22.2
Irian Jaya	na	na	19.8	18.8

Notes: na—Not available.
The figures are Singulate Mean Ages at First Marriage (SMAM) based on reports of current marital status.

Sources: Calculations by author based on the results of the 1964 *Sample Survey*, the 1971 and 1980 Population Censuses and the 1985 Intercensal Survey.

causes of early divorce (incompatibility) declined in importance, and more durable unions were formed.

In sum, the changing age at marriage and greater durability of union means that there has been a reduction of women at the youngest age groups being married, offset by an increase in the proportion in a state of current marriage at older ages (Hull and Mantra 1981:274–5). The impact of the former trend on fertility has been offset somewhat by the growing practice of premarital sex, about which we have little information. The proportion of women currently in a marital union during the childbearing period has fallen in Java from 78 per cent to 72 per cent.[2] This occurred because the proportion of currently single women rose dramatically from 9 per cent to 22 per cent, while the proportions of currently widowed and divorced fell from 6 per cent to 2 per cent and divorced fell from 7 per cent to 5 per cent, respectively. Java's experience is mirrored, in a less dramatic form, in the statistics for Indonesia as a whole, where the single proportion rose from 16 per cent to 26 per cent, while the widowed fell from 6 per cent to 2 per cent and the divorced fell from 5 to 3 per cent. The major point of these changes is that the transformation of the marriage systems of Indonesia was well underway before the New Order government came to power, but they reached the peak of their impact at precisely the time the government coincidentally began to promote fertility control through family planning.

Changes in desired family size

The impact of various other social changes on desired family sizes can be seen in Table 3.4. Where most Indonesians in the 1960s indicated a desire for at least a four-child family, the ideal by 1987 had fallen to around three, and for many people, to two. The desired family sizes also seem to reflect the regional patterns of fertility decline, and the relative length of operation of the family planning program. Though not shown in this table, it bears noting that, as in previous surveys, there is an inverse relation of desired family size and age, with younger women saying that even smaller numbers of children would be ideal.

The causes for this change in ideal family sizes may be summarised in terms of three major social changes. First, parents desire more for their children, including schooling, better food and clothing, and good employment opportunities in the modern sector. This makes having children more expensive. Second, as children spend increasing amounts of time in school, and as that experience often estranges them from family economic activities, the opportunity costs of having many children rises. They earn less for the parents. Third, the official government policies for family planning stress the benefits of a two-child family, and while slogans probably do not change minds directly, they do create images of what a 'good' family is, and these legitimate desires for fewer children than might have been common in earlier times.

Table 3.4   Reports of ideal family sizes, 1973–91

	Distribution of 'ideal' responses, Indonesia							
	Mean	1	2	3	4	5	6	+ Non-numeric responses
	(% of responses)							
1987	3.2	1.9	31.1	23.1	18.9	6.6	5.4	13.0
1991	3.1	1.7	34.3	21.5	16.7	5.0	5.1	15.6

	Mean ideal family size			
Region	1973	1976	1987	1991
Jakarta	—	4.4	3.0	2.8
West Java	4.1	4.1	3.0	3.0
Central Java	4.4	4.5	3.0	2.9
Yogyakarta	—	4.2	2.7	2.5
East Java	4.1	4.1	2.8	2.5
Bali	3.7	3.7	2.5	2.4
Java–Bali	—	4.2	2.9	2.8
Outer islands I[b]	4.9[a]		3.9	3.7
Outer islands II			3.7	3.6
Indonesia			3.2	3.1

Notes: [a] Average of responses for Sumatra and Sulawesi samples.
[b] Outer islands I and II refer to the year in which groups of outer island provinces were included in the National Family Planning Program. The groupings are:
I—Aceh, North Sumatra, West Sumatra, South Sumatra, Lampung, Nusa Tenggara Barat, West Kalimantan, South Kalimantan, North Sulawesi, and South Sulawesi (from 1974).
II—All remaining areas (from 1978–79). The sampling design of the 1987 Contraceptive Prevalence Survey omitted seven of these provinces, accounting for two-thirds of the outer island II population, and hence estimates for this region are heavily biased.
Question wording:
1973: 'What do you consider the best number of children for a woman to have?'(1973 Fertility Mortality Survey).
1976: 'If you could choose exactly the number of children to have in your whole life, how many children would that be?' (1976 Indonesian Fertility Survey q. 599).
1987 and 1991: 'If you could go back to the time you did not have any children and could choose exactly the number of children to have in your whole life, how many would that be?' (Biro Pusat Statistik, q. 611).
Sources: 1973—Demographic Institute (1974:34); 1976—BPS (1978:240–1); 1987—BPS (1989:64); 1991—BPS (1992:76, 78).

Declining mortality

Undoubtedly, another factor in changing desired family size has been the rapid reduction of infant and child mortality rates. Between the late 1960s and the late 1980s estimated infant mortality was nearly halved, as a result of improved nutrition, environment, and health services (see Table 3.5). Mortality has fallen dramatically both in urban and rural areas, with the rate of decline greatest in provinces which had already had lower mortality rates in the earlier period, such as Jakarta and Yogyakarta. Mortality remains high in the eastern part of the country, with an estimated 145 infants out of 1000 not living to their first birthday in West Nusa Tenggara, and East Nusa Tenggara, Irian Jaya, Maluku and East Timor having infant death rates above the national average. Child mortality—deaths to children between the ages of one and four—has also declined. The level was estimated at around eight to ten in 1985, representing a 60 per cent decline since 1965.

The relationship between falling mortality and falling fertility works in both directions: a perceived greater chance of infant and child survival mitigates against the 'insurance effect', whereby parents have more children than actually desired in order to ensure that an ideal number of surviving children is reached. On the other hand, contraceptive use and lower fertility contribute to declining infant mortality by lengthening the interval between births and eliminating some births among very young and older women, where risks of infant death are higher. Thus, later marriage, more stable marriages and overt desires to restrict family size in a context of increased child survival are all trends which, while rooted in the early independence period, reached fullness during the New Order. These provide the setting in which people might be expected to make decisions to restrict fertility.

Changes in contraceptive use

Table 3.6 shows the growth in the apparent use of various contraceptive methods, and the steady growth in the variety of methods available to women. In comparison with neighbours such as China, Vietnam and the Philippines, Indonesian couples enjoy ready access to a wide variety of methods. Use of the pill and IUD grew over the 1970s and 1980s, but recently women have increasingly turned to injectables and the contraceptive implant Norplant, as well as sterilisation, as means of limiting their family size (Ross and Poedjastoeti 1983). Vasectomy, one of the most popular and cost-effective methods of contraception in developed countries, is not popular among Indonesian males, due in part to religious objections, and in part due to government hesitance in promoting the method. The 1987 and 1991 surveys were particularly thorough in ascertaining current use of contraceptives, including a number of questions to check against 'courtesy-biased' answers given to please the interviewer or attest usage falsely. Moreover, as Streatfield (1985) demonstrated, the quality of reporting varies greatly from survey to survey and between the census or surveys and routine clinic data. Nonetheless, time trends of the most clearly comparable data show a steady increase in acceptance and use of family planning. With half the women of childbearing age shown to be using a method, and most of these using a reliable and secure method, the magnitude of the fertility

Table 3.5   Infant mortality rates by province, late 1960s to late 1980s

Region	Late 1960s	Late 1980s
Indonesia	132	69
Urban	104	52
Rural	137	77
Sumatra	138	65
DI Aceh	140	57
North Sumatra	116	59
West Sumatra	157	71
Riau	139	65
Jambi	157	71
South Sumatra	147	70
Bengkulu	167	68
Lampung	148	69
Java	136	69
DKI Jakarta	122	38
West Java	164	89
Central Java	137	63
DI Yogyakarta	93	41
East Java	117	62
Nusa Tenggara	163	91
Bali	121	49
West Nusa Tenggara	219	145
East Nusa Tenggara	147	74
East Timor	na	82
Kalimantan	142	74
West Kalimantan	141	80
Central Kalimantan	123	56
South Kalimantan	168	91
East Kalimantan	100	56
Sulawesi	149	71
North Sulawesi	111	63
Central Sulawesi	142	89
South Sulawesi	160	69
Southeast Sulawesi	164	76
Maluku	150	75
Irian Jaya	111	79

Notes: na—Not available.
Data refer to deaths under one year of age per 1000 live births.
Sources: Late 1960s—BPS (1988:51); late 1980s—Kasto (1992:15).

decline is explicable. Of course, high rates of current use do not guarantee that fertility will continue to decline. Speculation on that point requires a synthesis of the information presented above.

Future fertility trends and their implications for population size

What of the future of Indonesian fertility? On the one hand, most of the institutional variables seem to be relatively well-entrenched, and certainly

Table 3.6   Contraceptive use by method, 1976–91 (% of currently married women)

Method	Survey results		
	1976	1987	1991
Pill	11.6	16.1	14.8
IUD	4.1	13.2	13.3
Injection	—	9.4	11.7
Condom	1.5	1.6	0.8
Tubectomy	0.1	3.1	2.7
Vasectomy	0.0	0.2	0.6
Norplant implant	—	0.4	3.1
Periodic abstinence	0.8	1.2	1.1
Withdrawal	0.1	1.3	0.7
Other methods	—	1.2	0.9
Total users	18.3	47.7	49.7
No method reported	81.7	52.3	50.3

Sources: 1976—BPS (1978:122); 1987—BPS (1989:34); 1991—BPS (1992:53).

those related to 'demand for children' are unlikely to be seriously changed in such a way as to lead to increases in the demand for larger families in the near future. The education system is still sufficiently expensive in relation to current incomes to make parents think very hard before expanding their family size. The employment market is still sufficiently tight for most young people to be concerned about getting and keeping a job before making commitments of marriage and family building. In short, the long-term changes associated with 'modernisation' in the society have been strongly reinforced by the more recent changes brought in under the banner of the New Order government. Short of catastrophic collapse of the economy, or radical reorientation of consumer desires, these demand factors seem securely established in Indonesia, and of greater strength among each succeeding generation. Thus, from this viewpoint, indications are that fertility will continue to fall.

The institutions surrounding the supply of services, be they in the form of contraceptives, sterilisation, abortion, or counselling and sex education, are more problematic. They have expanded rapidly over the past two decades, with the government institutions showing the greatest expansion, while private foundations and medical organisations have become very important as points of high quality and innovative service delivery, particularly in cities.

The government institutions are highly susceptible to variations in government budgets, and are still very dependent on foreign assistance for a large proportion of the contraceptives or raw materials for contraceptives. This is the reason the BKKBN has redirected so much of its effort to the development of privatised family planning services through its 'KB Mandiri' program. The target of this program is to have 50 per cent of the supply of family planning services privatised by the year 2000.

Private institutions providing services such as abortion or sterilisation are vulnerable to the possibility that pressure groups could force governments to inhibit or close their operations. It is on the supply side that ideological issues over moral and political implications of specific methods of family planning are most salient, and where it is possible to imagine conditions under which a substantial contraction of services could occur. For the time being, though, the Indonesian government is fully committed to making methods of fertility control widely available; there is no organised opposition to this activity, and aid donors have been forthcoming in providing financial support.

On this basis I would argue that fertility decline will continue for some time, and that there will be no rebound in TFRs before reaching the level of the two-child family—that is between 2.0 and 2.3 children per woman on average. Even that level should not be assumed to be firm. Given an increasingly modernised setting, Indonesia could follow the examples of developed nations, where fertility has dipped below the levels of long-term replacement. If it does so, it will be because of the development of economic and social institutions which further depress the desire for children.

The prospect of fertility levels which are below replacement level might unsettle many Indonesian policy-makers, but it is one that they should be prepared to confront in coming decades. At the same time, policy-makers will undoubtedly take a measure of comfort from the impact that declining fertility has on total population size. The fertility decline which has already occurred has meant a difference of thirty million people in the total Indonesian population: had fertility been constant at 1961 levels, the 1990 population would have been 210 million instead of 180 million. Projections made in 1961 and assuming no fertility decline calculated a population at the turn of the century of 280 million, compared to 1987 BPS projections of 208 million for the year 2000 (Table 3.7).

Even the BPS projections made in 1987 are being revised on the basis of the recently released results of the 1990 census, which showed a lower total population and hence implied lower population growth rates than had been anticipated. Until the census, BPS projections tended to be fairly conservative, assuming that fertility would not fall as rapidly as indicated by recent trends. The projections issued after the census have seriously reduced estimates of population in the medium term—a reduction of over eight million for the year 2000 projection and ten million fewer people in the year 2005. Alternative projections by the United Nations (1989), Gardiner (1989) and the World Bank (Bulatao et al. 1990) indicate other futures dependent on the timing of achievement of a two-child family (NRR or Net Reproduction Rate = 1) and the likelihood that fertility decline would stop

Table 3.7   Population projections (million persons)

	BPS[a]	BPS[b]	UN[c]	UN[c] Low	World Bank[d] Medium
1990	182.7	179.9	178.0	180.5	181.6
1995	199.6	194.4	189.8	194.8	197.9
2000	216.1	208.4	200.9	208.3	213.6
2005	231.4	221.2	210.1	220.6	227.8
2010	—	232.4	216.0	232.0	241.4
2015	—		221.0	253.6	254.9
2020	—		225.0	253.6	267.8
2025	—		227.8	263.3	279.8

Gardiner's projections[e]

	Low	Medium	High	Path to 250 million Fast	Path to 250 million Slow
1990	180.1	180.6	180.6	180.1	180.6
1995	194.6	196.5	196.8	194.6	196.5
2000	208.4	211.9	213.0	208.4	211.9
2005	221.8	226.9	229.4	221.8	226.9
2010	235.4	241.1	245.3	230.2	241.1
2015	248.5	254.7	260.4	233.0	254.7
2020	260.9	267.9	274.5	235.1	266.8
2025	271.7	279.8	287.1	240.8	276.6
2030	280.9	290.3	298.6	248.8	283.9
2035	288.6	299.0	308.5	257.0	288.3
2040	294.6	305.8	316.7	260.4	290.7
2045	299.0	311.0	323.0	260.9	290.9
2050	301.7	314.5	327.4	257.6	289.9
2055	303.0	316.6	330.4	255.0	287.6
2060	303.4	317.7	332.4	253.2	284.5
. . .					
2125	304.0	318.9	335.7	251.1	253.2

Sources: a BPS (1987:39).
b Mamas (1991:32). Assumption I, with NRR = 1 around the year 2005.
c United Nations (1989:406–7).
d Bulatao et al. (1990:192). Assumes NRR = 1 in the year 2005, and maintains that rate thereafter.
e Gardiner (1989, Table 1). In the first three variants NRR = 1 in 2000–05 (low), 2010–15 (medium), 2020–25 (high). The other two variants reflect patterns inherent in meeting the president's desire to stabilise the population at 250 million in the year 2050.

at that point rather than follow the example of developed countries and fall to a 1.5 or 1.8 average family size.

The Gardiner projections are particularly interesting in their implications for government policy debates. President Soeharto has called for population to be stabilised at 250 million in 2050, ironically the total which President Sukarno boasted the nation could support. According to Gardiner's projections, reasonable assumptions for either rapid or slow fertility decline both show the total exceeding 250 million before falling back to that number if the country sustained below-replacement fertility for decades. These assumptions seemed to strain credulity, and the government quickly dropped discussion of a 250 million projection target, and returned to consideration of the more conventional assumptions which produce much larger populations.

Although we should not lose sight of the fact that the total Indonesian population is still likely to attain 300 million before coming to a halt, there can be no doubt that the remarkable fertility declines which have occurred in the New Order period made a significant difference in the economic development challenges facing Indonesia. Obviously, too, it has and is making a difference to millions of parents wishing to provide better food, clothing, schooling and prospects to their children, and who see family spacing and limitation as important means to reach this goal.

LABOUR FORCE AND EDUCATION

Gavin W. Jones

This chapter will attempt to give something of the flavour of the dramatic changes that have taken place in employment and education over the New Order period by first presenting 'snapshots' of the labour force and educational situations early and late in the New Order period. Data shortcomings, however, preclude the presentation of a clear picture of the situation early in the period—say, in late 1966. Instead, the 1971 census data will be used to describe the prevailing situation after the regime had had time to create some order from the economic shambles inherited from the previous regime, but before the oil boom-fuelled developments of the 1970s really got underway. The second snapshot will relate to the period 1985–90, after the oil boom and embracing the period of export-oriented industrialisation.

The labour force

The profile in 1971 and 1990

Table 3.8 shows the profile of the labour force in 1971 and 1990. During the New Order period, the Indonesian labour force has more than doubled in size and become less Java-centric, less concentrated in primary industries, less rural and much better educated. The decline in agriculture's share has exceeded the decline in the rural share, implying a change in the structure of employment in rural areas, which is shown in Table 3.9. The share of non-agricultural activities in rural employment has increased steadily, the main gains being registered in trade, construction, manufacturing and transport.

Table 3.8   Labour force profile, 1971, 1990

Profile	1971	1990
Number of employed persons (million)	39.2	72.0
	%	%
Rural	85.2	73.3
Female	33.2	35.8
Aged 15–29	34.4	36.7
In Java	65.7	61.6
With no education	42.7	17.5
With completed primary education or above	28.8	54.5
With completed junior high school or above	7.0	23.0
In agriculture	65.9	49.2
In professional, managerial or clerical occupations	5.7	8.8
Of labour force unemployed:		
rural	8.2 (1.7)[a]	2.1
urban	12.5 (4.8)[a]	6.3
urban aged 15–24	16.0 (8.7)[a]	16.7

Note: [a] Numbers from Series C (the advance tables) are shown in brackets. For a discussion of the reasons for the wide differences between the two sets of figures (due mainly to a change in imputation rules), see Jones (1981, footnote 8).

Sources: BPS, Population Census 1971 (Series C and D); 1990 (Series S.1).

Table 3.9   Percentage distribution of rural employment by industry, 1971–90, Indonesia and Java (% of total)[a]

Major industry group	Rural Indonesia			Rural Java		
	1971	1980	1990	1971	1980	1990
Agriculture, hunting, forestry and fishing	75.4	71.4	64.4	71.0	66.7	57.7
Manufacturing	7.1	6.6	9.4	8.5	7.9	11.8
Construction	1.4	2.0	3.3	1.4	2.4	4.0
Trade, restaurants and hotels	8.3	9.2	11.0	10.7	11.5	13.8
Transport, storage and communication	1.3	1.6	2.5	1.3	1.7	3.0
Community, social and personal services	6.4	8.4	7.8	7.0	9.1	8.3
Other	0.1	0.6	1.4	0.1	0.5	1.4
Total	100.0	100.0	100.0	100.0	100.0	100.0
Number ('000)	33 414	41 531	52 737	21 775	25 540	30 322

Note: [a] Persons with activities not adequately defined have been allocated to industry groups on a pro-rata basis.

Sources: BPS, Population Census 1971 (Series C); 1980, Table 58.6; 1990 (Series S.1), Tables 31.6 and 33.6.

146

There has been a tendency for the female proportion of the labour force to rise, as a result of rising labour force participation rates. Just how much these rates have risen is hard to determine, because of difficulties in comparing different sources of labour force data (Jones and Manning 1992). The work force has remained very youthful, and although youth unemployment has been a concern, the main problem has been low productivity and low earnings rather than overt unemployment.

Labour force and employment early in the New Order

The 39 million employed persons in 1971 were heavily concentrated in rural areas and in agricultural pursuits. Of those who worked in urban areas, a high proportion (probably above 50 per cent) were in the informal sector, a sector varying greatly in its income levels and productivity but including vast numbers in low productivity occupations such as *becak* driving, petty trade, labouring and a range of personal services. The working age population was poorly educated: 45 per cent had no education at all, and less than one-third had completed primary school education. Low levels of literacy contributed to low productivity. One-third of the labour force was female and just over one-third was youthful (aged 15–29). In contrast with more wealthy nations, where as much as 40 or 50 per cent of employment was in professional, managerial and clerical occupations, in Indonesia these occupations provided less than 6 per cent of employment.

Agriculture dominated the employment structure, accounting for two-thirds of all employment. Agriculture, however, was not as dominant as it was in countries such as Thailand or India at that time, and this was especially the case in Java, where its share was only 61 per cent. There was a long tradition of cottage industries, trading, transportation and construction activities in rural areas of Java, reflecting both the complexity of its rural economy and the strong pressures on people to find alternative sources of income to those provided by peasant production on small plots or by agricultural labour. Many workers had multiple activities and it was somewhat unrealistic to force them to state one major economic activity, as required in the censuses.

While bearing in mind the shaky foundation for comparing industry shares, manufacturing was clearly playing a very limited role, providing less than 8 per cent of total employment. Although this was a rise on the 6 per cent recorded in the 1961 census, it was still well below the 11 per cent or so recorded much earlier in the 1930 census (Jones 1966, Table 2), and also well below the manufacturing share in countries such as Malaysia and the Philippines in the early 1970s. This may partly reflect the incomplete recovery from the economic stagnation of the 1960s, when capacity of manufacturing industry was severely underutilised (Palmer 1965).

Although some cities in Indonesia had grown very large (three of them exceeded one million in population), much of this growth was recent and resulted from rural–urban migration. Urban–rural links therefore remained strong, albeit restricted by the poor transport and communications infrastructure. One indication of this was the large numbers of urban-based workers who did some work in agriculture during the previous season. Of all workers living in urban areas of Java in 1971, 5.9 per cent worked in agriculture. But nearly 13 per cent of all urban workers had done at least some work in agriculture in the previous agricultural season, as had over 7 per cent of all workers even in the capital city, Jakarta. The latter figure is probably an underestimate because of the tendency for censuses to record migrant workers temporarily resident in the city at the place of their usual residence.

Overt unemployment was not very high,[3] and it was heavily concentrated among the young and better educated. A high proportion of the better educated were still looking for their first job. I argued at the time that this unemployment was fictional; indeed, that unemployment was in a sense a luxury that young, educated, middle-class work force entrants could afford while waiting for the right job to turn up, whereas their less fortunate counterparts had to be content with whatever was available (Jones and Supraptilah 1976). Subsequent information on the labour markets has provided no reason to alter that judgement. The crux of the problem of labour underutilisation was the inability of the economy to absorb workers in reasonably productive and remunerative activities. Underutilisation was therefore indicated mainly by short hours (or in some cases, excessively long hours of work) and very low earnings per hour (Jones and Supraptilah 1976). Multiple activities also reflected low productivity and poor earnings in the main occupation, requiring additional activities to make ends meet, both in rural areas and among groups such as schoolteachers and government employees in urban areas (Hugo et al. 1987:291–2).

The recent labour force and employment situation

The structure of the labour force could hardly have been expected to alter dramatically by 1990. After all, a young worker can expect to remain in the labour force for at least four decades, and the turnover of the labour force as new entrants replace those who retire or die is a very gradual process. Therefore almost half of the 1990 labour force were people who were already in the labour force in 1971. Nevertheless, some important changes were apparent by 1990 (see Table 3.8). Perhaps the most notable were in the size of the work force, which had reached well over 70 million, in the higher proportion working outside Java, due to higher natural increase and transmigration, and in its educational composition. The proportion with no education had fallen to 18 per cent, and the proportion with completed primary education or above was now over one-half.

The age structure of the labour force had not changed very much, but the share of female workers had risen, reflecting changed attitudes to women's work and changes in economic structure that appear to have favoured the kinds of work usually done by women. For example, in 1985, women held the following shares of employment in rapidly-growing occupations: paramedics (66 per cent), teachers (45 per cent), sales workers (43 per cent) and over 50 per cent in a number of subsectors of manufacturing. (Data at this level of detail are not yet available for 1990.)

The lower share of agriculture in total employment in 1990 than in 1971 was offset by rises in the shares of each of the other major industry groups, but construction and transport were the sectors whose shares rose most in relative terms, for males, and trade and services for females. The difficulty in interpreting these increases in share is the wide range of activities falling under the rubric of the broad occupational categories. For example, among males working in transport in 1985, there were slightly over one million drivers of motor vehicles and slightly over half a million *becak* drivers. The relative size of these groups had been changing, but we are not sure of the 1971 figures.

The role of the informal sector—usually defined in Indonesia to include the self-employed, unpaid family workers and agricultural labourers, though more complex definitions are sometimes used (BPS 1986: Table 4.2)—remained very important, though it probably accounted for a smaller proportion of the urban work force than in the early stages of the New Order period. One study based on the 1982 *Susenas* indicated that the informal sector accounted for 45 per cent of employment in urban areas (BPS 1986), while another study showed its share of urban employment to be 43 per cent in both 1980 and 1985.[4] Trends are difficult to measure, because much depends on the definition of the informal sector used, but the latter study suggested little change in the share of the informal sector between 1980 and 1985, despite the wider coverage of unpaid family workers in 1985.[5]

Some 'modernisation' of the occupational structure had taken place since 1971; for example, the share of professional, managerial and clerical occupations had risen from 5.7 to 8.8 per cent, and within occupational groups, there had been a shift from more traditional to more modern occupations (for example, from *becak* riding to driving *bemos* or taxis, and from operating *warungs* and street and market vending to working as shop assistants and in supermarkets and department stores). However, the extent of this shift is not easily determined from the available data.

There is no clear evidence from the unemployment data in Table 3.8 that unemployment had increased appreciably between 1971 and 1990. Indeed, *Sakernas* (National Labour Force Survey) data for urban areas show that crude unemployment rates for males were the same (6.9 per cent) in both 1976 and 1986 (Table 3.10). Open unemployment rates in urban areas were highest among young secondary school leavers aged 15–24; they fell very sharply among those aged 25–29 (but were quite high at the tertiary level in this age group). Among those aged 30 and above unemployment rates were very low for all educational levels in 1976, 1982 and 1986. The urban unemployed were dominated by first-time job seekers (over 75 per cent in the mid-1980s) and a high proportion of those actively looking for work reported durations of job search of less than six months (close to 60 per cent in 1986). However, as noted already, other symptoms of underutilisation need to be examined if we are to learn whether the labour

Table 3.10 Unemployment rates by age and education, urban Indonesia, 1976, 1986 (%)

Age/educational category	Males		Females	
	1976	1986[a]	1976	1986[a]
15–19				
<Primary	22.3	10.2	6.5	5.0
Primary	26.2	16.1	7.5	11.4
Lower secondary	32.3	20.3	25.9	21.6
All 15–19	26.3	21.2	9.9	16.6
20–24				
<Primary	11.5	8.1	3.0	4.3
Primary	13.9	12.2	8.3	6.1
Lower secondary	19.5	20.3	20.7	24.9
Upper secondary				
Academic	32.2	41.5	33.4	50.2
Vocational	27.6	35.1	21.9	25.5
All 20–24	18.2	26.1	14.4	24.4
25–29				
<Primary	3.0	5.5	2.0	2.0
Primary	4.7	3.6	3.4	2.0
Lower secondary	7.8	5.2	10.9	11.9
Upper secondary				
Academic	8.4	8.7	5.9	13.9
Vocational	5.8	11.3	9.1	8.5
Tertiary	7.4	19.6	13.6	15.6
All 25–29	5.8	7.1	5.5	7.0
All ages 15–64				
<Primary	5.1	2.5	1.7	1.8
Primary	7.1	4.2	5.5	4.5
Lower secondary	8.0	6.4	11.3	11.2
Upper secondary				
Academic	9.7	14.8	18.6	31.0
Vocational	10.6	11.8	12.1	11.7
Tertiary	1.9	6.9	9.3	14.4
Total	6.9	6.9	5.1	8.1

Note: [a] Diploma I and II graduates included in the upper secondary vocational school group.
Sources: BPS, *Sakernas*, 1976, 1986.

150

force is really more or less fully utilised than in earlier times. This will be examined in more detail in the following section.

The dynamics of labour-force change

What were the processes by which changes in the labour force had taken place? First, we should note their demographic underpinnings. Mortality rates were declining; fertility was also declining over this period, but the cohorts born in declining fertility times had not yet had time to reach the labour-force ages. The labour force was therefore growing more rapidly than at any previous period in Indonesian history: at about 2.8 or 2.9 per cent per annum. The broad-based age pyramid meant that numbers entering the labour force each year greatly exceeded those leaving through death or retirement. In the 1980s, this ratio in the case of males was about 4:1 (Keyfitz 1989). This high turnover rate, as we will discuss below, was responsible for sharp changes in the educational composition of the labour force: of males leaving the work force in recent years, most are illiterate; three of the four persons replacing each of them have a high school education (Jones 1992).

Change in female labour force participation over the period is a controversial issue, because of wide differences between different data sources in the recording of women as unpaid family workers (Jones 1986; Hugo et al. 1987, ch.8; Jones and Manning 1992; Korns 1987). It is clear, however, that in recent times there has been a tendency for these rates to increase (Figure 3.1). The rates were substantially higher in both urban and rural areas in 1987 than in 1977. Indeed the data imply that, but for this rise in participation rates, the female work force would have been almost six million smaller than that actually recorded in 1987. Although part of the substantial increase in rural participation rates across almost all age categories in the period 1982–86 must be considered an artifact of greater coverage of family workers in 1987 (Jones and Manning 1992), the substantial rise in the urban rates, which are subject to less uncertainty in judging whether women are in the work force or not, indicates that at least part of the rise was real.

Why did female participation rates increase?[6] Changes in these rates were no doubt determined by interactions between a number of factors, including trends in marital status, fertility, and education (all of which are basically supply-side factors) and economic conditions influencing the demand for workers in occupations where female employment is important, along with changing perceptions about what is suitable female work (which are basically demand-side factors). Supply and demand cannot be so neatly separated, however. For example, for many women, decisions about marriage, childbearing and education may not be divorced from labour-market considerations.

151

Figure 3.1   Female activity rates by age and rural/urban residence, 1977–87

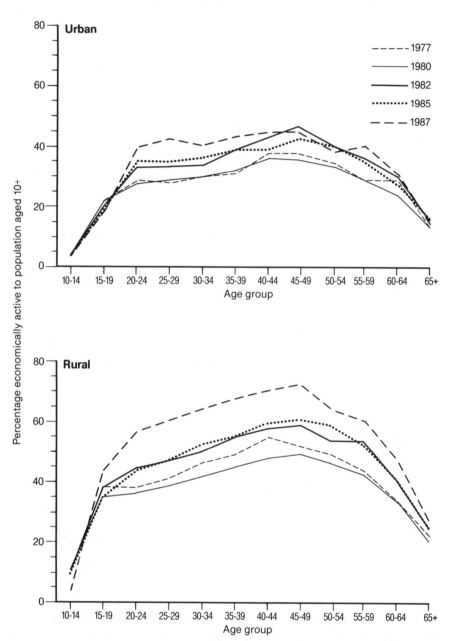

Source: BPS, unpublished data.

Rising ages at marriage and falling fertility undoubtedly have contributed to the growth of female employment, because participation rates have always tended to be higher for single than for married women and for women who do not have children of preschool age. Between 1977 and 1987, there may also have been a slight shift in the occupational structure towards occupations in which women are normally strongly represented. However, the most intriguing questions concern the effect on female employment of the changing education of both males and females as well as the effect of changing economic conditions.

Participation rates for Indonesian women have always differed markedly depending on the level of education (Widarti 1984; Jones 1986). A U-shaped pattern has prevailed, with the lowest rates for those with junior secondary school education and the highest rates for those with no education or tertiary education. This pattern has been maintained in the 1987 *Sakernas* figures (Figure 3.2). On balance, the changing educational composition of the female working-age population between 1977 and 1987 (a fall in the share of the uneducated and a rise in the share of those with completed primary school education and above) should have led, other things being equal, to a slight fall in the female participation rate, because the share of those with completed primary school and junior high school education, whose participation rates are low, increased the most.

Participation rates for women within different educational groups, however, are not static, but are influenced by economic trends affecting their job opportunities and desire to work, as well as by changes in perceptions about appropriate activities for women. Equally important, when education expands rapidly, as it has in Indonesia, the composition of educational attainment groups by economic class tends to change. Thus girls from lower socio-economic groups start to enter lower secondary education, and the motivations influencing work decisions of this group are likely to differ from motivations of earlier cohorts drawn more exclusively from the higher socio-economic groups.

Figure 3.3 shows that between 1977 and 1987, labour-force participation rates for women from each educational group have changed. To some extent the marked increases at primary and less than primary levels can be attributed to better coverage of unpaid family workers in 1987. At the younger ages, the rates rose at each educational level, but at the older ages, they rose only in the case of the uneducated and those with primary school education. We might hypothesise that the rise across the board at the younger ages reflects primarily a greater community acceptance of economic activity as appropriate for women, whereas at the older ages the rise among the less well-educated may reflect perceived economic pressures, particularly during the 1982–87 period.

The changing industrial structure of employment is quite difficult to

Figure 3.2   Female activity rates by age and educational attainment, 1977–87

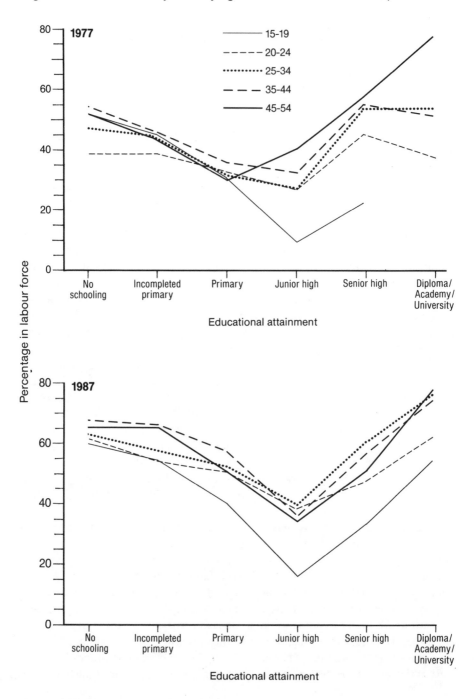

Sources: BPS, Sakernas, 1977, 1987.

Figure 3.3   Female activity rates by age for each educational attainment level, 1977–87

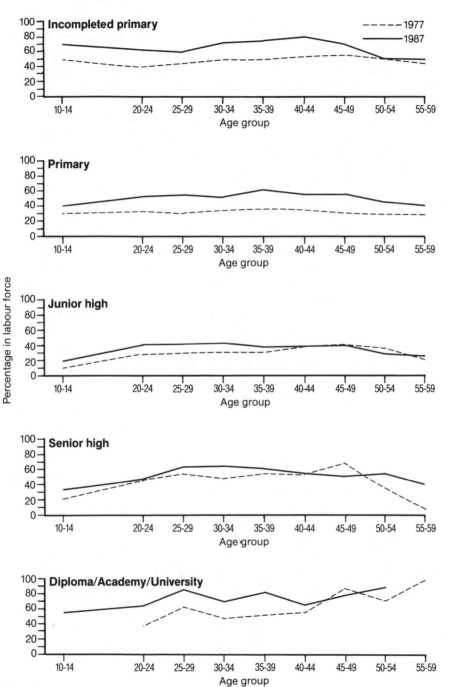

Sources: BPS, Sakernas, 1977, 1987.

determine because of comparability problems between the various data sources (Jones and Manning 1992). Table 3.11 summarises the employment changes which seem to have taken place between 1971 and 1990.[7] There were important differences in the pattern of employment growth over the 1970s compared with the 1980s. In the 1970s, non-agricultural employment grew rapidly, especially in the oil boom-supported service and construction industries, and to a lesser extent in manufacturing. Agricultural employment growth was sluggish, accounting for about 20 per cent of total employment growth. New agricultural jobs were heavily concentrated in the outer islands (partly as a result of the transmigration program) and although the agricultural labour force continued to grow on Java as a whole, it actually declined in about half the *kabupaten* in Java (Jones 1984: Figure 3).[8]

Slower economic growth rates in the 1980–85 period appear to have been associated with much less rapid growth in non-agricultural employment. This was counterbalanced by higher rates of labour absorption in agriculture on both Java and the outer islands than in the previous decade. Over the entire 1980s, agriculture apparently accounted for about 19 per cent of total employment growth in Java and 52 per cent in the outer islands. In Java, this was probably related to rapid rice-sector growth and agricultural diversification, but it appears also to be related to a decline in average hours worked, which hints at a possible return to the 'involutionary' patterns of the past.[9] Outside Java, transmigration, nucleus estate (*Perkebunan Inti Rakyat* [PIR]) schemes and the expansion of smallholder agriculture all help to explain strong growth in agricultural employment (Booth 1989a).

Lower recorded growth rates in non-agricultural employment in the first half of the 1980s were mainly the result of a marked slowdown in employment expansion in services and construction. Growth of employment in services remained sluggish throughout the 1980s, apparently reflecting in part the freeze on government-sector employment imposed in 1986; growth in this sector also favoured females over males, probably reflecting the important female role in the expanding occupations of nursing and teaching.[10] Employment in manufacturing grew at a heartening pace over the 1980s, rising substantially in the second half of the decade, from around 4.5 per cent per annum in 1980–85 to closer to 7 per cent per annum in 1985–90 (Manning 1992a:30). Trade and transport have also been important in employment growth, but (as with the expansion of labour absorption in agriculture), this appears partly to reflect growth of informal sector and low-wage work in response to difficulties in obtaining wage employment from the early 1980s (Hasibuan 1987).

Real wage trends indicate that Indonesia remained a labour surplus economy, with a relatively elastic supply curve of labour. It was only in the boom times of the late 1970s and early 1980s that real wages of unskilled labour rose markedly (Jones and Manning 1992). Lack of much advance in

Table 3.11 Growth of employment in Indonesia, 1971–90[a]

Sector	Share of employment (%)		Growth rates (% pa)		% of increment	
	1971	1990	1971–80	1980–90	1971–80	1980–90
Males						
Agriculture	66	50	1.4	1.5	29	30
Manufacturing	6	10	5.6	5.5	12	17
Construction	3	6	8.5	5.6	10	11
Trade	9	12	4.2	4.4	13	18
Transport	3	6	5.0	5.7	6	10
Services	12	13	5.9	1.6	26	8
Other[b]	1	3	12.9	6.5	4	5
Total	100	100	3.0	2.9	100	100
N (000)	26 184	45 490			8191	11 115
Females						
Agriculture	65	49	0.8	2.9	17	39
Manufacturing	11	15	3.4	5.4	16	19
Trade	15	20	6.0	4.5	35	23
Services	9	14	7.9	4.6	30	16
Other[c]	n	2	(13.9)	8.6	2	3
Total	100	100	2.9	4.0	100	100
N ('000)	13 026	25 118			3792	8298

Notes: [a] Excludes employment in Irian Jaya and East Timor. Responses classified as not stated/unclear redistributed on a pro-rata basis.
[b] Mining and public utilities.
[c] Construction, mining and public utilities.
n—Negligible.

Sources: Jones and Manning (1992, Tables 4 and 6). Based on BPS, Population Census 1971 (Series C); 1980 (Series S.1); and 1990 (Series S.2), Tables 31.7 and 31.8.

unskilled wages, however, has not prevented average wages from rising as a consequence of the changing composition of total employment; labour has tended to shift into more productive and higher paying jobs both across and within broad sectors of activity.

Changes in industrial structure were closely linked to urbanisation; the proportion of Indonesia's population living in urban areas rose from 17 per cent in 1971 to 25 per cent in 1985 and 31 per cent in 1990.[11] But even more important was the change in the employment structure in rural areas. Changes in industrial structure of employment can be disaggregated into three components: changes in the structure of employment within rural areas, changes in the structure of employment within urban areas, and a change in the proportion of workers living in urban and rural areas. Table 3.9 shows that the distribution of rural workers across industries changed quite markedly between 1971 and 1990, with a declining share of primary industries and a rising share of all other major industries. The structure of urban employment did not change very much. Overall, there were 18.8 million fewer workers in agriculture in 1990 than there would have been if agriculture's share of total employment had remained constant. Of this decline, changing rural employment structure accounted for 38 per cent, changing urban employment structure for 1 per cent and the rise in the urban share of employment for 61 per cent (see also Bendesa 1991).

A gradual shift in the occupational structure has accompanied the shift in the industrial structure. One key trend has been a rise in the share of professional, managerial and clerical occupations. There have been two reasons for this. First, there has been a shift towards employment in industries in which these occupations feature prominently. Secondly, within individual industries, there has been a shift towards a higher share of these occupations. But Indonesia is still in a very early stage of such structural shifts. Table 3.12 shows a much higher share of the professional, managerial and clerical occupations in each industry in Australia than in Indonesia, with Malaysia in an intermediate position.

Census and survey data on occupation cannot do full justice to occupational change in Indonesia, because traditional and modern (or low and high technology) occupations are often subsumed under the one occupational category. For example, different occupations in trade are not identified in such a way as to enable a split between hawking and street-vending and occupations in modern, highly-capitalised shopping complexes and supermarkets.

There is a range of evidence to suggest that the underutilisation of labour in urban areas had worsened, especially among females and young, upper secondary and tertiary educated in the mid-1980s compared with ten years earlier (Jones and Manning 1992:396–8). Unemployment rates had risen for these groups, and durations of unemployment also seem to have lengthened;

Demographic perspectives

Table 3.12   Proportion of PMC[a] occupations in total employment by major
             industries, Indonesia, Malaysia and Australia (%)

	Indonesia	Malaysia	Australia
	1985	1984	1986
Agriculture	0.0	0.9	73.0[c]
Mining and quarrying	10.7	24.2	31.2
Manufacturing	4.0	13.0	28.1
Electricity, gas, water	30.0	35.0	41.8
Construction	3.6	12.2	27.5
Commerce, trade	0.9	11.2	32.8
Transport and communication	10.2	28.1	29.7
Finance and insurance	61.6	77.4	71.6
Community services[b]	49.2	48.4	65.5
All industries	7.5	19.1	48.7

Notes: a PMC refers to professional, managerial and clerical.
         b Includes public administration and recreational services.
         c The 'managerial' occupation appears to include all self-employed farmers. In earlier
           years, PMC occupations contributed only about 2 per cent of total employment in agricul-
           ture. It should be noted that employment in agriculture constitutes only 6 per cent of
           total employment in Australia.

Sources: Indonesia—Intercensal Population Survey 1985; Malaysia—unpublished tables from 1984
         Labor Force Survey; Australia—1986 Census, Cross Classified Characteristics of Persons
         and Dwellings, Table C41.

in addition, the discouraged worker component among the young may have
risen quite substantially, especially among females (Manning 1989: Table
4). The upper secondary and tertiary graduates of the 1970s were fortunate
in that they entered the labour market with these scarce qualifications just
at the time when the economy began to boom. By contrast, these qualifications were less scarce in the 1980s and job opportunities were growing
less rapidly. Some data also suggest that underutilisation of workers in rural
areas (the proportion working short hours) increased during the 1980s, but
data comparability problems prevent any firm conclusions.

Employment change over the 1971–90 period was marked by important
regional differences. Non-agricultural employment grew at much the same
rate in Java and in the outer islands, but employment growth in agriculture
was both faster in the 1980s than in the 1970s and very much higher in the
outer islands than in Java. In the 1980s, agricultural employment grew by
3.3 per cent per annum in the outer islands compared with 1.2 per cent in
Java. In the same decade, manufacturing employment grew at almost the
same rate in Java and the outer islands, but there was considerable variation
within these broad regions, with Jakarta and West Java dominating in Java
and Kalimantan and Bali capturing a disproportionate share of growth in
the outer islands (Manning 1992:30).

A rate of agricultural employment growth in Java even as low as 1 per
cent per annum is higher than many would have predicted in the 1970s,

159

when limited land availability and technical change in agriculture were seen as severe constraints on further labour absorption. What appears to have happened is that despite the introduction of labour-replacing technology in rice agriculture (especially the sickle), rapid growth in agricultural output contributed to continued growth in employment in the early 1970s. In the boom period at the turn of the decade, labour was drawn out of agriculture both by the growth of employment opportunities in other sectors and by the expanded transmigration program. The economic slow-down of the early 1980s probably led to a return to agriculture by many as their principal source of employment, particularly given the continued rapid rates of growth in this sector up to the mid-decade. Part of the increase was in the secondary worker component, including women and children working relatively short hours. Despite this suggestion of less favourable labour-market conditions, real agricultural wages appear to have continued to increase in Java to the mid-1980s (probably related to the continued production growth in the sector, continued high levels of government spending in rural Java up to the middle of the decade, and a slackening of labour-supply pressures due to an expanded transmigration program), but to have stagnated after 1985.

In the outer islands, the slower growth of employment in other sectors and the role of the transmigration program must have boosted agricultural employment growth, and the expansion of smallholder cash cropping of non-rice crops has been of major importance (Booth 1989a). The major transmigration destinations remain relatively poor despite evidence that most transmigrants have bettered their conditions compared with what they could have expected had they remained in Java (World Bank 1988). Lampung illustrates most starkly the failure of transmigration to provide a major engine of growth for destination provinces. Its population more than doubled from 2.8 million in 1971 to almost 6 million in 1985, but agriculture continued to account for 75 per cent of employment in 1985, and high levels of poverty and environmental stress continue to prevail.

Labour unions remained weak over the New Order period, for a number of reasons (Manning 1992b). First, the banning of the leftist All-Indonesia Workers' Organisation (SOBSI) and removal of its leaders from the industrial relations scene greatly weakened the union movement. A unified trade union movement was seen by the military and their economic advisers as being in the best interests of political control, economic stability and growth, and this was achieved by the establishment of the government-backed All-Indonesia Labour Federation (FBSI) in 1973. Second, labour rights were curtailed through government intervention—including use of the military and police—in industrial relations processes. Over the New Order period, the only periods of substantial labour unrest have been from 1978 to 1982, and again in 1990 and 1991, the latter concentrated on foreign-owned firms in the low-wage footwear, garments and textile industries in the Jakarta region. The failure of such labour unrest to have much impact on wages and working conditions reflects on the third reason for union weakness—the continued labour surplus conditions which provided limited scope for union-led improvements.

Education

The profile in 1971 and 1990

One of the most significant achievements of the New Order regime has been the expansion of education to the point where universal primary education has been almost attained; this also means that illiteracy has almost disappeared among the younger population (see Figure 3.4).

Figure 3.5 gives some summary statistics on educational attainment of the adult population between 1961 and 1990. The biggest changes were in the proportions with no schooling (which dropped to 16 per cent in 1990) and with completed secondary education (which rose to 22 per cent in 1990). For the first time in Indonesian history, then, the secondary educated outnumbered those with no education. Female gains were relatively even greater than male. As far as current school attendance is concerned, the proportion at ages 7–15 rose from 55.6 per cent in 1971 to 87.6 per cent in 1985. The apparent slight decline in this figure by 1990 is more likely to reflect a change in definitions or procedures used in the census than a real decline.

The educational situation early in the New Order

Early in the New Order period, Indonesia was still far from reaching universal primary education, and male enrolments were still well above female, particularly at secondary and higher levels. This reflected a residual tendency to favour male education, particularly if a family's resources were not great enough to put all its children through school. Few rural children had access to a secondary school without travelling daily to a town, or moving to or boarding in such a town. Primary schools in rural areas provided little more than a roof to keep off the rain. The quality of teaching was low, and many teachers were forced to make ends meet by filling multiple jobs. Regional differentials dating back to colonial times were still evident—for example, in the relatively high educational attainment in Maluku and North Sulawesi and the relatively low attainment in Central and East Java, Bali and South Sulawesi (Jones 1976: Table 6). But the latter provinces lagged much less than they did previously, and this was particularly true of female education. Independence, then, had ushered in an era

Figure 3.4   **Literacy rates by age and sex, 1961–90 (% of literate population 10 years and over)**

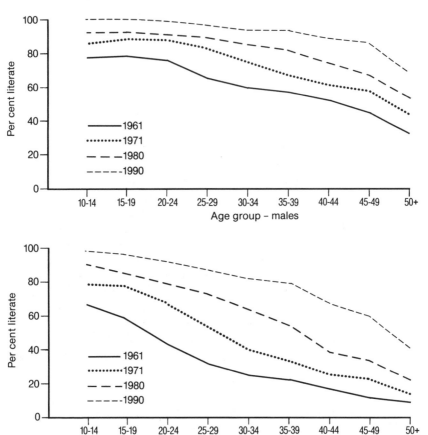

Sources: BPS, Population Census reports, 1961, 1971, 1980, 1990.

of even-handed development of education, albeit with serious shortcomings that were everywhere in evidence.

The recent educational situation

The coverage of education in 1990 was much higher at all levels than in 1971, and because of strong efforts in lagging regions, regional disparities had lessened. In addition to the near-attainment of universal primary education, enrolment ratios at the secondary and tertiary levels had also increased sharply. Junior high schools were now typically available in *kecamatan* towns, but historically poor access to schooling in the rural areas

Demographic perspectives

Figure 3.5   Indicators of educational progress, 1971–90

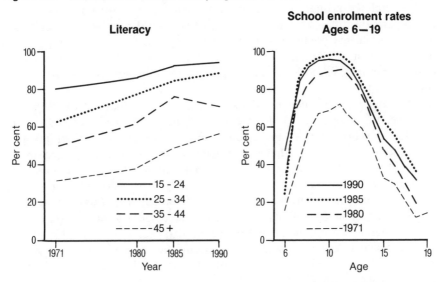

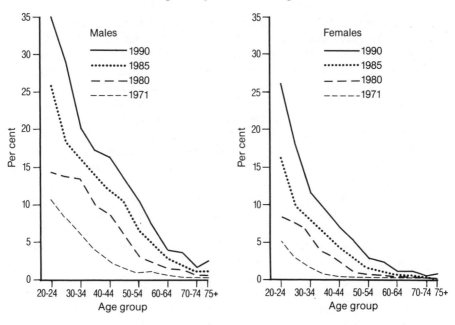

Sources: BPS, Population Census reports, 1971, 1980, 1990; *Supas*, 1985.

is reflected in a 59 per cent excess in the urban proportion of adult males with completed primary education compared with the rural proportion, and an 86 per cent urban excess in the case of women. Entry into the adult ages of better educated youth cohorts had markedly increased the average levels of educational attainment of the adult population, but the rapidity of the improvements resulted in a sharp age gradient in educational attainment (Figure 3.5).

The male–female gap in education was less pronounced by 1990. For example, whereas in 1971 there was a 45 per cent excess of males over females in school enrolments at ages 13–17, this excess had shrunk to 8 per cent by 1990. Nevertheless, females were still disadvantaged in the 1980s, most markedly so in Irian Jaya, Bali and West Nusa Tenggara. The ratio of females to males was considerably higher in non-Education Department schools, most of which are religious (mainly Islamic) schools, suggesting that many parents find it more acceptable to send girls to such schools than to more secular schools. It has also been argued that the relative female disadvantage in educational opportunities is greatest when schools are less accessible, because parents are reluctant to allow daughters to travel great distances (Oey-Gardiner 1991).

The dynamics of education change

The Indonesian government has placed strongest emphasis on the development of primary education, and it is noteworthy that the windfall gains in oil revenue in the 1970s were channelled, not into secondary schools, but into primary schools, and mainly in rural areas at that. This emphasis is entirely in accordance with the policy implications of rates of return studies, both in other countries and those few conducted in Indonesia. The findings of these studies will be summarised in a later section.

Rapid expansion of primary education in Indonesia, however, raises serious issues of quality. The high proportion of inadequately trained teachers, the very basic school buildings, the lack of teaching aids, the high level of absenteeism, particularly in the busy season in agricultural areas, and the high dropout rate before functional literacy is achieved, all serve to raise questions about the efficiency of use of the funds poured into primary education.

Compared to countries in ASEAN and in Northeast Asia, the proportion of eligible young people who enter tertiary education is very small (Table 3.13). It has increased markedly in recent years, with the proliferation of private institutions of higher education, of which there were 872 in 1990, attended by 1.2 million students, compared with 49 public institutions attended by about half that number of students (Oey-Gardiner and Suryatini 1990).

Table 3.13   Education enrolment in Asia (secondary and higher education enrolments as % of age group)

	Secondary education		Higher education	
	1965	1987	1965	1987
Indonesia	12	46[a]	1	7[a]
Philippines	41	68	19	38
Thailand	14	28	2	20
Malaysia	28	59	2	7
Singapore	45	71	10	12
Korea	35	88	6	36
Japan	82	96	13	29
China	24	43	1	2
India	27	39[b]	5	9[b]

Notes: Secondary school age range depends on national definitions. It is most commonly considered to be 12–17 years. The age range for higher education is taken to be 20–24 years.
[a] 1986.
[b] 1984.

Source: World Bank, *World Development Report 1990*, Table 29.

Now that universal primary education is on the verge of achievement and the primary school age population is growing very slowly, the emphasis in *Repelita V* (1988–93) has shifted to secondary education (Booth 1989a:23–7). Numbers of new entrants to lower secondary schools are projected to grow from 2.6 to 3.3 million and to upper secondary schools from 1.6 to 2.2 million over the plan period. These numbers imply that by 1994, enrolments in lower secondary schools will amount to two-thirds of children in the 13–15 age group, while upper secondary enrolments will amount to 45 per cent of children in the 16–18 age group, both figures representing a substantial rise on the proportions at the beginning of the plan period. Quality of secondary schools is much lower in rural than in urban areas (IEES 1986: ch.6, Table 6.9). Concern is frequently expressed over the declining quality of secondary education during recent periods of rapid expansion,[12] though the decline was fully expected by the government. Hard data to measure trends in quality, however, appear to be lacking.

Tertiary education enrolments are projected to grow even more rapidly, and this increases the urgency of dealing with issues of content and quality of tertiary education and of equity in the financing of education. On content, an international comparison suggests that the number of Indonesian tertiary students in the field of law may be excessive (Jones 1989b). The rapid expansion of the manufacturing and construction industries highlights the need to place more emphasis on engineering and technical education, not only at the tertiary level (for example, through a system of polytechnics) but also at the high school level. On quality, the shortcomings have been extensively discussed (Clark and Oey-Gardiner 1988; Keyfitz et al. 1989; Hill 1991). They relate to factors such as low salaries, necessitating additional jobs, a high proportion of poorly-trained staff in all but the few top universities, low levels of regional mobility among students and staff, lack of a tradition of critical scholarship and restrictions on academic freedom.

Although about half of the enrolments at the upper secondary and tertiary levels are in private schools, where students pay a high proportion of the tuition cost (Booth 1989a:27), the overall funding of education in Indonesia is such that the government is, as in most countries, subsidising tertiary education.[13] Meesook (1984) argues that present levels of subsidy to post-secondary education in Indonesia benefit the wealthy, so a policy of shifting part of the burden of finance to private rather than public funds would be justified on equity grounds. The poorest 40 per cent of income earners in Indonesia receive only 7 per cent of higher education subsidies, because low-income groups are grossly under-represented at this level of education. The highest 30 per cent of incomes receive 83 per cent of university subsidies.

The educational factor in employment and productivity

If educational development plays a role in economic growth, then the rapid educational advances over the past two decades in Indonesia should have contributed to its economic performance over that period. Were levels of educational investment appropriate? Was the mix between primary, secondary and tertiary education appropriate? What was the effect of broadened access to schooling on the subsequent educational composition of the labour force?

The importance of human resources in the spectacular economic development of Pacific rim countries over the past two decades has been stressed in a number of studies (Oshima 1988; Scitovsky 1986; Ogawa et al. 1993). There are a number of approaches to understanding the role of human capital in development, and to weighing the appropriate level of investment in human resources as compared with other developmental expenditures. Here we will summarise briefly the findings of studies which attempt to measure the rates of return to different levels of education.

Rates of return to different levels of education

Rates of return studies purport to show the return to society from investing in different levels of education. This has traditionally been done by finding the internal rate of return—that is the rate of discount which equates the present value of the streams of costs and benefits (the latter proxied by earnings) from a particular level of education. There are many weaknesses

in the approach,[14] but for what they are worth, the few available studies on
rates of return to education in Indonesia tend to conform to international
findings in showing highest returns at primary level and lowest for higher
education; private returns exceeding social returns (because students do not
pay the full cost of their schooling); and returns to education generally
exceeding the 10 per cent rule-of-thumb often used as the opportunity cost
of capital.

Byron and Takahashi (1989) estimated general returns to education in
Indonesia as a very high 15–17 per cent for each additional year of
schooling. Clark (1983) estimated the social return to secondary school,
based on a tracer study which enabled him to calculate returns after taking
into account the different periods of time waiting to get a job after gradu-
ation. He found that the return to senior high school (academic stream) was
32 per cent if the graduate found a job right away, and remained high (19
per cent) even if the graduate had to wait three years before finding a job.
The most recent comprehensive study was carried out by IEES (1986),
which combined detailed earnings and cost data to calculate internal rates
of return for 1982. The study found high rates to primary and junior high,
still higher rates to senior secondary (especially the academic stream) and
lower rates to university (10 per cent).

The changing educational composition of the labour force

The educational attainment of the working age population and of the labour
force in 1971 and 1990 is shown in Table 3.14. The average educational
level of the labour force had increased considerably; one estimate is 2.8
years of schooling in 1971 and 4.6 years of schooling in 1985 (Jones 1992:
Table 4). The level remains much lower than in Malaysia (over seven years),
however, or in the developed market economies (ten years or so).

For males, the educational attainment of the working-age population
and of the labour force differed very little, but for females a higher
proportion of the labour force than of the working-age population had either
no education or senior high school education or above, because of the higher
labour force participation rates among these educational groups. In any case,
for both males and females, by 1990 the proportion of the labour force with
secondary or tertiary education was much higher than in 1971, and the
proportion without schooling much lower. These changes were wrought by
better-educated cohorts replacing more poorly-educated ones: there was in
fact a sharp gradient in educational attainment, eloquently reflecting the
history of educational expansion in Indonesia; the working-age population
had only a 35 per cent chance of having completed primary school if they
were aged over 40, whereas those in their twenties had almost a 71 per cent
chance.

Working-age males (15–64) were divided into three large educational

Table 3.14 Population aged fifteen years and over, by educational attainment, 1971, 1990

Sex	Year	No schooling	Incomplete primary schooling	Completed primary schooling	Completed lower or upper secondary schooling	Academy or university education	Total
Males	1971	32.4	29.4	27.1	10.4	0.7	100
	1990	12.2	24.3	32.2	29.2	2.1	100
Females	1971	57.0	21.2	16.5	5.1	0.2	100
	1990	25.4	24.9	28.1	20.6	1.0	100
Both sexes	1971	45.2	25.1	21.6	7.7	0.4	100
	1990	18.9	24.6	30.1	24.8	1.6	100

Sources: BPS, Population Census 1971 (Series D), Table 18; 1990 (Series S.1), calculated from Tables 02, 06 and 29.

168

groups in 1990: those who had failed to complete primary school (34 per cent), those who had completed primary school (33 per cent), and those who had completed at least junior secondary school (33 per cent). Female workers were much worse off: 47 per cent had failed to complete primary school, and only 23 per cent had completed at least junior secondary school. In the case of both males and females, the urban work force was much better educated than the rural; even so, 29 per cent of working-age females in urban areas had not completed primary school.

Educational levels: industry and occupational groups

It is no surprise to discover that agriculture is the industry in which educational levels are lowest. In agriculture, only 5 per cent of workers had more than a primary school education in 1985; trade was next with 17 per cent, manufacturing with 18 per cent and construction with 19 per cent. The figure was 49 per cent in all remaining industries. More detailed information on education by industry would reveal wide differences in educational levels between employees in modern, capital-intensive sectors (such as large and medium manufacturing enterprises, supermarkets and shopping plazas) and those in traditional sectors such as cottage industries and the petty trade sector.

Accompanying the rise in educational levels of the labour force, there is normally a change in the occupational mix of available jobs, with an increasing share of the kinds of jobs usually performed by the high school and tertiary educated. For example, the share of agricultural workers declines along with the decline in agriculture's share of total employment, and the share of professional, managerial and clerical (P, M and C) occupations rises steadily. In Indonesia, the share of P, M and C occupations was still only 8 per cent in 1985, whereas in Malaysia it had reached 20 per cent, in Japan 33 per cent, and in Australia 46 per cent (Jones 1992:233).

There are two reasons why the share of P, M and C occupations rises. The first is that the structure of the economy shifts towards industries where the share of P, M and C occupations in the occupational structure is higher. The second is that, within individual industries, the share of P, M and C occupations rises over time as the industries modernise and their occupational structure becomes more complex. In the final section we will consider the issue of whether the growth of occupations considered suitable for the high school and college educated is likely to increase rapidly enough to absorb the rapidly growing number of graduates of these levels of education. Here we will simply examine the relationship between education and occupation in Indonesia in 1985.

Table 3.15 shows that workers with secondary and tertiary education are heavily concentrated in the P, M and C occupations; in turn, a high proportion of jobs in these occupations are held by those with secondary

Table 3.15 Occupation by education, 1985

Percentage distribution of occupations of employed population at each educational level

Main occupation	No schooling	Incomplete primary	Primary school	General high school		Vocational high school	Academy	University	Total
				Junior	Senior				
Professional	0.1	0.1	0.5	2.4	10.8	36.7	51.8	51.3	3.4
Managerial	0.0	0.0	0.0	0.2	1.4	0.3	3.8	5.3	0.2
Clerical	0.1	0.5	2.1	10.0	35.7	17.3	31.1	34.4	3.9
Sales	13.9	13.8	16.4	22.5	18.3	9.4	3.5	2.5	14.8
Service	3.4	3.2	4.3	5.7	4.5	3.5	1.2	0.8	3.4
Agriculture	70.8	64.3	53.0	30.8	9.8	11.2	2.3	2.0	55.1
Construction	—	—	—	—	—	—	—	—	—
Production	11.2	17.4	23.2	28.4	19.5	21.6	6.3	3.7	18.4
Total occupations	100.0	100.0	100.0	100.0	100.0	100.0	100.0	100.0	100.0
Numbers ('000)	13 562	21 489	17 233	3525	2194	3658	471	326	62 457

Percentage distribution of educational levels of employed population in each occupation group

Educational level	Professional	Managerial	Clerical	Sales	Service	Agriculture	Construction	Production	Total
No schooling	0.7	1.0	0.5	20.5	19.9	28.1	—	13.3	21.7
Incomplete primary	1.3	4.3	4.1	32.2	29.7	40.4	—	32.7	34.4
Primary school	3.7	7.3	14.7	30.7	32.2	26.6	—	34.8	27.6
Junior high school	3.7	7.1	14.0	8.4	8.4	3.1	—	8.5	5.6
Senior high school	10.7	32.6	30.9	4.2	4.2	0.6	—	3.6	3.5
Vocational high school	61.2	12.8	25.5	3.7	5.3	1.2	—	20.2	5.9
Academy	11.0	17.7	5.8	0.2	0.2	0.0	—	0.2	0.8
University	7.7	17.2	4.5	0.1	0.1	0.0	—	0.1	0.5
All education levels	100.0	100.0	100.0	100.0	100.0	100.0	—	100.0	100.0
Numbers ('000)	2151	98	2439	9180	2300	34198	—	11 445	62 457

Note: 'Primary school' includes those with incomplete junior high school; 'junior high school' includes those with incomplete senior high school; 'vocational high school' includes junior and senior vocational high school.

Source: Tabulations prepared from 1985 Intercensal Population Survey data tapes.

Table 3.16   Main occupations of better educated workers, 1985 (% distribution)

Main occupations	Junior high	Senior high or tertiary		
		Both sexes	Male	Female
Armed forces	2.7	2.1	2.8	0.1
Medical sciences	0.7	1.9	0.9	4.5
Teacher	2.2	26.2	19.5	45.6
Government office workers	1.7	6.5	7.7	3.0
Bookkeepers, treasurers, etc.	2.4	6.9	6.4	8.2
Clerical workers nec	4.2	10.9	11.0	10.4
Sales workers	19.5	9.2	8.8	10.4
Farmers	14.5	3.4	4.3	1.0
Farm workers and animal husbandry workers	13.0	3.1	3.3	2.4
Tailors and dressmakers	3.3	1.1	0.7	2.5
Carpenters, stonemasons and other building workers	4.1	1.8	2.4	0.1
Transport equipment operators	7.0	2.7	3.6	0.0
All other occupations	22.7	22.5	28.3	11.8
Total	100	100	100	100

Note: nec–Not elsewhere classified.

Source: Computer tapes of 1985 Intercensal Population Survey.

and tertiary education. Table 3.16 gives additional details about the specific occupations that account for most employment of the better educated. Whereas those with junior high school are widely distributed across occupational categories, at the senior high school level and above, employment in agricultural activities falls off dramatically, and production and transportation occupations also decline greatly in importance. Teaching is an extremely important occupation for the senior high school and college educated; among females with these levels of education, it provides almost half of all jobs.

In recent years, the growth of employment in P, M and C occupations in Indonesia appears to have been fast enough to maintain the proportions of the senior high school and college educated who find work in these occupations. In the final section, we will consider whether this favourable situation can be expected to continue in future.

Underutilisation of the better educated

Unemployment in Indonesia continues to be very much a phenomenon of the young, the better educated, and especially those who are both young and better educated. Table 3.17, showing the situation in 1990, portrays this pattern. Given the middle-class job search underpinnings of these unemployment rates, referred to earlier, the high rates need cause much concern

Table 3.17   Unemployment rates by age and education, urban Indonesia, 1990
(%)

Age group	Males	Females
15–19	18.7	15.1
20–24	16.1	17.5
25–29	5.6	7.8
30–44	1.3	1.6
45–64	1.0	0.8
All ages	5.6	7.6
Educational group		
None or incomplete primary	2.9	2.4
Completed primary	3.6	5.1
Lower secondary	6.1	9.4
Upper secondary	9.2	14.7
Tertiary	5.6	13.3
All educational levels	5.6	7.6

Source: BPS, Population Census 1990 (Series S.1), Tables 25 and 29.

only if there was evidence that they were starting to persist into older ages, or last for longer periods than before among the young. Unfortunately, although there is no evidence of high unemployment rates persisting beyond ages 20–24, there is some evidence of a lengthening of periods of unemployment among the young and better educated (see above).

Future prospects

Demographic dynamics

The 1980s was the last decade in which the numbers entering the labour force were largely unaffected by the fertility decline which began in the early 1970s. By the mid-1990s the youngest segment of the working-age population will have almost ceased to grow at all (Table 3.18), and the numbers in the labour force age groups as a whole will grow by 'only' 19 per cent during the 1990s, compared with 33 per cent during the 1980s. The 1990s will remain a problem period for employment. The problem of finding enough jobs for the growing labour force will remain critical, but as the 1990s progress, attention will shift more to the issues of 'age dualism' in the labour force (a rapidly growing older and poorly-educated segment and a slowly growing and well-educated younger segment) and the problem of altering the structure of employment quickly enough to provide 'acceptable' jobs for the rapidly growing number of educated young labour force entrants. (The paradox here is that, although the number of youthful

172

labour-force entrants will cease to grow, the number of well-educated youthful entrants will be increasing rapidly due to the sharp rise in schooling levels among this cohort.) By the first decade of the next century, growth of the working-age population will have ceased to be a major problem in itself.

Growth rates of the labour force, however, could continue to be pushed up by rising labour force participation rates among women. It is difficult to prognosticate on likely trends. Factors making for a continued rise in these participation rates include a continued shift in the balance of employment opportunities towards occupations in which females are strongly represented, and changing perceptions of female roles in a rapidly modernising society. Rising levels of education may also make for rising participation rates, as the proportion of well-educated women, for whom the opportunity costs of not working are high, rises. But the net outcome of rising education levels is indeterminate, because in absolute terms, the largest increase will be in the junior high school educated, the group which currently has the lowest participation rates of all women. The key will probably be changing perceptions about female roles, and this is difficult to forecast.

The projected ageing of the working-age population is shown in Table 3.18. The share of those aged 15–29 will decline steadily, whereas the share of those of mature age will continue to rise. These growth differences may be even more pronounced with respect to those actually in the labour force, because lengthening periods of education are certain to delay the entry of many young people into the labour force. This has implications for labour mobility; older workers are less geographically and occupationally mobile, and this is particularly the case for poorly-educated older workers. Age dualism in the labour force is likely to be particularly pronounced in respect of mobility, because it is mainly the young, much better educated workers

Table 3.18   Indonesia: index of growth of labour force age groups, 1990–2010
(1990=100)

	1990	1995	2000	2005	2010
All ages 15–64	100	110	119	127	134
15–19	100	102	104	106	111
20–24	100	114	116	118	121
25–29	100	117	133	136	139
30–34	100	111	130	149	153
35–44	100	124	146	167	194
45–64	100	110	126	148	174
Ratio, population aged 30–64/15–29	1.062	1.111	1.221	1.384	1.528

Source: Calculated from unpublished projections by age and sex supplied by the United Nations. The summary projections are published in United Nations (1991).

who will be competing for the kinds of jobs being created by economic and technological change.

Structural change

Notwithstanding the difficulties in comparing the allocation of employment across industries in different censuses and surveys, and the resultant deviations from the downward trend in agriculture's share in particular surveys, in general the downward trend over time is so clear as to be irrefutable. This trend will no doubt continue—but how rapidly? A wide range of possibilities emerge from international comparisons (Table 3.19). The shift out of agriculture in Indonesia during the New Order period (–1.4 per cent per annum over the 1971–85 period) has been much more rapid than in India or the Philippines but much less rapid than in Peninsular Malaysia, Taiwan or the Republic of Korea. Continuation of the Indonesian rate of decline to the year 2000 would see Indonesia with well under half (45 per cent) of its employment in agriculture by that year. But the Philippines' rate of decline would leave the percentage above 50 per cent, whereas Malaysian rates of decline would lower it to 36 per cent and Korean rates even lower. What is clear is that agriculture will continue to play a very major role in the employment structure, but never again will it be as dominant as it was early in the New Order period.

In examining which sectors will be counterbalancing the declining share of agriculture, attention always focuses on manufacturing, even though it is less prominent in the employment structure than are trade and services. The emphasis on manufacturing is probably not misplaced, however, because apart from the possibility that its share will rise quite rapidly, the pivotal role of manufacturing in raising production and providing 'spin off' employment in other sectors is well-known.

Manufacturing still employs a smaller share of the labour force in Indonesia than in its ASEAN neighbours, though its share is similar to that in India. A 6.7 per cent growth rate of employment is projected for this sector during *Repelita V*. This may be rather optimistic, given the still high potential for displacement by large, modern factories of large numbers of workers from labour-intensive areas of manufacturing, although it is consistent with the rate of manufacturing employment growth achieved in the second half of the 1980s. But even if this target were achieved, manufacturing would absorb only 19 per cent of the total labour force growth during this period, because of its still small base.

The prospects for employment in other sectors are clouded by the 'umbrella' nature of the trade, transportation and services sectors, covering informal sector activities of many kinds as well as modern supermarkets and shopping centres, air transport and government services, to name a few. The informal sector will continue to play a role as 'employer of last resort',

Table 3.19   Shift in employment share by major industry sectors, selected Asian countries (%)[a]

	Country/indicator					
	Indonesia			Philippines		
Broad industry group[b]	1971	1985	1971–85[d]	1970	1980	1970–80[d]
A	67.5	55.4	–1.4	55.1	52.7	–0.4
M	11.0	15.9	2.6	20.8	20.4	–0.2
S	21.5	28.7	2.1	24.1	26.9	0.3
Total	100.0	100.0		100.0	100.0	
n(m)	41.3	62.5		11.8	14.2	

	India			Republic of Korea		
	1961	1981	1961–81[d]	1960	1980	1960–80[d]
A	76.6	69.4	–0.5	67.2	26.0	–4.7
M	12.7	15.7	1.1	10.9	34.4	5.7
S	10.7	15.0	1.7	21.9	39.6	3.0
Total	100.0	100.0		100.0	100.0	
n(m)	188.2	222.6		7.0	15.0	

	Peninsula Malaysia			Taiwan		
	1971	1985	1971–85[d]	1970	1980	1970-80[d]
A	61.8	27.3	–2.9	60.5	25.2	–3.1
M	13.8	29.4	2.7	12.0	37.1	4.0
S	24.4	43.3	2.0	27.5	37.7	1.1
Total	100.0	100.0		100.0	100.0	
n(m)	2.1	4.6		6.1	9.0	

Notes: [a] Shift denotes rate of change in percentage points in employment share per annum since the previous period. Persons with activities not adequately defined have been allocated to industry groups pro-rata.
[b] A denotes agriculture, hunting, forestry, fishing, mining and quarrying.
M denotes manufacturing, electricity, gas, water, construction, transport, storage and communication.
S denotes trade, restaurants, hotels, financing, insurance, real estate, business services, community, social and personal services.
[c] Unadjusted data.
[d] Shift per annum.

Sources: Indonesia: BPS, Population Census 1971 (Series C); Intercensal Population Survey 1985 (Series 5). Peninsular Malaysia: 1957 and 1970 Population Censuses and 1985 Labour Force Survey. Korea: 1960—Population and Housing Census of Korea, Vol. 2, Table 14, p.168; 1971 and 1985—United Nations, *Statistical Yearbook for Asia and the Pacific*, 1979 and 1988. Taiwan: 1975 and 1985, Directorate-General of Budget, Accounting and Statistics, Executive Yuan, Republic of China, *Statistical Yearbook of the Republic of China*. Philippines: 1970, 1975 and 1980 Population Censuses. India: 1961, 1971 and 1981 Censuses of India, Subsidiary Table B-1.6(i): 3; Table B-1, Part A: 16; and Table B.3: 238, in that order.

so it will continue to grow as a residual if other kinds of employment do not increase rapidly enough. International experience would suggest that S sector employment as a whole will continue to increase its share, but that how quickly employment in modern and traditional activities within the sector will increase will depend on the pace and pattern of economic growth in relation to the continuing, though slowing, growth of the labour force.

The occupational structure in Indonesia is sure to change considerably, for reasons mentioned above. The rise in the share of P, M and C occupations within individual industries is still in its early stages, and can proceed much further (see the comparison between Indonesia, Malaysia and Australia in Table 3.12). It turns out that between 1971 and 1985, the industry shift effect accounted for 79 per cent of the rise in the share of P, M and C occupations in Indonesia, and the changing occupational composition of industries for just over one-fifth (Jones 1992). But the compositional effect within industries could well become more important in future.

Geographical shifts

Java's share of Indonesian employment is certain to continue falling; lower fertility than elsewhere is now being translated into a levelling-out in the growth of labour-force entrants, resulting in slower labour-force growth than elsewhere. On top of this is a continued net outmigration from Java, fuelled more by spontaneous movement than by organised movement under the transmigration program. It is difficult to forecast precisely where most of these migrants will go: Lampung has continued to attract large numbers despite being closed to transmigration, and this suggests the importance of its large Javanese population, proximity and cheap transport. If such factors continue to be important, it is southern Sumatra (though not Lampung, whose growth slowed markedly in the 1980s) rather than Irian Jaya or Central Sulawesi that is likely to attract most migrants. Much will also depend on patterns of industrial development, because future migration is unlikely to be as focused on agricultural settlement as in the past.

The expected decline in Java's share of employment is perhaps less worthy of attention than are likely trends in employment within Java, and the regional distribution of employment of the better educated. On the former, there has been a significant westward shift in the balance of employment in Java, with West Java–Jakarta's employment growing by 110 per cent between 1971 and 1990, compared with 57 per cent in the rest of Java. Present patterns of development can be expected to perpetuate this westward drift, although diseconomies of agglomeration in the Jabotabek region could foster the stronger growth of the counter-magnet of Surabaya in future.

As far as employment of the better educated is concerned, there has been a drift of such people to Java for a long time, thus offsetting the higher educational levels enjoyed by many outer island provinces. Whether this drift will continue will be greatly influenced by development policy and its effect on industrial location and infrastructure development.

Education–occupation 'mismatch'?

Will the tendency for the more rapid growth of employment in occupations in which the better educated have traditionally worked be sufficient to absorb the rapidly-growing number of the better educated joining the work force? Almost certainly not. The educational developments of the 1970s and 1980s, together with those expected in the Fifth Five-Year Development Plan period and beyond, will result in very sharp increases in the well-educated groups within the labour force (Keyfitz 1989; Jones 1992). In one set of projections, the rate of growth of the number of 'potential workers' (aged 20–64) with senior high school education will be 7.5 per cent per annum over the 1985–95 period and 6.5 per cent per annum over the 1995–2000 period. The rate of increase of the tertiary educated would be even faster— 13.6 per cent and 10.5 per cent, respectively (Jones 1992: Table 8.7).

The increased supply of better-educated workers has already led to a narrowing of earnings differentials by educational level (Keyfitz 1989:50–2), and further narrowing can be expected.[15] This will no doubt both deter some young people from continuing their education at the tertiary level and, on the demand side, encourage structural changes in favour of sectors which utilise educated manpower. Nevertheless, in the short to medium term, the rapid growth in the number of better educated is certain to outstrip the growth of professional, managerial and clerical jobs, many of which are in the now slowly growing public sector. Drastic changes in expectations will therefore be required as the 'scarcity rent' enjoyed until recently by the better educated disappears, and many are forced to adjust to narrowed earnings differentials or to take jobs previously considered inappropriate for the better educated.

Notes

1 See IPPA (1971) for comments on legal issues.
2 The percentages here are proportions of women aged fifteen to 49, weighted by their fecundity, as estimated by the theoretical maximum human fertility found among the Hutterites of North America.
3 There are major discrepancies between the Series C report on the 1971 census (based on a 10 per cent subsample of the census returns giving detailed characteristics of the population) and the Series D figures, based on the full 3.8 per cent sample of the total population. The Series C report gives an unemployment rate for males and females, respectively, of 2.4 and 1.5 per cent, whereas the Series D report gives figures of 7.5 and 13.0 per cent. The

main reason for the discrepancy was the change in imputation rules after the Series C figures were published. Normally the full sample data (Series D) would be preferred, but there is ample evidence that Series C is preferable for comparison with other data sources, and that Series D exaggerates the level of unemployment. For a fuller discussion, see Hugo et al. (1987:367–72).

4   Calculated from data in Muliakusuma and Trisilo (1988).

5   Other important studies on the informal sector in Indonesia include Hidayat (1978), Wirosardjono (1985), Widarti (1984) and Manning, Tadjuddin and Tukiran (1984).

6   The following paragraphs are drawn from Jones and Manning (1992).

7   These growth rates are based on the Series C (preliminary) figures of employment in 1971, as these are more appropriate than the Series D figures for measuring employment change.

8   The declines were concentrated particularly in the eastern half of East Java, the northern coastal strip of Central and West Java and much of the southern area between Yogyakarta and Tasikmalaya.

9   In 1990, over half of those working in agriculture in Indonesia worked less than 35 hours a week and roughly one-third less than 25 hours.

10   Other sources of data give conflicting estimates for the growth of government employment over the 1980s. See Booth (1992:292–5).

11   Changing urban definitions influenced these changes. The more realistic definitions employed for the 1980 census and subsequent enumerations, leading as they did to somewhat higher recorded urbanisation than the 1971 definitions would have, overstated the rise in percentage urban since 1971 (Hugo et al. 1987:86–8).

12   'The quality of the typical SMA graduate continues to decline to a level that is probably equivalent to that of the SMP before the beginning of rapid expansion of secondary education' (IEES 1986:77).

13   It has been argued that tuition-free higher education, which on the surface appears egalitarian, tends to favour children from rich rather than poor families, even after allowing for the fact that richer families pay more in taxes to support public universities (Hansen and Weisbrod 1969; Blaug 1982).

14   Most recent studies use a 'Mincer function' which does not incorporate careful cost analysis, including on the cost side only private earnings foregone. Earnings differentials are used as a proxy for increased productivity resulting from more education. Adjustments are sometimes made for factors such as productivity growth over time, the probability of the person being employed at a given age, and the need to attribute part of the earnings differential not to the 'pure' effect of education but to factors such as ability, social class background and motivation that are correlated with proceeding further in school. The latter class of adjustments are normally quite arbitrary (Gannicott 1990:46–9; Blinder 1976; Jones 1988:18–21; Psacharopoulos 1981; Blaug 1976).

15   It should be noted that this temporal lowering of the earnings premium on senior high and tertiary education throws into serious doubt the use of rates of return studies to guide future educational investment unless suitable adjustment is made in these studies for sharply altered earnings prospects.

4

Resource utilisation and the environment

Joan Hardjono

By comparison with most of its neighbours, Indonesia is a resource-rich country. Yet while its islands have been endowed with fertile soils, forests of tropical hardwoods, and minerals that include oil and natural gas, these resources are by no means uniformly distributed throughout the archipelago. Soils that favour intensive agriculture are concentrated very largely in Java and Bali, whereas oil and most minerals are located in the other islands, as are the country's forest resources. At the same time there are parts of the archipelago, like the islands of Nusa Tenggara, that lack not only good soils but also forests and mineral wealth. These spatial disparities in the pattern of resource location, reflected as they are in the distribution of population, constitute a factor that inevitably influences the nature of all policies relating to economic development in Indonesia.

More important today than the question of resource distribution is that of utilisation. The present state of the environment throughout much of Indonesia raises questions that government and community alike have only recently begun to be aware of, though their full dimensions and significance for national development in the years ahead still remain obscure for most people. Stated very briefly, they relate to the changes that are taking place in the condition and extent of the country's natural resources. In the case of land and water resources these changes involve degradation, which has been defined as the process of ecological adjustment from an originally stable level to a lower and often less-stable level of productivity (Shaxson, 1991:3). In the case of non-renewable assets like minerals, changes have tended to imply depletion. So increasingly evident are the signs of deterioration in the country's resource base that political confidence in the

179

availability of abundant natural assets as the foundation for sustainable economic growth in coming years may well be misplaced.

With implementation of the Fifth Five-Year Development Plan (1989–94) now approaching completion, it is an appropriate time to look at the way in which Indonesia has used its natural resources since the mid-1960s. This chapter considers the ecological and environmental consequences of population growth and economic development, and examines the major implications of the past approach to resource utilisation for the sustainability of development in future years.

The islands that make up Indonesia cover an area of 1 919 443 sq. km or just on 192 million hectares, though the total area of the country is 7.7 million sq. km if seas are included. Some 70 million hectares of land are used for agricultural purposes and settlements, while a total area of 113.4 million hectares is classed as forest land (see Table 4.1). Of this, almost 27 per cent consists of protection forest while production forest amounts to 57 per cent; national parks and nature reserves account for just over 16 per cent, that is, 18.7 million hectares, which represents almost 10 per cent of Indonesia's total land area.

Three interrelated factors have bearing on the problem of resource degradation and depletion, namely, natural forces, population growth and the development process itself. The role of the first factor can be seen in the results of the weathering process, which over the centuries has worn down the mountain chains in the interior of the larger islands and created broad coastal plains in many regions, as the gradual linking of Mt Muria to the mainland of Java illustrates. Now located on the coast of Central Java, this mountain, whose northern slopes are the site suggested for Indonesia's first nuclear power station, was an island separated from the town of Demak by a navigable strait when Dutch traders first reached Java in the seventeenth century. The same process of water-induced erosion and sedimentation has led to a gradual narrowing of the Strait of Malacca, which has become too shallow to permit safe passage for the larger vessels that once used it, and to the creation of broad stretches of swampland in Kalimantan. Yet while the high rainfall that characterises most parts of Indonesia has been a major factor, ENSO-related droughts have also played a role in shaping the natural environment of the islands of the archipelago, especially in the Nusa Tenggara region (Brookfield 1991).

The consequences of morphological conditions that favour erosion have been accelerated in recent years by human activities. The increase in population from 91 million in 1961 to almost 180 million in 1990 has created a need for more food, which has necessitated expansion in agriculture and has raised the demand for clothing, housing and fuel. It is the comparatively rapid growth in human activities in recent times that very

180

largely explains the emergence of many of the environmental problems that beset Indonesia today.

Nevertheless, not all man-induced changes are a direct consequence of the demands created by rapid population growth. The nature of the development process itself has also had implications for the environment. The change of government that occurred in Indonesia in the mid-1960s led to the adoption of development policies that have of necessity focused more on the economy than on the nation building that characterised the period between 1945 and 1965. While the achievement of economic stability and growth as major elements in overall national development has enabled basic needs to be met, the orientation of development policies, particularly in certain sectors, has also exerted considerable influence on the direction of resource exploitation both in Java and in the other islands of Indonesia.

As a consequence of the interaction of these factors, a steady deterioration is occurring in land resources in most parts of Indonesia. The Department of Forestry, which, besides dealing with forestry matters, is also responsible for soil conservation and rehabilitation on slopes over 8 per cent, defines degraded land (*tanah kritis*) as land that is undergoing erosion,

Table 4.1   Indonesia: land utilisation, 1989 (million hectares)

Type of land use	Java	Sum-atra	Kali-mantan	Sulawesi	Nusa Teng-gara[a]	Irian Jaya/Maluku[b]	Total
Home-lots	1.65	1.74	0.73	0.45	0.19	0.29	5.05
Rice-land[c]	3.45	2.26	1.28	0.83	0.41	0.01	8.24
Dry fields	3.17	4.15	2.26	1.82	0.94	0.95	13.29
Grassland	0.05	0.55	0.34	0.59	0.87	0.48	2.88
Fish-ponds	0.14	0.11	0.04	0.11	0.01	0.01	0.42
Wooded land[d]	0.31	4.14	3.14	1.41	0.86	10.46	20.32
Estates	0.67	5.16	1.90	1.34	0.35	0.86	10.28
Agric. land temporarily uncultivated	0.09	3.39	2.87	1.23	0.75	1.41	9.74
Forest land[e]	3.01	25.18	36.67	11.29	3.37	33.91	113.43
Other land[f]	0.68	0.68	4.71	−0.15	1.10	1.27	8.29
Total area	13.22	47.36	53.94	18.92	8.85	49.65	191.94

Notes: [a] Nusa Tenggara refers to Bali, West and East Nusa Tenggara and East Timor; East Timor is included only in figures for total area and forest land.
 [b] Figures for Irian Jaya and Maluku refer to 1982–83.
 [c] 'Rice-land' includes irrigated, rain-fed and swampland used for rice.
 [d] 'Wooded land' refers to land covered in wood-producing trees, shrubs and bamboo, planted or otherwise, outside the authority of the Department of Forestry.
 [e] 'Forest land' is land classified in 1984 as being under the authority of the Department of Forestry.
 [f] The residual 'other land' is the difference between the total area of the region and the sum of all other land. It includes land occupied by inland water bodies, reservoirs, roads, cemeteries, sports fields, airports and the like. It also reflects discrepancies between figures from different agencies for forest land.

Source: BPS (1990c).

land whose productive capacity has been reduced by erosion, and land whose hydrological performance is disturbed. Table 4.2 shows the distribution of the 12.9 million hectares of land that was classed as degraded by the Forestry Department in 1989. Within the various islands some provinces are in a worse condition than others. Some 14 per cent of all land in North Sumatra and 26 per cent in Bengkulu is degraded, while the figures for North Sulawesi and Southeast Sulawesi are 21 and 20 per cent respectively (BPS 1990c:219). In East Nusa Tenggara, 59 per cent of forest land and 30 per cent of land outside official forest areas is in a similar condition. Yet population density at 68 persons to the sq. km in this province in 1990 is lower than the figure of 93 for the whole country, bearing out Soemarwoto's point (1991:213) that land deterioration is not necessarily related to population density.

Java

The environmental problems evident in Java today stem largely from the nature of the agricultural systems that have been adopted in upland areas, the modifications that are being made to traditional land-use patterns on the lowlands, and the rapid expansion that is occurring in various urban-sector activities. In different ways these problems are a reflection of the interaction between demographic factors and the development process, though the part played by natural forces cannot be overlooked, as the 1982 eruptions of Mt Galunggung in West Java demonstrated. In that year an estimated 6.9 million

Table 4.2   Indonesia: degraded lands, 1989

Region	Population density per sq. km (1990)	Forest land[a]		Remaining + land[b]	
		Area (million ha)	% degraded[c]	Area (million ha)	% degraded[d]
Sumatra	77	25.18	5.6	22.18	10.4
Java	813	3.01	2.9	10.21	11.6
Nusa Tenggara[d]	115	3.37	30.7	5.48	22.4
Kalimantan	17	36.67	4.9	17.27	6.8
Sulawesi	66	11.29	9.7	7.63	12.7
Maluku	25	5.10	6.0	2.35	14.1
Irian Jaya	4	28.81	na	13.39	na
Indonesia	93	113.43	—	78.51	—

Notes: [a] 'Forest land' is land classified in 1984 as being under the authority of the Department of Forestry.
   [b] 'Remaining land' is the difference between the total area of the region and the area under the authority of the Department of Forestry.
   [c] For definition of 'degraded', see text.
   [d] Nusa Tenggara refers to Bali, West and East Nusa Tenggara and East Timor.

Source: BPS (1990c, 1990d).

tons of volcanic ash and sand were ejected, much of it ultimately passing into the Citanduy and other river systems of Tasikmalaya and Ciamis Districts.

The uplands

With more than a quarter of the island consisting of slopes over 30 per cent and an average annual rainfall of 2650 mm, Java has an extremely high rate of natural erosion (Pearce et al. 1990:73). The suspended sediment yields of rivers in Java are among the highest in the world, as Douglas and Spencer (1985:60–3) have shown in their discussion of weathering processes in tropical environments. Yet while a high rate of erosion has long been a characteristic of the uplands of Java, acceleration in environmental deterioration in recent decades can be traced largely to the shortage of land in relation to the needs of a constantly growing population (Palte 1989; Nibbering 1988, 1991). The response to this shortage has been agricultural extensification, a process that has led to the clearance of forests on higher land and the establishment of land-use and land-management systems that are often poorly suited to the physical conditions that prevail. Some idea of the expansion that has occurred can be obtained from the fact that between 1980 and 1989 the area under dry-field cultivation of non-rice crops in Java rose from 2.92 to 3.17 million hectares, an increase of almost 1 per cent per year.

While lower mountain slopes can be cultivated without any threat to the long-term sustainability of production if suitable cropping patterns and cultivation techniques are adopted, the steady movement of the agricultural frontier up the inherently unstable slopes of upper watersheds is creating environmental problems with far-reaching effects. In these areas, the stability that once existed under natural forests has been disrupted by the introduction of forms of land use that leave soil exposed to the heavy rains of the wet season. Because of heavy surface run-off the rate of water infiltration declines, which means that even in areas of very high rainfall the amount of moisture available within the soil for plant growth is often inadequate. At the same time, there is a reduction in the plant nutrients contained in the soil. As erosion progresses, land-use patterns become characterised by a much lower level of productivity.

Population pressure as such is not the only factor contributing to this upward movement of the agricultural frontier. As a consequence of national policies directed towards self-sufficiency in rice production, the cultivation of secondary food crops or *palawija* (a term that takes in dry rice, maize, sweet potatoes, soybeans, peanuts and mung beans) has since the late 1960s been increasingly transferred to non-irrigable land at higher altitudes. In foothill areas this land was already being used for food crops, usually in conjunction with smallholder commercial crops like tobacco, but in many parts of upland Java the shift has meant the making of completely new fields. The growth that has taken place in the production of *palawija* crops since 1970, limited as it has been by comparison with the increase in rice production, is primarily a reflection of expansion in planted area rather than in output per unit of land. Various government programs have been formulated with the stated aim of improving yields of secondary food crops. But by comparison with irrigated rice, these crops have received very little attention, even though they have always played a role in food-consumption patterns in most regions and the government itself has launched a number of campaigns urging the nation to diversify eating habits away from rice. As Palte (1989:206, 208) has noted, the rural credit programs introduced by the government since the early 1970s have on the whole bypassed the uplands, while the extension services provided during the same period have not been designed to cater for the wide variety of crops and cropping patterns that are characteristic of upland agriculture.

The expansion in arable farming on upper mountain slopes, however, is not explained exclusively by the need for land for subsistence food crops, as the rapid growth that has occurred in commercial vegetable production in Java since 1970 demonstrates. Considerable stretches of land where soils are of volcanic origin are now planted with vegetables like cabbages and potatoes. This form of land use is particularly evident in districts within trucking distance of major towns and cities, where the demand for these products has been encouraged by the government campaign during the early 1970s to improve levels of nutrition, and has been further stimulated by improved urban incomes. Vegetable production has continued to expand because it is an extremely profitable form of land use, though there is clear evidence that the techniques developed by cultivators are responsible for soil deterioration and erosion in many places (Hardjono 1991:145). Since freshly cleared land is initially very fertile due to the reserves of organic material within the soil, vegetable growers tend to make new fields rather than to improve their cultivation techniques. At the same time, since most upland vegetable crops require good drainage, farmers are generally unwilling to terrace their fields. Yet local government authorities are reluctant to discourage this form of land use, as it provides considerable employment, with labour inputs far higher than for irrigated rice. This highlights the land-use dilemma now faced in much of Java, where the lack of alternative employment makes it difficult to prevent arable farming in upper watersheds.

In those parts of Java where plantation agriculture involving perennials like tea and rubber was once the dominant form of land use, the expansion of food-crop cultivation on steep slopes has to a certain extent been facilitated by the fact that the question of neglected estates has not been handled satisfactorily. In the years immediately after the nationalisation of

Dutch property in 1957, the government converted the larger and more productive foreign estates into state plantation companies (PTP), but nothing was done at the time about the smaller estates. Much of this land was subsequently occupied by squatters, who used it for the cultivation of annuals. The post-1965 regime adopted a policy of selling the usage rights (*hak guna usaha*, or HGU) for these smaller estates to private companies, the assumption being that the buyers would rehabilitate and operate them as the previous owners had. Profits from the cultivation of tree crops, however, have not been commensurate with the financial investment required for replanting, especially since the government did not extend any credit for estate rehabilitation to the private sector until well into the 1980s. Despite clauses in the HGU agreements concerning appropriate land use, many of the purchasers have found it more profitable to rent the land back to the local food-crop cultivators who were already utilising it. Thus in these areas the change in land use has occurred in two stages, with the initial move from primary forest to the cultivation of perennials having relatively little adverse environmental impact by comparison with the more recent shift from perennials to annuals.

Attempts made since the early 1980s to have former estate land returned to perennials have given rise to some major confrontations between cultivators and government authorities. This relatively recent government interest in estate production has been closely related to policies designed to increase the export of commodities other than oil and natural gas so as to compensate for the decline in oil revenue since 1983. Reflecting as it does a tendency for policy-makers to look back to the pre-independence period, when Indonesia's comparative advantage in the production of tropical crops made the country a major exporter of sugar, tea, rubber, tobacco and other commodities, efforts to raise output of agricultural export products today face two major constraints. The first is the constantly growing domestic demand for these same products, while the second is the conflict of interests now occurring throughout Java with increasing frequency as different parties put forward claims to use the land on which these crops are cultivated for other purposes.

Apart from encouraging the rehabilitation of both state and private estates, the promotion of export crops has also exerted influence on the land-use patterns of small farmers in upland Java. When prices for certain commodities have risen, farmers have responded by expanding the area under those crops, as has happened in the case of tea. Having increased their hectarage, smallholders have then reacted to falling prices by underplanting tea bushes with food crops, a fact that in itself reduces the productivity of tea holdings (Etherington 1974). In the case of annuals the response is somewhat different. The area under cassava, for example, expands and contracts in accordance with prevailing policies concerning the export of dried cassava chips (*gaplek*), which, while forming a foodstuff in some parts of Java, are exported to Europe in pellet form as animal feed (Hardjono and Maspiyati 1990). From the environmental point of view there are serious dangers in this response pattern, for, when prices fall or government policies change, upland fields where extensification has occurred are frequently left unplanted and exposed to erosion.

The upper slopes of Java are also suffering from the effects of the constant removal of trees for timber and fuel purposes. The progress that has taken place since 1970 in the improvement of infrastructure, while enabling rural producers to market their goods, has had a negative environmental impact in that the extension of surfaced roads has provided illegal timber-cutters with access routes to forested uplands. Only a small proportion of the wood is used by local people for their own domestic needs. The greater part of tree-felling is commercially oriented in that those involved often obtain their whole livelihood from the sale of timber and firewood or the production of charcoal, while others in need of supplementary or seasonal income likewise turn to this occupation since the products are always marketable. There is an ever-rising demand for timber for house construction and furniture-making in both rural and urban areas. At the same time, many rural and urban households, unable to afford the cost of kerosene for domestic purposes, cook on stoves that burn wood, while large numbers of small industrial undertakings that range from urban bakeries to lime-firing and the making of bricks and tiles are dependent on wood-burning production processes. Dick (1980) has argued that a point should be reached at which it will become profitable for farmers to cultivate fast-growing trees for fuel purposes, but as yet there is very little evidence of this happening on a scale large enough to have a meaningful effect on erosion rates. Meanwhile, attempts to encourage small industry to use fuel sources other than wood have not been successful because of relative costs, a fact of some significance in the current drive to expand small-scale industry in the interests of generating non-farm employment in rural areas.

Although some of the trees that are cut down come from privately-owned land, the greater part of the wood used for timber and fuel purposes originates from government land (*tanah negara*), that is, land not privately owned and land classed as state forests. While these forests officially cover 3.013 million hectares of land, representing some 22 per cent of the whole of Java, satellite imagery shows the area under permanent tree cover to be closer to 7 per cent (Potter 1991a). The figure of 1.28 million hectares, calculated by the Directorate-General of Reforestation and Land Rehabilitation for degraded land in Java in 1989 (BPS 1990c: 219), represents an increase of more than 50 per cent on the 1987 figure of 0.84 million hectares from the same agency.

While the 1960 Basic Agrarian Act refers to conservation of the land itself as obligatory and states that, where land is neglected, ownership rights can be withdrawn by the state, there is no specific legislation that can control land use on private property. Thus farmers cannot be prevented from felling trees or cultivating annuals on steep slopes if the land is theirs. Where state forests are involved, there are legal sanctions against timber-cutters. Yet while there have been recent instances of such persons being prosecuted (*Pikiran Rakyat*, 10 March 1991), the consistent enforcement of legislation is virtually impossible. Furthermore, as Machfud (1989) has pointed out, the social and political costs of punitive action against illegal occupants of forest land are high. Monitoring is made particularly difficult by the tendency, which goes back to the rigidly enforced controls of colonial days, for rural people to regard prohibitions on entry as applicable only to areas actually planted by the state forestry agency, such as the teak forests of Central and East Java. Natural forests are seen as an open-access resource to which all should have entry.

In an attempt to deal with erosion in upland areas, the Department of Forestry has carried out programs of reforestation (*reboisasi*) in official forest zones and of regreening (*penghijauan*) on privately-owned land. Yet despite special funds made available since 1976 through the *Inpres Penghijauan* (Presidential Instruction on Regreening) program, success has been limited, the main problem being the difficulty of persuading farmers to adopt a long-term view of land use and of preventing further incursions into forests. To avoid disputes with cultivators, the Forestry Department has for some years permitted the temporary cultivation of annuals between rows of small, newly-planted trees in a system of intercropping (*tumpangsari*). But the system has not worked well because of the reluctance of farmers to relinquish the land as trees grow bigger and require more space. Even more to the point, it has encouraged cultivators from outside the immediate area to clear more land without permission in the expectation that it too would be reforested. The occurrence of a number of major natural disasters in the form of flash floods, directly traceable to the abuse of the *tumpangsari* system, has led to its being discontinued in many watersheds in Java (Hardjono 1991:148–9). In its place the Department has introduced what it terms a 'social forestry' program, the aim of which is to involve local residents in the maintenance of reforested areas by allowing them to intercrop fruit and fodder trees but not vegetables and other annuals with timber species. With only 3040 hectares replanted in this way by 1988, however, progress is very slow.

Other approaches have been adopted by the government on a much larger scale to deal with land degradation in the uplands of Java. Since the 1970s a number of watershed management projects have been undertaken with foreign assistance in an attempt to show farmers how to adopt better agricultural systems in the double interests of soil conservation and higher household incomes. The major projects have been the FAO/UNDP supported Upper Solo Watershed Management and Upland Development Project in Central Java (McComb 1974), the Citanduy River Basin Development Project funded by USAID in West Java (Huszar and Cochrane 1990; Huszar 1991) and the Dutch-assisted Kali Konto Watershed Management Project in East Java (Murdiono and Beerens 1991). They have involved among other things the introduction of such techniques as bench terracing and crop rotation as well as the use of green manure and the inclusion of livestock in land-use systems. The Kali Konto and the Upper Solo projects have proved relatively successful; in the former case the introduction of perennial crops helped household incomes to rise significantly while in the latter the planned resettlement of large numbers of farm families under the transmigration program enabled conservation measures to operate effectively. The Citanduy project, which was commenced in 1982 as a follow-up to the earlier Citanduy I flood control and irrigation project, has been only a 'qualified success' (Huszar and Cochrane 1990:124); while soil loss was reduced in some places, a serious problem still remains and there is no conclusive evidence of overall improvements in levels of farm income. On the whole, these projects have demonstrated that solutions to soil conservation which are technically viable in temperate, low-rainfall climates are less effective in Java's uplands. Even bench terracing does not make as much difference to the rate of soil loss as is normally assumed, nor do check dams and other engineering works have as much effect as might be anticipated (Murdiono and Beerens 1991).

Attempts to improve the productivity of farming systems face a constraint in the fact that there is far greater ecological diversity in these areas than is found on the lowlands, even though most uplands share a common problem in that they have a relatively poor physical base. The greater part of upland Java has sedimentary soils whose natural fertility is low and which should not be used for foodcrops; volcanic soils of higher fertility occur only in certain areas. Efforts to promote better forms of land use and management must therefore be tailored to site-specific needs. As soil loss and impoverishment continue, the agricultural base is being irretrievably weakened. Yet, while farmers may be conscious of the fact that farm output is declining, their limited employment options encourage them to remain on the land and to encroach even further upon forests wherever possible.

Apart from technical aspects, the very different socio-economic conditions of Java make approaches that are effective elsewhere less successful in Java. In subsidised projects designed to alter well-established systems of land use, returns have to be high enough to persuade cultivators to maintain the recommended cropping patterns and inputs when financial assistance ceases. Otherwise they tend to plant whatever crop offers the highest returns, switching from one to another commodity as relative prices change, and, although convinced of the benefits of animal husbandry, they tend to sell their livestock when in financial difficulty.

The government has also adopted various legislative approaches in its efforts to restrict cultivation of land considered to be in a critical condition or at least potentially susceptible to erosion. Government Regulation No. 33 of 1970, for example, states that land above 500 metres is to be under protective forest (Palte 1989:113). This ill-considered and inappropriate regulation was modified in 1980 by Decision No. 837 of the Minister for Agriculture, the aim of which was to limit further upward expansion of cultivation by designating zones of protective forest beyond whose boundaries arable farming would not be permitted. Although zones are defined in terms of slope, soil erodibility and rainfall intensity, this approach has proven ineffective because even detailed specifications of this kind cannot hope to make adequate allowance for the wide variations in physical conditions that exist at the micro level.

The lowland and coastal environment

The effects of land degradation in the uplands extend far beyond the immediate vicinity and are felt in the form of increased sedimentation on the lowlands, where the deposition of silt alters the flow of major rivers, reduces the storage capacity of reservoirs and impairs the ability of irrigation canals to carry water to fields. In the dry season the level of water in the lower courses of many rivers drops drastically, often to the point where irrigation supplies can no longer be relied on unless pumping units are installed to raise water into canals (Hardjono 1987:28). Yet in the wet season flooding is common. While regular inundation of the lowlands has occurred for centuries, causing the coastal plains to be steadily extended, the increased frequency of floods is now having an adverse effect on some of the most important achievements of recent development projects in that infrastructure is often damaged, if not destroyed. At the very least economic activities outside the agricultural sector are slowed down by the temporary inability of roads, bridges and railway tracks to function effectively.

Sedimentation and subsequent flooding are by no means explained only by the farming systems in operation at higher altitudes. Other forms of human activity also play a part, especially since demographic pressures now compel people to live in areas where physical conditions discouraged settlement in past decades. This is particularly true of river banks and low-lying areas, where the occupations that support many of these people, like the excavation of sand for the building industry, encourage erosion. The government is increasingly faced with requests for financial assistance from people who are affected by natural disasters, usually in the form of floods, because they have moved onto land that should not be occupied, let alone cultivated. At the same time, expansion in unsealed roads, the digging

of unpaved ditches for drainage purposes in villages and towns, and horti-
cultural practices in the neatly-kept home gardens that are so much a feature
of Central and East Java all contribute to surface erosion on the lowlands.
Landslides, both natural and man-induced, likewise cause large quantities
of earth to pass into water courses. Even the techniques developed by
farmers to level their rice fields exert an effect since running water,
temporarily diverted from streams for this purpose, is used to carry away
excess soil in many areas, particularly in West Java (Diemont et al. 1991:9).

While the lowland environment has been feeling the effects of erosion
and sedimentation for many years now, the rice-intensification program
introduced in the late 1960s has had ecological implications of an
unanticipated nature. In the years immediately preceding 1965, Indonesia
had become increasingly dependent on imports of rice, with more than one
million tons imported annually during the early 1960s (Mears and Moeljono
1981). In 1968 domestic production was only 11.4 million tons of milled
rice (*beras*). Conscious of the implications of inadequate supplies of the
basic food staple, the New Order government has for political more than
economic reasons made the attainment of self-sufficiency in rice production
a major commitment. Given the advantages of the Green Revolution technology that had been developed in the early 1960s and the traditions of
intensive rice cultivation that had long prevailed, the new regime chose
further intensification of production in existing rice-growing areas as the
quickest way to raise domestic output. A large-scale program of extension
services known as *Bimas* (*Bimbingan Massal*, or 'Mass Guidance') was
implemented to bring the new technology of high-yielding varieties (HYV)
to rice growers. Considerable financial investment was made in the rehabilitation and extension of irrigation networks, while domestic production of
the chemical fertilisers that had to be used with the new seeds was greatly
expanded.

In the mid-1970s, however, when the returns to government investment
were becoming evident in greatly increased annual rice output, a serious
threat to production policies appeared in the form of a pest known as *wereng*
or brown planthopper (*Nilaparvans lugens*). Although new rice varieties
were released in an attempt to overcome the problem, these were in turn
affected by *wereng*. The reason lay in the fact that genetic diversity had
been greatly reduced and rice plants were therefore more vulnerable to
disease and destruction by insects. The fact that farmers were applying very
large quantities of fertiliser and insecticide, both of which were heavily
subsidised, made crops even more susceptible.

The problem was temporarily overcome at the end of the 1970s by the
introduction of different rice strains. Extensive research had enabled Indonesia to expand its own breeding program and to develop new varieties
suited to local conditions. It was this that led to the achievement of

190

self-sufficiency in 1984, when output reached 26 million tons of milled rice. In 1985 and 1986, however, *wereng* reappeared, reflecting the fact that the genetic base on which self-sufficiency rested had become even more slender and that the broad-spectrum insecticides applied by farmers in ever-larger quantities were in reality continuing to destroy the natural enemies of the brown planthopper rather than the planthopper itself (Fox 1991:75).

The Indonesian government responded by introducing a new policy of integrated pest management that involved a ban on the use of 57 varieties of insecticide in rice cultivation as from November 1986 and the phasing out of all pesticide subsidies by 1989. As yet, however, this biological approach to pest control applies only to rice; there is no restriction on the use of prohibited pesticides on other crops. Farmers still use large quantities on secondary food crops and especially on vegetables, even though research has shown that the same concept of non-chemical control of pests is applicable to crops like cabbages (Sudarwohadi 1987).

Associated with the new approach to pest control is a different attitude to the continuous planting of rice on the same land. Under the influence of the campaign for rice self-sufficiency, cropping patterns on irrigated land had undergone a shift from one rice and one other food crop every year to three rice crops. This monocultural pattern, made possible by the fact that HYVs require a much shorter growing period than the older, long-stalked types of rice, was a further encouragement to the spread of pests. Since 1987, however, diversification in cropping patterns has become a major agricultural policy (Tabor 1992:186). In a reversal of the situation of the early 1970s, when non-HYV rice crops were destroyed on many occasions by government authorities, farmers are now being encouraged to grow two rice crops followed by a secondary food crop or a lowland vegetable crop like chilli or eggplant. Even so, rice is still by far the major food crop in Java and in 1989 some 62 per cent of all rice land was producing at least two crops of irrigated rice a year (BPS 1990a:5). Many small farmers are now reluctant to alter their cropping patterns because they have found that with three HYV crops a year they can at least meet their household rice needs. Large farmers are more attracted by a shift away from rice, for with rice prices still government-controlled, other commodities can be much more profitable.

The ecological implications of monoculture are not the only reason for the reorientation in government policy. The reduction in emphasis on rice reflects the attempt to increase the output of other agricultural commodities as part of the export diversification drive noted above and is also related to the current government policy of promoting agro-processing industries in rural areas. There is, however, a basic constraint upon realisation of these other objectives for the government still insists that self-sufficiency in rice production must be maintained.

Quite apart from the ecological, economic and political considerations inherent in this policy, the question arises of whether self-sufficiency is indeed sustainable. Estimates of population and consumption trends suggest that demand will increase by up to 3 per cent a year and that by the year 2000 as much as 42.2 million tons of milled rice will be needed by comparison with an output of 30.4 million tons in 1989 (Fox 1991:81). It will therefore be necessary to improve yields from existing *sawah* in Java and also from *sawah* in regions outside Java, especially in major production centres in South Sulawesi, North Sumatra, West Sumatra and South Sumatra. The development of hybrid rice, which could enable average yields to increase by 20 per cent (Fox 1991:82–3), indicates the direction that policy-makers may have to take to maintain self-sufficiency, though its introduction would require considerable technical and economic readjustment of long-established agricultural practices.

Meanwhile, a major contribution to the maintenance of self-sufficiency could be made by the permanent allocation to rice of land currently used for the rotational cropping of rice and sugarcane. Proposals have long been made that cane cultivation should be completely moved from Java, which, with 72 per cent of Indonesia's 365 500 hectares of cane, produced 83 per cent of the country's sugar in 1988 (BPS 1991b:35). The major constraint on development outside Java has always been the lower soil fertility and less reliable water supplies of most regions, but research into non-irrigated cane cultivation has demonstrated the technical feasibility of developing land in other islands for this crop (Brown 1989). Expansion outside Java has already begun, the main production region being Lampung, which had almost 8 per cent of total area in 1988. Even so, the government is still reluctant to give serious attention to the complete transfer of this crop, largely because considerable investment has been made in the rehabilitation of the older mills established in Java in colonial days. As it is, the small increase in sugar output resulting from the smallholder cane intensification (*Tebu Rakyat Intensifikasi*, or TRI) program that was introduced in Java in 1975 reflects extensification rather than the intended intensification, for cane has displaced both rice and *palawija* in the competition for land and water (Brown 1982:41, 44). Nevertheless, pressure to use well-irrigated land in Java for rice and other food crops may ultimately lead the government to reassess the advantages of a basic change in sugar production policies.

Environmental problems can develop not only from the introduction of a new form of land use like upland vegetable cultivation but also from excessive expansion in a traditional system, as is illustrated by the rapid growth that has taken place in aquaculture along the coasts of northern Java, Bali, South Sulawesi and eastern Sumatra (especially Aceh and Lampung) since the early 1980s. For many decades fish farmers in Java have bred shrimp and milkfish in brackish-water ponds known as *tambak*. Constructed close to the sea, the ponds are dependent on tidal forces to carry water into the manmade channels that lead to and drain them. In developing this form of aquaculture, fish farmers have relied on gathering the necessary shrimp larvae and milkfish fry from natural hatcheries found in coastal swamps and mangrove forests.

In response to high world prices in the early 1980s, the government introduced an intensification program (*Intensifikasi Tambak*, or *Intam*) designed to raise shrimp production. The aim was to encourage the replacement of traditional extensive methods of shrimp breeding by semi-intensive and intensive techniques through the provision of cheap credit. Semi-intensive techniques involve the use of supplementary shrimp feed, and of pumps to increase the rate of water exchange. In the intensive system, where shrimp densities are much higher, shrimp are dependent almost entirely on manufactured feed; in place of brackish water, pure sea water is pumped into the ponds, where it is mixed with fresh water (Rice 1991:167). But despite the credit program, productivity remains low. While the area of *tambak* in Java has expanded at approximately 9 per cent a year, the increase in per-hectare yields has been not more than 1 per cent (Tarrant et al. 1987:9), reflecting the technical difficulties that impose constraints on intensification.

Among the problems that producers of shrimp and milkfish face is contamination of fresh water supplies by toxic substances originating from fertilisers and pesticides used elsewhere on agricultural land, and from industrial waste as cities like Jakarta and Surabaya spread to east and west. At the same time siltation of the channels that bring sea water to both extensive and semi-intensive ponds has become a major constraint on the efficient exchange of water. With reduced efficiency in drainage, *tambak* are also affected by flooding, to the point where some stretches of ponds along the northern coast of Java cannot be used in the latter half of the wet season. Rather than utilise ordinary coastal land, investors now prefer to convert irrigated rice fields to *tambak* because, besides requiring less expenditure on construction work, existing fields are usually above flood level. Expansion of this kind, however, is discouraged by the government, as it poses a threat to the policy of rice self-sufficiency. In Bali, where investors continued to ignore government regulations concerning the conversion of *sawah* to ponds, the provincial governor ordered the opening of channel outlets and the drying of some 300 hectares of *tambak* at the end of 1990 (*Kompas*, 15 January 1991), highlighting the conflict of interests, both environmental and economic, in land use in Indonesia today.

Shrimp now form an important export commodity but the gain in revenue may in the longer term be offset by environmental consequences. The removal of mangrove and other swamp forests due to expansion in *tambak* since 1980 far exceeds the impact on these forests of small-scale collectors of timber and firewood over the past several decades. The consequence of destruction of a resource, encouraged as it has been by the government credit program, is not just the loss of trees. As Vannucci (1988:216) has stressed, 'shrimp ponds built on clear-felled mangrove land cease to be economically viable enterprises after a couple of years because natural recruitment of larvae is no longer possible'. With the destruction of the spawning grounds of the larvae and fry on which aquaculture depends, the future of the fishfarmers themselves is threatened. Attempts to develop the hatchery production of milkfish fry have so far been unsuccessful (Tarrant et al. 1987:34), while in the case of shrimp larvae the cost of modern hatchery technology puts this source beyond the reach of Indonesian producers. Fish farmers raising shrimp and milkfish are now increasingly dependent on the transportation of larvae and fry from other parts of the archipelago, where coastal mangroves are still comparatively undisturbed.

The government has endeavoured to protect both the coastal environment and the future of the shrimp industry itself through regulations that permit the establishment of ponds no closer than 400 metres to the coastline, the aim being to prevent removal of the mangrove forest adjacent to the sea. In Java, however, destruction has already taken place and the damage is irreparable. There would now appear to be no scope for further conversion of mangrove swamps to *tambak* in this island, which means that, despite problems of sedimentation and contamination, yields must be raised in existing ponds if shrimp production is to remain high.

Meanwhile, inshore fish stocks along the northern coast of Java are becoming increasingly depleted as a consequence of two factors, namely, the growth in the number of households that obtain their income from this resource and the destruction of the habitat of certain species of fish that has followed the removal of coastal forests and mangroves (Soegiarto 1986). At the same time, coastal and in particular deltaic areas are increasingly affected by pollution of various kinds. Silt and residue from agricultural inputs are not the only problem. Chemicals originating from industrial activities are washed into the rivers that eventually reach the Java Sea, to the detriment of the inshore fishing industry. The continued discharge of domestic and industrial waste by rivers that flow through urban areas makes the situation around harbours even worse, particularly since the north-coast port towns are expanding more rapidly in size than towns elsewhere in Java.

Quite apart from the effects of pollution, other factors have exerted a negative effect on the marine environment in areas close to urban settlements. In an attempt to obtain building materials, contractors have removed beach sand and excavated coral atolls, usually by blasting with explosives. Rice (1991:171) has observed extensive reef damage caused by the use of explosives in Jakarta Bay, on the west coast of Lombok and even off the southwest coast of western Timor. Such exploitation of the environment leads to changes that cannot be controlled or reversed. The destruction of reefs has an adverse effect on fish breeding, which is exacerbated by the fact that wave direction is altered and coastal erosion accelerated. The dredging of river estuaries, essential to keep shipping routes open as siltation rates increase, similarly influences the forces that shape the marine land-scape and ultimately affects the fishing industry.

Progress in technology has likewise had an impact, as is illustrated by the case of trawling, expansion in which was already causing depletion of fish in coastal waters during the 1970s (Bailey 1988:34–5). In an attempt to ensure that the livelihoods of subsistence fishermen dependent on tradi-tional methods were not destroyed by competition from larger boats using mechanised equipment, the Indonesian government in 1980 announced a presidential decree (No. 39 of 1980) prohibiting the operation of trawlers in the waters of western Indonesia; in 1983 the ban was extended to most of the country. Policies often have unanticipated consequences in other subsectors, however. Burbridge (1988:172) has noted that, as a consequence of the ban on trawling in the Strait of Malacca, there has been increased private sector and government investment in *tambak* development, which in turn has led to further destruction of coastal forests along eastern Sumatra. Like fishermen in Java, local households dependent on coastal and marine-capture fisheries in the Strait of Malacca are now finding that the destruction of mangroves means a loss of breeding grounds for other forms of marine life.

Nevertheless, marine-capture fisheries some distance offshore offer pos-sibilities for further development. Indonesia's fish resources are relatively abundant, if production is seen in relation to the country's 5.8 million sq. km of seas. Of this, 3.1 million sq. km represent territorial waters within the twelve-mile limit while the Exclusive Economic Zone covers an addi-tional 2.7 million sq. km (Haeruman 1988:218). Output from marine fisheries has always been very low, however. Soemarwoto (1991:223) has estimated that Indonesia's average annual production of marine fish was only a little over ten kilograms per capita in the 1982–85 period; in terms of area, it amounted to less than a quarter of a ton per square kilometre of sea in 1986. Yet while there is scope for much greater exploitation of pelagic fish in seas away from the coasts of northern Java and eastern Sumatra, expansion in this direction requires large, capital-intensive boats and equip-ment, which puts the resource beyond the reach of traditional fishermen. Meanwhile, the problem still arises of foreign fishing vessels operating in the less frequently patrolled eastern waters of the archipelago, where fish stocks are relatively abundant.

The urban environment

Java's environmental and ecological problems are by no means limited to rural and coastal areas or to the agricultural sector. As population grows and rapid diversification takes place in the economy, the coastal plains are being used increasingly for non-agricultural activities that affect the environment both directly and indirectly. Java, with its comparatively well-developed infrastructure, abundant manpower and extensive markets is still far ahead of the other islands as the focus of industrial development. Of the 75 industrial estates in Indonesia in April 1991, 62 were located in Java, with 40 concentrated in West Java (*Swa*, August 1991). The trend will certainly continue, for 18 000 hectares of land in this province alone have been set aside for factory development since Presidential Decree No. 53 of 1989 made it possible for the private sector to invest in industrial estates. The construction of more toll roads, such as the planned link between Bandung and Cikampek (Cementation 1990), will provide support for further expansion of these estates.

Although erosion is already causing a depletion of topsoil throughout Java, good soils close to major coastal cities like Jakarta and Surabaya and inland cities like Bogor and Bandung are being increasingly built on, causing further loss of one of Java's main resources. The West Java Irrigation Service has found that more than 57 000 hectares of arable land in this province was converted to non-agricultural uses between April 1984 and March 1991 (*Suara Pembaruan*, 28 June 1991). In the period between 1969 and 1985 new irrigation facilities were constructed to provide water for 1.2 million hectares of land but the function of one-quarter of that land had already changed by the end of the 1980s (*Kompas*, 18 April 1991). The conversion of irrigated land represents a double loss in that considerable investment was made in the improvement of water reticulation networks on this land during the 1970s. The fact that new land has been brought under dry crops on mountain slopes has not compensated in terms of output, for the decrease in agricultural land has occurred precisely in the best irrigated and most fertile areas. At a time when population is still growing, it will be increasingly up to farmers in other parts of the country to maintain rice self-sufficiency and produce the other foodstuffs needed in Java.

The new uses for which land is needed include not only industrial sites but also airports, roads and other infrastructure. At the same time, growth in the numbers of people living in urban areas has encouraged rapid and totally unplanned expansion in residential settlements close to industrial centres while improvements in the incomes of a part of the urban population have raised the demand for land for the construction of modern housing complexes. While it can be argued that the per-metre productivity of industrial land is far higher than that of *sawah*, long-term environmental and social aspects must also be taken into consideration, a view implicit in Presidential Decree No. 33 of 1990, which restricts industrial development on agricultural land. Apart from implications for food production, the conversion of land to industrial and other purposes has an indirect environmental impact in the form of labour displacement. Whether they sell their land directly to industrialists or whether it is resumed by the government for development projects, owners at least receive some financial payment, but the tenants and agricultural labourers who were once employed to cultivate it obtain no compensation for their loss of livelihood. Without the skills to obtain jobs in newly-established factories, many move to upland areas to find work in farming or timber-cutting.

The expansion in industry and infrastructure that has made a sizeable contribution to economic development over the past two decades has also stimulated the building industry. With construction now an important sector in the economy, there has been rapid growth in subsidiary activities to meet the demand for building materials, which include land-fill, lime, bricks, tiles and cement. Quite apart from the fact that the materials used for such purposes represent non-renewable resources, these activities tend to be destructive of the environment. The digging of open quarries close to urban areas to obtain land-fill material has created huge holes and rendered the land virtually useless for any other purpose. These excavations are not the undertakings of village people who use manual methods to obtain a few cubic metres of sand per day but of urban-based contractors. So great is the scale of their operations, made possible by mechanisation in the form of bulldozers and other heavy equipment, that district authorities often try to intervene in the interests of the environmental security of local communities. While it has been suggested that excavation sites should be restored to an environmentally satisfactory condition after exploitation (RUDS 1989:121), enforcement of policies of this kind is difficult. In most areas the techniques used by producers of bricks, tiles and lime add a further dimension to the damage already done to the environment in that wood is used to fire kilns, thus encouraging greater deforestation in the uplands.

At the same time there are major problems associated with the depletion and contamination of water resources. Even if greater efficiency could be achieved in the use of water for agriculture, Java's non-agricultural future could well face constraints in the lack of water for industrial and domestic purposes alike. It has been estimated that residential and industrial demand in urban areas will be more than four times greater in the year 2000 than it was in the mid-1980s (Douglass 1991:256). Urban water authorities throughout Java are having increasing difficulty in even maintaining current supplies of piped water to households, let alone obtaining additional sources of water to enable them to extend the reticulation systems. Much of the country's urban population, even in middle-class residential areas, is still dependent on shallow wells for household water. As deforestation continues, natural infiltration and storage of water in foothill regions is declining, and in recent years there have been frequent disputes over rights to the use of the water from mountain springs, sometimes between the municipal governments of adjacent cities like Jakarta and Bogor and sometimes between public and private interests.

With city water services unable to provide adequate and reliable supplies for domestic and industrial purposes alike, factory owners have resorted to the sinking of deep wells on their own premises, but this approach too is encountering the same problem of reduced availability because the water table in Java's major urban areas has been falling steadily for some years. So much water is lost in surface run-off that the quantity absorbed into the ground to replenish natural underground reservoirs has begun to decline. A recent study of urban development in the Bandung metropolitan area noted that groundwater from the deep aquifer below the city is already over-exploited for public and private water supplies (RUDS 1989:101, 103). In the heavily-industrialised area of Tangerang on the western periphery of Jakarta, automatic equipment installed in 1989 has registered a drop in the water table of 0.4 metre per month. With ever greater abstraction of groundwater, coastal areas in northern and western Jakarta are now seriously affected by the intrusion of salt water, which by 1985 had reached a point fifteen kilometres inland by comparison with one only five kilometres from the sea in 1970 (Douglass 1991:254). Salt-water intrusion below the city is not only increasing the contamination of groundwater but also causing problems of stability for the foundations of high-rise buildings in these sections of the city.

Over and above the problem of depletion of water resources is that of water quality. The recent expansion in companies that produce bottled drinking water is an indication of the fact that it is not sufficient nowadays for households just to boil water obtained from wells or even from piped supplies in some areas. As already noted, chemical pollutants are flowing into water courses from agricultural land, while in built-up areas the inadequacy of sewerage and garbage disposal systems is reflected in the discharge of household waste of all kinds into rivers and stormwater channels intended for drainage purposes. Industrial effluent is adding to the problem, largely because inadequate attention has been given to its disposal in plans for individual factories and for industrial development as a whole. As a result, groundwater in urban areas is becoming polluted by the downward movement of contaminated surface water. In the more densely populated parts of Bandung the quality of the water from the shallow aquifers that supply household wells is decreasing sharply and the high degree of pollution already poses a threat to public health (RUDS 1989:105).

With the introduction of the 'clean river program' (*Program Kali Bersih*, or *Prokasih*) by the Minister for Population and the Environment, an attempt is being made to improve the quality of urban rivers (KLH n.d.). Initiated in 1989 with twenty rivers in eight provinces, *Prokasih* has now been expanded to 25 waterways in thirteen provinces. The focus of the program is on sections of these rivers where pollution is caused by both industrial and household waste. Standards for industrial effluent have been prepared and are being gradually introduced, while attempts have been made to restrict human settlement along river banks (Bapedal 1990). Even so, with steady growth in both population and industry, it is proving difficult to deal with river pollution and the subsequent effects on estuaries and coastal waters. Rice (1991:172) and Tarrant et al. (1987:33) have drawn attention to the critical state of Jakarta Bay, which is a striking illustration of the extent to which the entry of pollutants can cause deterioration of the marine environment.

One of Java's major problems today is the growing inadequacy of the electricity network. Despite a tenfold increase since the early 1970s, supplies of power can barely meet present needs, let alone the expansion expected in industrial demand during the 1990s. Java has tended to depend on hydro-electricity, which now offers very little scope for further development. Apart from the fact that there are very few sites suited to the construction of new reservoirs, many of those built in the past twenty years as part of overall economic development strategies are now being affected by siltation to the point where their service life is likely to be much shorter than anticipated, for the original designs did not allow for such high rates of erosion in upstream areas. Added to this is a growing conflict of objectives in the management of reservoirs. Most were designed as multipurpose projects that would provide water for irrigation and urban needs, both household and industrial, as well as power for industrial expansion. The requirements of the industrial sector cannot be ignored, especially if man-ufacturing is to make a major contribution to exports. Yet the government continues to declare its determination to maintain rice self-sufficiency, which will obviously demand the regular reticulation of adequate water to *sawah*.

So far, oil has been widely used for small-scale power generation, though the importance of this commodity in the export trade and the fact that reserves are being depleted rapidly has led the government to turn to other sources of energy in recent years. In view of predictions that imports of oil will be necessary by the year 2000, attention is now being given to the country's large, virtually unexploited deposits of low-sulphur, low-ash coal, which are located in the southeastern corner of Kalimantan and in western Sumatra. Between 1986 and 1990 coal production rose from two million tons to 11.2 million tons, of which 42 per cent was exported and the remainder used domestically, mainly for power generation. Meanwhile, the construction of a geothermal power station, in operation since the early 1980s at Kamojang near Garut, has demonstrated that the immeasurable fields of steam beneath Java's volcanoes offer a sustainable and environ-mentally-attractive source of energy. Even so, policy-makers are now investigating the feasibility of nuclear energy to provide the necessary support for further industrialisation, though construction of a reactor will require considerable financial investment, not to mention political determination in the face of Indonesia's small but growing anti-nuclear movement.

The steady expansion of built-up areas, involving what are literally wall-to-wall factories and residential areas that have no yards or gardens, has environmental implications in that the run-off of rainwater from impermeable surfaces is accelerated. While urban planners agree without hesitation that green belts are needed around cities like Jakarta and Surabaya, the demand for land for other purposes tends to take precedence. Plans drawn up in the early 1970s for the development of Jakarta made allowance for zones where vegetative cover was to be maintained or re-established. But these green belts, limited in area as they were, are today being sacrificed to the needs of industrial growth and expansion in infrastructure.

While urban expansion has created environmental problems, it is itself increasingly affected by environmental degradation elsewhere and in particular the hydrological consequences of the changes now occurring in land use throughout Java. Sections of towns like Semarang are still subject to regular flooding despite considerable expenditure on improvements in drainage, and financial resources have to be diverted every year to local flood relief as well as to the repair of infrastructure. The situation is even worse in the so-called Jabopunjur corridor—which takes in Jakarta, Bogor, Puncak and Cianjur—for as residential, industrial and recreational activities spread southwards beyond the Jakarta–Bogor conurbation and encroach upon the tea estates and forests of the Puncak hills, the environmental damage is having repercussions for Jakarta itself (Douglass 1988) in the form of sudden floods caused by siltation of the rivers and canals within the city, as well as shortages of water for domestic and other purposes.

In looking to future developments, a prominent Indonesian economist predicted in the mid-1970s that by the end of the century population increase would make Java 'an island city', characterised by a mixture of semi-urban and semi-rural features (Sumitro 1977:102). With Jakarta already the world's eighth largest city in 1990, the trend in this direction is both obvious and irreversible, a fact that points to the urgent need for land-use planning that will restore ecological balance and for political will on the part of government authorities to enforce decisions relevant to the environment.

The other islands

Environmental problems relating to the utilisation of land and water resources are by no means limited to Java, for of the 36 watersheds described as being in a critical condition, 23 are to be found in the other islands. The accelerated deterioration that has become evident in the natural environment in regions outside Java in recent years is very largely the consequence of induced alterations in land use, just as it is in Java. These changes, however, reflecting as they do the specific physical characteristics of the other islands and the nature of the resource exploitation policies that have been adopted, differ somewhat from those found in Java. Nevertheless, the removal of trees, whether it be for agricultural extensification or for commercial timber exploitation, ultimately leads to the same consequences that have followed deforestation in Java. Erosion is having similar effects in the form of sedimentation and reduced soil fertility.

Two points must be noted, however. Firstly, while the dichotomy between Java and the other islands still holds true to a certain extent where general land-use patterns are concerned, it is by no means as clearly defined as it once was, when 'Outer Indonesia' could be characterised as a region in which land utilisation was based predominantly on various swidden systems (Geertz 1963a). The tendency to generalise about conditions in the islands other than Java and Bali disguises the fact that there are significant differences between and within these islands and that their environmental problems are by no means identical. Secondly, while population increase in recent years has been rapid outside Java and in many provinces has exceeded that of Java, the absolute numbers of people seeking a livelihood are still much smaller than in Java. Government policies concerning the utilisation of resources, in particular those relating to transmigration and forestry, have been more significant in these islands than in Java in terms of impact on the environment.

Much of the degradation that has taken place in the other islands has had its origins in the rapid extensification of agriculture. In some cases, agricultural extensification has been related to modifications made to traditional systems of land use like shifting cultivation and smallholder cash-crop agriculture, while in others it has been connected with the resettlement policies of the transmigration agency and with activities in the forestry subsector. The fact that expansion in farming has almost always taken place on marginal land very largely explains why environmental problems have increased. It has been estimated that some three million hectares of land in these islands were converted to tree-crop cultivation alone between 1971 and 1986 (Booth 1991:54). Not all of this land was forested, however. Much had reached varying degrees of degradation and was already covered in secondary vegetation that was evidence of human interference with natural ecological systems in earlier times. Where cleared land has been abandoned, *alang-alang* grass (*Imperata cyclindrica*) becomes established very rapidly and renders the land virtually useless for any purpose. There are an estimated 16 to 20 million hectares of this grass in Kalimantan and Sumatra, and the area is increasing at a rate of 100 000 to 150 000 hectares per year (Tarrant et al. 1987:22).

Shifting cultivation

It has become common in many circles in Indonesia to blame the deterioration in land resources outside Java on the continued existence of shifting cultivation (Tjondronegoro 1991b:26). In particular, those who wish to see Indonesia's current logging policies retained argue that the greater part of the damage done to forests is the work of non-sedentary cultivators who practise slash-and-burn agriculture. Yet although governments, forest services and international forestry agencies attribute tropical deforestation principally to shifting cultivation, the environmental movement holds the commercial logging industry responsible, as Byron and Waugh (1988:57) have noted.

In its traditional form shifting cultivation is a sustainable mode of production and does no permanent damage to resources. After making clearings in forested areas, cultivators grow subsistence food crops for two or three years and then move to another part of the forest as soil fertility declines, leaving the process of natural regeneration to restore the land to its original state. In more developed systems they plant tree crops, usually rubber, on their clearings and return to tap the trees some six or seven years later, if market prices for latex are high enough to warrant the output of labour. For the system to be sustainable, the fallow period must be long enough to permit fertility to be restored before the same land is again cleared and planted, a requirement less easily observed as population densities rise. It has long been the Indonesian government's stated policy to reduce the area under shifting cultivation, which agricultural planners regard as a wasteful form of land use. Yet how this can be done effectively has never been made clear, for government programs conducted by the Department of Home Affairs to resettle even small, isolated groups of shifting cultivators as sedentary farmers have been a failure (Tjondronegoro 1991a). Other approaches might be more beneficial. Whitten et al. (1987:580) have pointed out that much could be achieved by improving strains of the crops that shifting cultivators grow, introducing new species and identifying the best species for reforestation of fallow slopes.

In any discussion of shifting cultivation a distinction must be made between the two extremes of this form of land use. At one extreme there is the traditional, self-sustaining system that aims to meet subsistence needs, while at the other there is a greatly modified and far less-sustainable system of land use that is completely market oriented. In the latter system cultivators with access to equipment like chain saws fell primary forest in order to grow dry rice for sale in nearby markets (Tarrant et al. 1987:22). Because of the scale of their operations, which are frequently related to commercial timber-cutting, erosion is encouraged and land quality quickly deteriorates. In the traditional system, cultivators move not because they find it easy to prepare new fields but because they do not have the technology to utilise the poor-grade soils of the forests. In the modified form, which is increasingly common, cultivators with mechanised equipment do not require the same large input of manual labour to make new clearings. Seeking to obtain the maximum return from the temporary fertility of the soil, they often cultivate not only rice but also high-value crops like pepper (Kartawinata and Vayda 1984). Ultimately, however, the lack of a sustainable land-management system leads to a point where, despite the application of chemical fertilisers, the decline in soil fertility makes economic returns too low for cultivation to be worthwhile.

The question of shifting cultivation highlights an issue that is relevant to both resource utilisation and environmental deterioration, namely, that of open-access resources. Where common property systems have long been in existence, a breakdown in traditional forms of management usually follows changes in land use. While demographic pressure can bring about these changes, more frequently they are policy-induced and stem from government decisions to use the land itself or the resources associated with it for certain purposes. The nature of traditional tenure in islands like Kalimantan is such that a change in land use can be readily introduced by national and provincial level agencies, as has happened in the allocation of forestry concessions and in the designation of land for transmigration settlements. While these are the most obvious examples, the announcement that a private company has been given the right to harvest sago palms on an 85 000-hectare concession in Irian Jaya (*Swa*, August 1991:90) highlights the destiny of a virtually non-renewable resource to which local people have always had open access.

Cash-crop and livestock systems

Shifting cultivation is but one form of land use outside Java and Bali. For many decades agricultural production in the other islands has tended to focus around the sedentary cultivation of commercial crops by smallholders. An estimated 18 million people in these other islands obtain their livelihood from this form of agriculture (Barlow 1991:85), which in some areas also involves the cultivation of food crops and the raising of livestock. The 1983 Agricultural Census recorded some 7.7 million hectares of land throughout the country under smallholder cash crops by comparison with less than 1.2 million hectares under estate production.

One factor that has always influenced expansion in smallholder agriculture is the nature of markets, for cultivators of rubber, coffee, and other export crops are directly affected by world conditions. It was the existence of international markets that originally stimulated expansion in smallholder agriculture side by side with estate production not only in Indonesia but elsewhere in the tropical world during the colonial days of the nineteenth and early-twentieth centuries (Booth 1988a:195). As a result of export orientation, local prices for these commodities have tended to fluctuate with trends prevailing in the international economy, and this in turn has affected levels of both intensification and extensification in their production.

During the 1950s and 1960s Indonesian smallholder and estate agriculture alike suffered from a general decline but the smallholder sector has been much slower to recover than the estate sector, which has been more favoured by government policies. In the years following 1967, when the lowest point was reached in harvested areas and output in the estate sector, the government initiated a series of loan-financed programs designed to raise productivity in the interests of greater export earnings. With assistance directed exclusively towards government estates, private estates could not undertake rehabilitation until the early 1980s, when low-cost credit was extended to this sector also. The rise that has occurred in estate production is traceable almost entirely to the higher yields made possible by the application of new cultivation technology rather than to expansion in area. Only in the case of palm oil has there been any significant increase in hectarage because of new plantings. With the high international prices that prevailed in the 1970s, such serious attention was given to this crop that Indonesian palm-oil estates now have higher yields than Malaysian estates and, as Booth (1988a:211) has pointed out, appear to be at the forefront of world technology. Unfortunately, their technical advantage has been undermined by changes in market conditions, with world prices for crude palm oil at the end of 1990 only a third of what they had been six years earlier.

The smallholder sector presents a very different picture. Growth in output has been the result of extensification rather than of improvements in yields. In terms of planted area Indonesia's most important smallholder crops are coconuts in Sumatra, Kalimantan and North Sulawesi, rubber in Sumatra and West Kalimantan, and coffee in the southern provinces of Sumatra. Aware that this sector has potential for much greater development, the government has attempted to assist smallholders to raise yields but relatively little has been achieved. As a result, these cultivators have maintained and even increased output by resorting to the replication of traditional technologies on ever-wider stretches of land (Booth 1991:44), a trend that represents another facet of the process of agricultural extensification now taking place outside Java.

Various approaches have been adopted to the provision of assistance for smallholder cash-crop farmers in recent years (Barlow 1991:98–101). Until the mid-1970s small-scale efforts were made to provide extension services and to make improved planting materials available in scattered areas. But results were negligible since only better-off farmers had the money to purchase them. A group farming approach was then introduced to help rubber smallholders in North and West Sumatra with replanting and processing, but it proved costly as it was both capital and management-intensive. A similar though much less expensive attempt was made through the program for 'rejuvenation, rehabilitation and expansion of export crops' (*Peremajaan, Rehabilitasi dan Perluasan Tanaman Ekspor*, or PRPTE), which focused primarily on rubber and coconut producers outside Java and on tea smallholders in Java. Success was limited in all regions, largely because of inadequate technical inputs and extension work. The most recent approach has involved the nucleus estate and smallholder concept (*Perusahaan Inti Rakyat*, or PIR). Under this scheme, credit facilities are made available to both government and private plantation companies to enable them to establish small nucleus estates and to provide the necessary managerial, technical and processing support for farmers who already cultivate land in the immediate area of the estate and for those who choose to resettle on allocated smallholdings in the vicinity.

Traditional systems of livestock production are to be found in some regions, particularly in the drier parts of eastern Indonesia, where physical conditions are generally unfavourable to agriculture. As Barlow (1991:94) has pointed out, the main resources of these systems are the animals themselves, together with human labour and extensive areas of land. They usually exist in conjunction with food-crop cultivation, which not infrequently involves some kind of rotational farming because of the inherent infertility of the soils. To intensify such forms of land use is difficult without external inputs. As a result, an increase in population usually leads to deterioration in the resources on which the system is dependent. It is a combination of these factors that explains the low farm incomes and high level of land degradation in many parts of East and West Nusa Tenggara.

In some regions the continued expansion of the cultivated area and the acceleration of environmental degradation are a direct reflection of population growth. In Lampung and South Sumatra, for example, expansion in the cultivation of both food crops and smallholder cash crops, notably coffee, on mountain slopes has resulted in widespread deforestation and is leading to consequences similar to those caused by expansion in arable farming in upland Java. Although coffee is not an annual, it is comparatively short-rooted; the fact that it is now being grown on extremely steep slopes where soil is far from stable has led to disastrous landslides and floods. But expansion in agriculture is not the only cause of erosion. There is constant felling of trees for fuel and timber, for in southern Sumatra high population densities have created a growing demand for these basic necessities, just as they have in Java.

Apart from the direct effects in the uplands, there are also consequences for farmers at lower altitudes, where deposition of sediment is occurring at a rate no slower than in Java. The Belitang irrigation area, which is one of the major rice-producing centres of South Sumatra, exemplifies the process. Wet-rice cultivation in this area is dependent on irrigation water from the Komering River, which is a major tributary of the Musi. The course of the Komering has now widened and become so shallow because of sedimentation that in the dry season the water level is lower than the intake point for the canal network, which means that water is not available at the time when it is most needed (Hardjono 1978). Man-induced landslides in the upper watershed have been responsible for the destruction of hundreds of hectares of rice land elsewhere in the Komering valley (Meijerink et al. 1988). This process has led to excessive siltation of the Musi itself, which is among the most environmentally critical of all rivers in the country. The additional pollutants that it accumulates as it passes through the city of Palembang, with its one million residents, make it one of the main targets of the *Prokasih* campaign to clean up urban rivers. Other islands have similar problem areas. In South Sulawesi, the Saddang watershed, whose lower sections form the province's main centre of wet-rice cultivation, is in an equally critical state. Under the rainfall conditions that prevailed between 1968 and 1984, the erosion rate in some parts of the upper watershed was as high as 660 tons of soil per hectare per year (Sinukaban 1991), which is some 35 per cent greater than the rate in the Upper Citarum watershed of West Java.

The condition of watersheds like the Saddang warrants special attention because, as pointed out above, maintenance of national rice self-sufficiency will require much higher yields from existing wet-rice production centres outside Java as population grows and the area of irrigated land in Java decreases with expansion in industry. Relatively new and long-awaited irrigation projects like the Way Rarem in Lampung, which was designed to enable transmigrant farmers to convert dry fields to wet rice (Hardjono 1977:53), are now proving less effective than originally anticipated because upland erosion is causing rapid siltation of distribution channels. Although in 1989 there was a total of 4.8 million hectares of rice land in the islands of Sumatra, Bali, Nusa Tenggara, Kalimantan and Sulawesi, less than 18 per cent of this land had technical or semi-technical irrigation and only 28 per cent could produce more than one crop of rice a year (BPS 1990b:5). Money, labour and time are needed to transform land into irrigated fields and with only 45 000 hectares of new *sawah* prepared outside Java in 1989–90, progress is slow. Even allowing for a change in government policy concerning rice self-sufficiency, serious attention will have to be given to agricultural development in the other islands, as they will still have to provide increasingly large supplies of other foodstuffs for Java.

Transmigration

Transmigration, both government sponsored and spontaneous, has been a major element in the extensification of agriculture in the islands outside Java in the years since 1950. While the primary aim of transmigration has always been reduction of population pressure in Java, the government has frequently referred to the development of underutilised land in other parts of the country as further justification for promotion of this program. In the years since 1986, however, a number of factors that include first and foremost the high cost of fully-supported resettlement and the difficulty of obtaining suitable settlement sites, has resulted in a reduction in the scale of government-funded transmigration. Other factors that have led to a curtailment of the program include the slow economic growth of many settlements and their failure to contribute significantly to regional development (Babcock 1986), low incomes among transmigrants in many areas, the social impact of the new settlers on local communities and the effect of resettlement projects on the environment.

These various shortcomings of the government-funded transmigration program are to a certain extent interrelated. During the 1976–86 period, government hopes of achieving a meaningful impact on population densities in Java were expressed in excessively high annual targets. Attempts to shift large numbers of people in a relatively short period of time, however, resulted in poorly-planned settlements that had few prospects for economic growth because of the marginality of the land on which they were located, the introduction of land-use systems totally unsuited to the sites and the inadequacy of the farm inputs and general infrastructure provided for settlers (World Bank 1988).

Transmigration settlements are classified by the Department of Transmigration according to the type of land use intended to provide the economic foundation of the new villages. The three broad types are irrigated rice growing, tidal (*pasang-surut*) rice growing, and dry farming. Settlements of the first type are rarely established today, the reason being the lack of suitable topographical conditions for the impounding of water and the high cost of providing the necessary irrigation infrastructure. In pre-independence days the Dutch colonial government had established a number of settlements under its 'colonisation' scheme (Pelzer 1945; Amral Sjamsu 1960). Since the more successful projects were those located in areas where irrigated rice growing had been introduced, such as Metro in Lampung and Belitang in South Sumatra, post-independence transmigration authorities regarded irrigation as an essential part of resettlement planning until the early 1970s, by which time it had become apparent that there was very little land outside Java that was unoccupied yet had the potential for Java-style irrigation (Junghans 1974).

The second type of transmigration settlement, based on *pasang-surut* (or tidal rice) cultivation, represents an attempt to modify a traditional system of land use in swamplands. In past decades cultivators in the coastal areas of southern Kalimantan and eastern Sumatra had found that they could make use of the tidal influence in estuaries to lift water onto fields made along river banks. By digging ditches at right angles to the river itself, they could spread the tidal effect somewhat further inland. Until the mid-1980s government policy in transmigration favoured this type of settlement. There were two main considerations: it was believed that a contribution could be made to national rice production, and land acquisition was not difficult since the swamplands were comparatively underpopulated. Despite the total fail-ure of a number of attempts to develop tidal projects in South Kalimantan in the 1960s and in eastern Sumatra in the early 1970s, the government maintained this policy for several years, largely because the early success of the Delta Upang settlement in South Sumatra had suggested that tidal-rice cultivation was a viable form of land use. This particular settlement had prospered because of its location on the alluvial soil of an island in the Musi estuary but others fared less well, mainly because of unsuitable sites. To benefit from tidal forces, the location must be carefully chosen. If it is too close to the mouth of the estuary, salt intrusion, especially in the dry season, limits crop cultivation, yet if it is too far upstream the tidal effect is insufficient to lift water into irrigation canals (Hardjono 1977:73). Even where the river regime is suitable, the acidic soils characteristic of swamp-lands can produce only one crop of rice a year, while other crops like maize, cassava, chilli and cooking herbs cannot be grown.

This points to a basic weakness in planning. Policy-makers overlooked the fact that traditional rice growing in tidal areas is essentially a form of shifting cultivation. As Collier (1980) has shown, local farmers cultivate rice for no more than two or three years, during which time they plant coconut seedlings on mounds within the rice fields. They then begin clearing more land in preparation for the time when the initial fertility of the soil is depleted. The swamp soils are so acidic that coconuts are virtually the only perennial that can be grown, a reflection of the fact that these coastal regions form the natural habitat of the coconut palm. Subsequent land degradation has been a feature of many of the unsuccessful tidal projects, for neglected fields soon become covered in *alang-alang* grass. Where attempts have been made to drain swamps, the extremely fragile soils have broken up rapidly, making the land useless for farming since the process cannot be reversed.

While rice cultivation in tidal swamps appears to be one way of utilising underdeveloped land, in reality it is sustainable only if the clearing–culti-vation cycle is repeated over a very long period of time, which implies that population must remain small. Transmigration planners, however, designed projects as permanent settlements, allocating transmigrants the same two-hectare holding given to settlers in other ecological conditions and no opportunity to move to new land when fertility declined. This explains why settlers have frequently left tidal projects or at least sought supplementary income from timber-cutting in swamp forests. Many of the disasters of the early 1980s, which brought widespread criticism to the whole transmigration program, in fact occurred in tidal projects (Hardjono 1986). Resettlement experiences in these areas demonstrate the point made earlier: when a traditional form of land use is expanded in scale, the same results in terms of output and sustainability cannot be expected.

The third and by far the most common type of transmigration settlement involves dry farming. With very limited areas of good but unoccupied soils available, many of the sites allocated by provincial authorities for the establishment of settlements consist of land that has been cleared and abandoned by shifting cultivators in relatively recent times and is in various stages of deterioration. Indeed, part of the argument for the establishment of large-scale settlements on degraded land has lain in misguided notions of 'soil conservation'. This fact in itself indicates why many settlements have failed to develop, for it was the marginality of the land that caused previous cultivators to abandon it. Of the 800 000 hectares cleared between 1980 and 1986 for transmigration purposes, some 300 000 hectares were under secondary forest and scrub, while 200 000 hectares were not forested at all, indicating recent use by shifting cultivators and timber-cutters; the remaining 300 000 hectares were in logged-over primary forest (World Bank 1990a:33). The introduction of sedentary systems of dry farming has done little to improve land quality, since transmigrants have been no better equipped in terms of agricultural technology to utilise poor-quality soils than were earlier cultivators.

Related to the question of resettlement policies is another aspect relevant to ecological deterioration. Traditional forms of control over the utilisation of resources, in particular those in swamplands, have disappeared in the face of government policy-making. With the introduction in the post-1965 period of a uniform administrative structure of districts and subdistricts throughout the country, there is no place for traditional authorities and so the advantages of local resource management have been lost. While the administrative reorganisation was unquestionably necessary in the interests of expansion in educational, health and other services, a price has been paid in that public servants now make the decisions that community leaders once made. This issue of traditional forms of land management and environmental control, like the question of open-access resource utilisation, is one to which government-planning agencies in all spheres have given very little attention.

In addition to government-sponsored resettlement, spontaneous transmigration has been taking place on an increasing scale in recent years. Some of this movement is a direct result of the establishment of fully supported projects, with unsponsored newcomers following relatives and friends. Indeed, the expectation that investment in projects would encourage more people to move from Java of their own accord has always been one of the justifications for high expenditures on the government-funded program. Not all internal movement, however, has been related to government-planned transmigration, as is illustrated by the spontaneous resettlement near Samarinda in East Kalimantan of pepper growers originally from South Sulawesi (Kartawinata and Vayda 1984). At the same time there is also movement within the various islands of local people in search of better incomes. Many of these completely spontaneous settlers enter forestry concessions, following logging roads to obtain a source of livelihood in the form of either timber and firewood for sale or land for farming. These people, however, are 'merely the secondary agent of land clearing, after logging', as Byron and Waugh (1988:54) have stressed. While their activities retard the natural generation of trees, it is impossible to disaggregate the damage they do from that done by loggers.

Although there has been a considerable reduction in the number of transmigrants funded and resettled by the government, it is impossible to prevent completely spontaneous resettlement, involving not only people from Java but also those seeking to move from overcrowded areas like southern and central Lampung. The fact that there are no procedures by which newcomers who do not move under the government-organised trans-migration program can acquire land encourages them to settle in a totally unplanned manner that generally leads to negative consequences for the environment. A recent report (World Bank 1990a:36) draws attention to the need 'to free underutilised and degraded land for development, to facilitate land transfer and to ensure fair treatment of buyers and sellers', for without rational land markets outside Java it will be impossible for measures to be introduced to protect forests and watersheds from further degradation.

The forestry subsector

The question of the environmental impact of the forestry policies adopted by Indonesia since 1967 has provoked considerable argument, particularly in the context of the debate concerning the effect on global climate of the felling of tropical rainforests. In the present discussion no attempt is made to examine the wider implications of the reduction that has been taking place in the forests of the Indonesian archipelago. Rather, the focus is on local ecological consequences and on the sustainability of forestry activities.

When the New Order took over government in the mid-1960s, there was urgent need for sources of revenue. It was in this situation that the somewhat hastily formulated Basic Forestry Act of 1967 was ratified. The hardwoods of Kalimantan and other islands were perceived as an easily-harvested commodity that could be sold immediately, rather than as a resource to be managed efficiently in the interests of sustainable revenue. Little thought was given either to the fact that hardwoods are not a readily-renewable resource or to the environmental implications of widespread logging. It was only in the mid-1980s that new perceptions began to appear, reflecting both greater general concern within Indonesia about the environment and a certain amount of pressure from international sources.

The Indonesian logging industry has passed through two distinct phases and is about to enter a third, with the expansion planned for the pulp and paper industry during the 1990s (*Swa*, August 1990). The first phase took in the years from 1967 to 1979, while the second has covered the period since 1979 (Potter 1991b:181). During the first period the industry focused on the export of logs, the reason being that relatively little capital investment was required for this form of production, returns could be obtained quickly and profits were good because efficient Japanese mills had the capacity to pay high prices (Byron and Waugh 1988:60). The introduction of a ban on log exports in 1980 marked a change in the direction of the industry. Today most wood leaves the country in the form of plywood and veneer with the exception of a small amount of sawn timber. With the introduction of a new export tax on this product in March 1989, revenue from sawn wood fell by 80 per cent in the following year, but plywood continued to lead among Indonesia's non-oil export commodities until it was displaced by textiles in 1991.

The reason for imposition of the 1980 ban on log exports lay in an attempt on the part of government policy-makers to gain value added by ensuring that processing was done within the country. Large-scale investment in plywood factories, which in 1990 numbered 114, resulted in Indonesia moving from its 1979 position as the world's largest exporter of logs to that of the world's leading plywood exporter by 1982, though the rate of expansion ultimately had a negative effect on world prices for this commodity (Lindsay 1989:119). World prices have continued to fall, for expansion in the plywood industry, both in Indonesia and elsewhere, had been premised on the assumption of constant growth in Japanese demand, which had been high during the 1970s but has now been very largely met.

It has been argued that, despite the expansion that has occurred in the forestry industry since 1967, Indonesia has not received even half of the value of timber felled in those years, since only a small proportion of economic rent has been captured (Repetto 1988). In a study of logging in East Kalimantan prior to 1977, Ruzicka (1979:73–4) found that 'government collections averaged only around 35, 42 and 80 per cent of the rents earned by large, medium-sized and small producers respectively' and that differences in production efficiency 'resulted in substantial variations in the amount of rent generated from each hectare of "average" forest land'. Commenting on more recent trends, a World Bank (1990a:16) report concludes that because of the declining level of rent collection during the 1980–85 period, the timber industry in effect received a government subsidy of $1.2 billion. Lindsay meanwhile has pointed out that an inefficient rate of expansion in processing facilities has been one of the results of the ban on log exports and concludes that 'the environmental costs of maintaining the present forestry policy, which is resulting in 900 000 hectares of deforestation annually, is likely to dwarf . . . foreign exchange losses' (Lindsay 1989:121–2).

It is difficult to form an impression of the future potential of the forestry subsector because of the lack of precise information about the extent of untouched forests or of the relative contributions made to forest depletion by indigenous cultivators, resettled farmers and loggers. Preliminary figures from the FAO Forest Resources Assessment 1990 Project (cited in Potter 1991a) indicate that 56 per cent of the country (some 107.5 million hectares) was still under forest in 1990, by comparison with 21 per cent in the Philippines and 28 per cent in Thailand. Within Indonesia, the island of Java had the minimum with a figure of only 7 per cent for forested land, while the maximum was to be found in Irian Jaya (82 per cent). Between 1982 and 1990 an average of 937 000 hectares of land per year was deforested, a figure that excludes the effects of the 1983 fire which destroyed some 350 000 hectares of forests in Kalimantan (Potter 1991a). The 544 private concessions recorded in June 1989 covered 56.3 million hectares, which represents a sizeable portion of the country; more than half of this area is in Kalimantan, while Sumatra has almost one-quarter (Potter 1991b:202).

From the environmental point of view, the activities of loggers have much the same effect as those of farmers, though there is an important difference in that the introduction of a suitable agricultural system can prevent land deterioration when trees are removed. When forests are cleared and not replaced by another form of vegetative cover, *alang-alang* grass normally becomes established. But before this happens, exposure of the soil leads to accelerated erosion, for the heavy falls of rain typical of most forested regions in Indonesia cause the topsoil to be washed away. Certain technical aspects of logging increase the damage. Daylighting zones in the form of cleared land along logging roads, for example, as well as skidding roads and log yards, are left exposed in the process of timber extraction (Potter 1991b:184). On the whole, the rivers of the other islands now have rates of sedimentation similar to those of Java, though without the same pollution from other sources except in major urban areas like Palembang and Medan.

So far, the focus in the Indonesian forestry industry has been on production rather than on the sustainable utilisation of resources. Awareness of threats to the future of the industry led the government some years ago to introduce a selective cutting policy (*Tebangan Pilihan Indonesia*, or TPI) under which felling is in theory based on a 35-year cycle, with sections of concessions worked in blocks and trees under a certain size left to reach maturity. Far from helping to maintain forests or to make the logging industry more efficient, this policy has had the opposite effect, in that considerable damage is done to the remaining trees when larger ones are extracted. Moreover, with the removal of the best trees, genetic erosion is likely to occur since the trees that remain to produce seeds tend to be not only smaller but also inferior in quality (Whitten et al. 1987:481). While government policy requires logging companies to replant, incentives for enrichment planting of secondary forests are inadequate (Tarrant et al. 1987:7), as are those for the replanting of clear-cut land. The reason is that the reforestation levy on each cubic metre of extracted timber, although raised to $10 in July 1990, is too small to cover costs, despite the fact that it can be reclaimed after replanting is done. The fact that forestry leases are restricted to twenty years is another factor that discourages loggers from looking ahead to long-term prospects and to methods of ensuring that the industry itself remains sustainable.

Since 1987 the government has attempted to maintain the industry, if not the environment, through a replanting program that operates in conjunction with the development of timber estates (*Hutan Tanaman Industri*, or HTI). The aim is to establish forests of fast-growing softwoods that can provide raw material for the expanding pulp industry. Unfortunately, the present approach would appear, if anything, to be encouraging further felling of hardwoods. Timber companies are willing to establish plantations of soft-woods only when they are first given a concession of existing hardwoods that can be logged immediately (*Kompas*, 23 December 1988). To overcome this problem, the government has announced a policy of permitting timber estates to be established only on degraded land, but it remains to be seen whether pulp companies will find conditions attractive enough to invest in replanting.

Other constraints that may operate against the successful development of industrial forests include the fact that Indonesia is embarking on its program of timber estates at a time when fast-growing species like eucalypts have been planted on a large scale throughout the Pacific region, which means that the price of pulp is likely to fall steadily in the near future. Indonesia, which may not possess a comparative advantage in softwoods, could find it difficult to export the pulp and cheap timber thus produced, yet the scale of present plans is such that domestic markets are not likely to be able to absorb output. Ecologically, the replacement of natural forests by estates of eucalypts or similar trees should be carefully considered since any monoculture offers the possibility of pest attacks, as was demonstrated in the mid-1980s, when insects destroyed large stretches of planted *lamtoro gung* trees (Sp. *Leucaena*), a species that had previously proved effective in reducing soil loss and providing fuel-wood in dry-farming areas in Java and Nusa Tenggara (Metzner 1976). The diversity of the rainforest, which can never be reproduced, has always protected it from such threats.

From the economic point of view Indonesia may find that in the long term a timber estate will have far less value than a rainforest since the price

213

of tropical hardwoods is almost certain to rise as resources elsewhere become depleted. Research into the regeneration of hardwood species has so far had only limited results, though recent success in identification of the mycorrhizae necessary for the growth of dipterocarps offers prospects for their future cultivation. To transfer research findings to the field on a commercial basis, however, will not be easy. The fact that these slow-growing trees take several decades to reach maturity makes the practical application of research work less attractive to investors, who prefer relatively quick harvests of softwoods.

In the interests of sustained yield management of the forest resource, three general approaches have been suggested. The first involves a complete end to logging as the most effective way to preserve the environment, but with domestic demand rising it would be difficult to prevent illegal felling, even if exports were banned. The second approach involves the possible use of price mechanisms to reduce the rate of forest destruction, though a strategy that was based on raising the price of forest products could also encourage smuggling; in any case, as Zarsky (1991:68) points out, to be effective as a conservation measure price strategies would have to increase the market value of the forest area as a whole and not just the price of economically valuable hardwoods. The third approach is that of 'debt-for-nature swaps' whereby certain portions of debts are purchased by international bodies and then cancelled in return for the funding of local measures directed towards environmental conservation. No matter which, if any, of these approaches is adopted, there will always remain a major constraint on effective forest protection in the difficulty of preventing small-scale removal of timber by local saw-millers. As it is, authorities are finding it hard to stop the felling for timber purposes of West Kalimantan's *tengkawang* trees, a species of dipterocarps that produces illipe nuts, which are valuable for the oil that they yield.

Conclusion

A Minister of State for Development Supervision and Environment (changed in 1983 to Population and Environment) was appointed in 1978 and environmental legislation was passed soon afterwards in the form of Statute 4 of 1982 concerning Basic Provisions for the Management of the Environment and Government Regulation No. 29 of 1986 concerning Environmental Impact Analysis (Koesnadi 1989). However, it was only at the end of the 1980s that progress began to be made in the handling of environmental issues. The establishment of the *Badan Pengendalian Dampak Lingkungan* (Bapedal, Environmental Impact Management Agency), which officially came into existence on 5 June 1990 through Presidential Decree No. 23, is evidence of the greatly heightened government awareness of the importance of the environment and at the same time official recognition of the lack of adequate procedures by which environmental policies and regulations can be enforced. This new agency, of which the minister is the head, has national-level status. Independent of any department, it is directly responsible to the president. To support it in its task, special training has been provided for officials from departments like Industry and Justice, as they will be responsible for the implementation of legal proceedings in environmental matters. Since early 1991 *Bapedal* has made considerable progress in dealing with industrial pollution in urban areas. Factory owners have been told that if they do not take measures to prevent the disposal of effluent into rivers and the discharge of waste substances into the air, their business permits will be cancelled and legal action taken against them. Many factories, including the large cement plant at Cibinong near Jakarta, have responded by installing equipment to deal with pollutant waste.

One trend that has made the task of *Bapedal* easier is the growing awareness on the part of local communities of their right to live in a better physical environment. Many of the cases investigated by *Bapedal* have been the direct result of community protests about pollution that interferes with daily life. In Bekasi, for example, complaints have been made about paper factories that discharge waste into a river used for household water supplies and about other factories whose effluent has polluted *tambak* to the point where fish farmers have gone out of business. Similar complaints about waste water from the dyeing sections of textile factories in Tangerang have led to a suspension of their business permits. The highly-polluted Tapak River in Semarang has likewise attracted the attention of *Bapedal*, which has forced factory owners to install waste treatment plants.

The activities of *Bapedal* in attacking the problem of industrial waste disposal are tending, however, to divert public attention from less easily resolved questions of government policy in other matters relevant to the environment and to the sustainability of development. While there is wide community support for measures designed to clean up the highly visible pollution of urban rivers, the consequences of resource depletion, whether related to erosion in the upper watersheds of Java or to the effects of forestry and other land-use policies outside Java, are less frequently considered. Policy-making in these various spheres lies with individual government departments. Yet although all departments are now required to have internal monitoring units to assess the impact of their own activities on the environment, these units can only offer advice; decisions continue to be made at a higher level. Furthermore, this approach only strengthens the long-established pattern of sectoral policy-making. In the environmental conditions that now prevail throughout Indonesia, a regional approach is essential in all questions of how land and other resources are to be utilised, if sustainability is to be a major objective in national development strategies.

5
Cultural expression

Barbara Hatley

The focus of this chapter is creative expression through symbolic forms—performed arts, literature and mass media. That is to say, 'culture' in its formal sense rather than the more inclusive understanding of customs, ideas, patterns of association, the total way of life of a group of people. Yet symbolic forms, embodying the preoccupations and perceptions of those who create and 'consume' them, are of course part of a broader culture, in turn shaped by and inseparable from social, political and economic forces. The dramatic changes taking place in economy, society and politics in Indonesia during the New Order period are documented elsewhere in this volume. Assessing the way such changes have affected cultural perceptions and practices is a more complex, less quantifiable task. The following review of symbolic forms produced in particular social contexts during the New Order period pretends to no glib 'answers' to this question. The diversity of these forms and their contexts rules out any attempt to establish inclusive, uniform trends. Rather an attempt is made to highlight those patterns which emerge from documentation of cultural developments in their full, 'messy' variety. How these developments differ from the culture of the Old Order, how they arise out of social and political conditions, and what they suggest about the contemporary viability of the concept of a unitary 'Indonesian culture' are key questions informing this process.

Certainly the developments described in other chapters—rapid economic growth, increases in overall prosperity and in relative impoverishment, and strengthening of the state apparatus and emasculation of alternate political structures—have resulted in enormous changes in the facilities for and conditions of cultural expression. But evidence of the overall direction of

216

these changes is complex and confusing. Economic growth, for example, with its creation of a boom in the publishing industry, has made books, once rare and limited, a familiar and accessible commodity, and has stimulated the appearance of an ever-increasing variety of magazines and newspapers. The main market for these products is presumably the urban middle class, in keeping with their burgeoning consumption capacity, reflected elsewhere in grand new shopping complexes and roads perpetually jammed with private cars. But educational expansion has also created a vast literate public in villages and urban *kampung*, eager for access to written material. At the same time, audio–visual media—film, pop music, radio and particularly television, whose audience is estimated to have increased twentyfold during the late 1970s and early 1980s[1]—have likewise experienced enormous expansion. All this results in the exposure of ever greater numbers of people to expressions of a modern *national* culture, city based, employing the national language—Indonesian—and deriving originally from western models.

Active participation in Indonesian cultural forms is open to a broader spectrum of people than in the past. Small town and village high school pupils stage poetry readings and form pop music bands; labourers and *becak* drivers rehearse along with college students in modern theatre groups. One possible effect of the process is a greater sense of identification with such national culture, no longer seen as something remote, artificial, or the monopoly of a city elite. Also, the participation of a more diverse, heterogeneous population might be expected to have an eventual enriching effect on the culture itself.

But more important and more deleterious, many commentators suggest,[2] is the uniformity of thought and expression imposed by modern mass media. Bland images of urban prosperity, consumerist values and conformist sentiments, prized for their 'modernity', prevail over previously varied and autonomous regional modes of expression; the standardised Indonesian language of mass media and formal public communication undermines local linguistic diversity. Art forms and crafts of humble rural folk decline under the onslaught of mass-produced goods and media. The poor become dispossessed culturally as well as economically, consumers rather than producers of their own entertainment and cultural discourse.

Which is a more accurate representation of contemporary Indonesian cultural reality: Indonesian culture becoming more viable as it encompasses a wider public, or national media obliterating local diversity and creativity? Is it possible that both processes are taking place at the same time? Bound up with these questions is the related issue of state ideological control and intervention in cultural production. For the state contributes substantially to the bland ideological uniformity of the mass media, as it defines the limits of politically acceptable cultural expression. Through these information channels as well as through the educational system, and through its ubiquitous institutions and public rituals, it instils a particular vision of the world and walls out others. Government cultivation of traditional, regional art forms has meanwhile been seen to exacerbate the distancing of local communities from their own cultural expression, as performances are appropriated to new settings and 'developed' in accordance with outside values (see, for instance, Acciaioli 1985). Yet from other sources it is clear that state support, funding the program of institutes of the arts, fosters creative innovation in classical performing arts as well as more modern forms;[3] government-provided facilities and organisational networks encourage cultural activities at local community level.[4] Whatever its artificial aspects, state support for regional cultural forms does assist practitioners of these forms to maintain their art and strengthen its image against the tide of conformist modernity.

In the survey of contemporary cultural forms which follows, these issues are not addressed in a direct, systematic fashion. Rather, through the discussion there emerges reflection on issues of national and regional cultural identity, of commercialisation and westernisation, the viability of local cultural forms, the dominant role of the state in cultural production, and possibilities of resistance to this domination. The framework is one of a roughly chronological review of developments in art and entertainment forms in their social context from the late 1960s to the present day. To order the daunting task of documenting a veritable kaleidoscope of cultural expression over an extended time period, 'national' cultural forms such as modern Indonesian literature and theatre are distinguished from regional arts, and these in turn from mass media such as film, popular music, television and the press.

Such categorisation follows standard Indonesian practice, in which the term 'modern' is used to designate those cultural forms which arose with intensive western cultural contact and nationalist activity in late colonial times, which employ the national language, *bahasa* Indonesia, and which have currency throughout the archipelago. By contrast, forms based in particular regions, expressed in local languages and following long-established aesthetic models are described as both 'regional' and *tradisional*, 'traditional'. The English terms 'media' and 'mass media' are meanwhile widely used in Indonesia, to refer to the press and electronic media. In adopting these categories I acknowledge their inherent ambiguities and contradictions. When significant innovation occurs in a regional cultural form, is it still to be regarded as 'traditional'? Can the term 'traditional' apply to regional performances like *ludruk* and *kethoprak*, which developed into their present form only during the twentieth century? Surely films and popular music are as 'Indonesian' and 'national' in scope as literature and painting?[5] Here the terms are employed entirely for practical ends, to help order a complex body of information, with no normative assumptions.

Beginning the discussion with modern literature, theatre and art might seem to give inappropriate precedence to cultural forms of relatively limited public interest, compared with television, film or well-loved, long-entrenched traditional arts. The choice relates to the historical prominence of such forms in defining Indonesian culture, growing out of their relationship with nationalism, and the symbolic importance they still hold as 'barometers' of freedom of cultural expression vis-a-vis the state. The bannings of the *Manikebu* manifesto in Sukarno times, of Rendra's plays in the 1970s, Pramudya's novels in the 1980s, and recently the satirical comedies of the troupe Teater Koma, become major political events, attracting attention from far wider circles than would normally read novels or watch plays. Admittedly, also, the much greater documentation available for developments in the sphere of modern, national art, in the form of published original works, press reviews and academic articles, makes it easier to discuss these forms as a kind of base from which to move on to other areas.

Traditional, regional cultural forms with their long-established social roles are discussed next. Here the focus is mainly Javanese, because my own experience is in this area, and published material on the other islands is scant. But evidence from other regions, drawn on wherever possible, does seem to show continuities with the Javanese case. Finally, the mass media, once again necessarily concentrating on relatively well-documented examples, as expressive forms most closely integrated with rapid contemporary changes in society and economy, raises challenging questions for the future.

In each case discussion will first focus on structures and institutions for production and 'consumption' of the form. Dominant features arising out of these circumstances of production are then explored, along with alternate or problematic trends. Two general chronological periods can be identified— an early period of establishment of new patterns and institutions, often also of enthusiastic florescence and relatively liberal expression, lasting into the mid to late 1970s, followed by a time of greater technical and intellectual sophistication, but also of greater concentration of resources and control, less broadly-based activity, tighter censorship and greater influence of factors of wealth.

Beginnings

The transition to the New Order period is recalled in standard interpretation of recent Indonesian history as a catalyst for growth and florescence in cultural expression as in other fields of activity. Writers and modern theatre performers talk of liberation from the domination of political issues, from constant confrontation with artists of opposing political affiliation, and of freedom to pursue personal creativity. The speakers here represent, of course, the 'victors' in the final political clash which ended the old era and ushered in the new. Their account excludes the perspectives of their opponents, the leftist writers who were killed or imprisoned or fled during the communist purges of 1965–66, for whom the transition brought annihilation, on both the personal and professional level, rather than growth. In fact, the cultural forms of the earliest New Order years, in themselves, often by their very paucity and limited expressiveness, provide evidence of the traumatic rupture to Indonesian social and cultural life which occurred during those years. A few strident battle poems celebrating the 1966 student demonstrations against Sukarno,[6] a dozen or so short stories set during the time of the massacres, many curiously dry and flat, reflecting perhaps the strain of emotion still repressed, guilt inadequately expunged through writing[7]—these are the works of modern Indonesian literature documenting this period. In Indonesian-language theatre, very little activity seems to have taken place until late 1967. In modern film, great numbers of foreign films flooded in, particularly with the lifting of the ban on American works previously imposed by left-nationalist unions; but local productions were few. The regional performing arts, at least in Java, where many performers had had close links with the communist party, underwent a long period of quiescence. Apart from a few long-established, state-supported troupes in the big cities, professional theatre groups disbanded. Actors feared reprisals, nervous authorities suspected large gatherings of people, community celebrations of the kind usually marked by a theatrical performance were hardly being held. Not until the early 1970s did professional troupes performing regional popular theatre such as *ludruk* and *kethoprak* reassemble, now with links to the armed forces rather than political parties. Amateur, community-based groups reappeared a few years later.

By the early 1970s, however, a new period of growth, of initiation of new cultural institutions and activities had begun as part of more general processes of economic and social development. A shift had taken place in the structures of cultural production, as in polity and society generally, from rivalry between competing political groups to control by a strong centralised state. And the superior financial resources and wide-reaching authority of the New Order made possible the implementation of policies with far-reaching consequences for cultural activity. One thinks of the expansion of the education system, in particular, though the provision of new schools under the *Inpres* (Presidential Instruction) scheme; of campaigns for newspapers to reach villages (*koran masuk desa*); of the rapidly extending access to television, through private ownership and government-provided sets in community halls. Outside the ambit of direct government activity, but facilitated by the economic conditions state policies had encouraged, came mushrooming growth of newspapers and magazines, and gradual establishment of a burgeoning publishing industry.

In all three spheres of cultural expression to be discussed here—modern, national arts, regional forms and popular media—new institutional frameworks established at this time were crucially important to the development of the form.

National culture—modern art, literature and theatre

Structures and institutions

Production of modern Indonesian literature and the arts in the early New Order period was facilitated and dominated by three major institutions—the literary journal *Horison*, the Taman Ismail Marzuki (TIM) arts complex, and the new publishing houses which began operations at this time. In November 1968, as part of the development of the capital by energetic city governor Ali Sadikin, the TIM arts complex was opened in Jakarta.[8] TIM provided facilities for theatre performances and rehearsals, for art exhibitions and films, and for poetry readings and literary discussions. The literary magazine, *Horison*, had been founded earlier by a group of prominent writers from the liberal, 'rightist' camp in the literary-political polemics of the late Sukarno years—Mochtar Lubis, H.B. Jassin, Goenawan Mohamad, Taufik Ismail—as an artistic expression of the change of social and political order, a medium for literary works embodying the newly-released creative energies of the times. Interaction and debate among the writers and critics of *Horison* and other intellectuals of the capital gained a physical forum and live audiences at TIM. TIM at that time represented for artists and cultural enthusiasts a space relatively free of ideological restriction to meet, discuss, exhibit and perform.

TIM also maintained a more popular face, providing entertainment and facilities for a wider cross-section of the Jakarta population. Performances of traditional theatre forms from Central and East Java attracted large audiences from among Jakarta residents of Javanese origin. For a time there were also well-attended stagings of the local Jakarta folk theatre *lenong*, but these eventually lost momentum, perhaps because of the difficulty of recreating at TIM the intimacy and spontaneity of *lenong* in its original humble community setting. A more successful and lasting theatrical initiative of the Jakarta government during this period was the organisation of annual festivals of youth theatre, *teater remaja*. In community centres all over the city, local groups would compete to represent their area in the finals, held with considerable fanfare and judged by top performers at TIM.[9] These competitions continue today, based now in the regional youth centres rather than at TIM. One major aim of their introduction, some have said, was to provide young people with alternate recreation to cheap westernised culture, to 'keep them off the streets'. At the same time, theatre provides for urban youth a vital medium of expression of their sense of identity, of their confusions and frustrations, with competitions constituting an important stimulus for theatre activity. Some of the more successful actors, meanwhile, go on to become established theatre performers.

Besides serving the people of the capital, TIM also provided a model for the establishment of local art and cultural centres in major regional cities during the 1970s. The Den Pasar arts centre Werdi Budaya, for example, was established in 1976; the Solo *taman budaya* (regional arts centre) in 1979, and its Yogyakarta equivalent in 1980. Like TIM, such centres provide a location for performances and rehearsals of modern theatre as well as traditional performing arts and newly-created dance spectacles (*sendratari*), along with literary discussions and poetry readings. In their regional settings they also play an important role, through policies of presentation of performances, and conduct and content of cultural seminars, in the process of defining and transmitting local cultural identity. Their significance in this context is explored later in discussion of developments in the regional arts.

In the field of production and marketing of literary works, the early 1970s onward saw the growth of several large, commercial publishing houses associated with major daily newspapers and magazines. The proprietors of the national daily *Kompas* founded Gramedia publishing in 1970, producers of the *Sinar Harapan* (now *Suara Pembaruan)* newspaper established their publishing arm Sinar Kasih, while Grafitipers, set up to publish light, popular fiction in the early 1970s, later took on the national weekly *Tempo*, along with many 'serious' literary works. Additionally, several government publishing houses (the old, Dutch-established Balai Pustaka, revived and revamped; and the newly-founded Pustaka Jaya, prolifically productive during the 1970s) and large numbers of small, private printeries flourished briefly and then disappeared alongside the major firms. In striking contrast to the situation at the end of the Old Order period, when economic problems, including a chronic shortage of paper, slowed publication to a trickle, and authors had great difficulties publishing their works, opportunities now abounded.

Dominant trends in artistic expression

By its publication policies, *Horison* set the standards for 'serious' literature, providing models which writers all over Indonesia attempted to emulate, and its critical essays defined the dominant literary issues of the time (Hill 1984; Foulcher 1987). Likewise, the discussions and performances at the TIM arts centre, generously reported in the national press, served to establish key literary and cultural issues and exemplify the latest dramatic and poetic approaches and styles. In modern arts and literature, as in politics, administration or business, the capital city constituted the defining centre, the *pusat*: an invitation to appear at TIM constituted artistic recognition for regionally-based writers, artists and performers. The critical views and creative works of a group of writers who frequently wrote for *Horison* and participated in discussions at TIM—figures such as Asrul Sani, H.B. Jassin, Mochtar Lubis, Danarto, Budi Darma, Abdul Hadi, Sapardi Djoko Darmono—thus came to set the prevailing standards for serious literary activity. A more extended network of writers and performers who also have close links with the arts centre and whose work has achieved recognition and acclaim would include the dancer and choreographer Sardono W. Kusumo, playwright–directors Putu Wijaya and Arifin C. Noer, novelist and chairman of the Jakarta Arts Council in the early 1970s, Umar Kayam, and poets Soebagio Sastrowardojo, Toeti Heraty and Goenawan Mohamad.

What were the dominant characteristics of literature produced under these circumstances? And what kinds of relationships can be drawn between literary patterns, their process of production and the broader social environment?

Two major trends are observable amid the individual variation in these writers' works. First, aesthetic experimentation, a non-realistic, sometimes surreal and absurdist mode of expression, and a concentration on philosophical and metaphysical themes; secondly, reference to indigenous, regional cultural traditions. In some cases the two trends come together, in poems styled after the incantatory 'verbal magic' of mantra, for example, or absurdist plays invoking motifs and characters from traditional regional myths (Sumardjo 1984; quoted in Foulcher 1987).

Somewhat similar trends are observable in the field of visual arts. The individualist, modernist approach to art theory and practice, centred in Bandung, which had previously been contested by more populist, engaged movements in Yogyakarta and elsewhere, now achieved ascendancy (Holt 1967; Miklouho-Maklai 1991). The approved art of the time is described as 'characterised by individual expression, internationalism and decorative works in the abstract or realist style'. Particular artists, meanwhile, focused on traditional themes such as regional dances and ceremonies (Miklouho-Maklai 1991:16–18).

A key element in an impressive outburst of creativity in the early New Order period, included in such works as the mythic, magical short stories of Danarto's *Godlob* (1974), the intuitive, symbolic, intensely personal poetry of Soebagio Sastrowardojo's collection *Daerah Perbatasan* (1970), and Toeti Heraty's thoughtful and witty reflections on male–female relationships in *Sajak 33* (1974), is the freedom to give expression to experiences and perspectives denied legitimacy by the prescribed concerns of literature in the preceding period. Pre-1965 concentration on social and political themes, expressed in realistic mode, had rendered inappropriate (and unpublishable) symbolic reflections on psychological, spiritual and meta-physical dimensions of existence. Among the burst of publications of the early New Order period were a number of works produced earlier but only in the New Order years deemed acceptable by censors and publishers, most notably the absurdist novels of Iwan Simatupang, written in the 1960s but appearing posthumously in the early 1970s (see, for example, Simatupang 1969, 1972).

That this creative energy should continue through the 1970s to be directed into non-realistic, absurdist works has given rise to varying inter-pretations. To some observers this trend reflects mere imitation of western literary models. The novelist and critic Budi Darma asserts, however, that such writings are grounded in chaotic social conditions similar to those that gave rise to absurdist literature in Europe (Budi Darma 1989). Hill (1984) suggests that the surreal images and settings of much writing of this period, unrelated to contemporary social problems and issues, accords with official suppression of political organisation and analysis, and with the universalist, ahistorical literary perspectives of its authors. Similar views were expressed by supporters of the concept of *sastra kontekstual* (contextual literature) in the mid-1980s, to be discussed in more detail later. Sri Rahayu Prihatmi (1985), by contrast, sees such works as engaging with reality inasmuch as they express rebellion against it, rejecting conventional dogma and materi-alistic concerns; Tickell (1986) likewise explores the socially subversive functions of fantasy.

Regional cultural reference in the modern literature and drama of the 1970s, according to Foulcher (1978), differs from that of earlier historical periods in terms of its sophistication and conscious intent. Rather than naively and unconsciously drawing on their regional literary traditions, or conversely shunning them in an attempt to be western and modern, these authors display a mature, almost detached appreciation of their indigenous culture, selecting from it in accordance with their own creative purpose. Foulcher cites as examples the novelettes *Sri Sumarah* by Umar Kayam, and *Bila Malam Bertambah Malam* by Putu Wijaya, poetry by Soebagio Sastrowardojo, and the Rendra play *Kisah Perjuangan Suku Naga*. This process of appropriation of regional cultural elements meanwhile takes place in a context of extensive state support for regional performing arts and literary traditions. This government attention to regional traditions was intended to give substance to national cultural identity, in place of the populist–nationalist political vision of earlier years, and to counter the cultural influence accompanying new economic and political ties with the west (Foulcher 1990; Hatley 1993). On an individual level, traditional rituals and performances were gaining new currency with the urban middle class, enhancing prestige and perhaps providing a sense of cultural continuity amid rapid social change. The regional reference of modern literature might be seen to contribute in its own way to this broader process of construction of cultural identity.

Both literary trends of the 1970s, non-realistic, absurdist modes of expression and evocation of regional cultures, clearly relate in a different way to their social environment from literature of the preceding decades. Absent is the intent of direct engagement in social and political processes. The literary and artistic images of the early 1960s, depictions in realistic mode of the sufferings and preoccupations of the *rakyat*—the ordinary people—disappear, along with their authors' sense of participation in social debate and political struggle.

Within this framework of the conditions of literary and artistic production in the 1970s, through absurdist images and indigenous cultural elements, some artists reflect on perceived social problems. Two examples are the works of Arifin Noer and Putu Wijaya, playwright–directors whose theatre groups performed and rehearsed at TIM through the 1970s. Both Arifin and Putu had once performed with the dramatist Rendra in Yogyakarta; both established their own groups in Jakarta on a model similar to Rendra's—collectives of young people who rehearsed together constantly under the tutelage of a leader who wrote and directed all their plays.

Common to several of Arifin's plays is the motif of the 'little man' at the bottom of society struggling to survive in a hostile world, symbolised by sinister controlling figures and bizarrely tortuous representations of everyday encounters. In *Kapai-Kapai* (Gropings), the errand-boy, Abu, abused and mistreated by his boss, disparaged by his wife, hounded by religious zealots, physically battered by fate, nevertheless maintains faith in a dream of wealth and glory dangled before him by a team of crafty manipulators—until, just as he achieves the dream, these figures put him to death. In *Tengul,* the title figure attempts to escape his poverty-stricken existence through gambling, but achieves success only through promising his soul and sacrificing his wife to a mysterious supernatural being. In both these plays Arifin draws on images and forms of expression from indigenous folk tradition, particularly that of his Javanese north-coast (*pasisiran*) birthplace, Cirebon. In *Kapai-Kapai* there are children's games, exchanges of four-line poems (*pantun*) and a segment of popular theatre; in *Tengul* the power to whom Tengul sells his soul is a local deity of the north-coast regions. These elements are juxtaposed with other images and language modes, perhaps to convey a sense of the fragmented cultural world of character and playwright, and of modern Indonesians generally.[10]

Putu Wijaya's Balinese cultural background also inspires his theatre; not through identifiable symbols or images, he says, but rather through the whole atmosphere of the play and its emotional impact. Like Balinese performances, his plays are above all *tontonan* (spectacles), working through emotional empathy and absurd humour rather than structured plot and dialogue. Through bizarre images and events, his plays evoke feelings of alienation and confusion among urban Indonesians amid changing social norms, and ridicule egotistical, corrupt social practices (Rafferty 1990).

For both these dramatists, an important early influence, as already noted, was their contact with the playwright and poet Rendra. Rendra's activities in the 1970s—based outside the capital, in the central Javanese city of Yogyakarta—producing plays which directly engaged with social and political processes, in fact stand somewhat apart from the processes described so far, connecting in a different way with their social context. Because of his powerful influence on subsequent modern theatre activity, particularly in Central Java, his work warrants particular attention.

Rendra: an alternate model of artistic production

For Rendra, regional cultural traditions coloured not only his creative works but also work relations, lifestyle and philosophy, mixed eclectically with influences from foreign sources. Returning from study in the United States in 1967, Rendra established a theatre troupe, not in Jakarta, the modern, westernised capital, but in tradition-steeped Yogyakarta in Central Java. Troupe members lived in rented houses around Rendra in a semi-rural *kampung* on the outskirts of the city, supporting themselves at individual jobs but also cultivating a piece of land together, and gathering frequently for instruction from Rendra in philosophy and social analysis as well as dramaturgy. Outsiders were invited to talk to the group on subjects of their own expertise. An American doctor resident in Yogyakarta, for example, instructed them about nutrition and the control of epidemic diseases such as cholera and dengue fever. The pattern is intriguingly reminiscent of aspects of a traditional *pesantren* residential school, with Rendra as the powerful, respected teacher, the *kiyahi*, and of the communal lifestyle of touring Javanese popular theatre groups. Another key inspiration was surely Rendra's understanding of the commune movement as he had encountered it in America—the bohemian appearance and lifestyle of the actors, their long hair, jeans, and late-night carousing created an image more rebelliously 'modern' and western-influenced than traditionally Javanese.

Rendra's first performances on returning to Indonesia—before the American sojourn he headed a group as actor and director, but not as playwright and 'guru'—were abstract, scriptless, non-linear dramas, influenced by contact with western avant-garde theatre. There followed adaptations to a Javanese context of the western classics, *Oedipus*, *Lysistrata*, *Macbeth*, and *The Caucasian Chalk Circle*, employing Javanese costumes and *gamelan* musical accompaniment. In the mid-1970s came his original plays *Mastodon dan Burung Kondor* (The Mastodon and the Condor), *Kisah Perjuangan Suku Naga* (The Struggle of the Naga Tribe) and *Sekda* (The Regional Secretary). Settings and dramatic styles became more and more explicitly

Indonesian. *Suku Naga*'s location in the fictional kingdom of 'Astinam' (Astina is the name of the realm of the 'baddies' in *wayang* dramas), the use of a *dalang* narrator and a *wayang*-like dramatic structure all served to associate the satirised rulers of the kingdom with the leaders of the Indonesian state. Like the queen of the play, Indonesian authorities had allowed the appropriation of isolated lands for the establishment by foreign interests of a huge mine. *Sekda* is located straightforwardly in a Yogyakarta *kampung* on Independence Day; in a farcical 'play within a play' *kampung* residents satirise the behaviour of pompous, avaricious government officials responding to a rural epidemic with bogus 'seminars' and charity bazaars. The interaction of the officials recalls the comic routines of local popular theatre forms, while a virtuous doctor who denounces their irresponsibility proposes an alternate approach to the epidemic drawn straight from the lectures of Rendra's American doctor friend.

Rendra denies any deliberate intent to invoke Javanese cultural 'tradition'. Instead, indigenous elements arise as the most effective medium to convey the story he wishes to tell in the social context of its performance. In the case of *Suku Naga*, a *wayang* palace scene provides a golden opportunity to satirise the self-aggrandisement and corruption of contemporary officials. The narrator's critical comments on the action, departing from the traditional *dalang*'s role of simply reproducing established characterisations and relating events, may be intended as a model for a more participatory, critical approach to state affairs among the contemporary Indonesian public.

Rendra's plays clearly made reference to actual events and issues, and engaged in direct political debate. Their criticisms of state policies and personnel resulted in a ban by the Yogyakarta authorities on performances by Rendra's troupe in the Bengkel theatre, between 1974 and 1978. At the same time, rehearsals for performances in other cities continued to be held on an open area in front of Rendra's house, where large crowds gathered to watch. On two occasions when the prohibition was lifted, in 1977 for a performance of *Sekda* and 1978 for *Suku Naga*, the capacity crowd of students and other youthful supporters filled a local sports hall and roared with approval at each swipe at state authority. The same huge crowds, reacting with similiar excitement and approval, greeted Rendra's readings of his poetry—savage portraits of greedy decadent leaders, confused, corrupted youth and suffering poor he called 'pamphlet poems' (*sajak-sajak pamflet*).[11]

Rendra was giving voice to the mood of unrest and dissatisfaction widespread among young people at this time. These were the years of the Malari riots and trials, the student white paper, the campus protests of 1977–78. The abstract, non-realistic Jakarta-produced art and literature of the 1970s has been seen to accord with a general depoliticisation of cultural

227

expression induced by the policies of the New Order state: Rendra's realistic, politically critical plays and poems give vent to feelings of disillusionment with and alienation from that state being experienced by the middle of the decade in particular segments of New Order society. Students who had vigorously supported the rise to power of the New Order now felt betrayed by its perceived failures—the corruption, repression, and lack of concern with social justice.

While Rendra's poetry readings were giving expression to political dissatisfactions, a movement developed in the visual arts protesting against the perceived elitism and remoteness from real social issues of art institutions and art practice. In late 1974 a group of young artists and art students sent a flower tribute to the judges of a major painting exhibition at the Taman Ismail Marzuki, expressing their condolences on the 'death of Indonesian painting'. The *Gerakan Seni Rupa Baru* (Indonesian New Art Movement), rejecting the concept of 'fine art' and 'the elitist language of avant-gardism', held their own exhibitions of mixed-media assemblages, found objects, sculpture and photomontage, making reference—sometimes humorously satirical, sometimes brutally shocking—to social issues. Several such exhibitions took place between 1974 and 1979; then they stopped. Cessation of the group's activities at this point is attributed by some to loss of momentum and direction. Artists themselves blame the increased political repression of the late 1970s, as student leaders were arrested and university campuses were occupied by the military, for forcing them into silence (Miklouho-Maklai 1991:23–30, 76–7).

In Rendra's case, the connection between political events and artistic practice is very clear. By 1978, as the mood of confrontation heightened, Rendra was spending much time out of Yogyakarta, talking to student groups and reading his poetry at campus gatherings and in student dormitories. In July of that year, after a bomb exploded during one his poetry readings at TIM, Rendra was arrested and imprisoned on the grounds that his activities threatened public order. On release he was totally banned from public performance, a ban which was to remain in force for seven years. The Bengkel theatre of Yogyakarta disappeared and was never re-established— the new, post-1986 Bengkel, based just outside Jakarta, operates in a very different social environment, its performances sponsored by wealthy impresarios, with occasional overseas tours. But though Rendra and his troupe were gone, their legacy remained. Some contemporary performers recall their intrigue and fascination watching Bengkel's *kampung* rehearsals; later they established their own groups, likewise based in humble neighbourhoods, comprised of local youths, rehearsing in whatever space there was available. They too staged performances drawing on regional cultural traditions—historical and mythological themes, with traditional musical accompaniment—which were seen to address contemporary political issues.

It is Rendra's role as a catalyst for this kind of activity, his voicing of shared political sentiments otherwise suppressed, his popularisation of knowledge from outside Indonesia relevant to the contemporary situation, his overall embodiment of more general trends, which have made him a particularly important figure in Indonesian cultural life. His work encapsulates and in some cases initiates key trends in Indonesian modern arts in the mid to late 1970s—the re-emergence of political concerns, a focusing on regional cultural traditions, and the involvement in the production of modern Indonesian culture of greater numbers of young people of modest social circumstances, with some education, living in the regions. He may be seen as a key influence in the development of a distinctive style and mode of production of modern theatre performances in the regions, in particular the central Javanese cities of Yogyakarta and Solo—socially critical, with a regional cultural focus, *kampung*-based, and with close ties to their social environment.

Before following up into the 1980s the development of regionally-oriented literature and theatre, along with other trends in the production of modern Indonesian culture, let us look briefly at the situation of the original, regional forms, on which the modern works draw, in the first half of the New Order period.

Regional cultural forms in the 1970s

As mentioned earlier, after 1965 the New Order state became very active in the cultivation of regional performing arts and cultural forms, to a much greater degree than governments of the past. In this respect it took over and expanded roles previously played by the political parties. Between the late 1950s and mid-1960s, in the latter years of the Old Order, regional performing arts had received much attention and support from political parties and organisations, in particular from the communist-linked cultural institute *Lembaga Kebudayaan Rakyat* (Lekra) (Institute of People's Culture). McVey (1988) writes of the debates between communist figures over *wayang kulit*, Javanese shadow puppet theatre. With its stories of kings and courts and celebration of hierarchical 'feudal' values, yet its enormous ongoing influence in contemporary times among the Javanese masses, how could *wayang* be mobilised to promote more progressive social messages? The nationalist party, the PNI, had contacts with *dalang* through its affiliated cultural organisation, the *Lembaga Kebudayaan Nasional* (LKN) (National Cultural Organisation), establishing, for example, a school to teach both the art of *wayang* and PNI ideology (Brandon 1967:216).

Popular theatre, melodramatic plays enacted by human performers on the commercial stage, with historical or contemporary themes and settings, offered more clear-cut opportunities than *wayang* for conveying contemporary messages. Here political groups, particularly the communist movement, were very active. In Central Java, Bakoksi, a federation of *kethoprak* troupes aligned with the communist party, the PKI, formed in Yogyakarta in 1957, held congresses and discussions, and promoted better conditions for theatre performers. Instrumental in the formation of Bakoksi and working in direct association with it was Krido Mardi, one of the best-known professional troupes in Java, which also operated a school for young performers. In response to these activities, a rival *kethoprak* organisation, *Lembaga Kethoprak Nasional* (LKN) (National Kethoprak Association), with links to the PNI, was also established. In East Java both political parties and the armed forces were involved in promoting the local theatre form *ludruk*. The famous Ludruk Marhaen troupe was communist-connected, while the army supported the group Tresno Enggal. A PKI-aligned *ludruk* association, Lembaga Ludruk, was very active, with the cultural association of the PNI once again responding with its own initatives (Brandon 1967). Folk performances of particular regions, such as the dance pageant *reyog* in Ponorogo, were likewise sponsored by local branches of the major political parties, to encourage popular support (Kartomi 1978). Political rallies were frequently accompanied by performances of regional theatre forms.

The picture just described relates specifically to Java, where the communist movement was strongest, and where cultural activities of other political groups seem to have been stimulated largely in reaction to communist initiatives. Since the Muslim parties took little interest in theatre, politicisation of theatre activity centred on the conflict between the PKI and PNI. In other areas of Indonesia patterns of suppport for regional performing arts presumably reflected local political rivalries, with the dominant political power as the most influential sponsor.

It was the New Order state, then, which took over the role of chief sponsor of regional performing arts after the political changes of 1965–66, by eliminating the communist movement and bringing an end to the effective power of the political parties. The stated aim for such support was to preserve and nurture the traditional performing arts, and to engage them in the processes of societal development which the government sought to promote. There was no doubt also some sense of obligation—and opportunity—to build up an artistic infrastructure crushed and demoralised by the killings and imprisonments, and to replace old ideological connotations of theatre forms with new ones.

In the field of *wayang kulit*, in April 1969, coinciding with the official start to the first Five-Year Development Plan on 1 April, meetings were held in Jakarta with puppeteers from all over Indonesia. The group was addressed by several ministers including President Soeharto himself, who exhorted the *dalang* to assist in the achievement of the Five-Year Development Plan by arousing the peasants to their responsibility to contribute, in areas such as agricultural development and birth control. Further meetings were foreshadowed, along with the formation of a *dalang* organisation. In July of the same year, the Indonesian Association for the Art of the Dalang, best known by its abbreviated title, Ganasidi, was established in Semarang. The major initiator was General Surono, the then commanding officer of the Central Javanese military district, who saw the organisation as a forum to stimulate the devotion of *dalang* to their art 'in conformity with the government's policy' (van Groenendael 1985:147). In its initial phase Ganasidi was restricted to Central Java, with the Central Java military regional branches of several government departments (Information, Education and Culture) sharing patronage and sponsorship. In 1971 a *dalang* organisation encompassing all of Java and Madura, Pepadi, was formed, with Ganasidi as an affiliate. Among the activities promoted by the organisation were training workshops for young *dalang* and conferences to document the knowledge of older *dalang*, as custodians of traditional lore which might otherwise vanish with their passing.

Government departments were also directly involved in the cultivation of *wayang*. They sponsored performances of *wayang* forms now rarely seen, such as *wayang klithik*, with the aim of stimulating public interest (van Groenendael 1985:131), and experimented with a shortened time framework—3–4 hours rather than a whole night—and with the use of the Indonesian language rather than Javanese. There have been several week-long national *wayang* festivals in Jakarta since the early 1970s, with displays and performances purporting to represent the whole archipelago, and a permanent *wayang* museum has likewise been established.

While new initiatives such as these have attracted attention from *wayang* practitioners, intellectuals and those with special interest in the arts, it has been state-supported *wayang* performances of a more standard type which have had impact on the general public. Most prominent are the weekly broadcasts of *wayang* performances through the state radio network Radio Republik Indonesia (RRI). On Saturday nights several major Javanese cities—Jakarta, Yogyakarta, Solo and Surabaya—in rotation host the all-night show. Such broadcasts, accessible through transistor radios in even the most remote villages and poverty-stricken slums, are enormously popular. A performance for RRI, so it is said, has the same significance today for a young *dalang* aspiring to fame and fortune as did a performance at court in days of old (van Groenendael 1985:129).

Another context for state-supported *wayang* is celebration of official occasions, such as Independence Day, Armed Forces Day, the opening of an election campaign, and the anniversaries of institutions of all kinds. *Wayang*, with its reputation as the 'highest' of art forms and its history of cultivation in the Javanese courts, is a natural choice of performance for a contemporary state, authoritarian and hierarchically-structured, which attempts to appropriate to itself the grandeur and mystique of court culture. Audiences, as always, consist of invited guests of the same social circle as the host (here state officials and other members of the local elite), who attend for reasons of social obligation, and crowds of uninvited onlookers (now generally poor villagers and *kampung*-dwellers) who come because they love *wayang*. Along with official occasions of this type, another opportunity for performances, frequently involving the most highly-paid and prestigious *dalang* in the country, are private family celebrations of high-ranking government officials.

Classical dance, a cultural form somewhat marginalised under the egalitarian ideology of the Sukarno years, because of its direct stylistic and social connections to the court, has during the New Order come into its own. Whereas in the early 1960s choreographers of Javanese dance were encouraged to concentrate on new, populist works such as *tari petani* (farmer's dance) and *tari nelayan* (fisherman's dance), or dance dramas with heroic themes, in the 1970s the restoration, documentation and transmission of classical traditions became a legitimate focus of attention. In Yogyakarta private classical dance schools and organisations holding classes and rehearsals in *pendhapa* (open pavilions of aristocratic homes), experienced a boom in membership. Leading figures in these organisations, who also held positions in the Department of Education and Culture, obtained subsidies to research and revive court dances not performed since colonial times. Much attention focused on the documentation and reproduction of pure Yogyakarta-style (as opposed to the more common Surakarta-style) classical dance and music, with the state-run conservatory high school, Konri, producing several books on the subject.

By the late 1970s the governor of the Yogyakarta Special Region, the ninth Yogyakarta sultan, had established an arts council for the region, with the stated aim of revitalising the traditional arts. The council, in cooperation with several other government departments, formed a committee for Yogyakarta-style classical dance presentation, focusing on the revival of the court dance drama, *wayang wong*. The aim was to encourage appreciation of the form, especially among young people, for use as a source of information and study, and to develop its potential for tourism. The first performance, in March 1981, involving seventy dancers of differing ages and backgrounds, attracted great interest and excitement (Kam 1987).

In the case of the popular drama forms of *kethoprak* in Central Java and *ludruk* in East Java, it was the armed forces who initiated their revival after the upheaval of the mid-1960s that claimed a great many actors as victims. By 1970 the East Java Brawijaya regiment was supporting three *ludruk* troupes, involving a number of surviving actors from the previous communist-linked troupe Ludruk Marhaen.[12] In 1971 in Central Java the *kethoprak* troupe Sapta Mandala was formed under the patronage of the seventh district command of the Diponegoro regiment, with the well-known dancer and cultural figure Bagong Kussudiardja as formal head. It likewise included a number of former members of the communist-aligned Krido Mardi, along with several tertiary-educated teachers and civil servants who had begun to perform at student rallies before 1965. This direct military involvement presumably reflected a perceived need for strong control over theatre forms which had previously had populist, leftist connections and connotations. It can also be explained in terms of protection for actors with previous communist links: though they would not normally have received permission to work because of their past, military patronage gave them the opportunity to perform.

In addition to these groups, the city government of Yogyakarta sponsored the formation in the early 1970s of a *kethoprak* group to perform at the Taman Hiburan Rakyat (THR) (People's Entertainment Park). Kethoprak Mataram, the troupe maintained by the state radio station RRI, continued its hugely popular weekly broadcasts. Such broadcasts had begun in 1935 under the Dutch government radio station Mavro and continued after independence through RRI. In other Central Javanese cities, notably Solo and Semarang, where commercial *wayang orang* dance drama constituted the local popular theatre form, the state-subsidised troupes established in the 1950s and 1960s continued to perform, albeit to dwindling audiences. A significant development for the regional performing arts in general, and *kethoprak* in particular, was the establishment in the early 1970s of regional stations of the RRI television network. By the mid-1970s a policy of rotation of troupes for the weekly *kethoprak* television broadcast produced vigorous efforts by local groups to attract attention and prove their suitability for appearance on television.

Many independent theatre groups were also performing by the mid-1970s. In Yogyakarta, five *kethoprak* troupes played commercially each night in the vicinity of the city, and another performed several times a month. From time to time the East Javanese troupe Siswo Budoyo, famous for its glamorous decor and technical tricks, would come to Yogyakarta on tour, performing on the main square for 2–3 months. Other groups gathered more occasionally, when hired to perform on the occasion of a family or community celebration. Meanwhile, myriad amateur groups based in *kampung* neighbourhoods were particularly active about the time of Indonesian Independence Day, preparing to perform in the *malam kesenian*, a kind of community concert representing the climax of local celebrations. Many such groups had been established or had recently regrouped after a period of post-coup inactivity. A degree of official involvement was in evidence here, inasmuch as the impetus for regrouping often came from the head of the *kampung* or village, wanting to encourage cultural activity in his area, and the main occasion for performance was a state celebration such as Independence Day. Yet the zealous commitment of *kethoprak* players and the huge, enthusiastic crowds at their performances suggest that the state connection simply facilitated autonomously vital, popular activity. Performance content, I have suggested elsewhere, expressed a sense of community identity and a 'grassroots' notion of 'Indonesianness' rooted in local experience, rather than ideas absorbed from outside (Hatley 1982).

Where amateur theatre activity did come under more direct influence from the state was through the numerous festivals, competitions and sessions of instruction for actors organised by national and regional offices of the Department of Education and Culture, and the Department of Information. National festivals involved evening performances at the TIM cultural centre in Jakarta by troupes representing the different provinces, and daytime discussions documenting and analysing the various theatre forms. In regional festivals and competitions, groups from each administrative district (*kecamatan*) vied to compete at the next highest regency (*kabupaten*) level. Such contests involved instruction during rehearsals by visiting officials in artistic matters, and often also about ideological 'messages' to be included in the show. Information sessions or 'upgradings' focused on the need to improve performance standards, by such methods as streamlining dramatic structure, on the model of western dramaturgy, and portraying characters in a realistic manner, rather than according to traditional stereotypes. *Kethoprak* seems to have been given particular attention, in documentation of past and present performance styles and exhortations to make innovations. The stated aim for these measures was to enrich and improve the form, to build up its reputation, and to make it appealing to 'all levels of society'. The Sapta Mandala group, with its skilled, experienced players and connections in high places, became engaged in many efforts of this kind. Attention was devoted to reproducing more accurately the language of the Javanese courts, as well as the conventions of court dress; to more careful use of blocking and stage movement and more streamlined dramatic structure; and to experiments with complete written scripts rather than traditional improvisation of dialogue.

What major trends may be discerned in the traditional performing arts of this period? What was the effect of the change in sponsorship of both performances and programs of 'cultivation' of theatre forms from political parties to the state? What kind of impact on performance content and style resulted from the kind of activities just described?

In regard to *wayang kulit*, as already suggested, innovative measures such as the shortening of performance length and use of Indonesian language, though of considerable, ongoing interest to *wayang* practitioners and afficionados, have had minimal impact as yet on standard *wayang* performances. Just how *wayang*'s dramatic elements, ancient and hallowed as they are understood to be, may have been affected by changes in contemporary social and political order is a complex question. Presumably one should look in the first instance for change in relatively superficial areas rather than basic structure, and for shifts in perception and interpretation.

An important feature of *wayang* in the Old Order, many accounts suggest, was perceived political reference. The monthly *wayang* performances at the presidential palace were seen to reflect on the standing of particular political figures, through portrayal of *wayang* characters associated with them, and to hint at Sukarno's planned future strategies. On a local level, performances sponsored by a particular political party would implicate rival groups in evil, underhand practices through association with the 'villains' in the story performed. In the depoliticised atmosphere of the New Order, routine *wayang* performances evoke no such expectations. Direct political reference seems limited to the context of election campaigns. Performances sponsored in the 1970s by the government political party, Golkar, frequently featured a *wringin* (banyan) tree, the party symbol, as a sacred object won by the heroes of the story from their enemies (van Gronendael 1985; personal experience). In the 1971 elections the PNI countered with performances such as one I attended depicting established kingly authorities (read 'government and Golkar') as corrupt and flawed, and the rebel against this authority, the alternate source of power, as strong and virtuous. Today the Golkar-sponsored banyan tree *wayang* continue, but with the further emasculation of the political parties, and strict monitoring of their activities, oppositionist performances are rare.

Regarding the nature of *wayang* performances in general during the 1970s, Ward Keeler remarks on the prevalence of a 'blanket category' of *lakon* (story) 'deemed appropriate to almost all occasions' (contradicting the standard wisdom that stories are chosen to fit the purpose of the performance) and thus 'performed more often than any other type of story' (Keeler 1987:180). This concerned the receipt of a mystical boon or *wahy'u*, destined for the virtuous Pendawa brothers, but involving first a protracted struggle with their rivals, the Korawas. Keeler himself does not suggest reasons for this phenomenon, nor comment on the possibility of social influence. A fairly obvious speculation, however, might relate this bland uniformity of theme to the current depoliticisation of *wayang*, in contrast to its earlier intense political involvement. Such stories may have represented a safe option for puppeteers wishing to avoid any imputation of political inference, which audiences, too, found comfortably non-threatening. In one particular area of performance, direct comment is in fact sometimes made on the effect of depoliticisation. The humour of the clowns is said to be more obscene now than in the past, concentrating exclusively on sexual innuendo, now that political jokes are no longer an option.[13] But if political reference is no longer overt, *wayang* retains its age-old capacity for veiled, incidental critique. At three in the morning, when the dignitaries have gone home, one can hear audiences roaring with laughter at comments they immediately connect with current political issues.

A theme to be followed up later, in discussion of *wayang* in the 1980s, is a development arguably of much more wide-reaching significance than shifts in story content and humour—the introduction of cassette tapes. Marketed widely from the early 1970s on, cassette tapes along with radio broadcasts (often in combination, as amateur radio stations play specially-produced tapes) have had a major impact on *wayang* 'consumption'. While a live *wayang* performance remained the appropriate, esteemed means of celebrating life-cycle occasions such as marriages and circumcisions, a far cheaper option became available, in the form of *wayang* cassettes, relayed over loudspeakers to entertain guests. Individuals could buy tapes of their favourite *dalang* to play at home at their leisure, as well as tuning in to frequent radio broadcasts. Whether this should be seen as an undermining or an expansion of *wayang*'s clientele and social import will be explored later.

In the *kethoprak* field, actors and directors commented on a distinct shift they perceived in the type of *lakon* most frequently performed. Stories of the historical kingdoms of Java, particularly those set in the time of the late Mataram dynasty, understood as the core repertoire of the form, were far outnumbered in the early 1970s by *dongeng*, tales with fantastic, fictional settings. The shift was attributed mainly to political factors—historical stories, played in the past in such a way as to project strong political reference, were now avoided by performers, anxious to avoid suggestion of political bias, and deemed less interesting by audience members, no longer relevant to social life. *Dongeng*, on the other hand, with their fictional settings and fantastic events, allowed the use of glamorous costumes and spectacular technical effects. These fitted the mood of a society opening up to new consumer goods and technological advances, and of audience members seeking entertainment and distraction rather than edification following the traumas of recent historical experience.[14] By the late 1970s the avoidance of historical stories, or at least *lakon* set in the Mataram period, seemed less general. While *dongeng* still predominated on the commercial stage, performances for competitions, festivals and television broadcasts often played out stories with a historical setting. Naturally these portrayed political leaders in ways supportive of the authority of the contemporary state—there was none of the ridiculing of kingly figures nor championing of the rights of the people said to have been characteristic of leftist performances in Old Order times.

As regards style of performance, the kind of innovations promoted in government-organised discussions and upgradings began to have an impact

in a limited way. While performances held in village and *kampung* settings
in celebration of local events continued to follow long-established patterns—
lasting from around 10 p.m. until early morning, improvised, rambling and
relaxed in structure, and highlighting humorous elements—commercial performances were seen as necessarily more streamlined and serious. Directors
explained this in terms of pressures from paying audiences—viewers were
better educated than in the past, more exposed to different media and a
faster pace of life, and thus more demanding of a dramatically interesting
performance. The specific innovations proposed at upgradings and experimented with by groups such as Sapta Mandala drew cautious reactions from
actors. The use of written scripts drew much criticism from older, experienced actors, who complained not only of the difficulty of learning by rote,
but even more of the reduction of spontaneous creativity and loss of
adaptability to particular social circumstances. Yet the requirements of
television broadcasts in particular, demanding brevity and exact timing, have
promoted the use of memorised scripts, the reduction of traditional features
and development of a style of performance closer to Western drama and
film. Through television and live appearances by the prestigious group Sapta
Mandala this model of performance is said to have become widespread (Kus
Sudyarsono 1989).

Television broadcasts served as a site of innovation also in *wayang
orang* dance drama, with extensive use of colourful technical effects and
segments of more naturalistic interaction between characters in place of the
standard stylised patterns of movement and speech. But such experimentation did not seem to flow through to commercial troupes, in the first
instance; no doubt because of the difficulty and expense of reproducing
such effects on stage. For from the early 1970s onwards, most commercial
wayang orang troupes have been suffering declining audiences and severe
economic difficulties. The legendary troupes Sriwedari in Solo and Ngesti
Pendawa in Semarang, enormously popular and famous in their heyday in
the 1950s and 1960s, regularly attract audiences of only a few dozen, and
at best a few hundred on Saturday nights. They survive only through
government subsidies. Other less famous and less fortunate groups have had
to sell off costumes and properties, cut down the number of performances
each week, or in some cases disband altogether.[15]

Performers and observers of *wayang orang* all relate the decline in
interest in the form to the changing times, albeit with different emphases
and solutions. Some blame competition from modern entertainment media
such as videos and films. Others see the need for radical changes in the
form to make it appealing to contemporary tastes, a need not responded to
by its practitioners in their adherence to classical, court-derived dramatic
conventions.[16] Performers and fans of other forms have asserted that the
fixed story repertoire and stylised mode of *wayang orang* are simply not

amenable to the kind of adaptation to contemporary social conditions which is possible with, for example, *kethoprak*. *Wayang orang* provides nothing to compare with the zany humour, fast pace and up-to-the-minute reference which brought great popularity in the late 1970s to the relatively new form, *srimulat*.[17] Meanwhile, amid such depressed conditions elsewhere, in the capital of Jakarta, with its myriad modern entertainments, two *wayang orang* troupes, the large, well-endowed Wayang Orang Bharata in Senen, and a smaller group in North Jakarta, continue to thrive. Presumably their performances attract mainly ethnic Javanese residents of the city, renewing contact with their Javanese cultural roots, their outlay on such entertainment facilitated by the relatively high wages and strong economic conditions of the capital. Included here are perhaps both members of the lower middle-class groups (petty traders, minor clerks and the like) most likely to watch commercial *wayang orang* in Central Java, along with some of the more educated, middle-class people who in Yogyakarta and Solo would identify instead with the prestigious court style *wayang orang* taught by the private dance schools.

Might there be implications here for possible future roles of the traditional performing arts? With the decline of their former 'agrarian-feudal-aristocratic' basis of support and source of meaning (Umar Kayam 1981), might new constituencies and meanings emerge amid the flux of urbanisation and modernisation? Clearly the natural, almost 'organic' connection between particular population groups and their cultural forms changes with the increasing penetration of modern national culture and mass media. Models from the new media, it has been suggested, impel shifts in the form of the traditional performance itself. Later, in reviewing developments through the 1980s, we shall note similar changes in both the form and the pattern of 'consumption' of traditional performing arts. First, however, let us look at the new mass media themselves, as they developed during the 1970s.

Mass media in the 1970s

While the cultural forms surveyed so far have been importantly *influenced* by the economic growth and concomitant social changes of the 1970s, mass media such as films, magazines and pop music have been directly and immediately shaped by these developments. The growth of an increasingly affluent, educated middle class, aspiring to modern knowledge and skills, plus investors eager to take advantage of their potential, facilitated the publishing boom of the 1970s and 1980s. Along with new newspapers and popular novels appeared glossy magazines—first the news magazine *Tempo*, then the women's magazines, such as *Femina*, *Sarinah* and *Kartini*, and an ever-growing flood of magazines directed to specific social groups and interests, such as home beautification, business, sports activities, even a man's magazine—the 'Indonesian *Playboy*', *Matra*. Likewise, popular music found a thriving market among young people, referred to today as *remaja* ('youth', 'teenagers'), with its suggestion of subcultural tastes in leisure and entertainment, rather than by the Old Order term *pemuda*, with its implications of political activism.[18] The film industry, opening up to foreign imports after the lifting of trade union bans imposed in the late Sukarno years, was flooded with overseas products, and during the first years of the New Order period very few Indonesian films were made. But in 1967 a levy was introduced on foreign films, with the money being used to finance Indonesian productions. By 1971, partly through this method of tapping into the import market, and partly through a general expansion of the economy, the number of Indonesian-made films produced per year had increased considerably. The state television service, established since 1962, became a real mass medium only in the second half of the 1970s, once improved incomes allowed sizeable numbers of people to purchase sets. This period of booming oil revenues also saw the launching of the Palapa satellite, capable of relaying television broadcasts all over the country, the introduction of colour television, and the erection of many ground relay stations.

Structures and institutions

While, as we have seen, state institutions assumed the dominant role in sponsoring traditional and modern national arts in the early New Order period, popular mass media was largely funded and controlled by commercial interests. The state performed monitoring and regulatory functions. Radio and television networks constituted key exceptions, where state control was direct. State television, TVRI (Televisi Republik Indonesia), through its central and regional stations, held a complete monopoly on television broadcasting until the late 1980s, when the first private channel RCTI (Rajawali Citra Televisi Indonesia) was established. Moreover, in accordance with guidelines stating that 'TVRI . . . as a part of the Department of Information . . . is a public relations instrument of the government' (Quinn 1989:3), state television is required to cover all public activities of heads of government departments, all state ceremonies, and openings of new projects and the like. Radio broadcasting, by comparison, has become more open and diverse, with large numbers of local private stations springing up since the early 1970s alongside the long-established state network. These stations are not, however, permitted to produce their own news bulletins, but must relay news from the state system. Direct reporting of national affairs and state activities may be deemed too important and influential a function to be entrusted to independent commentators. It is presumably this perception of the enormous reach and influence of media such as radio and television which impels such strict overall government control.

Independently-produced media such as magazines, films and popular music are controlled through censorship codes designed to protect state security and social harmony. Film is seen to be subject to particularly strict censorship rules (Sen 1987:131), as first the written scenario, then the film itself must be submitted to the authorities for approval. Once again, this policy presumably reflects government perceptions of film's wide popular influence. Such censorship is carried out by the *Badan Sensor Filem* (BSF), the contemporary equivalent of the censorship boards which have overseen Indonesian film-making since Dutch times.

For a short period in the early 1970s, according to Sen (1987), there were attempts to open this board to wider public participation, including the appointment as board members of liberal intellectuals and artists such as Goenawan Mohamad, Arief Budiman, Asrul Sani and Syuman Jaya. This was also a period of active government support for local film production, through the levy on imported films, a program of reduction of imports and a requirement that importers must fund local productions. In the mid and late 1970s, however, changes of government personnel saw a shift from a cultural nationalist approach to more security-oriented, pragmatic, pro-business policies in regard to the film industry, resulting in a narrowing of participation and concentration of wealth and control. Representatives of government departments took control of the censorship board, and new, more detailed censorship guidelines were announced. Protection measures for local production were watered down and the interests of the big importing firms strengthened by the removal of importing restrictions and their consolidation into large consortia.

A clear division emerged between large, powerful business conglomerates involved in the importing and distribution of foreign films, and small-scale independent capitalists engaged in indigenous film production. Powerful business groups established large luxury cinema complexes in the major cities, with ties to particular import conglomerates. Here foreign films attracted affluent, middle-class audiences, while locally-made films played in more modest city theatres and in small towns to audiences consisting mainly of lower-class groups. A 1975 regulation that every theatre, including the big 'super halls', must show Indonesian films for at least four days per month does not seem to have had much impact—the hoped-for expansion of the market share for local film has not really taken place. Moving into the 1980s, the power and wealth of the big importer conglomerates have continued to grow, as local producers lament the lack of meaningful government support.

The field of magazine and popular fiction publishing is dominated, like that of 'serious' literature, by the big publishing houses associated with the daily newspapers. Their activities, too, are subject to standard censorship procedures—all book titles must be cleared by the Attorney-General's Department before sale, and magazines require, like newspapers, a publishing licence, which is subject to recall by the Department of Information.

Trends in mass media content

Although too diverse a field for comparison at a detailed level, popular media of the early New Order period can nevertheless be shown to share a broad common aspect—a preoccupation with 'glamour', embodied in images of a luxurious westernised lifestyle, and with material goods, ideas and practices drawn from western models.

For example, Goenawan (1974) describes how Indonesian films of the late 1960s and early 1970s focus on the domestic and leisure activities of wealthy urbanites. The settings feature modern living rooms, cars, restaurants and nightclubs, and displays of luxurious material possessions and sumptuous clothes. The work activities of the protagonists, meanwhile, if depicted at all, are indicated in shots of a modern office of unspecified location, purpose and institutional association. For the mundane world of work is of little interest in films which function for their audiences as wish-fulfilling fantasies, as 'dreams which can be bought'. The very attendance at movies of this kind, in cinemas with names such as Grand, Royal and Rex, contributes to a fantasy of affluence and luxury.

Women's magazines meanwhile provided their readers with glamorous visual images of, and an abundance of information about, international fashions, in clothes, home decoration and recipes, along with occasional suggestions as to how these might be adapted to Indonesian conditions. Popular fiction of the 'true romance' variety, likewise set in affluent, urban locales, flourished in the early New Order period. And in popular music, in a total reversal of the Old Order bans, songs of western rock groups like the Rolling Stones and Deep Purple, and of Indonesian counterparts like the Rollies and God Bless, were played constantly over amateur radio stations, and performed live in the rock concerts which started to be staged in large Indonesian cities. 'Soft rock' love ballads lamenting the singer's loss and loneliness also filled the airwaves. Together with radio, this ever-increasing exposure was ensured by the phenomenal growth of the cassette industry, which started with one state company, Lokananta, at the beginning of the 1970s, and grew to a multitude of producers whose tapes are sold everywhere from luxury supermarkets to village stalls.

Many commentators have criticised the popular media as shallow, derivative and greedily commercial, trading on the escapist desires and unsophisticated, uncritical tastes of lower-class consumers. But Goenawan's explanation of the themes and style of 1970s films, in the context of socio-political conditions of the period, help flesh out these judgements, and create a fuller picture of the workings of the mass media generally. For audiences leading drab, circumscribed lives, constrained by ongoing poverty, films provide exciting dreams and reflect a material prosperity until recently denied and frowned upon, even as an aspiration. Now suddenly celebrated, they provide a legitimate if unattainable fantasy. Understandable, then, is the exaggerated, unrealistic glamour of the film imagery, the fairytale quality of themes and plots. Also relevant here, perhaps, are earlier observations on trends in regional performing arts during this period, the preference for light, entertaining plots in *wayang* performances, and glamorous, glittering fantasy settings rather than political themes on the *kethoprak* stage. But as Indonesian society changes and develops, and the social and cultural expectations of audiences mature, so too, Goenawan predicts, will tastes in performance.

Indeed, moving into the mid-1970s, significant developments do begin to take place in media content. Sen (1987) writes of a shift from around 1974 onwards in the themes of films. In keeping with a sense of disillusionment with New Order economic policies, in their failure to bring generalised prosperity, the fascination with the glamorous lives of the wealthy of Jakarta began to weaken, and there appeared films set among villagers and the urban poor, depicting relations between the haves and the have nots. Always observed, however, is a rule of self-censorship, whereby tensions and contradictions raised in the course of the film are resolved in a happy ending depicting harmony between rich and poor. A film such as *Pengemis dan Tukang Becak* (The Beggar and the Becak Driver), for example, illustrates Sen's characterisation well in its extended, realistic depiction of the struggle for survival against poverty and heavy-handed authority of a *becak* driver and a household servant, who has run away with the neglected child of her rich, self-absorbed employers. It ends in a surprise reconciliation with the employers, who happily accept back into their household both servant, *becak* driver and a stray waif picked up along the way.

In popular music, the mid-1970s saw the rise of new forms incorporating more indigenous musical influences, and employing more varied and socially-aware lyrics. Most prominent was *dangdut*, a mixture of western pop with Malay–Indian–Middle Eastern rhythms and sounds drawn from the *orkes Melayu* tradition, itself originating from a blending of Arab, Indonesian and European musical styles in colonial Indonesia and Malaya. The onomatopoeic term *dangdut*, coined around 1973, refers to the heavy, catchy beat of the music, which, according to one commentator 'practically shook young listeners, compelling them to toss off their footgear and *bergoyang* (rock) to the music' (Frederick 1982:110). Sometimes the simple lyrics accompanying the beat contained a sharply-honed message about the gap between rich and poor or greed among social leaders, evoking an enthusiastic response from lower-class *kampung*-dwelling youth who made up the bulk of *dangdut* enthusiasts. Particularly in the hands of the acknowledged 'king' of *dangdut*, Rhoma Irama, who through the 1970s staged hugely popular live concerts and starred in numerous films, the music became increasingly Islamic in flavour, with lyrics bearing moral, proselytising messages and even including Koranic phrases. This accorded with a popular revival of Islam at this time among the urban masses, and with the activities of the oppositionist Islamic political party, PPP, for which Rhoma Irama campaigned in the 1977 and 1982 elections.

More sophisticated in style and social base than *dangdut*, and very appealing, for example, to student groups, were the thoughtful, socially-analytic ballads of Leo Kristi, and later the more explicitly political songs of Gombloh and Iwan Fals.[19] Greater indigenous input into popular music was implemented on one level by Guruh Sukarnoputra, show-business star and son of former President Sukarno, with his blending of *gamelan* and western classics to accompany exotic, spectacular dance shows and, at the 'grassroots', through adaptations into regional languages and musical styles of Indonesian pop songs.

Developments in the 1980s

These developments in popular music and film, the emergence of a degree of social and political critique, and of varied interplay between national and regional cultural forms, foreshadow trends important for Indonesian culture as a whole in the 1980s and 1990s. Cultural expression in the first decade of the New Order has been broadly characterised in terms of growth, experimentation, eager openness to outside influences, at times extending to uncritical consumption and imitation of western models. A liberality of expression, yet virtual absence of direct political reference, has been attributed to the generally apolitical ideological climate as well as the impact of specific mechanisms of control. Writers remember this as a time of innocence and growth, when creative artists, as providers of vital legitimacy to the new political regime, were relatively well-respected and feted.

In the mid to late 1970s certain shifts took place in these patterns, varying in form and implication between different cultural media. Key political developments of this period, such as the tightening of government control after the expression of popular disaffection of the Malari riots of 1974 and the student protests of 1977–78, contributed significantly to changes in the sphere of modern national culture. Mention has been made already of the activities at this time of the playwright and poet Rendra, in first giving voice through his work to political frustrations experienced by his youthful audiences, and then being gaoled and banned from performance in a repressive backlash. Arts institutions generally tightened their policies of sponsorship and censorship. For the traditional performing arts and mass popular culture, changes of an economic nature were probably even more important than political ones, as large corporations tightened their hold on the film industry and moved into pop music and newspaper/magazine production. Meanwhile, technological advances, large-scale government investment plus strengthened public buying power brought television to the countryside as well as to the city, to ever more remote areas, with a dramatic impact on local cultural forms.

Yet the very strength of these trends, towards strict political–ideological control, and towards commercialisation and westernisation, stimulates reactive alternate developments. Modern theatre in the regions becomes a vehicle both for critique of authoritarian control and for education in alternate perspectives; regional cultures become newly important foci of identity as 'modernity' and affluence spread.

National media in the 1980s

Structures and institutions

A feature of the production of national cultural forms in the 1980s generally agreed upon by commentators is a decline in the dynamism and authority of the two predominant institutions of the early New Order period, the Taman Ismail Marzuki arts centre and the literary journal *Horison*. As activities at TIM through the mid-1970s are seen to have embodied a flourishing of creative energy in a relatively free climate of expression, so restrictions imposed on the centre's administrative structure and operations in the late 1970s and 1980s have been linked with a narrowing of political vision and artistic focus. Reviewing TIM's history on the occasion of the centre's twenty-first anniversary in 1990, Goenawan (1990) recalls, for example, the effect of the replacement in 1977 of Ali Sadikin, the liberal Jakarta governor who initially established TIM and oversaw its semi-autonomous operation. The centre's funding was reduced and members of its staff made government appointees. Particularly after the banning from public appearance of the poet Rendra, following an incident at one of his poetry readings at TIM in May 1978, a political atmosphere hostile to all non-conformist expression became established. Performances of traditional art forms from the regions, regarded as politically 'safe', increased in frequency over more 'unpredictable' modern theatre. Other commentators (such as Hill 1984, 1993) report on a reduction of the diversity of viewpoints represented on the Jakarta arts council, the body overseeing TIM's administration, with a 'rightist' orientation predominating. Literary discussions likewise became dominated by a small group of writers (D. Hill 1984, 1992; Sumardjo 1984).

In the late 1980s, however, with talk of openness and democratisation in the political arena, the performing space at TIM likewise opened up to more diverse expression. Rendra was again able to read his poetry and perform plays. The group Teater Koma, under the leadership of dynamic, productive playwright and director Riantiarno, performed lively, colourful musicals satirising political corruption and injustice, most notably the *Bom Waktu* (Time Bomb) trilogy of plays, to enormous popular acclaim, and with no adverse reaction from the authorities. In 1990, however, Koma's play *Suksesi*, on the taboo theme of presidential succession, was banned; subsequently, permission was refused also for performance of another Koma play and a Rendra poem. A delegation of artists protested to parliament and to security forces and were sympathetically heard. Nevertheless, a dark mood of pessimism produced by the bannings settled over the artistic community about the prospects for creativity in such a repressive climate.

TIM meanwhile continues to struggle with another problem just as serious as political restriction, that of economic survival. In late 1990 a new arts foundation, involving some leading entrepreneurs, was formed to provide financial advice and support to the centre. A major challenge to TIM's viability is competition for audiences with newer, more glamorous performance venues. These include the Pasar Seni at the Ancol recreation complex in North Jakarta, the theatre at the Taman Mini Indonesia Indah (Beautiful Indonesia in Miniature) complex and most recently the Gedung Kesenian at Senen. Reopened after restoration in 1988, this elegant colonial building with its white marble columns and chandeliers quickly became the prestige site for modern theatre performances. Rendra's group has performed there on a number of occasions, and the building constitutes a most desirable locale for middle-class audiences attending Teater Koma's colourful, entertaining shows.

Larger, more ambitious spectacles, such as the glittering dance pageants staged by Guruh Sukarnoputra, or the poetry readings-cum-rock concerts in which Rendra has participated in recent years, make use of sports stadiums, or the huge Balai Sidang building at Senayan. Such grand shows, with their massive outlay of resources, are made possible by the recent entry into the world of theatre and performing arts of wealthy sponsors—large companies and individual entrepreneurs, such as Rendra's backer, the oil-tanker magnate Setiawan Djody. The giant cigarette producers Bentul and Jarum proclaim their sponsorship of theatre performances in banners swathed around the stage and in glossy programs: the red and white decor and costuming of a Guruh Sukarnoputra spectacular corresponds both with the symbolic colours of the Indonesian nation and the trademark hues of the sponsoring company, Revlon cosmetics.

Likewise in the case of the literary magazine, *Horison*, the availability of other avenues of expression and other media such as daily newspapers and magazines is seen to contribute to a perceived loss of momentum.

Editors of the journal comment favourably on the encouragement of literature by so many newspapers in the capital and the regions (Jassin 1989),
but they concede the difficulty for *Horison* as a 'little' magazine, with very
limited circulation, to compete for quality works with newspapers and
popular magazines able to offer far greater exposure and higher fees. In this
situation they hope simply that *Horison* can continue to provide a forum
for more experimental pieces by younger authors, less appropriate to a
popular mass medium (Djoko Damono 1989). Ironically enough, at the same
time, it is assistance from the more popular media which enables *Horison*
to maintain its existence at all. In an editorial on the occasion of the journal's
twenty-fifth anniversary, Mochtar Lubis comments on subsidies from the
national daily *Kompas*, the news weekly *Tempo* and the women's magazine
Femina which have ensured *Horison*'s longevity, in contrast to the financial
fragility and eventual failure of earlier literary magazines (Lubis 1991).

A favourite form for literary expression in the popular press is the
serialised story, which may be published separately later as a novel. An
often-quoted example is Marga T.'s novel *Karmila*, first serialised in
Kompas, then published by the newly-established Gramedia press in 1974,
to such enthusiastic public response as to require reprinting an astonishing
eleven times. While *Karmila*'s success is outstanding, other novels of this
type, focusing on the romantic and domestic concerns of youthful, middle-
class protagonists, categorised by critics as 'popular' as opposed to more
weighty 'serious' literature, flourished in Indonesia in the late 1970s and
1980s. As in the case of *Karmila,* many of the authors are women; likewise,
it is conjectured that women are well represented among the readers of these
novels, drawn largely from the expanding middle classes, produced out of
the economic growth of the New Order period. In contrast to the success
of these works, publishers of 'serious' literature struggled to promote and
sell their publications (Hill 1993:251).

Dominant trends

The creative works and critical views of writers associated with the Jakarta
arts centre and the *Horison* journal continued to set dominant trends in
modern literature into the 1980s, albeit under the impact of the developments
described above. Several commentators (Foulcher 1987, 1988; Hill 1993)
suggest a narrowing of the creative breadth which characterised the literary
expression of the early 1970s, paralleling the tightening up of the liberal
political mood of the earlier period. Anti-realist, ahistorical, apolitical tendencies hardened into a restrictive orthodoxy. The poet Sutardji Calzoum
Bachri announced an artistic credo of freeing language from the burden of
meaning, to return to its earlier magical, ritual function. The abstract, playful
manipulation of sound and written form in his poetry has been much praised
for its innovation, but concerns have also been raised about potential

annihilation rather than liberation of meaning. The work of the storyteller Danarto, author of the rich, mythic fantasies of the 1974 collection *Godlob*, has also been seen to lose imaginative force with a shift into an abstract, 'reference-free' dimension, in his 1982 collection *Adam Ma'rifat* (Foulcher 1987, 1992).[20] Exhibitions of painting and sculpture at TIM and other venues in the capital likewise attracted much criticism for their superficiality, abstraction and conformism, from much wider circles than the tiny group of students who criticised such exhibitions in 1974 (Miklouho-Maklai 1991:92–3).

As in the 1970s, however, anti-realist techniques in the hands of some artists evoke key dimensions of contemporary social experience. The fiction of the ever-productive Putu Wijaya might be seen to suggest, through its bizarre happenings and shifting perspectives, something of the post-modern nightmare of life in Jakarta for ordinary people.[21] And Leila Chudori (1989) likewise reflects through the surreal events of her stories on the distortions of 'real life' in conditions of repression. In modern theatre in recent years, major attention has focused on the extraordinary popular success of the troupe Teater Koma, with its satirical comedies combining social critique with music, raunchy humour and entertaining spectacle. Their patronage by affluent middle-class audiences provides theatrical reflection on one dimension of contemporary Jakarta life—its booming wealth. But in TIM's down-at-heel back theatres or other modest locations in the city, small, lesser known groups project a very different experience of contemporary social reality. Darkly surreal plays by groups such as Teater Sae and Teater Kubur project through disjointed action and dialogue the confused consciousness of their subjects, the urban underclass, their traditional structures of meaning dissolving, bombarded with ideology and advertising messages. An intense energy of expression conveys the depth of their frustration and pain.

Meanwhile, through the 1980s, in an alternate development to predominant anti-realist expression, there appeared several major works of prose fiction, realistic in style, and grounded in Indonesian history and ongoing social reality. Mangunwijaya's *Roro Mendut* trilogy, set in the courts of seventeenth-century Java, clearly reflect on contemporary issues of political control and resistance and female autonomy, while his *Burung-Burung Manyar* explores questions of political and personal loyalty during the Japanese occupation and revolution. Ajip Rosidi's novel *Anak Tanah Air* and N.H. Dini's *Jalan Bandungan* are set in the post-independence period, focusing on the experience, respectively, of a writer involved in politically-committed literary movements before the 1965 coup, and of the unwitting wife of a communist cadre who becomes a political prisoner.

The year 1979 saw the release of many thousands of political prisoners still remaining in detention without trial following the events of 1965–66. Whether their reappearance, and the issues involved in their reabsorption into society, served as a catalyst for the re-emergence in literature of historical consciousness and moral concerns is an intriguing question. Writers and artists from this group who attempted to re-enter the artistic community and resume creative life encountered much hostility and discrimination. Most writers are now forbidden to publish original works, critical articles or even translations. Yet the most famous of them, Pramudya Ananta Tur, continues to be widely read despite bans on his works, and to hold almost legendary stature among the young and politically critical. His *Bumi Manusia* quartet of novels, created while in prison—published, banned, then circulated clandestinely following their banning—constitutes the quintessential example of the historically grounded, socially referential literature of the 1980s. Set at the turn of the twentieth century, and tracing the growth of the early nationalist associations, the novels both provide young Indonesians with insight into a vital, little discussed period of their history and suggest illuminating parallels with the present day.

In a parallel development in the visual arts in the mid-1980s, two major realist painters came to the fore. Dede Eri Supria portrays in meticulous photorealistic detail, on huge, dramatic canvases, ordinary people of Jakarta engaged in their daily activities amidst a landscape of sophisticated glass and concrete skyscrapers—a juxtaposition almost surreal in its incongruity. And indeed, architectural elements of the paintings are often portrayed in semi-abstract fashion; the contrast with the warts-and-all reality of the figures reinforces the metaphor of separation and alienation. While Dede simply presents such scenes to the viewer, Semsar Siahaan, a young artist from Sumatra, assumes a very definite political stance in his paintings and line drawings of oppressed workers and bloated capitalist bosses, portrayed in a style strongly reminiscent of German expressionist models.

Another alternative to the anti-realist approach of the TIM circle of artists and writers is represented by works drawing on regional cultural traditions. Such literature in its various forms contributes to an ongoing, flourishing process of invocation or invention of 'tradition' in New Order society,[22] giving expression to particular social perspectives. In contrast to the literature of the 1970s, invoking regional traditions in a transformative, experimental way, a central body of works of the 1980s conveys traditional reference of a much more direct, celebratory, nostalgic kind. Traditional myths are retold, regional language expressions quoted and regional cultural values extolled. Javanese cultural reference predominates. Linus Suryadi's *Pengakuan Pariyem*, a long prose poem in mixed Indonesian and Javanese which celebrates a Javanese servant girl's joyful acceptance of her lot, provides a particularly rich example of the trend. The use of a female figure to embody the esteemed regional tradition is common to these works. In this time of rapid social change, one might conjecture, women in the home in traditional social roles, even traditional dress, serve as appropriate symbols of cultural continuity, preserving conservative social values.

Works of this type, often produced in the regions, may be seen to embody alternate but complementary perspectives to the dominant literary trends of the capital. They also accord with the attention directed by state authorities to esteemed, court-connected Javanese cultural traditions. But other voices from the regions directly challenge the dominant trends of the centre, and the cultural policies of officialdom.

In 1984 a conference was held in Solo endorsing the notion of *sastra kontekstual* (contextual literature)—literature produced out of and meaningful in terms of particular social circumstances. Participants questioned the legitimacy of the concept of universal aesthetic standards applicable to all literary expression, and criticised mainstream writers and critics for attempting to impose such standards on Indonesian literature as a whole. For one of the leading figures at the conference, Ariel Heryanto, the key issue was denial of the possibility of universals, given socially-constructed reality. All cultural products can be understood and assessed properly only in their context. For others, including sociologist Arief Budiman, the emphasis was more practical, the need for production of literature appropriate to the social reality of ordinary Indonesians. Rather than aping the themes and styles of established writers in the capital, young people should write about issues of concern in their own environment. A number of 'mainstream' Jakarta writers responded with angry denunciation of the contextualists for reviving the dangerous views of communist-linked Lekra, in their endorsement of socially-engaged literature. A lively, heated debate continued over a number of months in newspapers, journal pages and literary discussions, as documented in the compilation *Perdebatan Sastra Kontekstual* (Contextual Literature Debates) (Heryanto 1985). The issue of contextual literature has since faded from attention in dominant literary discussion. But, in the regions, writers and cultural activists attempt many contextually-grounded activities—such as readings of poetry in simple, everyday language about local social problems; and art lessons encouraging village children to draw the natural and social world they see around them, rather than idealised images from books and television.

Among practitioners of modern theatre in the regions, particularly Central Java, the notion of socially-oriented and involved performance has developed and spread since Rendra's Bengkel group lived and rehearsed in their Yogyakarta *kampung* in the 1970s. Dinasti, a group founded by several ex-Bengkel actors, became well-known in the early 1980s for performances of political–philosophical dramas set in Javanese royal courts, followed by sessions where audience members and actors discussed the social issues raised by the play. Other groups performing in Yogyakarta, Solo and other Central Javanese cities during the 1980s cultivated particular performing styles and themes. Gandrik in Yogyakarta, for example, staged colourful, folksy, humorous shows laced with social critique; Solo's Gapit portrayed the anger and desperation of poor local *kampung*-dwellers, pushed aside by the tide of 'development', using the blunt, earthy Javanese language these people themselves would speak. All groups conveyed reference to social issues, and fostered close engagement with audiences, with the post-play discussion becoming a standard feature of performances. Some performers have become involved in workshops and training programs sponsored by community-development groups, using theatre as a medium for promoting social conscience. Here, simple musical accompaniment, danced entrances and exits, folksy humour and dialogue including much Javanese, combine in a style reminiscent of village folk performances, designated *teater rakyat* (people's theatre). The familiarity and intimacy of such performances, it is hoped, will enhance communication and acceptance of their social message.

Such direct involvement in social action seems to be a particular characteristic of modern theatre activity in Central Java, influenced by a combination of factors—a strong network of non-government organisations, local history of politicisation of theatre, and contact between local actors and the Peta (Philippines Educational Theater Association) movement in the Philippines.[23] Reference to local cultural traditions, however, is a common phenomenon in modern theatre in the regions generally.[24] Some playwrights and directors speak of these traditions as a more natural idiom for their work than the models of western theatre; also central is the greater appeal to audience members of performances with a familiar style. The way in which modern theatre groups draw on regional history, myth and tradition in their performances often differs radically from the 'official', mainstream interpretations. Through satirical images of kings and courtiers, modern theatre groups express critiques of behaviour of contemporary power hold-ers. The 'little people', the villagers, figures of fun in traditional performances in their naive, bumbling ways, are depicted here as strong, shrewd battlers against an absurd social system.

Modern theatre groups frequently complain of lack of support for their activities from government institutions, focusing on issues such as access to performing spaces, granting of performance permission, and provision of subsidies. Government arts centres, they suggest, give preference to the traditional performing arts, seen as 'safe', apolitical and attractive to tourists. In fact, considerable variation occurs between arts centres in different regions in the degree of support for modern artistic expression, in accor-dance with local circumstances.[25] But as the actors' comments suggest, these centres serve generally as sites for interaction between 'modern national' and 'traditional, regional' performances, often projecting contrasting inter-pretations of cultural identity in the regions. Activities in the area of traditional arts predominate, with much direct involvement by the state.

Traditional performance in the 1980s

The government cultivation of regional performance traditions, documented earlier for the 1970s, continues and intensifies through the 1980s into the 1990s. Local forms are extensively documented through written reports and audio and video recordings, and performing groups are actively instructed and trained. The examples of several specific local art forms illustrate this process. In Ponorogo, East Java, for example, a grand, three-day competition between troupes from each local administrative district has been held each year since the early 1980s, performing the earthy, colourful dance pageant *reyog Ponorogo* long associated with this region. As before, national holidays and local events are marked with *reyog* processions, now with active government support and funding. Official brochures on *reyog*, prepared for its anticipated development as a tourist attraction, evade discussion of 'disreputable' aspects of its colourful history, such as association with invulnerability cults, homosexuality and leftist politics; stressed instead are its purported court connections. Concern for propriety has presumably helped motivate the substitution of 'real' females rather than the usual effeminately-attired males as horse dancers in a newly-created dance drama version of the form.[26]

In the Blora region in east Central Java, Widodo (1991) describes a process instigated by state officials during the 1980s, of transformation of local *tayuban*, village dance and drinking celebrations, into an officially-sanctioned art form, *seni tayub*, literally 'tayuban art'. Female dancers and male facilitators and musicians are given courses (*penataran*) of moral and technical instruction, on completion of which they gain certification as performing artists. Changes have been introduced in dress, dance style and musical accompaniment in keeping with the refined models of court art, and participants in the many *tayuban* competitions and festivals are judged on their adherence to these standards. Such activities, in Widodo's view, function as ritual celebrations of the hegemony of the state, here extending into the field of people's culture.

State-organised competitions and festivals of traditional art forms occur throughout Indonesia, as mentioned earlier for *kethoprak* in Central Java, and documented by anthropologists and ethnomusicologists for East Java, Bali, Central Sulawesi, North and South Sumatra, Madura, and elsewhere.[27] In addition, new performances with a traditional base, such as *sendratari* dance dramas, drawing on traditional dance movements in dramatisations of regional history and legend, which were first created in the dance academies, are now performed competitively by local groups (de Boer 1989; Soedarsono 1989). A key role of all such festivals, competitions and upgradings of regional performing arts is their perceived expression of the cultural identity (*jati diri*) of the particular area. Performances of local art forms

251

are seen to embody this spirit; local officials gain prestige and influence, and government structures legitimacy through the promotion of a distinctive artistic tradition giving expression to regional cultural pride.[28]

At another level, cultural bureaucracies and academic institutions, such as the dance, music and theatre academies (ASTI, ASKI, ISI) in regional cities, act as brokers promoting certain kinds of performances and standards. Students and teachers from these academies are frequently mobilised to perform for state occasions, both national and local, and for private celebrations. Graduates become teachers in local schools. Regional performing arts are promoted for tourism by both state bodies and private concerns, mostly in Bali but increasingly also in Yogyakarta, the second most popular tourist destination. In the field of written literature and cultural study, an important development during the 1980s was the *ologi* phenomenon—the establishment of centres for promotion of regional literatures and cultures, first an institute of 'Javanologi' in Yogyakarta, then 'Sundanologi', 'Balinologi' and others in their respective regions.

Government-initiated activities in the support and development of regional cultural traditions can be located and documented in a relatively straightforward manner. But what of cultural expression outside these structures? To what extent are regional performing arts, for example, still supported by their traditional constituencies?

Great variation naturally occurs between regions and genres. In Java *wayang kulit* continues to thrive. Though less widely performed live than in the past owing to the huge expense, radio broadcasts have increased, both through the RRI state network and on private stations, and the cassette trade flourishes. The best-known *dalang*, constantly in demand for institutional celebrations and the family rituals of the rich, as well as in the production of cassettes, have become very wealthy. Goenawan (1990) has commented on the unique position of *wayang kulit* among the Indonesian performing arts, with its established system of patronage providing skilled practitioners with a comfortable living. While large numbers of local *dalang* have now lost this living through socio-economic changes, in particular the advent of cassettes, for the privileged few life has never been better. And, through radio broadcasts and cassette tapes, *wayang* has become potentially more widely accessible than ever before.

Many individual Javanese today have little interest in *wayang*. Even among its afficionados, *wayang*'s social role is changing, as its ritual function declines. At the monthly performances on the southern square in Yogyakarta, for example, the chief attraction for most of the young men who make up the bulk of the audience is the *dalang*'s skill in puppet manipulation and his lively, risque humour. Yet a few report that they have come seeking words of wisdom from the *dalang*, or for some symbolic message from the performance to guide them through the uncertainties of these changing times. For as an ideology, the notion of *wayang*'s centrality to Javanese identity and spirituality lives on, assuring for the present the continued viability of the form.

Traditional performing arts without such elevated cultural connection, however, are not faring so well. Commercial *wayang orang* remains in a parlous state—the troupe Ngesti Pendawa in Semarang was almost forced to disband in the late 1980s, before rescue by the city government. Sriwedari in Solo likewise survives on subsidies. *Ludruk* in Surabaya is said to be long-extinguished as a commercial show; *srimulat*, the outrageous, humorous offshoot of *ludruk* which was enormously popular in the early 1980s, has since experienced an ignominious decline.[29] *Kethoprak*, which had been booming in the 1970s, declined dramatically as a live performance during the 1980s. In the Yogyakarta area in 1977–78 there were four or five professional troupes performing in and around the city each night. Since the mid-1980s there have been none. The RRI radio troupe performs two nights a month in their auditorium to a modest crowd of faithful fans—predominantly middle-aged to elderly village and *kampung* people. The standard commercial *kethoprak* show, in a barn-like prefabricated theatre with dirt floor, garishly-painted posters out front, exaggeratedly glitzy costumes and an uncertain sound system, indeed seems out of keeping with the slick, sophisticated mood of Yogyakarta in the 1980s. In Yogyakarta's 'sister' court city, Solo, however, where the pace of life is slower, and the inroads of national culture less advanced, one or two groups regularly perform, and a skilled troupe on a good night is still capable of attracting sizeable audiences.

Television broadcasts of *kethoprak*, meanwhile, have remained popular through the 1980s. Though the front rooms of television-owning homes in villages and *kampung* may not be quite as crowded now as in the late 1970s, when television *kethoprak* was a wondrous novelty, broadcasts still attract wide audiences. Active marketing strategies are implemented to maintain this interest. A mystery story is played out in serial form over a number of weeks, for example, and a competition run by a Yogyakarta newspaper for viewers to solve the puzzle—guess the killer, spot the disguised identity, and the like—with prizes for winning entries.[30]

For more localised performance genres, and for regional music, cassettes more than television constitute the transforming new medium of reproduction and transmission. Not only western-style pop songs but many types of regional music are available on cassette: taped local musical forms fill the air in even the most remote villages, and in Sumatra, in particular, are played constantly over the loudspeakers of inter-city buses. Like *wayang kulit* puppeteers, musicians have been hard hit by this development. Taped renditions by top musicians replace local ensembles in providing music for ritual celebrations, and dancers not only practise but also frequently perform to the accompaniment of cassette tapes rather than a *gamelan* orchestra (Sutton 1985a:27). Here, too, however, outstanding performers can gain prestige and popularity through recordings. And local performance traditions, hitherto unknown or little valued outside their own area, have gained increased exposure and recognition through their recording on cassette (Sutton 1985a:35–9).

Trends in style and content

For a number of observers, the two developments outlined above—cultivation by state authorities and transmission via commercial mass media—have had a negative impact on the content and meaning of regional performing arts. State appropriation of regional folk performances in the manner of *tayuban* cultivation in Blora has been seen to involve a process of sanitisation, refinement and 'bourgeoisification', in the course of which the form loses much of its original dynamism and spontaneity (Widodo 1991:19). Government-sponsored presentations of ritual dances as mere aesthetic display without religious function are said to hasten the loss of traditional cosmological values (Acciaioli 1985), being seen as frequent competitions and festivals to gobble up local resources, and promote emphasis on novelty and superficial glamour (Soedarsono 1989). Yet in a particular local context, even the highly-regulated circumstances of a government-organised revival have been shown to provide villagers with valued access to a long-suppressed performance tradition and its associated spiritual meaning (Aragon 1992:11). Similarly, the format of a regular, officially-sponsored competition, in the specific case of *sendratari* in Bali, has been seen to stimulate creativity and bring to the fore many talented young performers (de Boer 1989). Meanwhile, the benefits in both money and prestige for participants in officially-sponsored performances are undeniable, whatever the larger function of these activities. Clearly 'state cultivation of regional arts' is no monolithic activity, amenable to blanket assessments, but varies greatly in impact according to local social circumstances, the nature of the performance tradition, and the approach of particular officials. In many cases, funding and organisation by the state is essential to the maintenance of the form.

In the case of penetration by commercial media, a frequently-mentioned and much-feared effect is that of standardisation and homogenisation of regional music, dance and theatre genres. The technology of television, radio and cassettes facilitates propagation of a single prestigious style, which then shapes the tastes of consumers, and renders local regional variants no longer attractive. Local diversity of expression is undermined, and regional styles are likely to die away. But, again, this picture appears much too simplistic. In the field of Javanese *gamelan* music, for example, cassette stores in regional cities indeed stock a preponderance of tapes in the dominant style of the court city of Solo. This style of music is broadcast by local radio stations, imbibed by audiences and played by musicians. But such shops are also likely to hold many tapes of local musical genres produced in recent years, which are often more popular than those in the Solo style. Cassette salespeople, radio employees and musicians all agree that there is more heterogeneity of musical expression now than ten or fifteen years ago (Sutton 1985b:58). Newly-available technology, business interests and state promotion of the concept of local cultural identity seemingly work together to encourage cassette reproduction of local performance traditions. As well as celebrating cultural identity, commercial cassettes may also help consti-tute new values and cultural orientations. Susan Rodgers suggests this role for Angkola Batak taped dramas on themes of kinship relations and adjust-ment to city life, played on buses travelling between the Angkola homeland and the North Sumatran capital city of Medan (Rodgers 1986).

Movies and television are also frequently cited as a potential threat to the very survival of regional performance genres. Television, in particular, spreading exponentially during the 1980s into ever more isolated areas and more modest homes, has surely contributed significantly to the decline of commercial performance of forms like *wayang wong* and *kethoprak*. Yet the case of *kethoprak* also suggests potentially complex, multi-faceted interac-tion between modern mass media and regional performing arts. The style of *kethoprak* presented on television—fast-paced, compact, using written scripts and cinematic techniques—has had a major impact on expectations of the form. Inasmuch as rambling, improvised live performances are judged too predictable and unexciting by comparison, and fall from favour both as commercial shows and as entertainment at ritual celebrations (Widodo 1991), the very success of *kethoprak* in adapting to the new medium of television can be seen to undermine its traditional legitimacy. At the same time, however, television, together with other new dramatic media, offers a model for innovation in this still changing and evolving theatrical form.

At a government-organised seminar in 1990, *kethoprak televisi* (televi-sion *kethoprak*) was identified as a discrete new genre, like *kethoprak lesung*, the simple folk play accompanied by rhythmic rice-pounding music from which the form is said to have originated, or *kethoprak pendapan*, the style it took on when cultivated in aristocratic houses during the 1920s. *Kethoprak televisi* falls within a broader category of performance established at the seminar, *kethoprak garapan*—literally 'worked on *kethoprak*'—dis-tinguished from conventional *kethoprak* by its influence from western drama and film. Performances of this type, emphasising dramatic structure, using a written script, varying the standard order of scenes through such tech-niques as flashbacks, and first cultivated by the Sapta Mandala troupe, have become the preferred model for such activities as competitions and festivals. These gatherings attracted enthusiastic audiences, yet interest in commercial, paid performances remained sluggish, until in late 1991 a new type of 'worked on *kethoprak*' burst onto the scene. In *kethoprak plesedan*, literally 'slipped *kethoprak*', the standard language, theatrical conventions and story outlines of the form were playfully subverted and standard characterisations changed, for humorous effect, and to allow for an occasional burst of social critique. Created through collaboration between *kethoprak* players and some modern theatre actors, the new form proved spectacularly popular, particularly with young people. All performances were sell-out successes.

Lively discussion took place, much of it recorded in the Yogyakarta press, about possible reasons for the popularity of such performances, and their impact on *kethoprak* as a whole. Was the absurd humour of such shows appealing as pure fun, or as an escape from the frustrations of contemporary life? Was it experienced by audiences as representative, in some ways, of a world without fixed standards, of shifting, manipulated realities? Would such performances kill off standard *kethoprak* or renew public interest, attracting audiences back to more conventional performances? Quite unexpectedly, however, by the end of 1992, *kethoprak plesedan* activities had come to an abrupt halt. In two separate incidents in the latter months of the year, performers playing with language on stage in *plesedan* fashion had been detained for subversion and imprisoned. The Sapta Mandala troupe, erstwhile initiator and main performer of *kethoprak plesedan*, announced a stop to such activity. Other groups seem similiarly discouraged. Whether or not this hugely popular new style might be revived in a less jumpy political climate, together with innovative *kethoprak* more generally, it provides evidence of regional theatre responding dynamically to its contemporary context. Rather than being swamped by new dramatic media, these forms interact with and adapt from them.

The commercial success of *kethoprak plesedan*, not only in Central Java but also at recent stagings in Jakarta, suggests the possibility of a further development in the field of *kethoprak* and other regional performing arts: investment and promotion by big entrepreneurs. One instance of *kethoprak* sponsorship by a well-known impresario did in fact occur recently, in Solo in January 1992. Hundreds of performers, including a famous film star and a princess of the Solo royal house, plus horses and an elephant, participated in this show, designated *kethoprak kolossal*, held at the Mangkunegaran palace and sponsored by Jakarta millionaire Setiawan Djody. Djody, together with a party of luminaries including Rendra, Umar Kayam and Islamic leader Abdurrachman Wahid, flew in from the capital to watch. Later in the same year, the show was taken to Jakarta, and presented at the miniature Indonesia theme park, the Taman Mini Indonesia Indah. Was this an isolated occurrence, stemming simply from Djody's stated desire to do something beneficial for his home city of Solo?[31] Or was it a harbinger of things to come, of *kethoprak*'s transformation into a mass spectacle on the model of events sponsored by Djody and others in the sphere of rock music and popular culture?

Modern mass media in the 1980s

In the production of popular mass media, the dominant development of the 1980s is most surely expansion of the role and influence of big money. Millionaire stars, competition between rival conglomerates, and import and distribution monopolies constitute familiar features of the contemporary media scene.

In the field of popular music, for example, Philip Yampolsky documents the fierce competition between major cassette companies for radio and television exposure, and their regional empire building through local-language versions of Indonesian pop hits (Yampolsky 1989). Companies pay large fees for television broadcast of videoclips of recent releases, said to function informally as advertisements for the recordings (Munger 1991). Rock music is seen to flourish under the sponsorship of Indonesia's three major cigarette companies, Gudang Garam, Bentoel and Jarum, vying to promote their products through huge festivals and concerts. Concert promoters grow wealthy and many new recording stars emerge (Sasongko and Katjasungkana 1991). The world of film production is dominated by the huge conglomerates which own the glamorous theatre complexes in the big cities, and hold monopolies on the import of foreign films, as well as the process of distribution to regional theatres.[32] Though the number of Indonesian films produced has risen in recent years (73 in 1989, and 96 in 1990), local film-makers lament the difficulties of financing and distributing their work, in a situation where educated, middle-class audiences prefer foreign-made films, and distributors cater to their tastes.[33] Films by serious directors which achieve success at the annual Citra awards regularly fare poorly at the box office, ignored by their natural clientele, the upper middle class, and too difficult for the less-educated masses who constitute the social base of Indonesian film (Said 1990). Through a wistful comparison with the thriving Indian film industry, Eros Jarot indicates a need for the government to give support to local film production through subsidies, facilities and restrictions on imports, and to encourage pride in national work, rather than allowing international market forces to be all determining (Jarot 1990).

In print-media production, the two established giants, the Gramedia group, producers of the daily *Kompas*, and Grafitipers, publishers of *Tempo* magazine, along with the producers of the afternoon daily *Suara Pembaruan*—conglomerates of companies built up from the profits of their original publication—have recently been joined by many new press ventures. The launch of the financial daily *Bisnis Indonesia* in 1985, financed by interests of the billionaire magnate Liem Sioe Liong, initiated a new trend for non-media business groups to become involved in newspaper publication. Motivated, it has been suggested, by business incentives together with the desire to establish a form of political power base, conglomerates have entered the press field in sizeable numbers. 'Every business group is only happy after it opens a bank, a supermarket and a newspaper' quips a *Tempo* journalist.[34] Established media interests have expanded their activities in response. Regional newspaper publishing has become a field of particularly intense competition, as big groups in the capital acquire interests in, and promote the circulation of, previously ailing local dailies. Major players are the *Jawa Pos* group in Surabaya, 40 per cent owned by Grafitipers, *Kompas*/Gramedia, and the Surya Persindo group, owners of the recently revamped Jakarta daily, *Media Indonesia*.[35]

Along with the expansion of dailies, various new tabloids presenting television, film and sports news have appeared over the period since the closure of the weekly *Monitor* over a heated religious controversy, for whose market they are competing. And new glossy magazines continue to appear. But recent reports indicate a faltering in the publishing boom, with the 1991 circulation of newspapers and magazines down one million from the previous year, to thirteen million, and the closure of five publication companies (*Tempo*, 15 February 1992).

A major reason cited for loss of press circulation is competition from television. Since 1988 three private stations have been established alongside TVRI, Rajawali Citra Indonesia (RCTI) in Jakarta, Surabaya Centra Televisi (SCTI) in Surabaya, and the educational station Televisi Pendidikan Indonesia (TPI). A recent change of government policy permitting these stations to broadcast their own news, rather than reproduce official RRI bulletins, along with their capacity, unlike TVRI, to include advertisements, is seen to have taken away both advertising revenue and news readership from the print media. The founding of these private stations has contributed to vast expansion in the overall Indonesian television system, with the addition of many new regional relay stations, transmitters and satellite ground stations, the installation of 300 000–400 000 parabola antennae, picking up programs direct from the Palapa satellite (*Tempo*, 6 July 1991), and an increase in the estimated viewing audience to around 120 million, or approximately two-thirds of the total population (Quinn 1989).

Trends in content

The existence of a booming, expanding consumer market and the dominance of big-business interests is often seen to produce superficial, ephemeral qualities in the mass media of recent years. Pop music records are produced speedily to make quick profits from an undemanding market, but lacking any distinctive qualities, they likewise quickly fade from attention: female singers achieve success because of their pretty faces, not because of their voices, and television video clips focus attention on glamorous costumes and fantasy settings, not on musical content (Piper and Jabo 1987). Song lyrics are criticised as shallow and stereotypical, constantly repeating the 'why, oh why?' lament of love gone wrong (Sylado 1977).

Indonesian-made films, all agree, are dominated by lightweight, farcical comedies and *silat* (martial arts) films with a legendary background. But whereas the makers of these films defend their products as simple, easily understood, and appropriate to the entertainment needs of their lower-class and lower-middle-class audiences (*Tempo*, 6 July 1991), others lament their lack of stimulating or enriching content (*Editor*, 24 November 1990), even designating their impact as 'poisoning' (*Tempo*, 1 December 1990). Such films sell well, it has been suggested, because of continuity with the conventions of regional popular theatre—legendary stories and spectacular technical effects—familiar to village and *kampung* viewers (*Tempo*, 6 July 1991), and as comic distraction from the harsh reality of contemporary lower-class life. Even those films treating more serious themes tend to project narrow, conservative social attitudes, particularly in the area of male–female relations (Sen 1981; Sita Aripurnomo 1990).

In the field of television, the differential treatment of state-owned TVRI, excluded from commercial activity and subject to a variety of official pressures from private stations free to follow market forces, has resulted in the overburdening of the state network with official propaganda and an overwhelming concentration by the private stations on imported rather than indigenous programs (*Tempo*, 6 July 1991). Popular literature, in the form of paperback books and magazine fiction, caters to a more affluent, educated audience than the majority film public, and thus deals with a broader range of themes and settings. But, in attracting readers with the latest youth slang and fashion reference, such fiction is also seen to restrict itself to a short-lived viability (Sumardjo 1977).

However, by no means are all observations of the contemporary mass media negative. Sometimes the same features described above are viewed from a more positive angle. The up-to-the-minute focus of popular literature, for example, can be seen to allow reflection on issues of immediate public interest, dealt with in a more open way than would be possible through the more tightly controlled news media. Expressed as 'heart-to-heart' communication between author and reader, such fiction also encourages individualism and openness rather than regimentation of thought (Parera 1988). In the specific area of gender relations, popular fiction, as an arena of strong participation by women as both producers and consumers, takes as themes issues of female concern such as work and marriage for women, social ostracism of divorcees, abortion, infertility, and even rape. While, at the level of the narrative, the problems raised by these issues are resolved without challenging established stereotypes, the very inclusion of these issues as fictional themes brings them into public discussion, and allows for questioning and imagining (Toeti Heraty 1989; Hellwig n.d.).

Several recent films have received commendation for their 'progressive' representations of women. *Roro Mendut*, a retelling of a Javanese legend, set in the kingdom of Mataram in the seventeenth century, is about a commoner girl who refuses to submit sexually to her aristocratic master; and *Cut Nya Dien*, the story of a renowned Acehnese heroine, commander of the military struggle against the Dutch in the Aceh war, are two key examples. Cut Nya Dien, in particular, like another courageous female opponent of Dutch colonialism, Nyai Ontosoroh in Pramudya Ananta Tur's novel *Bumi Manusia*, might be seen as an evocative symbol not only of the admirable strength of women but also of the power of popular resistance against unjust authority.

Yet the very force and breadth of these female characterisations as symbols can be seen to work against their representativeness as depictions of women. The exemplary bravery of Cut Nya Dien or the resolute defiance of the simultaneously gorgeously attractive Roro Mendut sets them apart from the social experience of ordinary women, too remote for identification. Indonesian film, in the business of 'selling dreams', under market constraints to represent the world in general, and women figures in particular, with maximum glamour,[36] is perhaps not the place to look for representation of the everyday. Where something closer to such cinematic representation does appear, however, in productions with settings and narratives familiar to viewers' own experience, is on television.

State-owned television, TVRI, has long broadcast drama programs, for which prominent directors and playwrights from the live theatre have been invited to produce plays. Since the mid-1980s, TVRI has also been producing its own movies, termed *sinetron* (*sinema elektronik*), shot on location rather than in the studio, in the manner of a commercial film. Constrained by the modest resources of TVRI, compared to those of the film industry, but also freed from the demands of commercial marketing, and subject to less stringent and formal censorship procedures, these films have been widely praised for their realistic treatment of serious themes in everyday settings. One of the most frequently mentioned is the 1988 *Sayekti dan Hanafi*, the factually-based story of a market coolie and her *becak* driver husband whose baby is withheld in a maternity clinic because they are unable to pay the bill. In her struggle to regain her child, Sayekti must contend with various professed 'helpers'—a journalist, a group of middle-class ladies, the market manager—all wanting to exploit her situation for their own ends (*Tempo*, 7 January 1989).

Dua Wanita (Two Women) examines the exploitative sexual attitudes and practices of a group of bureaucrats, and the interaction between the wife and mistress of one of them. Perhaps because these films were broadcast into their own homes, and depicted recognisable settings and occurrences, they were avidly discussed by viewers, many of whom felt moved to write letters to newspapers, expressing their opinions and reactions (Sunindyo 1993).

In the last two years, several classics of Indonesian literature, including the 1920 novel *Siti Nurbaya*, have been made into *sinetron*, once again stimulating great public interest and discussion.

Meanwhile, weekly episodes of the serial *Losmen*, about the daily problems of a family running a small hotel (*losmen*) in Yogyakarta, broadcast for several years in the late 1980s, attracted a huge and enthusiastic popular following. Issues such as the appropriateness of the adult daughter of the family, Sri, pursuing a career as a singer, or how the family should respond to the infidelities of Sri's husband, made absorbing and thought-provoking viewing. Such shows might be seen to reflect upon changing practices and values in areas of shared social experience, and to contribute to a popular discourse on how these issues might be handled. After a three-year break, *Losmen* has recently returned to television screens. Meanwhile, TVRI has produced three further serials, in this case with financial assistance but no direct involvement in production, from the government departments of health, transmigration and social welfare. The settings have been described as 'more easily recognisable' than those of *Losmen*, as the films completely eschew glamour, concentrating instead on excellent acting and realistic dialogue, in depicting common experiences in the arena of health care, family relations and transmigration (*Tempo*, 22 July 1989).

Popular music, with its glitter and ballyhoo, seems a world away from the simple and everyday. Even those genres which in the 1970s had a more populist image—*dangdut*, with its socially critical and moralistic lyrics and lower-class following, and the political ballads of youth heroes like Gombloh and Iwan Fals—have become part of the world of glamour and big money. After several years of decline in the early 1980s, *dangdut* has now revived with a vengeance, performed at elite Jakarta discos as well as *kampung* celebrations, broadcast constantly over television and radio, its cassette sales booming, and its performers wealthy enough to buy cars and build homes—even a neighbourhood mosque (*Tempo*, 25 May 1991). Iwan Fals, meanwhile, joined by rock performer Sawung Jabo and aspiring musician-cum-millionaire entrepreneur Setiawan Djody in a group called Swami, has produced cassette recordings selling over a million copies. In 1990–91, Djody sponsored a spectacular, extravagant live concert, *Kantata Takwa*, involving Iwan, Swami and the poet Rendra, which played in huge sports arenas in a number of cities before audiences of hundreds of thousands (100 000 in Jakarta alone). A far cry, for Rendra and Iwan both, from the impromptu campus gatherings of yesteryear.

And yet the lyrics of Iwan's songs, the themes he addresses on cassettes and in live performances, remain as sharply critical as ever. At the Solo staging of Kantata Takwa, it is reported that the whole stadium sang along with his 1990 hit *Bongkar* (Demolish): 'Oppression and abuses of power/ are too numerous to mention . . . We're fed up with greed and uncertainty.' In the context of a glittering, costly, technologically-sophisticated rock concert, there is surely irony in a message of protest against the system that makes these things possible. Yet, for youthful fans, Iwan is a much-needed hero, an idol voicing sentiments that they are afraid to express themselves (*Far Eastern Economic Review*, 24 October 1991), something like Rendra represented in earlier times, but with far greater media exposure.

Dangdut, too, maintains its own kind of social critique. Though most contemporary *dangdut* songs, like pop music generally, deal with themes of love and heartache, there are others voicing familiar protest at the gap between rich and poor, and at neglect of Islamic morality. Such critique is seen as an aspect of the straightforward quality of *dangdut*—no flowery metaphors but frank, literal reflection on issues of concern to its constituency.[37] For all the glitter and ballyhoo, it seems, and for all the shallow commercialism of much pop music and other contemporary mass media, there are ways in which these media connect with and give meaningful expression to the experiences and understanding of their public.

Conclusion

What is one to say in stepping back again from the minutiae to the big picture, trying to relate the preceding detail to the issues raised initially—the relationship of national to regional cultural expression, the viability of 'traditional' forms, the impact of commercialisation and westernisation, and the role of the state?

On all of these fronts there are complex trends. The new national media of press, literature, film, radio and television in the national language, Indonesian, continue to extend their reach, with profound effects on the perceptions and tastes of their audiences. Regional popular entertainment forms struggle to compete, but in many cases are dead or dying, no longer sufficiently engaging or relevant to attract their traditional constituency. At the same time, constructions of regional cultures have in their turn shaped national media such as Indonesian literature and theatre in complex and varying ways, reflecting on questions of identity and cultural politics. Films and television, too, depict regional narratives and settings, though still perhaps with the perspectives of the centre. Meanwhile, many traditional, regional cultural forms live on in new contexts, conveyed through different media, sometimes in dramatically changed form, with different kinds of patronage. Regional theatre genres no longer performed nightly on the commercial stage but by middle-class amateur groups, for self-development or simply for fun, or watched on television in a much streamlined mode; *wayang* watched at a commercial performance rather than a ritual celebration or simply heard rather than seen, in radio broadcast or cassette recording; regional music learnt from cassette rather than live demonstration; Javanese court theatre attracting much better audiences in cosmopolitan Jakarta than in the Javanese heartland—such are the developments documented here. Social changes give rise to new contexts and constituencies, to which living evolving cultural forms respond, in ways which might seem likely to sustain the form by totally transforming it.

Commercial interests and the activities of the state profoundly shape this picture. The all-determining power of big business in the modern mass media has been amply documented, including its frequent discouragement of local creativity. State activities focus on traditional, regional performing arts, seeking political control and legitimacy through creation of 'cultural identity'. In this context, modern artists, particularly in the regions, frequently feel ignored and stifled. Factors of political control plus difficulties of finance make autonomous cultivation of local, community cultural forms a rather rare occurrence. But quality films still get made; local people do put on their own performances, or derive their own pleasure and interest from state-supported ones. Writers of modern fiction continue to be read, with or without official blessing, and modern theatre groups do make their statements. One hopes it has been more than naive optimism which has led me to focus here on alternate developments to the oft-reported bland uniformity of contemporary Indonesian cultural expression, on the plurality of voices which can be heard, and on the energies and creativity of particular groups amid the whole.

Notes

1 Quinn (1989) cites this figure, based on Indonesian government and media sources.
2 At the *temu budaya* (cultural encounter) conference held in Solo in 1987, on the theme of identifying a 'people's culture', many of the speakers, for example, lamented the disappearance of distinctive, local forms of cultural expression, swamped by the power of modern mass media.
3 Tony Day made this point, with special reference to the dance and music academy ASKI in Solo, in addressing the conference on the New Order at the Australian National University in 1989.
4 An excellent example of community recreational and cultural activities facilitated by state structures are the *kampung* and village competitions and performances held in celebration of Indonesian Independence Day on 17 August. See Hatley (1982) for discussion of these activities.
5 For an incisive analysis of the meanings of 'modernity' and 'tradition' in the

Indonesian arts, as defined by practitioners, and debated in their problematic implications, see Lindsay (1985).

6 See Jassin (1968) for examples. Two of the best-known of such poems are *Tirani* (Tyranny) and *Seorang Tukang Rambutan Pada Isterinya* (A Rambutan Seller Talks to his Wife) by Taufik Ismail.

7 See Aveling (1975a) for English translations of a number of these stories.

8 See Hill (1993) for details of the process of the founding of the Jakarta Arts Council, the administrative body overseeing the operations of the arts centre, and the subsequent history of both the council and the centre.

9 A 1985 publication by the Jakarta Arts Council, *Gejolak Teater Remaja di Jakarta*, contains a discussion of the aims of these competitions, commentaries on their operation and on particular performances, and a list of the winning groups over a number of years.

10 Tickell (1976) gives a detailed analysis of the language of *Kapai-Kapai*; while Piper (1976) discusses Arifin Noer's plays and artistic concerns more generally.

11 These were first published in English translation by Harry Aveling as *State of Emergency* (1980b) and in Indonesian in the intriguingly-titled *Potret Pembangunan dalam Puisi* (Portrait of a Poet in Development) (1980a).

12 Information about the army connections of *ludruk* troupes in East Java and *kethoprak* groups in Central Java comes from my own research in East Java in the early 1970s and Yogyakarta in 1977–78.

13 Helen Pausacker, who studied *wayang* in Solo in the 1970s, reports this as a frequently-heard observation at that time (personal communication).

14 Among others, Pak Siswondo, owner and director of the Siswoyo Budoyo troupe and Pak Mugihardjo, director of the Sapta Mandala troupe, made these observations in personal communications—Pak Siswondo in Malang in 1971 and Pak Mugihardjo in Yogyakarta in 1977.

15 Occasional feature stories appear in the press about the struggle for survival of traditional art forms, with frequent mention of *wayang orang*. A long article, 'Sendyakala ning Wayang Wong' (Twilight of Wayang Orang), describing the poor crowds, parlous state of theatre buildings and pitiful earnings of performers, for example, appeared in *Tempo*, 18 February 1984.

16 This summation by the renowned Javanese essayist and cultural analyst Umar Kayam is quoted in the above-mentioned article on *wayang orang* (*Tempo*, 18 February 1984:52).

17 Siegel (1986) gives an intriguing interpretation of the enormous popular appeal of *srimulat* performances in Solo in the early 1980s, at the same time as the various forms of the *wayang* tradition, with their very different style and meaning, reportedly experienced a decline.

18 Sasongko and Katjasungkana (1991:52–3) quote Siegel's (1986) work on Solo in the New Order, in differentiating the term *remaja* from *pemuda* and analysing the significance of the *remaja* concept for contemporary popular culture.

19 Piper and Jabo (1987), in their review of the history of pop music in Indonesia, comment on the distinctive styles of these singers and the social content of their songs. In Fals' case, sharply critical lyrics have often caused problems in obtaining permission to perform.

20 In the mid-1980s the phenomenon of *sastra sufi*, literary works with Islamic imagery and themes, absorbed attention in literary discussions and in the pages of *Horison*, coinciding with an Islamic revival in Indonesian society as a whole. By the end of the decade, however, such literature had faded from attention in dominant literary media in the capital, though maintaining its importance in regional areas, sustained by direct connection with the Islamic movement in the wider society.

21 See, for example, his short stories in the Indonesian–English collection *Bomb* translated by Rafferty (1989). Foulcher (1992) points out that, although Putu's stories are open to the kind of reading suggested above, the very absence of a single authorial point of view or perspective of interpretation is one of their most interesting and innovative characteristics.

22 The concept of 'invented tradition' is introduced and defined by Eric Hobsbawm in Hobsbawm and Ranger (1983).

23 A number of Yogyakarta actors went to the Philippines in the early 1980s to take part in workshops organised by Peta, and to see in practice their use of theatre for social education among workers and farmers. The Peta workshops served as models for those held later in Indonesia, and for some individual performers the Philippine experience profoundly affected their theatre practice. Michael Bodden's PhD thesis (Comparative Literature, University of Wisconsin, Madison) describes this process in detail, with particular focus on the group Teater Arena in Yogyakarta.

24 See, for example, the West Sumatran playwright and director Wisran Hadi, who bases the themes of his many plays on Minangkabau legends and adapts the style of local theatre forms such as *randai* in performing them. So prolific and well-established is Wisran that many analyses of his work can be found among student theses and academic papers in his native Padang (Hatley 1991; Junus 1981).

25 Regional arts centres, *taman budaya*, present a program of performances, exhibitions and other activities through the year. Some activities are directly sponsored by the centre itself, in terms of funding and performance permission; for others, organisers must request space, and pay building rent and organise their own permits. Modern theatre groups are usually included in the second category. In Hatley (1993) I try to explain some of the differences in official attitudes towards the modern performing arts in the cities of Yogyakarta and Solo, looking at factors of local cultural politics and bureaucratic organisation.

26 These observations are based on discussions with officials and viewing of performances of *reyog* in Ponorogo in January 1988.

27 See, for example, Sutton (1988) on *gamelan* festivals in East Java; Picard (1990) and Hough (1992) on dance in Bali; and Acciaioli (1985) and Aragon (1992) on ritual performances in Central Sulawesi.

28 Sutton (1988) gives a most interesting analysis of the process of attempted creation of a province-wide East Javanese *gamelan* tradition from a variety of existing, locally-specific forms. He documents the ironies of a situation in which those charged with developing a distinctive tradition to 'bolster the status of the province in the eyes of the rest of the nation—especially the eyes of the Central Javanese' (p.99) teachers at the Surabaya performing arts

conservatory— have expert training in Central Javanese music, not local styles. Problems of popular acceptance naturally arise. For all these difficulties, however, Sutton reports that certain core East Javanese traditions have gained strength in recent years and appear likely to become the basis for the new 'East Javanese tradition'.

29 See, for example, the *Tempo* article 'Srimulat tak Mampu Terbang' (Srimulat is Unable to Fly), 24 June 1989, for an account of a failed attempt by the Jakarta *srimulat* troupe to recoup enormous debts, and their tarnished reputation through a gigantic performance which attracted only a fraction of the expected crowd.

30 Such competitions involve alteration to the system introduced in the 1970s of presentation of television *kethoprak* by various local groups in rotation. Competition serials require a fixed cast of skilled, experienced actors collaborating over many weeks. Standards of performance are higher, but the participatory quality is reduced.

31 In a speech preceding the performance Djody stated this as his motive in sponsoring the show, and reinforced this gesture with a further gift of Rp50 million to the mayor of Solo for public works in the city.

32 For a detailed discussion of these importing conglomerates and their networks of distribution, see the main report in *Tempo*, 29 July 1990, particularly the article 'Zaman Keemasan Kelompok 21'.

33 A tragic example of this phenomenon occurred with the film *Langitku Rumahku* (My House, My Sky) by director Slamet Rahardjo, winner of several Indonesian film awards in 1990, and shown to great acclaim at Cannes and a number of other international festivals with resulting sales for foreign distribution. The film was withdrawn after only one day's showing at Jakarta cinemas because of a reported failure to attract a stipulated minimum number of viewers on that day. Crass business interests, most commentators agreed, won out over the value of this excellent film about a friendship between two children. See *Tempo*, 1 December 1990.

34 The remark by the *Tempo* journalist is quoted in the *Far Eastern Economic Review*, 26 July 1990; the possible motivations of conglomerates in establishing newspapers is suggested in *Tempo*, 15 February 1992.

35 While the *Jawa Pos* group is particularly active in Eastern Indonesia, *Kompas* and Surya Persindo compete for circulation in Yogyakarta, Bandung, Aceh and elsewhere.

36 See Sunindyo (1993) and Hatley (1988) for discussion of the effect of these pressures on the representation of women in film, with particular reference to *Roro Mendut*.

37 Along with issues of social justice, other more earthy preoccupations are also seen to find expression in *dangdut* lyrics, including erotic sex (*Tempo*, 25 May 1991). But while some critics frown in disapproval, others, including Rhoma Irama, self-styled moral guardian of the *dangdut* scene, advise tolerance, within limits, of such expression as a reflection of the organic, living nature of the musical form.

6

Local society and culture

Patrick Guinness

Perhaps the most remarkable feature of Indonesia is its social and cultural diversity. Spread over Indonesia's 3000 islands are some 300 ethnic groups distinguished by name, language, custom, ecology and social organisation. Over a third of Indonesia's population belong to just one ethnic group, the Javanese. Even they further distinguish among themselves on the basis of subtle differences in language and culture, between those of the north coast, those of the former Mataram court as the heartland of things Javanese, and several other locations like the 'outer lands' of East Java. Ethnic cultures, as depicted in distinct language, social etiquette, dress, food, dance and theatre are of passionate interest to most Indonesians, constituting unfailing sources of conversation, particularly for those in urban or resettlement areas faced with this cultural diversity. Equally important are the religious differences between the various world religions—Islam, Hinduism, Buddhism and Christianity—and the wide range of beliefs and practices focused on local and ancestral spirit beings, such as the *kejawen* beliefs and practices of the Javanese. Less commonly discussed are the differences in social and political organisation, in agricultural practices and in the social values that also characterise these diverse groups.

Any attempt to stereotype the diverse cultures and societies of Indonesia of necessity conceals much of the richness of their diversity. In her

---

It has been a daunting task to attempt to do justice to the vast wealth of ethnographic material on Indonesian people and cultures over the New Order. The result is but a partial picture. I am especially aware of the meagre reference to writings by Indonesian scholars. Incomplete as it is, this chapter has benefited from copious comments by Greg Acciaioli and Joan Hardjono, and from earlier discussions with Jim Fox.

pathbreaking description of 'Indonesian cultures and communities', Hildred Geertz (1963) distinguished three broad types of Indonesian society: the strongly Hindu inland wet-rice areas; the trade-oriented, deeply Islamic coastal people; and the mainly pagan tribal groups of the mountainous interior regions. These broad categories rely on contrasts in ecology and economic activity among sedentary growers of wet rice, shifting cultivators of dry rice and root crops, and traders, between those communities organised around kinship groups and those organised territorially, and between localised expressions of religious faith and practice, and adherence to world religions. Yet, as Peacock (1973:132) pointed out, and Geertz herself admits, many groups such as the Batak, the Chinese, the Rotinese, the Ambonese and societies of New Guinea do not fit neatly into these typologies. Indeed, thirty years on from Geertz's classification, social and cultural changes among many of these peoples, fueled by competing claims to cultural orthodoxy, challenge the appropriateness of such distinctions.

This social and cultural diversity is the culmination of a number of factors. The pattern of arrival of these peoples, their isolation on far-flung islands and in jungle pockets, the contrasting ecological conditions to which they adjusted, and their subsequent contact with outside cultures and religions all played a part. The colonial period served only to formalise, at times even create, the differences.

The Dutch, and for a short time the British, colonial officials were quick to recognise this cultural diversity. They attempted to centralise control over the widely dispersed Indonesian peoples by recognising local leaders of diverse political traditions, and by codifying custom under what the Dutch termed *adatrecht* (*adat* law). This nineteenth-century exercise had the effect of freezing into written law what had previously been a continuing revision, review and reaffirmation of social norms and values through the consensus of elders and people in each ethnic group. However, the *adat* law written into the texts of Dutch colonial administrators allowed them considerable control over the cultural centres of the many ethnic groups all over Indonesia. The diversity was guaranteed, but ultimate authority over people's ways was centralised in the colonial regime.

One of the more important distinctions for Indonesians is the prominence of particular ethnic groups and their leaders in the political struggles and economic dynamism of independent Indonesia. Javanese are seen as dominant in government, as well as in population, and have dispersed widely throughout the country. Most urban residents throughout Indonesia have become familiar with at least a few phrases of the Javanese language and essentials of the social etiquette of Javanese neighbours. Minangkabau, Sundanese, Bugis and Acehnese ethnic groups are represented among the nation's proclaimed heroes. Various ethnic groups have also spread widely through the archipelago and are well recognised, such as the Batak and

Minangkabau of Sumatran origin, the Bugis of Sulawesi, and the Madurese from an island off the north coast of Java.

At Independence, Indonesians, with a few regional and ethnic exceptions (notably the Ambonese), declared their unity against Dutch colonial re-establishment. The nation's motto *Bhinneka Tunggal Ika* (Unity in Diversity), recognised both the euphoria of that victory and the challenge of the years to come.[1] Ethnic identity, whether of cabinet ministers, army commanders, or urban bus drivers and food sellers, was of critical importance to both urban and rural residents. The Sukarno years from 1946 to 1965 witnessed first the proud unification of the nation around the proclamation of independence, the establishment of a constitution, the invention of a national culture centred on a national language, and then, as the centre weakened, social and cultural conflicts that ripped the nation apart. In the various parts of the new nation—West Java, West Sumatra and South Sulawesi—local expressions of ethnic and religious autonomy erupted into war with the central government. In the national heartland of Java there were clear signs of vertical divisions (*aliran*), based on ideologies of Islam and of communism that threatened the stability of communities and the peaceful performance of ritual life (Geertz 1965). Patronage consolidated the vertical divisions, particularly in urban areas, though in Javanese villages there was evidence that ideological splits reflected an incipient class struggle (Wertheim 1977).

The New Order government embarked on a strategy of national stability and unification, secured by the armed forces, but dynamised by the program of development linked to five-year plans. The armed forces had an acknowledged role in that development under the policy of *dwifungsi* (dual roles), by which army personnel were dispatched throughout the archipelago to perform both military and civilian roles. Development became the means to introduce uniformities both of a material and cultural nature. The president took the title of *Bapak Pembangunan* (Father of Development), associated with the concept of progress (*maju*) towards a clean, orderly and 'modern' society. The emphasis of development was on material improvements, industrialisation, housing, schools, health clinics, rice intensification, and communications. These brought a rise in living standards throughout Indonesia, but they also brought a realisation of Jakarta's expanding control over many areas of people's lives. 'Development' became the means of legitimation for the New Order as it demonstrated the ability of the central government to bring material benefits to its subjects (Ariel Heryanto 1988, 1990).

'Modern' life patterns and consumerism, associated with the global capitalist economy, are the second force for change that has dominated the New Order. Television, newspapers, pop music and magazines, motorised transport, western dress, school or civil service uniforms, refrigeration, fast

269

foods, and many other elements of contemporary consumer society have introduced new elements into the cultural diversity of Indonesian society. Strategies of identity reflect not only cultural differences but the relative positions of these groups in this global phenomenon (Friedman 1990:324). At the same time an urban and rural middle class has emerged that is committed to the benefits of a capitalist economy and its consumer culture. But the influence of this change has affected the whole of society and perhaps, most significantly, the youth of urban and rural Indonesia.

A third force for undermining locally-based ethnicity within Indonesia during the New Order has been the political and cultural stress on monotheism. This cannot be separated from the influence of the New Order state, which has taken the ideological position that, without at least nominal commitment to one of the recognised world religions, individuals are atheistic and, by extension, communist sympathisers.

The actions of the state, the dynamism of capitalist development and consumer culture, and the consolidation of world religions pose questions for many peoples in Indonesia. While a number have adopted the models of modernity and progress disseminated from Jakarta with enthusiasm, critics identify this rather as a form of neo-colonialism, or Javanisation. Does the construction of an Indonesian society inevitably mean the undermining of social and cultural diversity, through the growth of a homogeneous 'modern' society, perhaps with direct government mediation? What exactly does *Bhinneka Tunggal Ika* mean in contemporary Indonesia? What are the social and cultural forms of the newly-constituted Indonesia and to what extent does local diversity reconstitute itself under the New Order? Are the local expressions of diversity a major threat to the New Order?

Local identity and external pressures for change under the New Order

Throughout the history of the Indonesian peoples, local traditions and expressions of social and cultural autonomy have been pitted against external pressures for change. Within contemporary Indonesia this dialogue continues between *adat*, as an expression of local identity and order, and the forces of external influence encapsulated in the state, the capitalist economy and its consumer culture, and world religious ideologies and practices. It is not a matter of local identity disappearing in the face of such forces, but of bending and transforming. While these external forces are intent on creating social and cultural forms that are more amenable to political and economic penetration, expressions of localised sentiment and identity persist, even as they draw on elements introduced as a result of these forces. Their strength is their claim on communal loyalties, fostered by an appeal to the past. This chapter will examine, whether they are identified as *adat* or not, these locally-diverse forms of society and culture, and their reinterpretation and transformation under the three major forces of the New Order. This is a dynamic interchange, not one to be characterised by 'obstinate backward tradition' versus 'modern progress'. Rather, at the local level the substance of group identity is constantly being reworked, subject to disparate claims by experts and populace, men and women, old and young.

In what follows the three external forces identified above will be examined in relation to their observed impact on local society and culture.

Unity and integration of the nation state

Liddle (1989:11) suggests that 'probably a majority of elite Indonesians are convinced that without paternalistic leadership Indonesia will dissolve into chaos because of mass backwardness and deep cultural divisions'. Through its emphasis on national culture, broadcast through a mushrooming network of primary and secondary education, and rapidly expanding radio, television and other mass media coverage, the central government has sought to replace traditional ethnic and territorial loyalties. Allegiance to the centre and the culture of 'modern' Indonesia is encouraged. This is mediated by the state's invention not only of a national culture, based on a common language, history and ritual, but of various provincial foci of identification, centred on regional administrations appointed from the centre, and often headed by retired military officers. The central government has also pro-moted an often curious amalgam of the region's artistic expression as emblems of this provincial identification. So national television features daily the dances and songs and dress of the respective provinces, without identifying the ethnic origins of each particular item. Similarly, in the Taman Mini Indonesia Indah, a tourist attraction outside Jakarta established under the auspices of the president's wife, each province is represented by one house, but this may contain an amalgam of architectural features and furnishings from the various ethnic groups that are based in that province. Stamps and national airline souvenirs also portray distinctive wedding costumes for each province, again ignoring the vast ethnic diversity within the province. The central elite has thus made a strong move to limit diversity through social and cultural codification.

Faced with the massive task of administering the world's fourth most populous nation of diverse cultures spread over this varied archipelago, the New Order government appealed to the *Pancasila* as the uniting ideology of the nation, a set of principles charted at independence. The *Pancasila* acknowledges commitment to belief in one God, a just and civilised human-ity, national unity, and people's rule through consultation and representation, to achieve social justice for all Indonesians. Its broad terms, however, have not always proved satisfactory to interests championing an Islamic state nor to those seeking the more specific delineation of human rights. The New Order's insistence that all community organisations, political parties and religious groups acknowledge this ideology as their sole principle challenged the diverse ideologies of these groups. It also challenged the status of 'tradition', particularly where that tradition included beliefs beyond the accepted meaning of monotheism. The promotion of the principles of *Pancasila* through *Pancasila* education courses which government employees, community leaders, business and private company employees had to attend reflected the strong emphasis on integration under the New Order state. *Pancasila* became the 'ideological obsession' of the government and the basis for state control of social movements (Bowen 1991:126)

The ritual of the New Order further promotes integration. President Soeharto appears daily on national television and newspapers as 'father' of the nation, above any divisive sectional interests. His picture, and usually that of the vice-president, hang in all government and village offices, and in many private homes and offices. Independence Day (17 August) is a day celebrated nationwide with marches, flag-raising, ceremonies and local celebrations. On this day each local community puts on its own mixture of sporting events, house or hamlet competitions, and drama and dance festivals, often with the financial support of the central government. Independence Day is the most significant of all rituals for those communities created by administrative decree, but its emphasis is less on independence than the expression of unity. In some areas, government programs such as family planning or the formation of new administrative divisions have been launched on Independence Day to foster their public acceptance.

The rituals continue through the year. Throughout the nation, school children attend in uniform and parade before the flagpole to sing the national anthem, and they attest to their loyalty at least one morning a week. Public servants do likewise, attending the office in uniform and parading at least one day a week. Government offices, even in isolated rural areas, display the picture of the president and vice-president, and include an 'operations room' on the model of a military command (or the state cabinet).

The push for integration and unity under the New Order was not without its opposition from local *adat*, religious and other interest groups, but the political authority and military strength of the central government ensured the relatively smooth implementation of its main policies. The development promoted from Jakarta sought a uniformity of planning and implementation throughout the nation. This was particularly evident in the legislation and administration of the Village Law.

Village Law and government

The New Order accelerated attempts to institute a system of national law and administration. In the process it differentiated *adat*, 'traditional law and custom', often linked with religion, from secular, and thus national, administration, just as the colonial government had done (Schulte Nordholt 1989). *Adat* is frequently characterised by the government as stagnant tradition to be modernised or transformed to allow development to take place. For example, in Bali government officials attempted to compile a full list of all existing *adat* regulations (*awig-awig*) and to 'synchronise' them with national priorities. This allowed the state to penetrate into local affairs by taking control of secular matters, symbolised by positions such as the village leader, and strategies, such as village development plans (Parker 1989). Throughout Indonesia the New Order channelled substantial development funds through new village-level institutions and programs, such as *Inpres Desa* for the financing of village schools, meeting halls, roads, bridges and other infrastructure, *Bimas* rice intensification, *Dulog/Bulog* rice purchasing and storage, BUUD cooperatives, LKMD and LMD village committees, rural banks and rural health centres. Villages were classified on a points system that was based on such institutional indicators, and were expected to progress from an undeveloped state, termed *swadaya* (innate resources), to a highly developed state, termed *swasembada* (self-sufficient), as quickly as possible. This was most easily done by the establishment of those institutions designated by the state, and its success entitled village communities to greater access to central development funding. The state thus embarked on a program of converting the social forms and political structures of the village into its own image, which was often at variance with local expressions of community, identity and autonomy.

Village government, for example, was transformed by the Village Law of 1979, implemented gradually through the 1980s. This stipulated the uniform formation of villages, called either *desa* or *kelurahan*, headed respectively by *kepala desa* and *lurah*. Below that level, village hamlets were to be called *dusun*. At first there was considerable resentment at this use of Javanese terms, *desa* and *dusun*, to define the administrative units of local society. In West Sumatra many Minangkabau criticised the law as undermining their *adat* through the substitution of a new term for the local unit *nagari* (Kato 1989:96). In Bali there was concern over the substitution of the term *dusun* for the term *banjar*.

But the imposition of central authority is more striking in the appointment of leaders to these units. Village and hamlet communities are able to nominate individuals to fill such positions, but the local subdistrict head screens potential candidates, calls for the elimination of those considered too independent, and appoints the leader from two nominations finally submitted to him. When the *desa* is 'upgraded' to *kelurahan* status, all salaried officials at both hamlet (now called *lingkungan*) and village level become civil servants whose obligations are entirely to the administrative hierarchy. By definition, *kelurahan*, unlike *desa*, no longer have the right to manage their own affairs (Warren 1986:222–3). These leaders become salaried civil servants, thus ensuring their primary loyalties are to the central and regional government rather than to their own 'electorate'. Their position is no longer vulnerable to local censure but is rather ratified and enforced by the authority of the state. The position of these appointed leaders is further reinforced by their control, in consultation with an advisory council of village elite (LKMD), of all development funds channelled to the village. Not only does this consolidate the authority of the village head and elite, it also gives them access to 'commissions' of various kinds in administering such funds.

These provisions sharply differentiate New Order village administration from that which preceded it. In Bali, under the new forms of administration, the local population has been virtually excluded from the formal political scene (Schulte Nordholt 1989:15). Warren (1986) suggests that the 1979 Village Law will 'freeze in place a top-down administrative structure which will exacerbate the lack of communication between the central government and the rural majority'. In Riau *adat* leadership has also been considerably undermined, as people have begun to bring *adat* problems to *desa* heads, whom they see as having more political clout, rather than to *adat* leaders. The *negeri*, the local unit over which the authority of *adat* leaders mainly applied, was disbanded under the Village Law (Kato 1989:105).

One of the most dramatic impacts of the Village Law has been the dissolution or amalgamation of established territorial units. In the densely populated parts of Bali, villages have been amalgamated into *kelurahan* with a new leader appointed from outside. Among the Rejang of Bengkulu in Sumatra, the *marga*, the territorial unit above village level, was abolished. Previously, the *marga* was only indirectly controlled by the central government, but after the reorganisation, the central administration reached to village level, controlling the election of village heads and administration, and taking over lands previously under the control of village and *marga*. This at first seemed more democratic, for the *pasirah* who headed the *marga* had been known to use their position for personal profit and gain. However, their demise brought the loss of comprehensive social order, ideology and morality among the Rejang. The formally-educated younger men who are being chosen as village leaders under the new law often have little interest in tradition, and the subdistrict head does not interest himself in it. With the undermining of the *pasirah's* authority, there are neither groups nor individuals who can guarantee the social order. What seems to have disappeared is any sense of a moral community capable of preserving and reforming traditions. Instead, young and old, and traditionalists and reformists are increasingly out of tune with each other (Galizia 1989).

In some parts of Sumatra the provincial or subdistrict government used the new law to its advantage by splitting up existing village communities into a number of *desa* to maximise their claims on central funding of village units. The village multiplication resulting from the Village Law tore apart the close relationship of *adat* and administration. In Riau, settlements previously linked by formal *adat*, social structure and Islamic observance within *negeri* 'villages' have become separate *desa* villages, responsive more to directives from the *kecamatan* (subdistrict) office than to *adat* loyalties to the *negeri*. The coordination of rice planting within the *negeri* no longer takes place. The building or maintenance of public facilities such as bridges, schools and mosques which served several villages formerly united as one *negeri* have increasingly become the responsibility of the one village where they are located. As a result, the central government has increased its control over villages, even removing the revenue sources previously prescribed by *adat*, such as the taxing of the commercial exploitation of forest products. Kato (1989) suggests that the implementation of the 1979 Village Law violated the spirit of the 1945 Constitution, which respected indigenous structures and 'original rights of areas which have special attributes'. *Desa* multiplication increased the amount of development money available at village level, but this was secured by sacrificing a sense of community rooted in *adat* and history. Under the new scheme, cooperation among *desa* heads became rare. *Desa* leaders sacrificed cooperation for competition for economic and political resources (Kato 1989:106).

The implementation of the Village Law was not limited to rural areas. In 1988 it was introduced into urban Yogyakarta with the creation of a new unit, the *kelurahan*, below the level of *kecamatan*, and staffed by appointed civil servants. Below the *kelurahan*, the former administrative units, *rukun kampung* (RK), were abolished and smaller *rukun warga* (RW) were instituted. The RK, while not necessarily an effective administrative unit, had developed into a communal unit of some significance (Guinness 1986). Its elected head was not a salaried official, and was at some liberty to interpret government instructions to suit the interests of those under his care, and to strengthen their claims and conditions wherever possible in negotiation with higher authorities. Communal ceremonies, such as on Independence Day or *Hari Raya Idul Fitri*, the end of the Muslim fasting month, were organised by the RK. RK committees had also been successful in helping the poor and marginalised through programs that made it financially possible for residents to arrange a circumcision for their sons, provided equipment for parties, and distributed meat through the local mosque on *Hari Korban* (Day of Sacrifice). The RK head was regarded with some respect and his advice and support sought on household and neighbourhood matters. Under the new Village Law the level of RK, each of which in Yogyakarta numbered several thousand residents, was officially disbanded, and a new unit, the *kelurahan*, containing several of the former RK, formed. The *kelurahan* is unlikely to develop any of the communality associated with the RK. Its administration is staffed by appointed civil servants who may not even reside in the area, and it includes in a wider territorial unit a number of residential communities with few, if any, pre-existing social links, and frequently separated by busy city streets (Guinness 1991).

The new smaller unit of *rukun warga* (RW), at least in the part of Yogyakarta where I did my research (Guinness 1991), corresponded to an existing informal community whose members attended the most important ritual occasions together, provided the community of mourning on the death of members, initiated sporting and recreational activities for youth, cooper-ated in work projects and rotating credit associations, and were intimately known to each other. This was the unit more likely under the 1988 changes to assume the community functions of the RK. However, *kampung* RWs were financially much weaker than the former RK, for wealthier streetside RK members in many cases now form their own separate RW. This new arrangement thus undermined the fragile, but financially important, links between *kampung* and streetside residents formerly united within the same RK. In addition, annual *Inpres* funds formerly distributed annually to each RK are now allocated to the *kelurahan*, to be shared among constituent RW in rotation, thus severely cutting the amount of such funds.

To impress upon the city population the significance of the new levels of administration, all *kampung* houses were renumbered consecutively—once when the *kelurahan* were formed in 1981 and again when the RW replaced the RK. The disruption of postal deliveries was only ameliorated by the fact that postal deliverers were able to rely on their own and residents' knowledge of personal identities. The changes tended to emphasise the arbitrary, but authoritative, nature of state control.

Although traditional local forms have been severely undermined by the standardisation and central control of the New Order government's village policies, new sites and forms of local identity and social and cultural autonomy are likely to emerge. Warren (1986:218) indicates the capacity of local *banjar* to 'provide the organisational basis for the promotion of collective interests which may not necessarily coincide with bureacratic determinations'. In one example, a *banjar* successfully resisted administra-tive and military proposals to exclude it from an improved water supply and it did so through appeal to *Pancasila* principles.

The homogenisation of farming practices

One of the key ingredients of the New Order's development program has been the intensification of agricultural production. This entailed introducing inputs, such as improved seeds with shorter growing cycles, that depended on efficient irrigation (for rice) and heavy application of fertilisers, herbi-cides and pesticides. In the irrigated areas of Java and Bali, West and South

Sumatra, and South Sulawesi, and scattered pockets elsewhere, this program has achieved impressive results that have taken Indonesia from being the world's biggest rice importer to being self-sufficient in rice. However, the program has also borne the heavy stamp of the central government's insistence on uniformity. One reason for this has been the centre's pre-occupation with rice as the staple food, and its conviction that a program that worked in one place (Java) must work elsewhere. For Javanese rulers, intense wet-rice cultivation has always been a means to sustain high population density and to maximise returns to land and capital. Both of these, ample labour and taxable income, have been the mainstays of the Javanese and Indonesian states (Dove 1986). Throughout Indonesia intensive cultivation of irrigated rice and plantation crops on the pattern of the inner islands has been pushed by the central government in opposition to extensive cultivation of swidden crops and the collection of forest products. The success of new agricultural settlements in the outer islands, for example, was often judged solely on their production of rice (Babcock 1986:170).

Swidden cultivators in the outer islands, however, make better use of their labour by cultivating both annual and perennial crops (Dove 1985, 1986). In the outer islands, it is labour rather than land which is usually in short supply. Diversity of crops and cultivation patterns is an important feature of farmers' adaptation to the ecological diversity of Indonesia. In the islands of Roti and Timor, where the ecology only permits rice cultivation in scattered pockets, dry-rice cultivation and animal grazing have given way to labour-intensive palm harvesting when population pressures dictate (Fox 1977). To the central government policy-makers, these practices are frequently seen as outmoded and backward, although in some parts of highland Java the central government has promoted dry-land (*palawija*) crops. In 1986 there was a further revision to this policy as the central government admitted there had been too great an emphasis on fertilisers, pesticides and one or two rice varieties (Fox 1989). 'Traditional' varieties of rice continue to be grown and to fetch a market despite their slower growth and high price.

Government efforts to achieve such standardisation are not always met with approval by farmers. In Rejang, peasants refused to accept government planting schedules on the basis that local knowledge of seasons, rainfall and crops was more trustworthy than plans hatched by agricultural officers in distant centres (Galizia 1989).

The transmigration program has been a key component of the government's agricultural development program. Although programs of resettlement from the inner islands to the more sparsely populated outer islands had characterised both colonial and post-independence governments, transmigration has been seen by the New Order government as a critical policy for reducing population pressure in Java, Madura and Bali, and later

Lombok and Lampung. Its justification has been couched in terms of first resettling landless and land-poor families in the sparsely populated outer islands; and second of contributing to regional development throughout Indonesia by raising agricultural production. Settlers from Java and Bali have been seen as experts in wet-rice cultivation, despite the fact that many transmigrants are landless labourers with no experience of farm management. Local conditions in transmigration settlements are commonly unsuitable for wet-rice cultivation anyway. Commonly, where conditions are suitable, local farmers are usually already adept at growing wet rice. The program has thus tended to ignore local farming knowledge. It is therefore not surprising that transmigration has sometimes been perceived by local populations as a crude attempt at 'Javanisation' of the outer islands, despite the fact that settlers also originate from non-Javanese groups.

The push for the settlement of inner islands farmers throughout the archipelago, while intended to further integrate the nation, has threatened to raise ethnic antagonisms. Transmigration settlements brought to the foreground problems of land tenure. The Agrarian Law recognises the precedence of *adat*, and when local authorities settle the status of a proposed transmigration area they attempt to do so in the context of local *adat*, which often does not recognise the alienability of land. This leads to anomalies of land ownership, frequently exacerbated by government's ignorance of people's cultural links with their environment (Aditjondro 1986:73). In addition, locals continue to recognise traditional claims on fruit trees, sago and coconut palms, and bamboo groves located on the proposed resettlement area. This frequently leaves land tenure in doubt, with transmigrants hesitant to cultivate land that has residual local claims over it. Conflict over land, as well as resentment of the superior facilities and services on transmigration settlements, historical antipathies and general cultural differences, and the heavy burdens placed on provincial services are all fertile sources of antagonisms (Babcock 1986:178—see also Hardjono 1977; Hasan Mangunrai 1977; Suratman and Guinness 1977). It is significant that these antagonisms have often further entrenched ethnic groups identifying with specific practices and customs, *adat*, that distinguish them from other groups.

The New Order government has acknowledged such difficulties by attempting to incorporate local residents in the transmigration settlements. In Irian Jaya a target was set of 25 per cent of all settlers to come from local Irianese. In addition, the bulk of official transmigrants to Irian Jaya come not from Java or Islamic societies, but from Hindu Bali and Christian populations in eastern Indonesia (Aditjondro 1986). Despite these measures tensions frequently remain. In the Kutai district of East Kalimantan, transmigrants from Java joined local Kutai farmers within the one settlement. Despite government administration of the commmunity, Kutai disputed some instances of settlement by outsiders and a degree of hostility and competition developed between the two groups. Kutai were accused by Javanese of exploiting them in the inital adjustment period by charging them highly for local seed materials, and as a result some Javanese moved away from Kutai-dominated areas of the settlement. For their part, Javanese were accused by Kutai of being stupid and untrustworthy (Clauss, Evers and Gerke 1988).

In other cases, the state has directly vilified *adat* as being old-fashioned and sterile. In Kalimantan the 'wastage' of ceremonial exchange in harvest rituals was condemned by the government because it committed production surplus to distribution within the community rather than sale without. Orders were given that all longhouses hold harvest rituals on the same day to prevent inter-longhouse visiting and the resulting large distributions (Dove 1985). The government insisted that harvest surplus could more efficiently be invested in capital improvements. However, this stance ignored the significance of longhouse ceremonial exchange, which was an acknowledgement of others' labour, rather than capital, as the scarce resource. The government's stance also encouraged consumer spending on manufactured articles distributed from industrial centres remote from these longhouse settlements. The increasing religious and political ties with the centre were thus paralleled by growing economic ties. In South Kalimantan the subdistrict head and local Muslim leaders railed against the expense of the *banjar sunaten* ritual, suggesting that it no longer was suitable to a 'modern' society (Hawkins 1989). Similarly, *sumbangan* exchange among Yogyakarta villagers has been on the decline because it is regarded as wasteful and backward by government and Islamic reform groups. This exchange system in many parts of Java provides the means whereby individuals and couples build up exchange partners to whom they contribute and from whom they expect contributions of cash or food at rites of passage. Instead, the government has encouraged them to invest in their houses, and in their children's education.

The appropriation of local ideology and cultural practice

The monopoly of power by the state included the appropriation of local cultural forms and often their representation, or misrepresentation, in new terms deemed more appropriate by the central government. *Adat* was thus institutionalised and ratified by the state, as it had been by the Dutch, but in this case certain selected ethnic customs contributed to the construction of a national tradition. This gave the appearance of a cultural continuity to state control. *Gotong royong*, a term that recognised forms of balanced and generalised reciprocity among Javanese villagers (Koentjaraningrat 1977), became a central item in the ideology of New Order Indonesia, but in its representation it signified villagers' obligations to provide disinterested support in the form of labour and materials to government-inspired programs. Its implementation frequently relied on coerced rather than voluntary labour (Bowen 1986). This obligatory service was praised as a true expression of a basic Indonesian value, the general spirit of selflessness. *Gotong royong* was touted as an essential element of community without which local development could not proceed. However, on some occasions under the New Order's interpretation it differed little from the corvée labour required of Javanese villagers by their feudal lord and by the Dutch colonial government. In one subdistrict of Yogyakarta in the 1970s RK-directed teams of 'voluntary' labour sank 106 wells, paved 78 per cent of the alleyways, formed-up 72 per cent of its storm drains, erected eleven community halls, built ten public bathhouses and nine kiosks and kept in good repair numerous other facilities (Sullivan 1990:12).

Similarly, the concept of *musyawarah*, signifying the recognition of consultation among all household heads before community decisions were made, became interpreted under the New Order as the process by which the central government, through its local officials, informed the community of its plans and wishes.

In urban areas the concept *rukun*, signifying harmony and the lack of overt tension or conflict within a community, was appropriated at independence in the terms for the lowest level administrative units, *rukun tetangga* and *rukun kampung*, and later *rukun warga*. *Rukun* was a concept highly valued by urban *kampung* (and rural) communities, who associated it with the need for tolerance of each other's religious and cultural differences, and a willingness to live harmoniously together (Guinness 1989). The New Order state with some success used this concept of *rukun* to propagate an ideology of neighbourly cooperation and solidarity to achieve urban improvements at very low cost to government. These communal units also provided the state with some stability, as they undertook the policing and social control of their own populations.

The appropriation of such traditional concepts by the state is not without its contradictions. In discussing *gotong royong*, Bowen (1986:556) suggests that 'the state depicts its demands as the channeling of ongoing, free, mutual-assistance labor into productive infrastructure projects . . . [while] the villager . . . sees the program as state demands that possess a tangible opportunity cost'. Such government demands for voluntary labour have different degrees of cultural and political legitimacy. In Java, familiar with more indigenous forms of *gotong royong* and *rukun*, there was at least grudging compliance and sometimes enthusiastic cooperation when the project proved popular. In the urban *kampung* of Central Java, *rukun* is the basis of the introduced administrative units, readily endorsed by established residents concerned about the diversity of social and economic conditions and cultural loyalties of newer migrants to the area. However, in other areas of Indonesia where these concepts were introduced there was less interest or support. Among the Gayo in Aceh, for example, where no tradition of communal labour exists, those who would like to work are simply paid a high wage to get the government-agreed task done. The village officials then rigged the books detailing the (imaginary) voluntary labour and materials contributed by the community (Bowen 1986).

A second area of cultural appropriation by the state concerned traditional rituals. In Bali, for example, the government sponsored traditional island-wide rituals, *Eka Dasa Rudra* in 1979, and *Panca Wali Krama* in 1989. These were modelled on pre-colonial royal rituals that legitimised, even created, the power of the ruler (Geertz 1980). Under Sukarno's government, a dramatically unsuccessful attempt was made to revive the *Eka Dasa Rudra* in 1963. On that occasion, the simultaneous eruption of the volcano Gunung Agung was believed to reflect on the illegitimate authority of the military commander and (Javanese) head of police in Bali who organised the ceremony. However, the successful staging of these ceremonies in 1979 by the New Order during which the governor of Bali, a Balinese and a Brahman, represented the Indonesian government, ratified him as the right-ful ruler of the island province.

In 1989 in Rejang, Bengkulu (Sumatra) the subdistrict head and the head of the agricultural department organised a fertility ritual called *Mdundang Binnia*, which was normally held only after a succession of crop failures. The ritual brought together several territorial units (*marga*) and was the occasion when elders discussed and informally agreed to changes in *adat*. The government officials resorted to the ritual only after all other attempts had failed to induce peasants to adopt new varieties of seed and to sow at the same time according to the government's schedule. The government scheme backfired, however, for farmers were not persuaded to fall into line with government planting schedules but complained instead that officials had shown scant regard for tradition by failing to foster the community deliberations that normally accompany such a ritual, and for ignoring the appropriate deities by using Islamic prayers (Galizia 1989).

A notable instance of government encouragement for traditional cere-mony is when these are seen as attractive to tourists. The temple festivals and cremations of Bali, and the mortuary ritual, including buffalo duels and cliff burials of the Toraja in the South Sulawesi highlands, are promoted by the government tourist agencies. The Tengger in East Java are encouraged to continue to perform the annual *Kasada* sacrificial festival at the mouth of Mt Bromo volcano. In the case of Bali, where the major domestic and international tourist demand is centred, government efforts are directed at regulating and perpetuating traditional arts and crafts (Picard 1990). *Banjar* 'hamlet' units are appointed to market these attractions and training schools set up to produce new generations of performers and artists. The Balinese are in many cases able to accommodate the tourist demands on these ceremonies, and thus do not totally surrender the meaning of *adat* to government authorisation. They have begun to perform the same ceremonies in two different contexts—as a ritual in the context of their community life, and as a theatrical performance for tourists (Miller and Branson 1989).

This emphasis on local tourist attractions has brought diverse impact in local areas. The volume of tourism has grown and large-scale domestic and foreign entrepreneurs have emerged. New cultural forms have emerged to satisfy the market, even while local creativity has been enhanced. Tourism has encouraged, even obliged, local groups to adjust their activities, both in livelihood and ritual, to the curiosity and demands of domestic and foreign visitors. Artistic talents have been promoted. New dances, for example, and new painting styles have emerged in response to tourist, and government, demand, to the extent that new dances such as the Ramayana have now become more popular among Balinese audiences than more traditional forms. Thus external pressures of the state and of tourism have brought transformations in Balinese artistic performance, and yet have not destroyed the sense that Balinese are expressing something central to their own identity in their performances and crafts.

The Toraja of South Sulawesi began to experience large numbers of tourists from overseas interested in witnessing their mortuary rituals. Initially they faced this growing tourist market with concern, as feast givers could not refuse gifts of meat, the traditional gift to participants, to any guest, whether kin or tourist (Crystal 1977). However, by the late 1970s, just as the number of tourists was reaching thousands, the Toraja themselves, many of them returning from employment outside the area, were investing ever-increasing resources acquired outside Torajaland in the mortuary rituals as a means of gaining recognition back home. The growth of tourism coincided with rather than caused a revival of interest in *Aluk to dolo*, Toraja's traditional religion, but it contributed to the lavishness of rituals as occasionally hundreds of foreign guests joined by foreign television crews were invited. Tourists became the justification for the extravagance of these ritual occasions, for which buffalo and pigs were slaughtered, and numerous houses were constructed temporarily for the visitors (Volkman 1985:170).

The promotion of tourism by the New Order helped to unify the country as government agencies and offices were established to service the industry and increasing numbers of domestic tourists travelled round the country. In Bali numerous government departments have the task of coordinating local services catering to the international and domestic tourist market. A large percentage of the profits of tourist traffic do not accrue to Balinese people, as airlines and travel agents and hotel and tour operators based in Jakarta or overseas control much of the tourist sector. However, Bali's own response has flourished with the provision of village accommodation and entertainment. Rice fields have been converted into guest houses and farm workers have become artists, souvenir sellers and masseurs. Despite central government intentions, large amounts of tourist dollars earned by village Balinese go unrecorded and untaxed, and most of the creative energies of Balinese artists remain outside government control.

Defining women's roles

The state has assumed a key role in the definition of gender roles. Women's roles as defined in such all-Indonesian associations as the PKK (*Pembinaan Kesejahteraan Keluarga* (Family Welfare Association) emphasise the domestic roles of mother and spouse, despite the evident involvement of women in a wide variety of labouring, entrepreneurial and managerial positions. In these formulations, women as important breadwinners, such as in trading or farming, have been ignored. Trading, in much of Indonesia an activity associated with women, is increasingly defined by government as a site of development requiring economic initiative, and thus by this logic the leadership of men (Branson and Miller 1988). Successful food stalls run by women in Jakarta, for example, were quickly taken over by men (Murray 1991:55–6). The state also encouraged the ideology of female passivity in industrial development as a means to the exploitation of women through low wages in factories (Murray 1991:127). Murray suggests that it is as prostitutes that some women in Jakarta have been able to assert their independence of state 'patriarchal' structures.

PKK branches have been set up in *desa* and *kelurahan* units throughout the country, usually with the wife of the local head as association head. The program emphasises five roles of the ideal wife—as a faithful companion, manager of the household, producer of the nation's future generation, mother and educator and citizen. Their meetings and programs stress such urban middle-class values as the two-child family, the importance of the mother being at home to care for her children, 'western' dress and cosmetics, and baking of foods such as bread and cakes. Little attention is paid to the necessities of earning an income, a familiar responsibility to most women in both urban and rural lower-income households (Sullivan 1983). However, *kampung* women treat much of this official ideology with scant regard and even amusement. They regard the urban middle-class values espoused in such ideology as inappropriate to their own economic and social situations. For urban *kampung* women, trading may well provide the household with subsistence needs, but it is conducted within the confines of their obligations to networks of neighbours and the values they espouse. The giving of credit and attention to gossip become important mechanisms in strengthening community attachments.

State pressures on local ideology and practice have thus produced a variety of responses, tending both to conform to and to resist government blueprints. State intrusions at the local level have not gone unresisted. Farming schedules have been rejected, resettlement projects opposed, women have flouted the espoused ideal, vilified practices have been continued, and national cultures have been subverted. There is considerable evidence of local attempts to protect local autonomy and identity.

In these cases there is always a peculiarly local response to pressures from the centre, a response which often draws on tradition, community, or ethnic sentiment for its justification. *Adat* is seen to be preserved, even as new ways are fashioned to meet the demands of the state.

The capitalist economy and 'modern' consumer culture

The promotion of a capitalist economy is a centrepiece of the New Order's development program. It has entailed enormous investment by the government in extending its bureaucracy and the country's infrastructure, itself supporting a growing band of subcontractors, exporters and importers, and thus encouraging the emergence of a distinct urban middle class identified with the images of that economy and with the consumers of its products.

Communications and mobility

The New Order government transformed social and cultural relations within the country through the improvement in communications. In the 1970s Indonesia set up its own satellite called Palapa to create a modern telecommunications system, able to beam television broadcasts from Jakarta throughout the country. This became an important means for the promotion of a national image and culture. In East Timor, for example, televisions were provided to all villages, with the national television and radio stations seen as primary ways to integrate dissident East Timorese into the nation.

In addition, the construction and upgrading of roads, railways, shipping and airports from Sumatra to Timor and Irian Jaya led to increased movement of people and goods across regional and ethnic boundaries. People from Aceh were able to travel by bus all the way through Sumatra and Java to Bali. Domestic movement for employment and recreation was thus encouraged. Business opportunities in Bali, for example, were no longer the prerogative of local islanders, and much of the profit and employment generated by tourism there went to non-Balinese. Indonesia's urban middle class became far better travelled and familiar with their country's tourist destinations, while Indonesians of all classes and ethnic groups moved around the country in search of education, employment or business opportunity.

The government's own resettlement program encouraged increased mobility in search of better opportunities, and official transmigrants were augmented by migrants moving of their own accord and negotiating for land with local owners. Problems both with land tenure and inadequate crop and farming knowledge of the different conditions of the outer islands led to extreme poverty among many settlers, which resulted in some returning to Java and Bali, and others drifting to employment centres away from the settlement. Diverse settlement patterns and rural poverty similar to the situation on Java became familiar in some transmigration areas such as Lampung.

Various dimensions of migration have been found in Indonesia for centuries. Some ethnic groups, such as the Minang, Banjar, Kabau, Iban and Bugis, were renowned traditionally for their mobility, as male status was earned through the *rantau*, 'journey outside or overseas'. However, even in Java, where there was a strong attachment of people to their natal village, Javanese undertook to commute or migrate seasonally in order to find work (Mantra 1981). For many poor rural Javanese households, however, migration was not an option (Hart 1986:203). Titus (1978) argued that there was little evidence for assuming an intrinsic, culturally determined difference in the propensity of Indonesians to migrate. He pointed out that as road networks improved under the New Order, highland Toraja in South Sulawesi became just as mobile as the lowland Bugis. Although Toraja have moved widely throughout South Sulawesi, they are yet to follow the Bugis into such far-flung corners of Indonesia as the markets of Irian Jaya and East Timor, or the fishing settlements of Kalimantan and Sulawesi. For the Toraja there are no historical precedents for extensive migration. They traditionally shunned unnecessary movement and encouraged family members to stay close to the 'centre'. Under the New Order opportunities for employment have opened up for Toraja people, of all social levels, all over Sulawesi and as far as Jakarta, but their 'centre' continues to be Torajaland, where they return to claim status through ritual ceremonies (Volkman 1985:132).

Promotion of a metropolitan way of life and the urban middle class

The New Order encouraged population movement through the promotion of images of a national culture associated primarily with Java, urban environments, and Jakarta in particular. Hildred Geertz (1963) alluded to the development of a metropolitan 'superculture', particularly in the nation's capital. The image of modern Indonesia promoted on the nation's television screens and through government broadcasts, and exemplified by the nation's leaders was that of the lifestyle of the educated urban middle class. Although never defined precisely, the metropolitan concept demanded a clean and orderly city, a dynamic and modern centre attractive to westerners, with priority given to motorised transport (Murray 1991). These development objectives led to the suppression of those petty enterprises that were seen to dirty the city or clog up its thoroughfares, such as cheap food stalls located on pavements, cheap pedicab transport services, cheap housing located along the waterways and railway tracks, prostitution, and services such as rubbish recycling, or the processing of construction materials from river sand or discarded bricks. Jakarta has largely eradicated the *becak* pedicab, and in many other cities it has been excluded from central areas, despite the arguments of many observers that it provided an accessible and economic form of transportation and an important source of employment (Budhy Tjahjati S. Soegijoko 1984).

The model for modern metropolitan Indonesian culture and society was derived not just from western urban middle-class patterns but from a Javanese feudal aristocracy. Koentjaraningrat (1985) identified the modern Indonesian urban culture as that of the Javanese *priyayi* (bureaucratic elite), whose origins were in court life, where they served as officials to the sultans of Java. In the court they had privileged access to the wealth and influence of the ruler, and in modern Indonesia the urban middle class have retained such privileges through access to the rewards distributed by the government in its development program. Their lifestyle, revolving around fine homes, complete with the most modern of consumer durables, and expensive clothing and eating habits, resembles that of the elite in affluent western countries. The prominence of this group in formulating the norms for the nation is illustrated in the ideological priority given to state-affiliated organisations like the women's movement mentioned above.

International and domestic investment channelled towards the larger urban centres has also helped to spawn this urban middle class of managers, financiers and professionals, characterised by their demand for a consumer lifestyle and for education for their children. Many of them also espouse values of equality and human rights that challenge the mode of operation of the Indonesian state (Dick 1985). The state has been under pressure to satisfy their demands, not only for urban consumer goods, infrastructure and services, but also for some moderation in its authoritarian practices.

The growth of this urban middle class is paralleled by the increasing acceptance by the masses of Indonesian consumer patterns associated with modernisation, such as 'western' clothing, pop music, staples such as bread, television programs, and the Indonesian language.

One of the ironies of such a promotion of the metropolitan 'superculture' is its perceived affiliation with the Chinese ethnic group. Some Chinese run prominent businesses as exporters and importers, and as traders throughout the archipelago. As such they are often perceived not only as exemplifying the lifestyle of this 'superculture' but also as being in some way responsible for it, as the importers of foreign consumer goods. This has led to an ambivalence towards the Chinese among both the state and the larger public. In one of the most dramatic moves in its development program, the New

Order government sought, soon after coming to power, to weaken the cultural identity of Indonesia's Chinese population. Chinese language publications, signs and schooling were banned, and Chinese small traders were outlawed from rural settlements. Chinese were encouraged to change their Chinese names to more Indonesian-sounding names, and to contribute financially to local developments. However, although citizenship has been extended to many Chinese, the New Order government still differentiates against them by terming them *Warga Negara Indonesia* (WNI), meaning Indonesian citizen, but in fact a term reserved exclusively for Chinese and certain others of 'foreign' origin.

The 'otherness' of Chinese for the Indonesian public was illustrated when Chinese businesses, particularly shophouses, became the target of Jakarta crowd fury in 1974 when demonstrations erupted over levels of foreign investment in Indonesia during the visit of the Japanese prime minister. Although Japanese goods such as cars were the initial target of the crowd's anger, the Chinese became a useful target for such anti-foreign sentiments. Bandung witnessed a similar demonstration in 1973, and Solo in 1980 when riots broke out following a traffic accident. In the latter case, one observer identified the mass reaction of burning and destroying Chinese shophouses and goods as a form of ritual cleansing, a disavowal of the extreme forms of materialism particularly identified with the Chinese population (Siegel 1986). Javanese are less willing to admit that similar lifestyles are also overtly displayed by the urban elite and middle classes.

The rural middle class and social polarisation in Java

The benefits of agricultural development and government rural projects were not realised equitably among all villagers. The advent of central funding and the legitimation of village elites under the New Order has led to the consolidation of a rural middle class modelling its consumer patterns on urban counterparts. Agricultural reforms have proved more capital intensive than labour absorbing. In rural Java the landless and poor with limited access to agricultural labour were forced into non-agricultural employment, generally with poor returns, while the village wealthy have been able to invest their agricultural profits in capital-intensive, high-return activities such as trading and moneylending and others employing rice-hullers and pick-up trucks, for example. Those who have fared worst in the agricultural changes have been the poorer women whose labour was displaced by rice mills and harvest contract teams and who have had less opportunity to venture to the city in search of employment. This polarisation in village society has become more marked under the New Order (White 1989).

In the Javanese lowlands, farmers achieved marked increases in output through higher-yielding seeds and multiple cropping. This encouraged larger landowners to take back land from sharecroppers or to lease out land on prepayment of multi-year contracts. Increasingly, profits were invested outside of agriculture in what were seen as more profitable ventures such as mini-bus transport or rice milling, or in status emblems such as housing, furniture or motor vehicles. In contrast, few of the rural elite accumulated large landholdings.

However, as a result of rural agricultural programs, rural enterprise became more evidently commercial in operation. Open harvest arrangements disappeared in many parts of Java, thus depriving the poor of access to harvest income, and labour exploitation re-emerged in the form of share-cropping (*kedokan*) (Hart 1988). Rural relations were thus marked by increasing exclusion and marginalisation of the poor. However, the change from open harvests to *kedokan* may not have been as widespread as first reported. Even small farmers were able to raise their incomes from the new technologies, enabling relative stability in the distribution of land owned and operated (Manning 1986).

The important factor in this change was the relative security of the rural elite (Hart 1988). Although their relation with the state was often contradictory, the strong control of the bureaucratic–military oligarchy at village level restrained any politicisation of village populations. Young (1990) emphasises in fact that .it is this dependence on the state that differentiates members of the rural middle class from their urban counterparts. Their access to the riches of development programs and agricultural packages has led them both to reinforce ties of patronage when it suits them and at other times to ignore traditional obligations for purely commercial operations. It is clear that village social formations are changing, but not necessarily in the direction of the 'autonomous pursuit of individual prosperity in impersonal markets' (Young 1990:149).

Where pesticides, fertilisers and improved seeds were introduced in the highlands of Java, farmers initially turned to vegetable cash crops, and instead of spending their market proceeds on Japanese consumer goods like farmers in the lowlands, they channelled them towards more elaborate festivals. In the Tengger highlands, while the wealthy sponsored such rituals, with particular stress on exchange with those of similar means, poorer villagers increasingly withdrew from ritual performance, shamed by their lack of resources. The purification rite, once the sacred duty of all families, was increasingly regarded as the obligation only of those who could afford it. In its place Hefner (1983a) suggested that more families would turn to the purchase of consumer goods, as in the lowlands, and downplay the importance of exchange relationships, as improved roads and transportation made their contact with consumer goods markets easier. Ritual exchange would thus further consolidate the status position of wealthy villagers.

In Toraja, land ritual has become the focus for the assertion of status by low-status villagers, including former slaves. Through education and employment outside the area, especially in the army and civil service, low-status Torajans are acquiring the wealth to hold rituals of an extravagance formerly associated only with those of high rank. Although there is change here in traditionally accepted social levels, the claim to status is still being made in a distinctly Torajan way (Volkman 1985).

Throughout Indonesia, rural elites have emerged that depend both on the authority and largesse of the state and the benefits of the expanding capitalist economy. Village populations are being polarised both by consumption patterns and by the state's support for the emerging middle classes. With these changes has come the questioning of established models of stratification and status etiquette and the establishment of new status distinctions.

The cultural, technological and administrative innovations of the New Order have not brought consensus as to the precise nature of status hierarchy. Uncertainty about status in New Order Indonesia reflects the decline of traditional status markers such as aristocratic birth or age in a society that increasingly stresses education and advancement through occupation, wealth and connections. In both town and village there is unmistakable evidence that the display of wealth in house style, possession of a motor vehicle, and clothes and jewellery has become important in status claims, alongside more traditional markers such as patronage, ritual and landholdings.

In areas of Java the ambiguities of status are reflected in changing language patterns. In Javanese the high speech level (*kromo*) was formerly used to show respect towards one's elders, those of noble birth or of official standing. In contemporary Indonesia the relative status of others is more uncertain, and the determination of correct speech levels of address more problematic. Standard *kromo* increasingly characterises the interaction between strangers rather than recognition through language levels of their differential status. Perhaps as commonly, standard Indonesian is used because it does not require the subtle differentiation of style. An unusual example of this is among the Tengger of East Java, where *kromo*, a speech level alien to the village community, is increasingly being used rather than Indonesian in addressing non-Tengger. Tengger regarded it as more important to assert their common Javanese identity than to identify themselves as Indonesians. In contrast, Tengger among themselves use their own dialect of Javanese, which, however, is denigrated by Muslim outsiders as being not just backward but also non-Muslim (Smith-Hefner 1989:266).

Industrialisation

The growth of the capitalist economy under the New Order is closely associated with investment in manufacturing. Industrial activity has been centred in and around the main urban centres, especially in Java, with their superior infrastructure of roads, ports, power and water. Factories have in turn attracted to the cities a large number of both inter-urban and rural migrants. Not all have been employed on the factory floor, for the emergence of such a work force has stimulated the growth of a variety of service industries, providing accommodation, food, and recreational needs for this work force. In both urban *kampung* and villages on the edge of urban areas a proletariat of wage-workers is emerging.

An important element of the urban work force has been the circular migrants and village commuters, whose social and cultural allegiances remain with their village communities despite their employment in the city. In many parts of Java improvements in roads networks and means of transportation mean that villagers can commute each day to city employment, using a combination of bus, mini-bus and even taxi-motorbike from the remotest locations. Migrants' proclivity to return seasonally to their village to take part in harvest or planting or attend rituals militates against the growth of a genuine proletariat in the town. Individuals maximise income by working beyond the farm and village and maximise security by protecting ties with village-based support systems. For these reasons, circular migration, in contrast to permanent migration, inhibits structural change and the inevitable capitalisation of the rural sector. The communal labour and petty commodity production options of the city provide a bare subsistence for village households already squeezed by rural transformations. Circular migration helps to perpetuate a wide margin of inequality between the elite of the wage-earning classes and the circulating petty commodity producer-peasant subsistence classes (Forbes 1980:23). In West Java the flow of remittances from urban workers can be absolutely critical to the well-being of many village households, providing the necessities of life rather than contributing to capital investment. In West Java, in those rural households with a member working in Jakarta, fifty to sixty per cent of household cash income came in 1973 through remittances from the city (Hugo 1977:65–6; 1982). In Ujung Pandang, about a third of pedicab drivers remitted money to rural areas, either for daily cash needs or for investment in land purchase or small stores. Sixty per cent of the drivers returned for planting of the rice crop in their home village and 68 per cent for its harvesting (Forbes 1978:69).

An emerging component of the industrial work force has been young, single women. Previously engaged in domestic work, farming or petty trade, these women, mostly in the 15–25 year age range, enjoy a certain sense of social and cultural independence in factory employment. They exchange the confines of village society, the dust and heat of farm work, for a job in a clean, air-conditioned, clock-regulated industrial environment, where they can mix freely with young people of both sexes, and earn cash with which to purchase 'modern' clothes and cosmetics. Not all village commuters to urban or industrial enterprises make significant contributions to household finances. Village women near Semarang in 1982 sought factory work for their own personal needs, rather than for the betterment of their village family (Wolf 1990). Wolf calculated that three-fourths of the approximately 6000 persons employed in nearby textile factories were females, most of whom were single and between the ages of fifteen and twenty-four. As a general rule, daughters of poor families volunteered for factory labour, although only when there was another able-bodied woman in the household to take up the necessary home duties. Few of these women contributed to household finances on a regular basis; indeed, many continued to be supported from home. The support of their village household allowed them to be recruited cheaply, and thus further guaranteed a cheap and profitable labour force. Their major contribution to their families was through periodic cash disbursements of rotating credit organisations (*arisan*), with which major items of furniture or household expenditure could be met. Their employment, while taking some of the financial strain of their upkeep off the family, produced new strains as their tasks within the household had to be taken up by others.

The peri-urban factories had considerable impact on village society, in some cases forming an industrial corridor stretching from one urban centre to the next, and adding to the group of landless within the affected villages (Wolf 1986:143). This new avenue of employment also brought challenges to traditional norms of conduct between young and old and men and women. In northern Central Java, daughters from the age of fifteen were finding work in nearby factories without their parents' approval or knowledge, thus challenging traditional norms of authority within the family. Migrant women labourers were regarded as particularly lax in terms of traditional morality, and were blamed for increases in robbery, sexual promiscuity and having children out of wedlock in the villages where they stayed (Wolf 1986:147). However, in West Java in 1978 young women were closely supervised in factory employment through an alliance between parents, village leaders and factory management (Mather 1983)

Factory working conditions are frequently less ideal than imagined by these young women. They commonly work long hours, in a constant state of exhaustion. In Jakarta a 1984 Health Ministry survey of women factory workers found that many of them had health problems such as anaemia due to inadequate nutrition, and gynaecological problems, and that factories in general had poor sanitation (Murray 1991:98)

In industrial employment women are usually paid a lower wage and employed in more menial tasks. Promotions for them are rare and unattractive in a male-dominated environment. Even in petty enterprises heavily dominated by women, such as market trade, the development priorities of the government are making these activities more attractive and available to men as their commercial opportunities are emphasised. As street-level trading was replaced by high-rise market building, men began to replace women—for example, in the sale of cooked food or herbal medicines (Murray 1991). Models of modernity, frequently associated with western society and implemented by male planners, challenge women's access to food and cash resources, and their participation in decision making.

Although very locally specific, mining also undermines the integrity of local groups and social order. In the Freeport Indonesia copper mine in southern Irian Jaya, local landholders were removed forcibly to make way for the mining operations. They received compensation only for disruptions to current gardens, and the mine paid them no land rent or royalties. Subsequent mining caused surface degradation, river-water pollution and destruction of wildlife, and helped to fuel resistance by locals in association with the Free Papua Organisation (OPM). The local Amungme sabotaged mining operations in 1977, and as a result the Indonesian military carried out reprisals, killing hundreds, perhaps thousands of villagers. Others were forcibly resettled in low altitudes, where twenty per cent of infants died because of lack of resistance to malaria (Hyndman 1988).

In Soroako, South Sulawesi, Inco nickel mine appropriated the land and livelihoods of local residents (Robinson 1986a). Although initially many Soroakans welcomed the mine because it promised them permanent employment and better living conditions, many were left unemployed and without the fields that had formerly supported them. They were the first to be laid off as mining activities were curbed, and their village site was inundated by large numbers of immigrants, resulting in increased demand on water supplies and degradation of the environment. As a result of their lack of access to land or employment, married women were confined to the home and the care of children. They became increasingly dependent on their husbands for a cash income to meet subsistence needs. As a result of mining employment, men's and women's worlds became increasingly segregated, with women having little knowledge of the men's working world.

In some cases status differentiation based on ethnic identity was confirmed by industrial policies. In the Inco nickel mine in Soroako (Robinson 1986a), where mine management functioned as a de facto government administration, Europeans were located at the top of the company pyramid; below them were Sundanese from West Java, then Javanese and Sumatrans in junior management and skilled categories. In addition to their higher wages, the top groups were rewarded with better housing and access to services such as the supermarket and hospital. Indigenous Soroakans, whose land had been appropriated for mine and town developments, and whose village had absorbed large numbers of migrant squatters, only had access to unskilled jobs, with minimal access to services within the mining town. These differences reinforced the notion of Soroakans, and Sulawesi people generally, as inferior, and Javanese, Sundanese and Europeans as superior ethnic groups. This only encouraged the Soroakans to interpret their situation in terms of ethnicity and to refer to ethnic identity and solidarity in challenging what they saw as injustices of the development process—their loss of land, lack of jobs, and poor access to housing, water and health services. This led them to differentiate even between themselves and others from Sulawesi who were similarly placed on the employment scale. The Soroakan indigenes, deprived of their land and with their housing areas and water supplies increasingly under pressure, characterised themselves as mere 'stepchildren of progress'.

Industrialisation thus had its victims as well as its beneficiaries. The high wages paid to skilled and managerial Indonesian staff on mining projects such as Inco or Freeport were in contrast to the marginalisation of local farmers. Similarly, timber operations along the south coast of Irian Jaya decimated the social and cultural life of the Asmat people. With the forest source of their livelihood destroyed, they found employment in logging camps, where they only became aware of their relative poverty and dependence on manipulative employers (Aditjondro 1985). The marginalisation of such groups tended to cultivate new expressions of localised identity based on perceived ethnic and cultural commonalities. In the case of Soroako or Freeport, such identity was expressed forcibly through conflict with company and state authorities.

Small-scale manufacturing and trading

The development of substantial infrastructure, services and employment within the city in conjunction with growing landlessness in villages has stimulated a flow of urban migrants who cannot all be absorbed by urban factories or formal sector employment. The influx of Indonesians from all over the country has been particularly evident in the major cities. Here earlier migrants act as patrons and hosts to later arrivals from home villages. Migrants, particularly circular migrants, live in *pondok* (dormitories) among their village mates and have their food and trading needs supplied by the *pondok* host (Jellinek 1978). Many set up petty enterprises distinguished by ethnic or regional or village associations. Particular foods are marketed by different ethnic groups, while members of a particular village or area often monopolise the trade in a particular item, or the filling of particular city employment niches (Firman 1991).

In both villages and towns, petty commodity producers provide goods and services that guarantee the cheap price of labour to the capitalist sector (Forbes 1980:18). Circulation of labour between peasant subsistence production and petty commodity production in village and town make both possible. The evidence from Java (Alexander 1987) and West Sumatra (Kahn 1980) indicates the persistence of petty commodity production as a viable

293

peasant existence, with production revolving around the deployment of family labour. The restriction of such enterprises to small-scale production was due not to lack of entrepreneurial skill but to the structural obstacles within the New Order economy. Kahn (1980) demonstrates how village blacksmiths in West Sumatra thrived during a period before 1965 when foreign imports of steel products were banned. Conversely, the opening of Indonesia to foreign capital after 1965 imposed severe restrictions on the growth of petty manufacturing into major indigenous industrial enterprise.

Petty commodity producers in both rural and urban settings retain, or identify with, many features of social and cultural behaviour identified by them as tradition, or *adat*. So markets all over Indonesia are characterised by complex bargaining procedures among a myriad of petty traders and their customers (Geertz 1963b; Alexander 1987). Government attempts to shift these traders into multi-storeyed buildings and formalise trading arrangements threaten rather than support their ways of conducting business and their livelihoods. Outside these formal markets, traditional marketing arrangements still flourish. Much of this 'traditional' economic behaviour has its own rationale (Murray 1991).

Many of these petty traders and manufacturers and providers of cheap services experienced 'the wheel of fortune' (Jellinek 1991). Their good fortune in occupying a niche in the urban market, providing goods or services in demand from a popular location, could as easily be undermined by government action against those occupying street sidewalks or obstructing traffic, or changes in consumer preferences or costs of manufacturing between homemade and mass-produced ice-cream.

As a result of these structural pressures, income in the small-scale sector remains stagnant or declines, while the availability of cheap services supports the low costs of reproduction of the wage labour force. Wealth generated in the small-scale sector is thus appropriated elsewhere. In Ujung Pandang, South Sulawesi, for example, owners of *becak* pedicabs extracted surplus wealth from the drivers who hired them. This was appropriated within the petty commodity sector. Further along the chain the city government taxed petty commodity producers such as pedicab owners and drivers, fruit sellers and pedlars of all kinds. There were few services provided to these entrepreneurs by the government to justify such taxes. Forbes (1981a:848) concluded that it was a way of taking wealth from the poor and distributing it in other parts of the economy. He pointed out from his research that the incomes of petty commodity producers had remained static or declined under the New Order, and that most had little surplus cash for investment.

Local neighbourhoods

As people move into the towns and cities in search of employment and

294

improved incomes, the distinctions between an urban middle class of high ranking civil servants and businessmen, and the lower classes both of waged workers, petty entrepreneurs, low-ranking public servants and the marginalised class of circular migrants and casual workers, have been heightened. The lower classes have been largely confined to off-street neighbourhoods (*kampung*), with the middle classes monopolising the streetside better-quality homes. *Kampung* residents, comprising two-thirds of the population of many towns, pride themselves on their 'traditional' communality and neighbourhood associations, and accuse streetsiders of aloofness, insularity and arrogance. Streetsiders speak contemptuously of *kampung* people as ignorant, uncultured and criminal. While most streetsiders have secure positions in the city's economy, many *kampung* dwellers eke out a living on their wits from day to day, producing cheap goods and services, and creating new opportunities in an already crowded environment. Frequently, *kampung* residents occupy a position outside the social and political norms of the wider, streetside-dominated urban society by supporting illicit economic activities, instituting their own law and order procedures, and ignoring the social and cultural associations of the outside.

Kampung also provide both formalised and squatter housing. Though some earlier squatters have gained security in title to the land they occupy, others build shelters perched beside railways, rivers or canals, with little hope of security of tenure. In Jakarta central city squatters in one *kampung* were moved out to allow the construction of multi-storeyed blocks of flats. Some of the former *kampung* residents with petty manufacturing industries chose to invest in the new units and thus retain their clientele, but most found themselves forced to the outskirts, where employment and entrepreneurial opportunities were limited (Jellinek 1991).

The impact of world religions

The state has assumed authority for defining and officially recognising the religions approved under *Pancasila*. Religion in the terms of monotheism thus defined is associated with progress, literacy, power, wealth and sophistication. Thus a Middle Eastern monotheism and the authority of holy scriptures have become the defining features of religion. 'Traditional' religions which fail to meet these criteria are seen as pagan customs (Atkinson 1983). The official policy thus guarantees religious freedom and tolerance to members of recognised world religions, while censoring localised 'traditional' beliefs.

Pressure on individuals to join a world religion was further enhanced by officially sanctioned suspicions that atheism was akin to communism. Thus in the early years of the New Order there was mass entry to the ranks of Islam, Christianity, Hinduism and Buddhism. Simultaneously, conversion offered a solution to perceived social backwardness.

The state took a hand in the formalisation of religious dogma and liturgy. In Bali, where Hinduism took many forms, many of which were in danger of not meeting the official requirements of monotheism, the government encouraged the establishment of *Parisada Hindu Dharma*, which was given the task of registering priests and formalising a liturgy. Later this body became affiliated to the association of functional groups, Golkar, under central government control.

The formation of *Parisada* facilitated the recognition of a number of local religions as satisfying the state requirements of monotheism. Through affiliation with *Parisada* and acceptance of its liturgy the followers of the Buda[2] religion of Tengger gained legitimacy for their 'traditional' practices, while at the same time preserving religious practices and beliefs distinct from their lowland Muslim neighbours. Among the Toraja, *Aluk to dolo*, 'the way of the ancestors'; among the Sidenreng-Rappang Bugis, the *to Lotang* (beliefs); and in Kalimantan the *Kaharingan* religious practices of the Dayak were also recognised by the state as religions through the agency of *Parisada*. In these cases, traditional religions became important ethnic markers, providing a sense of identity, continuity with the past, and moral worth.

Among the Javanese, *kebatinan* mysticism was also given religious recognition early in the New Order, despite some opposition from Muslim quarters. Leading figures in the New Order such as the president himself were known adherents of mystical beliefs and practices. Recognition of *kebatinan* was a challenge to the political influence of the Islamic and Christian parties.

Mulder (1978) emphasised a contradictory movement of Javanese to *kebatinan* mystical movements, facilitated by the support of the New Order military and administrative leadership for the recognition of such movements as religious. In 1970 Golkar, the government-dominated political organisation of functional groups, established a coordination body of spiritual and mystical leaders, and the position of mysticism appeared to strengthen through the 1970s. Mulder saw this not as an escape from modernity or Islam, but as a reflection of the underlying traditions of Javanese culture that pre-dated Islam and western influences. The late Sultan Hamengku Buwono, former vice-president and provincial head, placed importance in mystical powers and was revered for those by millions in Java and beyond (Kleden 1989). Kleden suggests that, whereas for the late sultan mysticism was an important link with the spiritual realm, for many Indonesians it is seen as a way of achieving practical and economic goals. In East Java such a mystical movement gained strength in the 1970s as a reaction to perceived malpractices and abuses of power in government circles, but declined in the

1980s as the security forces loosened their control of rural areas and development programs increasingly incorporated people within the centre (Raharjo Suwandi 1989).

The early years of the New Order thus saw a revival of forms of religious expression. Lyon (1980), in describing the increase in membership of *Parisada* Hindu movements in Central Java, traced it to the political resurgence of Islam following the 1965 abortive coup, as people scrambled to avoid identification as atheist and thus communist. During the 1970s that sense of urgency lessened and membership of *Parisada* subsequently declined. In Bali the *Pasek* movement challenged the authority of Brahmans and the hierarchical structures of Hinduism promoted by *Parisada*, but on the basis that *Pasek* commoners can trace their ancestry further back into the past than the Brahman priests (Schulte Nordholt 1989).

The persistence and flexibility of *adat* is matched by the continuing strength of religious persuasion. Despite government dismemberment of Islamic political parties, there are other areas in which Islam exerts much greater influence. In Kotagede outside Yogyakarta, for example, growing numbers of Muslims, under the influence of the Muhammadiyah organisation, commit themselves to daily prayer and to fasting, notwithstanding the ritual association of this town with the syncretist traditions of the royal courts of Yogyakarta (Nakamura 1983). In Central Kalimantan, Miles (1978) described how Ngaju Dayak people from upriver were drawn not only into the commodity and labour markets of the downstream *banjar* society, but into its religious and cultural ambit. Conversion to Islam aided their economic integration and led to perceived change in ethnic identity as well as they abandoned traditions associated with upriver cultures. However, among those Ngaju Dayak who supported Dayak political movements, an anti-Islamic stance in the form of adherence to traditional beliefs and practices became part of their identity.

In the Tengger highlands of East Java there has been a history of those of Islamic faith settling further and further up the slopes and putting pressure on the Tengger themselves to convert to Islam. On the middle slopes, improvements in roads and transportation, and the introduction of government administration and services and of cash crops (coffee) encouraged the in-migration of lowland Muslim farmers during the nineteenth century. Besuki village, for example, was settled by Madurese entrepreneurs and landless labourers who dominated the indigenous Buda community both politically and economically. By the 1970s Muslims were occupying leadership positions in the village and had persuaded many Tengger to adopt Islamic ways. The Buda priest there was resigned to the demise of traditional religious practices. Higher up, Buda practices and beliefs continued but were placed under new pressures in the 1970s with the central government's emphasis on standardising religious expression and belief. As a result, the

Tengger Buda communities sought to protect their autonomy through affiliation with Hindu *Parisada* organisations in Bali (Hefner 1986).

Islam's resurgence in Indonesia is demonstrated in the increase of *pesantren* schools and their students, the latter numbering 1.2 million in 1987 (Zamakhasari Dhofier 1989). The *pesantren* education involves both Islamic and secular subjects, and produces an Islamic counter to western concepts of modernisation and development. The growth of *pesantren* is associated with the move of the *Nahdatul Ulama* Islamic organisation from political to social and cultural roles.

Despite its formal political demise, Muslim leaders continue to wield strong social leadership. In Jepara, Central Java, Nahdatul Ulama leaders, Muslim merchants and politicians of the Islamic party PPP challenged government malpractices associated with competition for scarce government jobs and funding, and the rising consumer demands of the state elite (Schiller 1990). In East Java, where orthodox Islam increased in popularity, traditional culture such as the *tayuban*, a ribald, flirtatious dance, was in decline due to opposition from Muslim quarters. However, as Hefner (1987b) pointed out, it was also rejected by poorer villagers who questioned the conspicuous consumption of wealthy villagers through these status-centred rituals.

More recently, with signs of a greater fervency among Muslim adherents such as in mosque attendance and the wearing of the veil by Muslim women, the government has attempted to appease this potential opposition by funding the construction of mosques and prayer houses and by providing support to Muslim associations such as the recently established Muslim Intellectual Association (known by its Indonesian acronym ICMI). President Soeharto and his family recently completed the pilgrimage to Mecca.

East Timor has witnessed a surge of Catholic membership as a result of state vilification of traditional religion and the growing involvement of the church hierarchy in protesting the harsh treatment of local people by the state. Although under the Portuguese colonial regime the local priests represented an elite distanced from local concerns, under the Indonesian state they have become spokespersons for justice and freedom. In this case, religion is an emblem of an East Timor identity that unites the more differentiated ethnic groups there (Mubyarto, Loekman Soetrisno et al. 1991).

The growing emphasis on monotheistic religions has paralleled the growth in state control and consumer culture. However, the embrace of world religions may also indicate resistance to such centralising and homogenising tendencies. In other cases, local religious identity pits itself against the more global concerns of the world religions.

Local identity and expression under the New Order

Liddle (1989) suggests that Indonesia is both modern and indigenous at the same time. The local ethnic culture provides for the private life of its adherents most of what is intimate, warm and familial, while the national culture deals with public life. The New Order's Javanism, he says, has been open, flexible and tolerant enough to give other groups room to manoeuvre.

On the other hand, local expressions of identity can also be seen as a counter to the centralising strategies of the national elites. Despite the considerable emphasis put on national integration by the New Order, diverse local groups have continued to place their particular interpretations on the development process. Much of the incidence across Indonesia of ethnic, religious and status differentiation, and of participatory social order, can be interpreted in terms of continuing questioning of the New Order's stress on homogeneity and uniformity. These local expressions rely both on invocations of *adat* and on less traditional concepts. Thus Islamic organisations, and non-government organisations in general, have become the media through which alternative development options have been explored. Despite the New Order's intent to appropriate cultural meanings and symbols to the purposes of national integration, not all culture has been manipulated, and government has found it difficult to manage all aspects of the social and symbolic order.

Ethnicity in the city

Ethnic sentiments remain strong in most urban settings. Foods and crafts of local ethnic origin are a major feature of the informal urban sector. Ethnic neighbourhoods, encouraged under the colonial government, continue to retain some of their significance. Chinese, for example, continue to congregate and be associated with certain urban districts such as Kota, the old port area of Jakarta, where they concentrate on 'traditional' pursuits of trade and commerce (Persoon 1986). In urban Yogyakarta ethnic origins contribute to a *kampung* resident's status. Those from the cultural heart of Java are considered of superior standing to those from East Java, whose command of refined language and etiquette is considered inferior, and to those of non-Javanese ethnic origins. There is a strong suspicion of non-Javanese neighbours, unless they make an attempt to use the Javanese language and social etiquette. Even when they make such an attempt their lack of fluency may be ridiculed (Guinness 1986).

Even in the national capital ethnic affiliation persists and is regarded as essential for survival. The Minangkabau of West Sumatra, for example, of whom possibly a half live away from their home region, congregate in Jakarta in organisations linked to home villages or districts. They support new arrivals from Sumatra, helping them find employment, and

Minangkabau marriage remains largely ethnically endogamous. Cultural traditions are maintained, even in migration (Persoon 1986). Similarly, Batak associations remain strong in the cities of Java and Sumatra, performing essential services in the gaining of employment and the performance of ceremonies, particularly weddings, where it is important to have representatives of particular kin groups present (Bruner 1974).

The persisting strength of ethnicity in urban settings, even among the 'modern' urban middle class, reflects the continuing importance of a local focus for ever-changing expressions of identity. The form that ethnic identity takes in the city may be very different to its expression in the village. Ethnic groups may be widely dispersed over the city, such that members only come together on formal occasions, like organisation meetings or weddings. Their ethnic sentiments may be focused on the construction of an *adat* house or the securing of village land a thousand kilometres away in the home village. Ethnic identification is more self-conscious and more focused on its distinctiveness from other ethnic expressions. It proclaims a unity of some kind, however, with the society and culture of its origins. Urban ethnicity thus mirrors the continuing importance of local identity within the contemporary Indonesian nation.

Adat and religion under the New Order

Adat, as Bowen (1986) remarks, cannot be seen either as timeless indigenous philosophy or as cultureless external ideology. The tenacity of *adat* derives from its pivotal role in social change, providing both a sense of continuity to temporal and geographical discontinuity, and an ideal cultural operator by which authorities have 'translated' radically new ideas and practices into ideologically familiar terms. *Adat* renders change intelligible to the individual and group imagination, and as a social process it allows change to happen within an ordered system of social relations. *Adat* offers an opportunity to formulate a kind of counter identity at the local level, which may redefine and reinterpret authority when and where state structures are weak. Even national concepts, such as *Pancasila*, that are derived from traditional values, may become a forum for resistance and debate. *Pancasila* has been variously interpreted as Marxist socialism, or as defining the right to equity and mutual cooperation, or to tolerance and consultation, depending on the viewpoint and traditions of the individual or group concerned (Warren 1989).

Members of all societies in Indonesia selectively incorporate messages from larger socio-political and socio-legal systems into local practice, thus retaining a sense of social continuity. *Adat* both eases the introduction of new ideas and constrains their implementation to acceptable terms. Civil and religious courts among the Gayo in Aceh, Sumatra, have presided over dramatic changes in divorce settlements and inheritance law, for example;

though the central tenets of *adat* are popularly considered to remain intact. In this case, *adat* law has come under pressure from central government attempts to construct a national 'modern' code that recognises bilateral inheritance, individual ownership and the equal rights of men and women. Gayo people by indirect means rather than formal opposition negotiated their own versions of these changes, particularly where they threatened the communal residual right over village land. The force for change came from the widespread adoption of coffee cultivation, and led to farmers and their families challenging 'traditional' terms of land ownership. As a result, a divorced wife was recognised by both civil and religious courts, on the basis of *adat*, to have an equal share with her husband in jointly produced wealth. However, Gayo communities sought to limit the loss of land to outside residents by declaring that women who had left the community had already received their share of the inheritance in marriage gifts, and thus had no further claims on their natal family's land. Similarly, the rights of all sons and daughters to inherit was recognised by the courts, challenging the previous control by the oldest son.

Adat was put under pressure from two angles—that of market forces associated with the production of cash crops, and that of more fundamental Islamic interpretation of Shari'a law. Those challenges strengthened the position of uxorilocally married men, and eroded the authority of eldest sons to divide estates. However, the central tenet of Gayo *adat* enshrined in *sarak opat* (the four elements which identified the political and territorial entity of the village community—the ruler, his assistant, the religious official and the remaining common people) and village land has not been challenged (Bowen 1988:286).

Similarly, Minangkabau *adat* authorities in West Sumatra have been successful in preserving *pusako*, matrilineally inherited land, from division among non-members of the matrilineage, while recognising that earned wealth could be given to sons. While men's position in Minangkabau households has changed with their admission to their wife's home and the construction of many more nuclear family homes, the matrilineal system and matrifocality of Minangkabau society has not been undermined (Ng 1987:35). Among the Batak in North Sumatra the central ritual relationships of wife-givers and wife-takers remain intact despite the economic and political changes of the New Order (Bowen 1988).

Adat remains the foundation of corporate social life in contemporary Bali, with the *banjar* as a whole retaining rights over residential land and responsibility for burial and cremations. Fines are also imposed on individuals by the *banjar* for failure to participate in community activities (Warren 1986:215).

In Kalimantan growing population pressure under the New Order exerted pressure on social institutions. Where forest had traditionally been open to all, exclusive hunting rights over secondary forest came into force among the Kantu in West Kalimantan and changes were made in the devolution of land rights to allow households a share in secondary forest they had not originally cleared. These changes happened gradually and were always the subject of intense deliberation by *adat* experts. As a result, the changes were frequently seen to be in accordance with *adat* (Dove 1980). *Adat* in these cases had been altered, while retaining its authority and image of continuity with the past.

Adat, or alternatively 'traditional' religion, generally serves to distinguish a group from other ethnic or religious groups. Wana religion in Central Sulawesi, for example, is a catalogue of dietary and burial practices, healing measures, farming rituals, sexual propriety, ritual specialisation and government ties that distinguish 'pagan' Wana from Christian and Muslim neighbours (Atkinson 1983:690). The declaration of all food as edible for Wana is emphasised precisely because Muslims make such an important issue of diet. In contrast, Wana have adopted elements of their cosmology to emphasise their belief in one God and their acceptance of an afterlife in conformity with Muslim and Christian beliefs. Here local cultural traditions are in dialogue with world religious cosmologies, and pattern themselves on wider social and cultural systems (Atkinson 1983:694).

The importance of *adat* is not simply as a means to preserve ethnic identity, but as an attempt to maintain a cultural and moral legitimacy in the face of a dominant external state and culture. Among the Salu Mambi of South Sulawesi the adherence to *Ada' Mappurondo* among a dispersed population of swidden farmers interspersed with Muslim and Christian kin is centred on an annual headhunting ritual which frees the community of its mourning for those who died during the previous year. The ritual, which uses a coconut as a surrogate head, is a celebration of moral value and heroic virtue, shaping the community's historical consciousness. It assumes added importance because its adherents perceive their need to assert their identity in a multicultural society (George 1991).

Such a reaffirmation of moral worth, at both individual and community level, is found in myriad forms throughout Indonesia. Ritual speaking, for example, which is characteristic of diverse groups throughout Indonesia, may have lost its political or ritual signficance but is still important in communicating a generalised moral authority of society.

Conclusion

The New Order state has attempted to create a nation out of .the diversity of local cultures and societies. It has sought to construct a unity based on certain 'sacred' principles—the constitution, *Pancasila*, and particularly its statement of belief in one God, the office (and person) of the president, the national language, and national rituals such as Independence Day. Its claim to legitimacy in this task has been staked on improving the material welfare of the majority of Indonesian people, achieved through the national program of 'development'. This in turn has paved the way for the spread of capitalist and consumer cultures throughout the archipelago.

This chapter has traced the impact of these state-sponsored changes on local societies and cultures. Diversity of social and cultural forms has probably always been a feature of these islands. Various political regimes, including most recently the Dutch colonials, the state under President Sukarno, and the New Order have attempted to stamp a political uniformity on this diversity, often by recognising the diversity of local societies and cultures, while attempting to codify them and limit their potential to disrupt national objectives. This chapter has shown how local cultural and social expressions have both been legitimated by the state and on the other hand have struggled against the pressures of state directives and global culture. Instead of insisting on social and cultural homogeneity, an impossible task anyway, the New Order has attempted to create a 'floating mass' of peasants and urban workers. In such a formulation, local forms might be seen as surface phenomena, as flotsam drifting randomly together into particular cultural and social configurations. The underlying current, however, is of bureaucratic and military control and powerful consumer culture. What has intrigued observers of these New Order currents has been the persistent strength of local expressions. These are not to be explained by the obstinacy of tradition, a mindless resistance to change. They are rather flexible, ever-changing expressions of local identity.

In this chapter I have traced the accommodation and dialogue of local identity with these economic, political and ideological forces. The state has not reached any kind of cultural hegemony despite the widespread recognition of *Pancasila* and Independence Day. Instead, countless expressions of local *adat* reaffirm the importance of ethnic identity and of the specific formulations of moral worth. These can be interpreted as resistance, a culture of opposition to the hegemony the state is attempting to impose. They may also be viewed sometimes as a response to the growing intrusion of authoritarian religious dogmas or the spreading culture of consumerism. They are also the product of an ongoing local dialogue that includes many disparate voices, of men and women, old and young, literate and illiterate, of high and low socio-economic status and rank, within a constantly changing social and economic environment. These multiple voices within any local group provide a forum for the constant reformulation and reconstitution of *adat* and group identity within the wider political and economic environment. That these reformulations continue to produce a diversity of social and cultural forms in Indonesia is evidence of the vitality and creativity of Indonesian peoples within the dictates of the nation-state and the expansion of global consumerism. It may well be that such capacity at the local level to reinterpret and redefine meaning through the medium of *adat*, and to articulate local ritual and power relations with those of the wider society, fluctuates with the strength of the state, the capitalist economy and monotheistic doctrine. The contemporary history of New Order Indonesia demonstrates the resilience of such local expressions of identity.

Notes

1   It is interesting that this motto and the word *Pancasila*, signifying the 'Five Guiding Principles' of the Indonesian nation, are of Sanskrit origin. Their adoption as national emblems reflects the dominant Javanese influence in such matters.
2   Not strictly Buddhist, the Buda religion has many liturgical features similar to Hindu practices.

Bibliography

(*Note*: *BIES* refers to the *Bulletin of Indonesian Economic Studies*.)

Abeyasekere, S. (1987), *Jakarta: A History*, Oxford University Press, Singapore

Acciaioli, G. (1985), 'Culture as art: from practice to spectacle in Indonesia', *Canberra Anthropology* 8(1 & 2)

——(1989), 'Searching for good fortune: the making of a Bugis shore community at Lake Lindu, Central Sulawesi', PhD thesis, Australian National University, Canberra

Aditjondro, G. (ed.) (1985), *Pengaruh Penebangan Hutan terhadap Kesejahteraan Masyarakat di Asmat*, Yayasan Pengembangan Masyarakat Desa Irian Jaya, Jayapura

——(1986), 'Transmigration in Irian Jaya: issues, targets and alternative approaches', *Prisma* 41, pp. 67–82

Afiff, S. et al. (1980), 'Elements of a food and nutrition policy for Indonesia', in *The Indonesian Economy*, G.F. Papanek (ed.), Praeger, New York, pp. 406–27

Aidid, H. (1987), 'Islamic leaders' attitudes towards family planning in Indonesia (1950s–1980s)', MA thesis, Australian National University, Canberra

Akita, T. (1988), 'Recent economic development', in *Indonesian Economic Development: Issues and Analysis*, S. Ichimura (ed.), Japanese International Cooperation Agency, Tokyo

Alexander, J. (1987), *Trade, Traders and Trading in Rural Java*, Oxford University Press, Singapore

Alexander, J. and Booth, A. (1992), 'The service sector', in *The Oil Boom and After: Indonesian Economic Policy and Performance in the Soeharto Era*, A. Booth (ed.), Oxford University Press, Singapore, pp. 283–319

Amnesty International (1985), *East Timor: Violations of Human Rights—Extrajudicial Executions, 'Disappearances' and Political Imprisonment*, Amnesty International, London

Amral Sjamsu, M. (1960), *Dari Kolonisasi Ke Transmigrasi* (From Colonisation to Transmigration), Djambatan, Jakarta

Ananta, A. and Arifin, E.N. (1990), 'Sensus penduduk 1990: bukan kejutan' (Population census 1990: no surprises), *Warta Demografi* 20(12), pp. 3–12

Anderson, B.R.O'G. (1978), 'Last days of Indonesia's Suharto?', *Southeast Asia Chronicle* 63, pp. 2–17

——(1983), 'Old state, new society: Indonesia's New Order in comparative perspective', *Journal of Asian Studies*, 42(3), pp. 477–96

——(1988), 'Current data on the Indonesian military elite', *Indonesia* (45), pp. 137–62

Anderson, B.R.O'G. and McVey, R. (1971), *A Preliminary Analysis of the October 1, 1965 Coup in Indonesia*, Cornell Modern Indonesia Project, Ithaca

Anderson, B.R.O'G. and Kahin, A. (eds) (1982), *Interpreting Indonesian Politics: Thirteen Contributions to the Debate*, Interim Reports Series no. 62, Cornell Modern Indonesia Project, Ithaca

Anderson, K. (1992), 'Effects on the environment and welfare of liberalising world trade: the cases of coal and food', in *The Greening of World Trade Issues*, K. Anderson and R. Blackhurst (eds), Harvester–Wheatsheaf, London

Anderson, K. and Blackhurst, R. (eds) (1992), *The Greening of World Trade Issues*, Harvester–Wheatsheaf, London

Anderson, K., Hayami, Y. and Associates (1986), *The Political Economy of Agricultural Protection: East Asia in International Perspective,* Allen & Unwin, Sydney, for the Australia–Japan Research Centre, Australian National University, Canberra

Aragon, L. (1992), 'Suppressed and revised performances, the *Rego* songs of Central Sulawesi', Paper presented at the Association for Asian Studies Conference, Washington DC, 3–6 April

Ariel Heryanto (1988), 'The development of "development" ', *Indonesia* 46, pp. 1–24

——(1990), 'Introduction: state ideology and civil discourse', in *State and Civil Society in Indonesia*, Arief Budiman (ed.), Centre for Southeast Asian Studies, Monash University, Clayton, pp. 289–300

Arndt, H.W. (1971), 'Banking in hyperinflation and stabilisation', in *The Economy of Indonesia: Selected Readings*, B. Glassburner (ed.), Cornell University Press, Ithaca

——(1979), 'Monetary policy instruments in Indonesia', *BIES* 15(3), pp. 107–22

——(1980), 'Growth and equity objectives in economic thought about Indonesia', in R.G. Garnaut and P. T. McCawley (eds), *Indonesia: Dualism, Growth and Poverty*, Research School of Pacific Studies, Australian National University, Canberra

——(1984), *The Indonesian Economy: Collected Papers*, Chopmen Publishers, Singapore

Arndt, H.W. and Sundrum, R.M. (1975), 'Regional price disparities', *BIES* 11(2), pp. 30–68

——(1984), 'Devaluation and inflation: the 1978 experience', *BIES* 20(1), pp. 83–97

Asher, M.G. (1989), 'A comparative overview of ASEAN fiscal systems and practices', in *Fiscal Systems and Practices in ASEAN: Trends, Impact and Evaluation*, M.G. Asher (ed.), Institute of Southeast Asian Studies, Singapore

Asher, M.G. and Booth, A. (1992), 'Fiscal policy', in *The Indonesian Economy During the Soeharto Era*, A. Booth (ed.), Oxford University Press, Kuala Lumpur, pp. 41–76

Asia Watch (1988), *Human Rights in Indonesia and East Timor*, The Asia Watch Committee, New York

——(1990), *Injustice, Persecution, Eviction: A Human Rights Update on Indonesia and East Timor*, The Asia Watch Committee, New York

Asra, A. (1989), 'Inequality trends in Indonesia, 1969–1981: a re-examination', *BIES* 25(2), pp. 100–10

Atkinson, J. (1983), 'Religions in dialogue: the construction of an Indonesian minority religion', *American Ethnologist* 10(4), pp. 684–96

——(1989), *The Art and Politics of Wana Shamanship*, University of California Press, Berkeley

Aveling, H. (1975a), *Gestapu: Indonesian Short Stories on the Abortive Communist Coup of 30th September, 1965*, Southeast Asian Studies Program, University of Hawaii, Honolulu

——(1975b), *Contemporary Indonesian Poetry*, University of Queensland Press, Brisbane

Azis, I.J. (1989), 'Key issues in Indonesian regional development', in H. Hill (ed.), *Unity and Diversity: Regional Economic Development in Indonesia Since 1970*, Oxford University Press, Singapore

——(1990), 'Inpres' role in the reduction of interregional disparity', *Asian Economic Journal* 4(2), pp. 1–27

Babcock, T. (1986), 'Transmigration: the regional impact of a miracle cure', in *Central Government and Local Development in Indonesia*, C. MacAndrews (ed.), Oxford University Press, Singapore, pp. 157–89

Bailey, C. (1988), 'The political economy of marine fisheries development in Indonesia', *Indonesia* 46, pp. 25–38

Bapedal (1990), *Report on the Implementation of Prokasih*, Environmental Impact Management Agency, Jakarta

Barker, R., Herdt, R.W. and Rose, B. (1985), *The Rice Economy of Asia*, Resources for the Future, Washington DC

Barlow, C. (1991), 'Developments in plantation agriculture and smallholder cash-crop production', in *Indonesia: Resources, Ecology and Environment*, J. Hardjono (ed.), Oxford University Press, Singapore, pp. 85–103

Barlow, C. and Jayasuriya, S.K. (1984), 'Problems of investment for technological advance: the case of Indonesian rubber smallholders', *Journal of Agricultural Economics* 35(1), pp. 85–95

Barlow, C. and Muharminto (1982), 'The rubber smallholder economy', *BIES* 18(2), pp. 86–119

Barlow, C. and Tomich, T. (1991), 'Indonesian agricultural development: the awkward case of smallholder tree crops', *BIES* 27(3), pp. 29–55

Barrichello, R.R. and Flatters, F.R. (1991), 'Trade policy reform in Indonesia', in *Reforming Economic Systems in Developing Countries*, D.H. Perkins and M.

Roemer (eds), Harvard Studies in International Development, Harvard Institute for International Development, Boston, pp. 271–91

Bendesa, I.K.G. (1991), 'The decline in the agricultural share of the labour force in Indonesia: 1971–1985', unpublished PhD thesis, Department of Economics, Research School of Pacific Studies, Australian National University, Canberra

Bennett, C.P. A. and Godoy, R.A. (1992), 'The quality of smallholder coffee in South Sumatra: the production of low-quality coffee as a response to world demand', *BIES* 28(1), pp. 85–100

Binhadi and Meek, P. (1992), 'Implementing monetary policy', in *The Oil Boom and After: Indonesian Economic Policy and Performance in the Soeharto Era*, A. Booth (ed.), Oxford University Press, Singapore, pp. 102–31

Birowo, A.T. and Hansen, G.E. (1981), 'Agricultural and rural development: an overview', in *Agricultural and Rural Development*, G.E. Hansen (ed.), Westview Press, Boulder, pp. 1–27

BKKBN (1973), *Laporan Pelaksanaan Program Keluarga Berencana Periode 1968–1972* (Report on the Implementation of the Family Planning Program for the Period 1968–1972), Badan Koordinasi Keluarga Berencana Nasional, Jakarta

Blaug, M. (1976), 'The empirical status of human capital theory: a slightly jaundiced survey', *Journal of Economic Literature* 14

——(1982), 'The distributional effects of higher education subsidies', *Economics of Education Review* 2(3)

Blinder, A.S. (1976), 'On dogmatism in human capital theory', *Journal of Human Resources* 11(1)

Boediono (1990), 'Fiscal policy in Indonesia', Paper presented to the Second Convention of the East Asian Economic Association, Bandung

Boediono and Kaneko, T. (1988), 'Price changes', in *Indonesian Economic Development: Issues and Analysis*, S. Ichimura (ed.), Japanese International Cooperation Agency, Tokyo, pp. 283–305

Boeke, J.H. (1953), 'Population increase', in *Eastern and Western World*, S. Hofstra (ed.), W. van Hoeve, The Hague

Bolnick, B.R. and Nelson, E.R. (1990), 'Evaluating the economic impact of a special credit program: KIK/KMKP in Indonesia', *Journal of Development Studies* 26(2), pp. 299–312

Booth, A. (1986), 'Efforts to decentralize fiscal policy: problems of taxable capacity, tax effort and revenue sharing', in *Central Government and Local Development in Indonesia*, C. MacAndrews (ed.), Oxford University Press, Singapore, pp. 77–100

——(1988a), *Agricultural Development in Indonesia*, Allen & Unwin, Sydney

——(1988b), 'Central government funding of regional government development expenditures in Indonesia: past achievement and future prospects', *Prisma* 45, pp. 7–22

——(1989a), 'Repelita V and Indonesia's medium term economic strategy', *BIES* 25(2), pp. 3–30

——(1989b), 'Indonesian agricultural development in comparative perspective', *World Development* 17(8), pp. 1235–54

——(1990), 'The tourism boom in Indonesia', *BIES* 26(3), pp. 45–73

Bibliography

——(1991), 'Regional aspects of Indonesian agricultural growth', in *Indonesia: Resources, Ecology, and Environment*, J. Hardjono (ed.), Oxford University Press, Singapore, pp. 36–60

——(ed.) (1992), *The Oil Boom and After: Indonesian Economic Policy and Performance in the Soeharto Era*, Oxford University Press, Singapore

——(1993), 'Counting the poor in Indonesia', *BIES* 29(1), pp. 53–83

Booth, A. and McCawley, P. (1981a), 'Fiscal policy', in A. Booth and P. McCawley (eds), *The Indonesian Economy During the Soeharto Era*, Oxford University Press, Kuala Lumpur, pp. 126–61

——(1981b), 'The Indonesian economy since the mid-sixties', in *The Indonesian Economy During the Soeharto Era*, A. Booth and P. McCawley (eds), Oxford University Press, Kuala Lumpur, pp. 1–22

——(1981c), 'Conclusions: looking to the future', in *The Indonesian Economy During the Soeharto Era*, A. Booth and P. McCawley (eds), Oxford University Press, Kuala Lumpur, pp. 315–22

Booth, A. and Sundrum, R.M. (1981), 'Income distribution', in *The Indonesian Economy During the Soeharto Era*, A. Booth and P. McCawley (eds), Oxford University Press, Kuala Lumpur, pp. 181–217

Bourchier D. (1984), *Dynamics of Dissent in Indonesia: Sawito and the Phantom Coup*, Cornell Modern Indonesian Project, Interim Reports Series no. 63, Ithaca

——(1990), 'Crime, law and state authority in Indonesia', in *State and Civil Society in Indonesia*, Arief Budiman (ed.), Centre for Southeast Asian Studies, Monash University, Clayton, pp. 177–212

Bowen, J. (1984), 'Death and the history of Islam in highland Aceh', *Indonesia* 38, pp. 21–38

——(1986), 'On the political construction of tradition: gotong royong in Indonesia', *Journal of Asian Studies* 45(3), pp. 545–61

——(1988), 'The transformation of an Indonesian property system: adat, Islam, and social change in the Gayo highlands', *American Ethnologist* 15(2), pp. 274–93

——(1989), 'Poetic duels and political change in the Gayo highlands of Sumatra', *American Anthropologist* 91, pp. 25–40

——(1991), *Sumatran Politics and Poetics: Gayo History, 1900–1969*, Yale University Press, New Haven and London

BPS (1978), *Indonesian Fertility Survey 1976: Principal Report*, volumes I and II, Biro Pusat Statistik, Jakarta

——(1981a), *Penduduk Indonesia 1980: Menurut Propinsi dan Kabupaten/ Kotamadya* (The Population of Indonesia in 1980: By Province and Regency/Municipality), Seri L.2, Biro Pusat Statistik, Jakarta

——(1981b), *Penduduk Indonesia 1980: Menurut Propinsi* (The Population of Indonesia in 1980: By Province), Seri L.3, Biro Pusat Statistik, Jakarta

——(1986), *Pekerja Sektor Informal di Indonesia* (Informal Sector Workers in Indonesia), Biro Pusat Statistik, Jakarta

——(1987), *Proyeksi Penduduk Indonesia 1985–2005 Berdasarkan Hasil Survei Penduduk Antar Sensus* (Indonesian Population Projections 1985–2005 Based on the Intercensal Survey), Biro Pusat Statistik, Jakarta

——(1988), *Perkiraan Angka Kelahiran dan Kematian: Hasil Survei Pendukuk*

Antar Sensus, 1985 (Estimates of Birth and Death Rates: Results of the 1985 Intercensal Survey), Biro Pusat Statistik, Jakarta

——(1989), *National Contraceptive Prevalence Survey 1987*, Biro Pusat Statistik, Jakarta

——(1990a), *Luas Tanah Menurut Penggunaannya di Jawa* (Land Area by Utilisation in Java), Biro Pusat Statistik, Jakarta

——(1990b), *Luas Tanah Menurut Penggunaannya di Luar Jawa* (Land Area by Utilisation Outside Java), Biro Pusat Statistik, Jakarta

——(1990c), *Statistik Indonesia* (Indonesian Statistics), Biro Pusat Statistik, Jakarta

——(1990d), *1990 Population Census*, Biro Pusat Statistik, Jakarta

——(1991a), *Penduduk Indonesia: Hasil Sensus Penduduk, 1990* (The Population of Indonesia: Results of the 1990 Population Census), Biro Pusat Statistik, Jakarta

——(1991b), *Statistik Perkebunan Besar, 1986–1989* (Statistics for Large Estates, 1986–1989), Biro Pusat Statistik, Jakarta

——(1992), *Indonesia Demographic and Health Survey 1991*, Biro Pusat Statistik, Jakarta

Brandon, J. (1967), *Theatre in Southeast Asia* Harvard University Press, Harvard

Branson, J. and Miller, D. (1988), 'The subordination of the relatively autonomous market seller in Bali', in *Development and Displacement: Women in Southeast Asia*, G. Chandler, N. Sullivan and J. Branson (eds), Centre for Southeast Asian Studies, Monash University, Clayton, pp. 1–15

Brookfield, H.G. (1991), 'The dimensions of environmental change and management in the Southeast Asian region', Paper presented to the workshop on Toward a Sustainable Environmental Future for the Southeast Asian Region, Gadjah Mada University, Yogyakarta, May

Brown, C. (1982), 'The intensified smallholder cane programme: the first five years', *BIES* 18(1), pp. 39–60

——(1989), 'The sugar industry in Indonesia's outer islands', in *Observing Change in Asia: Essays in Honour of J.A.C. Mackie*, R.J. May and W.J. O'Malley (eds), Crawford House Press, Bathurst

Bruner, E. (1974), 'The expression of ethnicity in Indonesia', in *Urban Ethnicity*, A. Cohen (ed.), Tavistock Publications, London, pp. 251–80

Budhy Tjahjati S. Soegijoko (1984), 'Becaks as a component of urban public transport in Indonesia', *Prisma* 32, pp. 64–77

Budi Darma (1989), 'Literature under the New Order', Paper presented at a conference on Indonesia's New Order, Australian National University, Canberra, December

Budiardjo, C. and Liem Soei Liong (1984), *The War in East Timor*, Zed Press, London

Budiman, Arief (ed.) (1990), *State and Civil Society in Indonesia*, Centre for Southeast Asian Studies, Monash University, Clayton

Bulatao, R., Bos, E. Stephens, P. W. and My T. Vu (1990), *World Population Projections 1989–90 Edition: Short and Long-term Estimates*, Johns Hopkins University Press for the World Bank, Baltimore,

Burbridge, P. R. (1988), 'Coastal and marine resource management in the Strait of Malacca', *Ambio* 17(3), pp. 170–7

Bibliography

Byron, N. and Waugh, G. (1988), 'Forestry and fisheries in the Asian–Pacific region: issues in natural resource management', *Asian–Pacific Economic Literature* 2(1), pp. 46–80

Byron, R.P. and Takahashi, H. (1989), 'An analysis of the effect of schooling, experience and sex on earnings in the government and private sectors of urban Java', *BIES* 25(1), pp. 105–17

Caldwell, M. (1975), *Ten Years of Military Terror in Indonesia*, Bertrand Russell Peace Foundation, Nottingham

Cantor, D. (1982), 'Indonesia looks toward continued fertility decline', Appendix B in *World Population and Fertility Planning Technologies: The Next 20 Years*, Office of Technology Assessment, Congress of the United States, Washington DC

Cementation (1990), *Cikampek Padalarang Toll Road*, Phase 1 Report, Cementation International Ltd, London

Chudori, L. (1989), *Malam Terakhir*, Grafitipers, Jakarta

Clark, D. (1983), 'How secondary school graduates perform in the labour market: a study of Indonesia', World Bank Staff Working Paper no. 165, Washington DC

Clark, D. and Oey-Gardiner, M. (1988), 'Towards an environment for quality teaching in the state institutions of higher learning', unpublished paper, CPIS, Jakarta

Clauss, W., Evers, Hans-Dieter and Gerke, S. (1988), 'The formation of a peasant society: Javanese transmigrants in East Kalimantan', *Indonesia* 46, pp. 79–90

Cole, D.C. and Slade, B.F. (1992), 'Financial development in Indonesia', in A. Booth (ed.), *The Oil Boom and After: Indonesian Economic Policy and Performance in the Soeharto Era*, Oxford University Press, Singapore, pp. 77–101

Collier, W.L. (1980), 'Fifty years of spontaneous and government-sponsored transmigration in the swampy lands of Kalimantan', *Prisma* 18 (English edition), pp. 32–56

Collier, W. et al. (1973), 'Recent changes in rice harvesting methods: some serious social implications', *BIES* 9(2), pp. 36–45

——(1974), 'Comment' (on Timmer, 1973), *BIES* 10(1), pp. 106–20

——(1982), 'Acceleration of rural development in Java', *BIES* 18(3), pp. 84–101

Coppel, C. (1983), *Indonesia's Chinese in Crisis*, Oxford University Press, Singapore

Cribb, R. (ed.) (1991), 'The Indonesian killings of 1965–1966: studies from Java and Bali,' Centre for Southeast Asian Studies, Monash Papers on Southeast Asia no. 21, Monash University, Clayton

Crouch, H. (1974), *The 15th January Affair in Indonesia*, Dyason House Papers no. 1, pp. 1–5

——(1976), 'Generals and business in Indonesia', *Pacific Affairs* 48 (4), pp. 519–40

——(1978), *The Army and Politics in Indonesia*, Cornell University Press, Ithaca

——(1979), 'Patrimonialism and military rule in Indonesia', *World Politics* 31(4), pp. 571–87

——(1984), *Domestic Political Structures and Regional Economic Cooperation*, Institute of Southeast Asian Studies, Singapore

——(1985), 'Indonesia', in *Military-Civilian Relations in South East Asia*, H. Crouch and Zakariah Haji Ahmad (eds), Institute of Southeast Asian Studies, Singapore, pp. 50–77

——(1988), 'Succession in Indonesia', *Third World Quarterly* 10(1), pp. 160–75

Crystal, E. (1977), 'Tourism in Tana Toraja', in *Hosts and Guests: The Anthropology of Tourism*, V. Smith (ed.), University of Pennsylvania Press, Philadelphia, pp. 109–25

'Current data on the Indonesian military elite', *Indonesia*, various issues

Danarto (1974), *Godlob*, Rombongan Dongeng dari Dirah

——(1982), *Adam Ma'rifat*, Balai Pustaka, Jakarta,

Dapice, D.O. (1980a), 'An overview of the Indonesian economy, in *The Indonesian Economy*, G.F. Papanek (ed.), Praeger, New York, pp. 3–55

——(1980b), 'Trends in income distribution and levels of living, 1970–75', in G.F. Papanek (ed.), *The Indonesian Economy*, Praeger, New York, pp. 67–81

de Boer, F. (1989), 'Balinese *sendratari*, a modern dramatic dance genre', *Asian Theatre Journal* 6(2), pp. 179–93

de Wit, Y.B. (1973), 'The kabupaten program', *BIES* 9(1), pp. 65–85

Dedé Oetomo (1989), 'The ethnic Chinese in Indonesia', in *The Ethnic Chinese in Southeast Asia: Bibliographical Essays*, Leo Suryjadinata (ed.), Institute of Southeast Asian Studies, Singapore, pp. 43–96

Demographic Institute (1974), *Indonesian Fertility–Mortality Survey 1973, Preliminary Reports Numbers 1–6*, Faculty of Economics, University of Indonesia, Jakarta

Devas, N. and Associates (1989), *Financing Local Government in Indonesia*, Ohio University Center for International Studies, Monographs in International Studies, Athens

Dick, H.W. (1980), 'The oil price subsidy, deforestation and equity', *BIES* 16(3), pp. 32–60

——(1981), 'Urban public transport, parts I and II', *BIES* 17(1), pp. 66–82; 17(2), pp. 72–88

——(1985), 'The rise of a middle class and the changing concept of equity in Indonesia: an interpretation', *Indonesia* 39, pp. 71–92

Dick, H.W. (1987), *The Indonesian Interisland Shipping Industry: An Analysis of Competition and Regulation*, Institute of Southeast Asian Studies, Singapore

Dick, H.W. and Forbes, D. (1992), 'Transport and communications: a quiet revolution', in *The Oil Boom and After: Indonesian Economic Policy and Performance in the Soeharto Era*, A. Booth (ed.), Oxford University Press, Singapore, pp. 258–82

Dickie, R.B. and Layman, T.A. (1988), *Foreign Investment and Government Policy in the Third World: Forging Common Interests in Indonesia and Beyond*, Macmillan, London

Diemont, W.H., Nurdin, Mannaerts, C., Smiet, A.C. and Rijnberg, T. (1991), 'Re-thinking erosion on Java', Paper presented to the International Workshop on Conservation Policies for Sustainable Hillslope Farming, Solo, Indonesia, March

Bibliography

Dini, N.H. (1989), *Jalan Bandungan* (Bandungan Street), Djambatan, Jakarta

Djajadiningrat, Madelon (1987), 'Ibuism and priyayization: path to power?', in *Indonesian Women in Focus*, E. Locher-Schulten and A. Niehof (eds), Foris Publications, Leiden

Djoko Damono, S. (1989), 'Karya sastra yang baik tidak lagi ada di *Horison*' (Good literature no longer appears in *Horison*), *Horison* 24(12)

Donges, J.B., Stecher, B. and Wolter, F. (1974), *Industrial Development Policies for Indonesia*, Kieler Studien 126, J.C.B. Mohr, Tubingen

Douglas, I. and Spencer, T. (1985), *Environmental Change and Tropical Geomorphology*, George Allen & Unwin, London

Douglass, M. (1988), 'Land use and environmental sustainability of the extended metropolis. Jabotabek and Jabopunjur corridor', Paper presented to the Conference on the Extended Metropolis in Asia, East–West Center, Environment and Policy Institute, Honolulu

——(1991), 'Planning for environmental sustainability in the extended Jakarta metropolitan region', in *The Extended Metropolis: Settlement Transition in Asia*, N. Ginsburg, B. Koppel and T.G. McGee (eds), University of Hawaii Press, Honolulu, pp. 239–73

Dove, M. (1980), 'Swidden systems and their potential role in agricultural development: a case-study from Kalimantan', *Prisma* 19, pp. 81–100

——(1985), 'The agroecological mythology of the Javanese and the political economy of Indonesia', *Indonesia* 39, pp. 1–36

——(1986), 'The ideology of agricultural development in Indonesia', in *Central Government and Local Development in Indonesia*, C. MacAndrews (ed.), Oxford University Press, Singapore, pp. 221–47

Drake, C. (1989), *National Integration in Indonesia: Patterns and Issues*, University of Hawaii Press, Honolulu

Dunn, J.T. (1983), *East Timor: A People Betrayed*, Jacaranda Press, Brisbane

Edmundson, W. and Edmundson, S. (1983), 'A decade of village development in East Java', *BIES* 19(2), pp. 46–59

Ellis, F. (1990), 'The rice market and its management in Indonesia', *IDS Bulletin* 21(3), pp. 44–51

Emerson, C. et al. (1984), 'Mining taxation in Indonesia', *BIES* 20(2), pp. 107–21

Emmerson D.K. (1978), 'The bureaucracy in political context: weakness in strength', in *Political Power and Communications in Indonesia*, L.W. Pye and K.D. Jackson (eds), University of California Press, Berkeley, pp. 82–136

——(1983), 'Understanding the New Order: bureaucratic pluralism in Indonesia', *Asian Survey* 23, pp. 1220–41

Errington, S. (1989), *Meaning and Power in a Southeast Asian Realm*, Princeton University Press, Princeton

Esmara, H. (1975), 'Regional income disparities', *BIES* 11(1), pp. 41–57

Etherington, D.M. (1974), 'The Indonesian tea industry', *BIES* 10(2), pp. 83–113

Evers, H.D. (1991), 'Shadow economy, subsistence production and informal sector: economic activity outside of market and state', *Prisma* 51, pp. 34–45

Falcon, W. et al. (1984), *The Cassava Economy of Java*, Stanford University Press, Stanford

Fane, G. and Phillips, C. (1991), 'Effective protection in Indonesia in 1987', *BIES* 27(1), pp. 105–25

Feith, H. (1962), *The Decline of Constitutional Democracy in Indonesia*, Cornell University Press, Ithaca

——(1968), 'Suharto's search for a political format', *Indonesia* 6, pp. 88–105

——(1980), 'Repressive–developmentalist regimes in Asia: old strengths, new vulnerabilities', *Prisma* 19, pp. 39–55

Firdausy, C. and Tisdell, C. (1992), 'Rural poverty and its measurement: a comparative study of villages in Nusa Penida, Bali, Indonesia', *BIES* 28(2), pp. 75–94

Firman, T. (1991), 'Population mobility in Java: in search of a theoretical explanation', *Sojourn* 6(1), pp. 71–105

Fischer, J. (1990), *Modern Indonesian Art: Three Generations of Traditional Change 1945–1990*, Festival of Indonesia, Jakarta and New York

Forbes, D. (1978), ' "Peasants" in the city: an Indonesian example', *Southeast Asian Review* 2(2), pp. 75–95

——(1980), 'Mobility and uneven development in Indonesia: a critique of explanations of migration and circular migration', in *Population Mobility and Development: Southeast Asia and the Pacific*, G. Jones and H. Richter (eds), Australian National University, Canberra, pp. 51–70

——(1981a), 'Production, reproduction and underdevelopment: petty commodity producers in Ujung Pandang, Indonesia', *Environment and Planning A* 13, pp. 841–56

——(1981b), 'Population mobility in Indonesia revisited', *Prisma* 20, pp. 69–77

Foulcher, K. (1978), 'Image and perspective in recent Indonesian literature', *Review of Indonesian and Malayan Affairs* 12(2), pp. 1–16

——(1987), 'Sastra kontekstual (contextual literature), recent developments in Indonesian literary politics', *Review of Indonesian and Malayan Affairs* 21(1), pp. 6–28

——(1988), 'Roda yang berputar: beberapa aspek perkembangan sastra sejak 1965' (The revolving wheel: some aspects of the development of literature since 1965), *Prisma* 8

——(1990), 'The construction of an Indonesian national culture: patterns of hegemony and resistance', in *State and Civil Society in Indonesia*, Arief Budiman (ed.), Centre for Southeast Asian Studies, Monash University, Clayton

——(1993), 'Post-modernism, the question of history, some trends in Indonesian fiction since 1965', in *Culture and Society in New Order Indonesia*, V. Hooker (ed.), Oxford University Press, Singapore

Fox, J.J (1977), *The Harvest of the Palm*, Harvard University Press, Cambridge

——(1988), 'Village and the state: Indonesia's "Bantuan Pembangunan Desa" program', Paper presented at a conference on The State and Civil Society in Contemporary Indonesia, Monash University, Clayton, November

——(1991), 'Managing the ecology of rice production in Indonesia', in *Indonesia: Resources, Ecology and Environment*, J. Hardjono (ed.), Oxford University Press, Singapore, pp. 61–84

Fox J., Garnaut, R., McCawley, P., and Mackie, J.A.C. (eds) (1980), *Indonesia:*

Australian Perspectives, Research School of Pacific Studies, Australian National University, Canberra

Frederick, W. (1982), 'Rhoma Irama and the dangdut style', *Indonesia* 34, pp. 103–32

Freedman, R. (1986), 'On the tendency to underestimate the rate of social change: a cautionary note', *Research Report* 86–95, Population Studies Center, University of Michigan

Freedman, R., Khoo, S.E. and Supraptilah, B. (1981), 'Modern contraceptive use in Indonesia: a challenge to conventional wisdom', *Scientific Report* no. 20, World Fertility Survey, London

Friedman, J. (1990), 'Being in the world: globalization and localization', in *Global Culture: Nationalism, Globalization and Modernity*, M. Featherstone (ed.), Sage Publications, London, pp. 311–28

Funkhouser, R. and MacAvoy, P. W. (1979), 'A sample of observations on comparative prices in public and private enterprises', *Journal of Public Economics* 11, pp. 353–68

Galizia, M. (1989), 'State and ethnic identity: among the Rejang of Southwest Sumatra', *Prisma* 46, pp. 57–69

Gannicott, K. (1990), 'The economics of education in Asian–Pacific developing countries', *Asian–Pacific Economic Literature* 4(1), pp. 41–64

Gardiner, P. (1989), 'Population prospects in Indonesia: size, structure and distribution', Paper presented at a conference on Indonesia's New Order, Australian National University, Canberra, December

Garnaut, R.G. and McCawley, P. T. (eds) (1980), *Indonesia: Dualism, Growth and Poverty*, Research School of Pacific Studies, Australian National University, Canberra

Geertz, C. (1956), 'Religious belief and economic change in a Javanese town', *Economic Development and Cultural Change* 4(1), pp. 34–58

——(1960), *The Religion of Java*, The Free Press, Glencoe

——(1963a), *Agricultural Involution: The Process of Ecological Change in Indonesia*, University of California Press, Berkeley

——(1963b), *Peddlers and Princes: Social Change and Economic Modernization in Two Indonesian Towns*, University of Chicago Press, Chicago

——(1965), *The Social History of an Indonesian Town*, MIT Press, Cambridge

——(1980), *Negara: The Theatre State in Nineteenth-Century Bali*, Princeton University Press, Princeton

——(1990) 'Popular art and the Javanese tradition', *Indonesia* 50, pp. 77–94

Geertz, H. (1963), 'Indonesian cultures and communities', in *Indonesia*, R. McVey (ed.) Yale University South East Asian Studies, New Haven, pp. 24–96

Gelb, A. and Associates (1988), *Oil Windfalls: Blessing or Curse?*, Oxford University Press, for the World Bank New York

George, K. (1991) 'Headhunting, history and exchange in upland Sulawesi', *Journal of Asian Studies* 50(3), pp. 536–64

Gillis, M. (1982), 'Allocative and x-efficiency in state-owned mining enterprises: comparisons between Bolivia and Indonesia', *Journal of Comparative Economics* 6, pp. 1–23

——(1984), 'Episodes in Indonesian economic growth', in *World Economic*

Growth, A.C. Harberger (ed.), Institute for Contemporary Studies, San Francisco, pp. 231–64

——(1985), 'Micro and macroeconomics of tax reform: Indonesia', *Journal of Development Economics* 19, pp. 221–54

——(1989), 'Comprehensive tax reform: the Indonesian experience, 1981–1988', in *Tax Reform in Developing Countries*, M. Gillis (ed.), Duke University Press, Duke

Giridhar, G., E. Sattar and Kang, J.S. (1989), *Readings in Population Programme Management*, ICOMP, Kuala Lumpur

Girling, J.L.S. (1981), 'The bureaucratic polity in modernizing societies: similarities, differences and prospects in the ASEAN region', Occasional Paper no. 74, Institute of Southeast Asian Studies, Singapore

Glassburner, B. (ed.) (1971), *The Economy of Indonesia: Selected Readings*, Cornell University Press, Ithaca

——(1976), 'In the wake of General Ibnu: crisis in the Indonesian oil industry', *Asia Survey* 16(12), pp. 1099–112

——(1978), 'Political economy and the Suharto regime', *BIES* 14(3), pp. 24–51

——(1979), 'Budgets and fiscal policy under the Soeharto regime in Indonesia', *Ekonomi dan Keuangan Indonesia* 27(3), pp. 295–314

Gluck, C. (1985), *Japan's Modern Myths: Ideology in the late Meiji Era*, Princeton University Press, Princeton

Godoy, R. and Bennett, C. (1990), 'The quality of smallholder cloves in Maluku: the local response to domestic demand for a high-quality product', *BIES* 26(2), pp. 59–78

Goenawan Mohamad (1974), 'Sebuah pengantar untuk film Indonesia mutakhir: catatan tahun 1974' (An introduction to the latest Indonesian films: notes on 1974), *Prisma* 3, pp. 49–60

——(1990), 'Dari Ramayana sampai Rendra: sebuah eksperimen bernama "TIM" ' (From the Ramayana to Rendra: an experiment called "TIM" '), *Tempo* 10 November

Gray, C. (1979), 'Civil service compensation in Indonesia', *BIES* 15(1), pp. 85–113

Grenville, S. (1981), 'Monetary policy and the formal financial sector', in *The Indonesian Economy During the Soeharto Era*, A. Booth and P. McCawley (eds), Oxford University Press, Kuala Lumpur, pp. 102–25

Guinness, P. (1986), *Harmony and Hierarchy: Social Relations in a Javanese Kampung*, Oxford University Press, Singapore

——(1989), ' "Social harmony" as ideology and practice in a Javanese city', in *Creating Indonesian Culture*, P. Alexander (ed.), Oceania Publications, Sydney, pp. 55–74

——(1991), 'Kampung and the street-side: Yogyakarta under the New Order', *Prisma* 51, pp. 86–98

Habir, A.D. (1990), 'State enterprises: reform and policy issues', in *Indonesia Assessment 1990*, H. Hill and T. Hull (eds), Political and Social Change Monograph 11, Department of Political and Social Change, Australian National University, Canberra, pp. 90–107

Haeruman, H. (1988), 'Conservation in Indonesia', *Ambio* 17(3), pp. 218–22

Bibliography

Hansen, G.E. (ed.) (1981), *Agricultural and Rural Development*, Westview Press, Boulder

Hansen, W.L. and Weisbrod, B.A. (1969), 'The distribution of the costs and benefits of public higher education: the case of California', *Journal of Human Resources* 4(2)

Hardjono, J. (1977), *Transmigration in Indonesia*, Oxford University Press, Kuala Lumpur

——(1978), 'Access to land in a Javanese settlement in South Sumatra', Litt.B. thesis, University of New England

——(1986), 'Transmigration: looking to the future', *BIES* 22(2), pp. 28–53

——(1987), *Land, Labour and Livelihood in a West Java Village*, Gadjah Mada University Press, Yogyakarta

——(ed.) (1991), *Indonesia: Resources, Ecology, and Environment*, Oxford University Press, Singapore

Hardjono, J. and Maspiyati (1990), 'The processing of cassava starch in West Java: production and employment relations', Working Paper B–9, Institute of Social Studies, West Java Rural Nonfarm Sector Research Project, Bandung

Hart, G. (1986), *Power, Labor and Livelihood: Processes of Change in Rural Java*, University of California Press, Berkeley

——(1988), 'Agrarian structure and the state in Java and Bangladesh', *Journal of Asian Studies* 47(2), pp. 249–67

Hasan Mangunrai (1977), 'Evaluasi pengembangan transmigrasi di Sulawesi Selatan: suatu studi tentang integrasi transmigran dengan penduduk asli di daerah transmigrasi Luwu Sulawesi Selatan' (An evaluation of the development of transmigration in South Sulawesi: a study of the integration of transmigrants with the original population in the Luwu transmigration area of South Sulawesi), Southeast Asian Population Research Awards Program, Singapore

Hasibuan, Sayuti (1987), 'Labour force growth, structural change and labour absorption in the Indonesian economy', unpublished paper, Jakarta

Hatley, B. (1982), 'National ritual, neighbourhood performance: celebrating Tujuhbelasan', *Indonesia* 34, pp. 55–64

——(1988), 'Texts and contexts: the Roro Mendut folk legend on stage and screen', in K. Sen (ed.), *Histories and Stories: Cinema in New Order Indonesia*, Centre for Southeast Asian Studies, Monash University, Clayton

——(1991), 'Theatre and the politics of national/regional identity: some Sumatran examples', *Review of Indonesian and Malayan Affairs* (25)2

——(1993), 'Constructions of "tradition" in New Order Indonesian theatre', in *Culture and Society in New Order Indonesia*, V. Hooker (ed.), Oxford University Press, Singapore

Hawkins, M. (1989), 'Slametan in South Kalimantan', in *Creating Indonesian Culture*, P. Alexander (ed.), Oceania Publications, Sydney, pp. 159–74

Hefner, R. (1983a), 'The problem of preference: economic and ritual change in highlands Java', *Man* (N.S) 18, pp. 669–89

——(1983b), 'Ritual and cultural reproduction in non-Islamic Java', *American Ethnologist* 10(4), pp. 665–83

——(1985), *Hindu Javanese: Tengger Tradition and Islam*, Princeton University Press, Princeton

——(1986), 'On the political construction of tradition: gotong royong in Indonesia', *Journal of Asian Studies* 45(3), pp. 545–61

——(1987a), 'Islamizing Java? Religion and politics in rural East Java', *Journal of Asian Studies* 46(3), pp. 533–54

——(1987b), 'The politics of popular art: tayuban dance and culture change in East Java', *Indonesia* 43, pp. 75–94

Hellwig, C.M.S. (n.d.), 'Leila S. Chudori and women in contemporary fiction writing', unpublished paper

Heryanto, A. (1985), *Perdebatan Sastra Kontekstual* (The Contextual Literature Debate), Rajawali, Jakarta

Hidayat (1978), 'Peranan sektor informal dalam perekonomian Indonesia' (The role of the informal sector in the Indonesian economy), *Ekonomi dan Keuangan Indonesia* 26(4)

Higgins, B. (1958), 'Hatta and co-operatives: the middle way for Indonesia?', *The Annals of the American Academy of Political Science* 318, pp. 45–7

——(1968), *Economic Development*, W.W. Norton, New York

Hill, D. (1984), 'Whose left? Indonesian literature in the early 1980s', Centre for Southeast Asian Studies, Working Paper no. 33, Monash University, Clayton

——(1992), 'Recent developments in the Indonesian press', ASAA National Conference Paper, Armidale, July

——(1993), ' "The two leading institutions" Taman Ismail Marzuki and *Horison*', in *Culture and Society in New Order Indonesia*, V. Hooker (ed.), Oxford University Press, Singapore

Hill, H. (1982), 'State enterprises in a competitive industry: an Indonesian case study', *World Development* 10(11), pp. 1015–23

——(1983), 'Choice of technique in the Indonesian weaving industry', *Economic Development and Cultural Change* 31(2), pp. 337–53

——(1988), *Foreign Investment and Industrialization in Indonesia*, Oxford University Press, Singapore

——(ed.) (1989), *Unity and Diversity: Regional Economic Development in Indonesia Since 1970*, Oxford University Press, Singapore

——(1990a), 'Indonesia's industrial transformation: parts I and II', *BIES* 26(2), pp. 79–120; 26(3), pp. 75–110

——(1990b), 'Foreign investment and East Asian economic development', *Asian–Pacific Economic Literature* 4(2), pp. 21–58

——(1990c), 'Ownership in Indonesia: who owns what and does it matter?', in H. Hill and T. Hull (eds), *Indonesia Assessment 1990*, Political and Social Change Monograph 11, Department of Political and Social Change, Australian National University, Canberra, pp. 52–65

——(ed.) (1991), *Indonesia Assessment 1991*, Political and Social Change Monograph 14, Department of Political and Social Change, Australian National University, Canberra

——(1992a), 'Manufacturing industry', in A. Booth (ed.), *The Oil Boom and After: Indonesian Economic Policy and Performance in the Soeharto Era*, Oxford University Press, Singapore, pp. 204–57

——(1992b), 'Regional development in a "boom and bust petroleum economy":

Indonesia since 1970', *Economic Development and Cultural Change* 40(2), pp. 351–79

Hill, H. and Hull, T. (eds) (1990), *Indonesia Assessment 1990*, Political and Social Change Monograph 11, Department of Political and Social Change, Australian National University, Canberra

Hill, H. and Mackie, J.A.C. (eds) (1989), *Indonesia Update 1988*, Political and Social Change Monograph 8, Department of Political and Social Change, Australian National University, Canberra

Hobsbawm, E. and Ranger, T. (1983), *The Invention of Tradition* Cambridge University Press, Cambridge

Holt, C. (1967), *Art in Indonesia: Continuities and Changes*, Cornell University Press, Ithaca

Hooker, V. (ed.) (1993), *Culture and Society in New Order Indonesia*, Oxford University Press, Singapore

Hough, B. (1992), 'Contemporary Balinese dance spectacles as national ritual', Centre for Southeast Asian Studies, Working Paper no. 74, Monash University, Clayton

Howell, L. and M. Morrow (1974), *Asia, Oil Politics and the Energy Crisis: The Haves and Have-nots*, IDOC, New York

Hugo, G. (1977), 'Circular migration', *BIES* 13(3), pp. 57–66

——(1982), 'Circular migration in Indonesia', *Population and Development Review* 8(1), pp. 59–83

Hugo, G., Hull, T.H., Hull, V.J. and Jones, G.W. (1987), *The Demographic Dimension in Indonesian Development*, Oxford University Press, Singapore

Hull, T.H. (1978), 'Where credit is due: policy implications of the recent fertility decline in Bali', Population Institute Working Paper no. 18, Gadjah Mada University, Yogyakarta

——(1980), 'Fertility decline in Indonesia: a review of recent evidence', *BIES* 16(2), pp. 104–12

——(1981), 'Indonesian population growth 1971–1980', *BIES* 17(1), pp. 114–20

——(1983), 'Cultural influences on fertility decision making styles', in *Determinants of Fertility in Developing Countries, Vol. 2: Fertility Regulation and Institutional Influences*, R.A. Bulatao et al., Academic Press, New York, pp. 381–414

——(1986), 'Socio-demographic change in Indonesia', in *Fertility and Mortality: Theory, Methodology and Empirical Issues*, K. Mahadevan (ed.), Sage, New Delhi

——(1987), 'Fertility decline in Indonesia: an institutionalist interpretation', *International Family Planning Perspectives* 13(3), pp. 90–5

Hull, T.H. and Hull, V.J. (1977), 'The relation of economic class and fertility: an analysis of some Indonesian data', *Population Studies* 31(1), pp. 43–57

——(1984), 'Population change in Indonesia: findings of the 1980 census', *BIES* 20(3), pp. 95–119

——(1987), 'Changing marriage behaviour in Java: the role of timing of consummation', *Southeast Asian Journal of Social Science* 15(1), pp. 104–19

Hull, T.H. and Mantra, I.B. (1981), 'Indonesia's changing population', in *The*

Indonesian Economy During the Soeharto Era, A. Booth and P. McCawley (eds), Oxford University Press, Kuala Lumpur, pp. 262–88

Hull, T.H., Hull, V.J. and Singarimbun, M. (1977), *Indonesia's Family Planning Story: Success and Challenge*, Population Institute, Gadjah Mada University, Yogyakarta

Huppi, M. and Ravallion, M. (1991), 'The sectoral structure of poverty during an adjustment period: evidence for Indonesia in the mid-1980s', *World Development* 19(12), pp. 1653–78

Husken, F. (1979), 'Landlords, sharecroppers and agricultural labourers: changing labour relations in rural Java', *Journal of Contemporary Asia*, pp. 140–51

——(1984), 'Kinship, economics and politics in a central Javanese village', *Masyarakat Indonesia* 11(1), pp. 29–43

Huszar, P. C. (1991), 'Government incentives for soil conservation', Paper presented to the International Workshop on Conservation Policies for Sustainable Hillslope Farming, Solo, Indonesia, March

Huszar, P. C. and Cochrane, H.C. (1990), 'Subsidisation of upland conservation in West Java: the Citanduy II project', *BIES* 26(2), pp. 121–33

Hyndman, D. (1988), 'Melanesian resistance to ecocide and ethnocide: transnational mining projects and the Fourth World on the island of New Guinea', in *Tribal Peoples and Development Issues*, J. Bodley (ed.), Mountain View, Mayfield, pp. 281–98

Ichimura, S. (ed.) (1988), *Indonesian Economic Development: Issues and Analysis*, Japanese International Cooperation Agency, Tokyo

IEES (Improving the Efficiency of Educational Systems) (1986), *Indonesia: Education and Human Resources Sector Review*, ch. 2, Economic and Financial Analysis, Ministry of Education and Culture/USAID, Tallahassee

IISI (1992), *The Military Balance*, IISI, London

IPPA (1969), *Yearly Report*, Indonesian Planned Parenthood Association, Jakarta

——(1970), *Yearly Report*, Indonesian Planned Parenthood Association, Jakarta

——(1971), *Legal Aspects of Family Planning*, Indonesian Planned Parenthood Association, Jakarta

Islam, I. and Khan, H. (1986), 'Spatial patterns of inequality and poverty in Indonesia', *BIES* 22(2), pp. 80–102

Jackson, K. (1978a), 'Bureaucratic polity: a theoretical framework for the analysis of power and communications in Indonesia', in *Political Power and Communications in Indonesia*, L.W. Pye and K.D. Jackson (eds), University of California Press, Berkeley

——(1978b), 'The prospects for bureaucratic polity in Indonesia', in *Political Power and Communications in Indonesia*, L.W. Pye and K.D. Jackson (eds), University of California Press, Berkeley

Jarot, E. (1990), 'Teringat akan Raj Kapoor' (Shades of Raj Kapoor), *Tempo* 1 December

Jassin, H.B. (1968), *Angkatan 66* (The 66 Generation), Gunung Agung, Jakarta

——(1989), 'Sastra dalam surat kabar dan majalah' (Literature in newspapers and magazines), *Horison* 23(2)

Jayasuriya, S.K. and Manning, C.G. (1990), 'Agricultural wage growth and rural labour market adjustment: the case of Java 1970–1988', Working Papers in

Bibliography

Trade and Development no. 90/2, Research School of Pacific Studies, Australian National University, Canberra

Jayasuriya, S.K. and Nehen, I.K. (1989), 'Bali: economic growth and tourism', in *Unity and Diversity: Regional Economic Development in Indonesia Since 1970*, H. Hill (ed.), Oxford University Press, Singapore, pp. 331–48

Jellinek, L. (1978), 'Circular migration and the pondok dwelling system: a case study of ice cream traders in Jakarta', in *Food, Shelter and Transport in Southeast Asia and the Pacific*, P. Rimmer, D. Drakakis-Smith and T. McGee (eds), Australian National University, Canberra, pp. 135–54

——(1991), *The Wheel of Fortune: The History of a Poor Community in Jakarta*, Allen & Unwin, Sydney

Jenkins, D. (1984), *Suharto and his Generals: Indonesian Military Politics 1975–1983*, Monograph Series no. 64, Cornell Modern Indonesia Project, Ithaca

Johns, A.H. (1987), 'Indonesia, Islam and cultural pluralism', in *Islam in Asia. Religion, Politics and Society*, J.L. Esposito (ed.), Oxford University Press, New York, pp. 209–29

Jones, G.W. (1966), 'The growth and changing structure of the Indonesian labour force, 1930–81', *BIES* 4, pp. 50–74

——(1976), 'Religion and education in Indonesia', *Indonesia* 22, pp. 19–56

——(1977), *The Population of North Sulawesi*, Gadjah Mada University Press, Yogyakarta

——(1981), 'The Indonesian labour force since 1961', in *The Indonesian Economy During the Soeharto Era*, A. Booth and P. McCawley (eds), Oxford University Press, Kuala Lumpur, pp. 286–340

——(1984), 'Links between urbanization and sectoral shifts in employment in Java', *BIES* 20(3), pp. 120–57

——(1986), 'Differentials in female labour force participation rates in Indonesia: reflection of economic needs and opportunities, culture or bad data?', *Majalah Demografi Indonesia* 26, pp. 1–28

——(1988), 'Economic growth, changing employment structure and implications for educational planning in ASEAN countries', NUPRI Research Paper Series no. 47, Nihon University Population Research Institute, Tokyo

——(1989a), 'Sub-national population policy: the case of North Sulawesi', *BIES* 25(1), pp. 77–104

——(1989b), 'Expansion of secondary and tertiary education in South East Asia: some implications for Australia', *Journal of the Australian Population Association* 6(1)

——(1992), 'Dilemmas in expanding education for faster economic growth: Indonesia, Malaysia and Thailand', in *Human Resources and Development Along the Asia-Pacific Rim*, N. Ogawa, G.W. Jones and J. Williamson (eds), Oxford University Press, Singapore

Jones, G.W. and Manning, C. (1992), 'Labour force and employment during the 1980s', in *The Oil Boom and After: Indonesian Economic Policy and Performance in the Soeharto Era*, A. Booth (ed.), Oxford University Press, Singapore

Jones, G.W. and Supraptilah, B. (1976), 'Underutilization of labour in Palembang and Ujung Pandang', *BIES* 12(2), pp. 30–57

Junghans, K.H. (1974), 'Transmigration and agricultural production in Lampung', in *Transmigration in the Context of Area Development*, R. Soebiantoro (ed.), Transmigration Training and Research Center, Jakarta, pp. 68–83

Junus, U. (1981), *Mitos dan Komunikasi* (Myth and Communication), Sinar Harapan, Jakarta

Kahn, J. (1980), *Minangkabau Social Formations*, Cambridge University Press, Cambridge

——(1985), 'Indonesia after the demise of involution: critique of a debate', *Critique of Anthropology* 5(1), pp. 69–96

Kam, G. (1987), '*Wayang wong* in the court of Yogyakarta: the enduring significance of Javanese dance drama', *Asian Theatre Journal* 4(1), pp. 29–51

Kameo, D. and Rietveld, P. (1987), 'Regional income disparities in Indonesia: a comment', *Ekonomi dan Keuangan Indonesia* 35(4), pp. 451–9

Kartawinata, K. and Vayda, A.P. (1984), 'Forest conversion in East Kalimantan, Indonesia: the activities and impact of timber companies, shifting cultivators, migrant pepper farmers and others', in *Ecology in Practice I: Ecosystem Management*, F. Di Castri, F.W.G. Baker and M. Hadley (eds), Tycooly, Dublin; UNESCO, Paris, pp. 98–126

Kartomi, M. (1978), 'Performance, music and meaning of reyog ponorogo', *Indonesia* 22, pp. 85–130

Kasto (1992), 'Variasi tingkat kematian bayi dan harapan hidup di Indonesia menurut propinsi: hasil sensus penduduk 1990' (The variation of infant mortality and life expectancy in Indonesia by province: results of the 1990 population census), *Populasi* 2(3), pp. 13–23

Kato, T. (1977), 'Change and continuity in the Minangkabau matrilineal system', *Indonesia* 25, pp. 1–16

——(1989), 'Different fields, similar locusts: adat communities and the Village Law of 1979 in Indonesia', *Indonesia* 47, pp. 89–114

Keeler, W. (1987) *Javanese Shadow Puppets, Javanese Selves*, Princeton University Press, Princeton

Kelly, R. (1989), 'Property taxation', in *Financing Local Government in Indonesia*, N. Devas and Associates, Ohio University Center for International Studies, Monographs in International Studies, Athens, pp. 109–34

——(1993), 'Property tax reform in Indonesia: applying a collection-led implementation strategy', *BIES* 29(1), pp. 85–104

Keyfitz, N. (1965), 'Indonesian population and the European Industrial Revolution', *Asian Survey* 10, pp. 503–14

——(1989), 'Putting trained labour power to work: the dilemma of education and employment', *BIES* 25(3), pp. 35–55

Keyfitz, N., Oey-Gardiner, M. Clark, D. and Manaf, D.R.S. (1989), *Indonesian Universities at the Crossroads*, CPIS, Jakarta

Khong, C.O. (1986), *The Politics of Oil in Indonesia: Foreign Company—Host Government Relations*, LSE Monographs in International Studies, Cambridge University Press, Cambridge

Khoo, S.E. (1982), 'The determinants of modern contraceptive use in Indonesia: analyses of the effect of program effort', Working Paper no. 23, East–West Population Institute, East–West Center, Hawaii

King, D. (1982), 'Is the New Order a bureaucratic polity, a neopatrimonial regime or a bureaucratic–authoritarian regime? What difference does it make?', in *Interpreting Indonesian Politics: Thirteen Contributions to the Debate*, B.R.O'G. Anderson and A. Kahin (eds), Interim Reports Series no. 62, Cornell Modern Indonesia Project, Ithaca, pp. 104–16

Kleden, I. (1989), 'The changing political leadership of Java: the significance of Sultan Hamengku Buwono IX', *Prisma* 46, pp. 21–31

KLH (n.d.), *Prokasih: Clean River Programme*, Office of the Minister of State for Population and Environment, Jakarta

Koentjaraningrat (1977), 'The system and spirit of "gotong royong" ', *Prisma* 6, pp. 20–7

——(1985), *Javanese Culture*, Institute of Southeast Asian Studies and Oxford University Press, Singapore

Koesnadi Hardjasoemantri (1989), *Environmental Legislation in Indonesia*, 2nd edn, Gadjah Mada University Press, Yogyakarta

Korns, A. (1987), 'Distinguishing signal from noise in labour force data for Indonesia', Development Studies Programme Research Paper no. 1, Jakarta

Kus Sudyarsono, H. (1989), *Ketoprak*, Kanisius, Yogyakarta

Legge, J.D. (1961), *Central Authority and Regional Autonomy in Indonesia: A Study in Local Administration 1950–1960*, Cornell University Press, Ithaca

Leifer, M. (1983), *Indonesian Foreign Policy*, Allen & Unwin, London

Leinbach, T.R. (1986), 'Transport development in Indonesia: progress, problems and policies under the New Order', in *Central Government and Local Development in Indonesia*, C. MacAndrews (ed.), Oxford University Press, Singapore, pp. 190–220

Lerche, D. (1980), 'Efficiency of taxation in Indonesia', *BIES* 16(1), pp. 34–51

Lev, D.S. (1979), 'Judicial authority and the struggle for an Indonesia Rechsstaat', *Law and Society Review* 13(1), pp. 37–71

——(1987), 'Legal aid in Indonesia', Centre for Southeast Asian Studies, Monash Papers on Southeast Asia no. 44, Monash University, Clayton

——(1991) 'Becoming an orang Indonesia sejati: the political journey of Yap Thiam Hien', *Indonesia*, Special Issue on the Indonesian Chinese

Liddle, R.W. (1983), 'The politics of shared growth: some Indonesian cases', *Comparative Politics* 19(2), pp. 127–46

——(1985), 'Suharto's Indonesia: personal rule and political institutions', *Pacific Affairs* 58(1), pp. 68–90

——(1989), 'The national political culture and the New Order', *Prisma* 46, pp. 4–20

——(1991), 'The relative autonomy of the Third World politician: Suharto and Indonesia's economic development in comparative perspective', *International Studies Quarterly* 35, pp. 403–25

Lindsay, H. (1989), 'The Indonesian log export ban: an estimation of foregone export earnings', *BIES* 25(2), pp. 111–23

Lindsay, J. (1985), 'Klasik, kitsch, kontemporer: a study of the Javanese performing arts', PhD thesis, University of Sydney

Linus Suryadi (1984), *Pengakuan Pariyem*, Sinar Harapan, Jakarta

Lubis, M. (1991), '*Horison* 25 Tahun', *Horison* 25(7)

Lyon, M. (1980), 'The Hindu revival in Java: politics and religious identity', in

Indonesia: The Making of a Culture, J. Fox (ed.), Australian National University, Canberra

MacAndrews, C. (ed.) (1986), *Central Government and Local Development in Indonesia*, Oxford University Press, Singapore

McCawley, P. (1971), 'The Indonesian electric supply industry', unpublished PhD thesis, Australian National University, Canberra

——(1978), 'Some consequences of the Pertamina crisis in Indonesia', *Journal of Southeast Asian Studies* 9(1), pp. 1–27

——(1980), 'Indonesia's new balance of payment problem: a surplus to get rid of', *Ekonomi dan Keuangan Indonesia* 28(1), pp. 39–58

——(1981), 'The growth of the industrial sector', in *The Indonesian Economy During the Soeharto Era*, A. Booth and P. McCawley (eds), Oxford University Press, Kuala Lumpur, pp. 62–101

McComb, A.L. (1974), 'Land use and area development problems in the Upper Solo River Basin', in *Transmigration in the Context of Area Development*, R. Soebiantoro (ed.), Transmigration Training and Research Center, Jakarta, pp. 118–26

McDonald, H. (1980), *Suharto's Indonesia*, Fontana Books, Blackburn

McDougall, J.A. (1982), 'Patterns of military control in the Indonesian higher bureaucracy', *Indonesia* 33, pp. 89–121

Machfud, D.S. (1989), 'Social forestry in upland areas in Java', in Voices from the Field: Second Annual Social Forestry Writing Workshop, Environment and Policy Institute, East–West Center, Honolulu, pp. 54–71

MacIntyre, A. (1990), *Business and Politics in Indonesia*, Asian Studies Association of Australia Publications Series no. 21, Allen & Unwin, Sydney

McKendrick, D.G. (1989), 'Acquiring technological capabilities: aircraft and commercial banking in Indonesia', unpublished doctoral thesis, University of California, Berkeley

——(1992), 'Obstacles to "catch up": the case of the Indonesian aircraft industry', *BIES* 28(1), pp. 39–66

Mackie, J.A.C. (1961–62), 'Indonesia's government estates and their masters', *Pacific Affairs* 34(4), pp. 337–60

——(1967), *Problems of Inflation in Indonesia*, Cornell Modern Indonesia Project, Monograph Series, Ithaca

——(1970), 'The report of the Commission of Four on Corruption', *BIES* 6(3), pp. 87–101

——(1976), 'Anti-Chinese outbreaks in Indonesia, 1959–68', in *The Chinese in Indonesia*, J.A.C. Mackie (ed.), Thomas Nelson, for the Australian Institute of International Affairs, Melbourne, pp. 77–138

——(1980), 'Integrating and centrifugal factors in Indonesian politics since 1945', in *Indonesia: The Making of a Nation*, vol. 2 of *Indonesia: Australian Perspectives*, J.A.C. Mackie (ed.), Research School of Pacific Studies, Australian National University, Canberra, pp. 669–84

——(1985), 'The changing political economy of an export crop: the case of Jember's tobacco industry', *BIES* 21(1), pp. 113–39

——(1989), 'Indonesia political developments, 1987–88', in *Indonesia Update 1988*, H. Hill and J.A.C Mackie (eds), Political and Social Change Monograph

8, Department of Political and Social Change, Australian National University, Canberra, pp. 13–38

——(1990a), 'Property and power in Indonesia', in *The Politics of Middle Class Indonesia*, R. Tanter and K. Young (eds), Centre for Southeast Asian Studies, Monash Papers on Southeast Asia no. 19, Monash University, Clayton, pp. 71–95

——(1990b), 'Money and the middle class', in *The Politics of Middle Class Indonesia*, R. Tanter and K. Young (eds), Centre for Southeast Asian Studies, Monash Papers on Southeast Asia no. 19, Monash University, Clayton, pp. 96–122

——(1990c), 'The Indonesian conglomerates in regional perspective', in *Indonesia Assessment 1990*, H. Hill and T. Hull (eds), Political and Social Change Monograph 11, Department of Political and Social Change, Australian National University, Canberra

——(1992), 'Changing patterns of Chinese business in Southeast Asia', in *Southeast Asian Capitalists*, R. McVey (ed.), Southeast Asia Program, Publications on Southeast Asia, Cornell University, Ithaca

Mackie, J.A.C. and Sjahrir (1989), 'Survey of recent developments', *BIES* 25(3), pp. 3–34

McLeod, R.H. (1980), 'Finance and entrepreneurship in the small business sector in Indonesia', unpublished PhD thesis, Australian National University, Canberra

——(1984), 'Financial institutions and markets in Indonesia', in *Financial Institutions and Markets in Southeast Asia*, M.T. Skully (ed.), Macmillan, London, pp. 49–109

——(1992), 'Indonesia's new banking law', *BIES* 28(3), pp. 107–22

McNicoll, G. and Singarimbun, M. (1983), *Fertility Decline in Indonesia: Analysis and Interpretation*, Committee on Population and Demography, National Academy Press, Washington DC

McVey, R. (1971), 'The post-revolutionary transformation of the Indonesian army, part I', *Indonesia* 11, pp. 131–76

——(1972), 'The post-revolutionary transformation of the Indonesian army, part II', *Indonesia* 13, pp. 147–82

——(1982), 'The *Beamtenstaat* in Indonesia', in B.R.O'G. Anderson and A. Kahin (eds), *Interpreting Indonesian Politics: Thirteen Contributions to the Debate*, Interim Reports Series no. 62, Cornell Modern Indonesia Project, Ithaca, pp. 84–91

——(1988) 'The wayang controversy in Indonesian communism', in *Context, Meaning and Power in Southeast Asia*, M. Hobart and R. Taylor (eds), Southeast Asia Program, Cornell University, Ithaca

——(1992) 'The materialization of the Southeast Asian entrepreneur', in *Southeast Asian Capitalists*, R. McVey (ed.), Cornell Southeast Asia Program, Publications on Southeast Asia, Cornell University, Ithaca, pp. 7–33

Mamas, S.G.M. (1991), 'Penduduk Indonesia dan berberapa proyeksinya di masa mendatang dalam kaitannya dengan proses transisi demografi' (The population of Indonesia and some future projections, as related to the process of demographic transition), Paper presented to a workshop organised by the State Ministry for Population and Development, 25–26 March

——(1983), 'Proyeksi penduduk Indonesia 1980–2000' (Indonesian population projections 1980–2000), Paper presented to the Seminar Fertilitas Indonesia, 30 May to 1 June, Jakarta

Mangkusuwondo, S. et al. (1988), 'Trade policy options for Indonesia', in *The Uguguay Round: ASEAN Trade Policy Options*, M. Ariff and J.L.H. Tan (eds), Institute of Southeast Asian Studies, Singapore, pp. 38–64

Mangunwijaya, Y.B. (1978), *Puntung-Puntung Roro Mendut* (The Cigarette Butts of Roro Mendut), PT Gramedia, Jakarta

——(1981), *Burung-Burung Manyar* (The Weaverbirds), Djambatan, Jakarta

Manning, C.G. (1971), 'The timber boom with special reference to East Kalimantan', *BIES* 7(3), pp. 30–60

——(1986), 'Changing occupational structure, urban work and landowning class in six West Java communities: a view from the village', Paper presented at the Asian Studies Association of Australia Sixth National Conference, University of Sydney

——(1987), 'Rural economic change and labour mobility: a case study from West Java', *BIES* 23(3), pp. 52–79

——(1988), 'The green revolution, employment and economic change: a reassessment of trends under the New Order', Occasional Paper no. 84, Institute of Southeast Asian Studies, Singapore

——(1989), 'Employment trends in Indonesia in the 1970s and 1980s', Paper presented at a conference on Indonesia's New Order, Australian National University, Canberra, December

——(1992a), 'Survey of recent developments', *BIES* 28(1), pp. 3–38

——(1992b), 'Structural change and industrial relations in a labour surplus economy: the case of Indonesia', unpublished paper, Australian National University, Canberra

Manning, C. and Effendi, T.N. (eds) (1985), *Urbanisasi, Pengangguran dan Sektor Informal di Kota* (Urbanization, Unemployment and the Urban Informal Sector), Gramedia, Jakarta

Manning, C., Tajuddin and Tukiran (1984), 'Sektor informal, mobilitas pekerjaan dan kemiskinan: sebuah studi kasus di Dirapraja, Yogyakarta' (The informal sector, work mobility and poverty: a case study in Dirapraja, Yogyakarta), Population Studies Centre, Gadjah Mada University, Yogykarta

Mantra, I. (1981), *Population Movement in Central Java*, Gadjah Mada University Press, Yogyakarta

Mather, C. (1983), 'Industrialization in the Tangerang regency of West Java: women workers and the Islamic patriarchy', *Bulletin of Concerned Asian Scholars* 15(2), pp. 2–17

May, R.J. (ed.) (1986), *Between Two Nations: The Indonesia–Papua New Guinea Border and West Papuan Nationalism*, Robert Brook and Associates, Bathurst

Mears, L. (1978), 'Problems of supply and marketing of food in Repelita III', *BIES* 14(3), pp. 52–62

——(1981), *The New Rice Economy of Indonesia*, Gadjah Mada University Press, Yogyakarta

Mears, L.A. and S. Afiff (1969), 'An operational rice price policy for Indonesia', *Ekonomi dan Keuangan Indonesia* 17(1), pp. 3–13

Mears, L.A. and Moeljono, S. (1981), 'Food policy', in *The Indonesian Economy During the Soeharto Era*, A. Booth and P. McCawley (eds), Oxford University Press, Kuala Lumpur, pp. 23–61

Meesook, O.A. (1984), 'Financing and equity in the social sciences in Indonesia', World Bank Staff Working Paper no. 703, Washington DC

Meijerink, A.M.J., Van Wijngaarden, W., Asrun, S.A. and Mathuis, B.H. (1988), 'Downstream damage caused by upstream land degradation in the Komering River basin', *I.T.C. Journal* 1, pp. 96–108

Metzner, J.K. (1976), 'Lamtoronisasi: an experiment in soil conservation', *BIES* 12(1), pp. 103–9

Miklouho-Maklai, B. (1991), *Exposing Society's Wounds: Some Aspects of Contemporary Indonesian Art Since 1966*, Monograph no. 5, Flinders University, Adelaide

Miles, D. (1976), *Cutlass and Crescent Moon*, Centre for Asian Studies, University of Sydney, Sydney

Miller, D. and Branson, J. (1989), 'Pollution in paradise: Hinduism and the subordination of women in Bali', in *Creating Indonesian Cultures*, P. Alexander (ed.), Oceania Publications, Sydney, pp. 91–112

Moebramsjah, J. (1983), 'Management of the family planning programme in Indonesia', in *Views from Three Continents*, E. Sattar (ed.), International Committee on the Management of Population Programmes, Kuala Lumpur, pp. 6–21

Moebramsjah, H., D'Agnes, T.R. and Tjiptorahardjo, S. (1982), 'The national family planning program in Indonesia: a management approach to a complex social issue', Report to an ICOMP Conference, Kuala Lumpur, July 1982, National Family Planning Coordinating Board, Jakarta

Mohtar Ma'soed (1989), 'The state reorganization of society under the New Order', *Prisma* 47, pp. 3–24

Morfitt, M. (1981), 'Pancasila: the Indonesian state ideology according to the New Order government', *Asian Survey* 21(8), pp. 838–51

Morrisson, C. and Thorbecke, E. (1990), 'The concept of agricultural surplus', *World Development* 18(8), pp. 1081–95

Mortimer, R. (ed.) (1973), *Show Case State: The Illusion of Indonesia's Accelerated Modernization*, Angus and Robertson, Sydney

Mubyarto (ed.) (1982), *Growth and Equity in Indonesian Agricultural Development*, Yayasan Agro Ekonomika, Jakarta

Mubyarto, Loekman Soetrisno et al. (1991), *East Timor: The Impact of Integration*, Indonesian Resources and Information Program, Northcote

Muhaimin, Y.A. (1991), *Bisnis dan Politik: Kebijaksanaan Ekonomi Indonesia 1950–1980* (Business and Politics: Indonesian Economic Policy 1950–1980), LP3ES, Jakarta

Mulder, N. (1978), *Mysticism and Everyday Life in Contemporary Java: Cultural Persistence and Change*, University of Singapore Press, Singapore

Muliakusuma, S. and Trisilo, R.B. (1988), *Keadaan Pekerja Sektor Informal di Indonesia 1980 dan 1985* (The Situation of Informal Sector Workers in

Indonesia 1980 and 1985), Kantor Menteri Negara Kependudukan dan Lingkungan Hidup dan Lembaga Demografi Fakultas Ekonomi Universitas Indonesia (Office of the Minister of State for Population and Environment and the Demographic Institute, Economics Faculty, University of Indonesia), Jakarta

Munger, J. (1991), ' "Colourful rotten cake": pop music and television in Indonesia', Paper presented at a conference on Indonesian Music: 20th Century Innovation and Tradition, University of California, Berkeley, September

Murdiono, B. and Beerens, S. (1991), 'The socio-economic and institutional aspects of soil conservation in the Upper Konto Watershed, East Java', Paper presented to the International Workshop on Conservation Policies for Sustainable Hillslope Farming, Solo, Indonesia, March

Murray, A. (1991), *No Money, No Honey: A Study of Street Traders and Prostitutes in Jakarta*, Oxford University Press, Singapore

Myrdal, G. (1968), *Asian Drama—An Inquiry into the Poverty of Nations*, Penguin, Harmondsworth

Nakamura, M. (1983), *The Crescent Rises over the Banyan Tree*, Gadjah Mada University Press, Yogyakarta

Nasir Tamara (1990), 'Islam under the New Order', *Prisma* 49, pp. 6–30

Nasution, A. (1983), *Financial Institutions and Policies in Indonesia*, Institute of Southeast Asian Studies, Singapore

——(1989), 'Fiscal system and practices in Indonesia', in M.G. Asher (ed.), *Fiscal Systems and Practices in ASEAN: Trends, Impact and Evaluation*, Institute of Southeast Asian Studies, Singapore, pp. 19–62

Naylor, R. (1990), 'Wage trends in rice production in Java: 1976–1988', *BIES* 26(2), pp. 133–56

Nazaruddin Sjamsudin (1985), *The Republican Revolt: A Study of the Acehnese Rebellion*, Institute of Southeast Asian Studies, Singapore

Nehen, I.K. (1989), 'Insurance industry and employment in ASEAN', *ASEAN Economic Bulletin* 6(1), pp. 46–58

Nelson, G.C. (1986), 'Labor intensity, employment growth and technical change— an example from starch processing in Indonesia', *Journal of Development Economics* 24, pp. 111–17

Nelson, G.C. and Panggabean, M. (1991), 'The costs of Indonesian sugar policy: a policy analysis matrix approach', *American Journal of Agricultural Economics* 73(3), pp. 703–12

Ng, C. (1987), 'The weaving of prestige: village women's representations of the social categories of Minangkabau society', PhD thesis, Australian National University, Canberra

Nibbering, J.W. (1988), 'Forest degradation and reforestation in a highland area of Java', in *Changing Tropical Forests: Historical Perspectives on Today's Challenges in Asia, Australasia and Oceania*, J. Dargavel, K. Dixon and N. Sample (eds), Centre for Resource and Environmental Studies, Australian National University, Canberra, pp. 155–77

——(1991), 'Crisis and resilience in upland land use in Java', in *Indonesia: Resources, Ecology, and Environment*, J. Hardjono (ed.), Oxford University Press, Singapore, pp. 104–32

Bibliography

Nishihara, M. (1972), *Golkar and the Indonesian Elections of 1971*, Cornell Modern Indonesia Project, Monograph Series no. 56, Ithaca

Nugroho Notosusanto and Ismail Saleh (1968), *The Coup Attempt of the September 30th Movement in Indonesia*, Pembimbing Masa, Jakarta

Nurcholish Madjid (1985), 'An Islamic appraisal of the future of Indonesia', *Prisma* 35, pp. 11–26

——(1990), 'Indonesia in the future: sophisticated and devoutly religious', *Prisma* 49, pp. 77–96

Odano, S. et al. (1988), 'Financial development', in *Indonesian Economic Development: Issues and Analysis*, S. Ichimura (ed.), Japanese International Cooperation Agency, Tokyo, pp. 167–89

Oey-Gardiner, M. (1991), 'Gender differences in schooling in Indonesia', *BIES* 27(1), pp. 57–79

Oey-Gardiner, M. and Suryatini, A. (1990), 'Issues in Indonesian higher education policy making processes', Paper prepared for the International Conference on Economic Policy Making Process in Indonesia, Bali, 6–9 September

Oey Hong Lee (ed.) (1974), *Indonesia After the 1971 Elections*, Oxford University Press, London

Oey, Mayling (1982), 'The transmigration program in Indonesia', in *Population Resettlement Programs in Southeast Asia*, G.W. Jones and H.V. Richter (eds), Australian National University, Canberra, pp. 27–51

——(1985), 'Changing work patterns of women in Indonesia during the 1970s: causes and consequences', *Prisma* 37, pp. 18–41

Ogawa, N., Jones, G.W. and Williamson, J. (eds) (1993), *Human Resources and Development Along the Asia–Pacific Rim*, Oxford University Press, Singapore

Oshima, H. (1988), 'Human resources in East Asia's secular growth', *Economic Development and Cultural Change* 36(3), pp. S103–22

Palmer, I. (1965), 'The textile industry', *BIES* 2, pp. 34–48

——(1978), *The Indonesian Economy since 1965*, Frank Cass and Co., London

Palte (1989), *Upland Farming on Java, Indonesia*, Nederlandse Geografische Studies 97, Royal Dutch Geographical Society, Amsterdam; and Geographical Institute, University of Utrecht, Utrecht

Pangestu, M. (1987), 'The pattern of direct foreign investment in ASEAN: the United States vs Japan', *ASEAN Economic Bulletin* 3(3), pp. 301–28

——(1991a), 'Managing economic policy reforms in Indonesia', in *Authority and Academic Scribblers: The Role of Research in East Asian Policy Reform*, S. Ostry (ed.), International Center for Economic Growth, San Francisco, pp. 93–120

——(1991b), 'Foreign firms and structural change in the Indonesian manufacturing sector', in *Direct Foreign Investment in Asia's Developing Economies and Structural Change in the Asia–Pacific Region*, E.D. Ramstetter (ed.), Westview Press, Boulder, pp. 35–64

——(1991c), 'Macroeconomic management in the ASEAN countries', in *The Pacific Economy: Growth and External Stability*, M. Ariff (ed.), Allen & Unwin, Sydney, pp. 121–54

Pangestu, M. and Boediono (1986), 'Indonesia: the structure and causes of manufacturing sector protection', in *The Political Economy of Manufacturing*

Protection: Experiences of ASEAN and Australia, C. Findlay and R. Garnaut (eds), Allen & Unwin, Sydney, pp. 1–47

Pangestu, M. and Habir, A.D. (1989), 'Trends and prospects in privatization and deregulation in Indonesia', *ASEAN Economic Bulletin* 5(3), pp. 224–41

Panglaykim, J. and Arndt, H.W. (1966), 'Survey of recent developments', *BIES* 4, pp. 1–35

Papanek, G.F. (ed.) (1980) *The Indonesian Economy*, Praeger, New York

——(1985), 'Agricultural income distribution and employment in the 1970s', *BIES* 21(2), pp. 24–50

Parera, F.M. (1988), 'Perkembangan industri novel populer di Indonesia' (The development of the popular novel industry in Indonesia), *Prisma* 8

Parker, L. (1989), 'Brassika, Bali: the village as a target for government intervention', Paper presented at a conference on Indonesia's New Order, Australian National University, Canberra, December

Parlindungan, A.P. (1981), 'The case of the estates in East Sumatra', Paper presented to the Policy Workshop on Agrarian Reform in Comparative Perspective, Sukabumi

Parsons, J.S. (1984), 'What makes the Indonesian family planning programme tick?', *Populi* 11(3), pp. 5–19

Patten, R.H. and Rosengard, J.K. (1991), *Progress with Profits: the Development of Rural Banking in Indonesia*, International Center for Economic Growth, San Francisco

Patten, R. et al. (1980), 'An experiment in rural employment creation: the early history of Indonesia's kabupaten development program', in *The Indonesian Economy*, G.F. Papanek (ed.), Praeger, New York, pp. 155–82

Peacock, J. (1973), *Indonesia: An Anthropological Perspective*, Goodyear Publishing Company, Pacific Palisades, California

Pearce, D., Barbier, E. and Markandya, A. (1990), *Sustainable Development: Economics and Environment in the Third World*, Edward Elgar, London

Pearson, S. et al. (1991), *Rice Policy in Indonesia*, Cornell University Press, Ithaca

Pelzer, K.J. (1945), *Pioneer Settlement in the Asiatic Tropics*, Institute of Pacific Relations, New York

Penny, D.H. (1969), 'Indonesia', in *Agricultural Development in Asia*, R.T. Shand (ed.), Australian National University Press, Canberra, pp. 251–79

Penny, D.H. and Singarimbun, M. (1973), *Population and Poverty in Rural Java: Some Economic Arithmetic from Sriharjo*, Cornell International Agricultural Development Mimeograph 41, Cornell University, Ithaca

Perkins, D.H. and Roemer, M. (eds) (1991), *Reforming Economic Systems in Developing Countries*, Harvard Studies in International Development, Harvard Institute for International Development, Boston

Persoon, G. (1986), 'Congelation in the melting pot: the Minangkabau in Jakarta', in *The Indonesian City*, P. Nas (ed.), Foris Publications, Dordrecht, the Netherlands, pp. 176–96

Picard, M. (1990), 'Cultural tourism in Bali: cultural performances as tourist attractions', *Indonesia* 49, pp. 37–74

Pinto, B. (1987), 'Nigeria during and after the oil boom: a policy comparison with Indonesia', *World Bank Economic Review* 1(3), pp. 419–45

Bibliography

Piper, S. (1976), 'Modern Indonesian drama: an analysis of four plays by Rendra and Arifin C. Noer', BA Honours thesis, Department of Indonesian and Malayan Studies, University of Sydney, Sydney

Piper, S. and Sawung Jabo (1987), 'Musik Indonesia dari 1950-an hingga 1980-an' (Indonesian music from the 1950s to the 1980s), *Prisma* 5, pp. 8–23

Pitt, M.M. (1991), 'Indonesia', in *Liberalizing Foreign Trade*, D. Papageorgiou et al. (eds), vol. 5, Basil Blackwell, for the World Bank, Cambridge, Mass., pp. 1–196

Poffenberger, M. and Zurbuchen, M. (1980), 'The economics of village Bali: three perspectives', *Economic Development and Cultural Change* 29(1), pp. 91–133

Poot, H. et al. (1990), *Industrialization and Trade in Indonesia*, Gadjah Mada University Press, Yogyakarta

Posthumus, G.A. (1971), *The Inter-Governmental Group on Indonesia*, Rotterdam University Press, Rotterdam

Poston, D. and Gu Baochang (1987), 'Socioeconomic development, family planning and fertility in China', *Demography* 24, pp. 531–51

Potter, L. (1991a), 'The onslaught on the forests', Paper presented at the Workshop on Toward a Sustainable Environmental Future for the Southeast Asian Region, Gadjah Mada University, Yogyakarta, May

——(1991b), 'Environmental and social aspects of timber exploitation in Kalimantan, 1967–1989', in *Indonesia, Resources, Ecology, and Environment*, J. Hardjono (ed.), Oxford University Press, Singapore, pp. 177–211

Pramudya Ananta Tur (1980a), *Bumi Manusia*, Hasta Mitra, Jakarta

——(1980b), *Anak Semua Bangsa*, Hasta Mitra, Jakarta

——(1985), *Jejak Langkah*, Hasta Mitra, Jakarta

——(1988), *Rumah Kaca*, Hasta Mitra, Jakarta

Psacharopoulos, G. (1981), 'Returns to education: an updated international comparison', *Comparative Education* 17(3), pp. 321–41

Pye, L.W. and Jackson, K.D. (eds) (1978), *Political Power and Communications in Indonesia*, University of California Press, Berkeley

Quinn, G. (1989), 'Monopoly and diversity in Indonesia's television news', Paper delivered at a conference on Indonesia's New Order, Australian National University, Canberra, December

Rafferty, E. (1989), *Putu Wijaya in Performance*, University of Wisconsin, Madison

——(1990), 'The new tradition of Putu Wijaya', *Indonesia* 49, pp. 103–16

Rafferty, E. and Sears, L.J. (eds) (1988), *Bomb: Indonesian Short Stories by Putu Wijaya*, University of Wisconsin, Madison

Raharjo Suwandi (1989), 'The Embah Wali movement, East Java: a Javanese quest for justice in the New Order', Paper presented at a conference on Indonesia's New Order, Australian National University, Canberra, December

Ravallion, M. (1988), 'Inpres and equality: a distributional perspective on the centre's regional disbursements', *BIES* 24(3), pp. 53–71

Ravallion, M. and Huppi, M. (1991), 'Measuring changes in poverty: a methodological case study of Indonesia during an adjustment period', *World Bank Economic Review* 5(1), pp. 57–82

Reeve, D. (1985), *Golkar of Indonesia: An Alternative to the Party System*, Oxford University Press, Singapore

——(1990), 'The corporatist state: the case of Golkar', in Arief Budiman (ed.), *State and Civil Society in Indonesia*, Center for Southeast Asian Studies, Monash University, Clayton, pp. 151–212

Rendra (1979), *The Struggle of the Naga Tribe* (translated by H. Aveling), Queensland University Press, Brisbane

——(1980a), *Potret Pembangunan dalam Puisi*, Lembaga Studi Pembangunan, Jakarta

——(1980b), *State of Emergency* (translated by H. Aveling), Wild and Woolley

Repetto, R. (1988), *The Forest for the Trees? Government Policies and the Misuse of Forest Resources*, World Resources Institute, Washington DC

Repetto, R., Magrath, W., Wells, M., Beer, C. and Rossini, F. (1989), *Wasting Assets: Natural Resources in the National Income Accounts*, World Resources Institute, Washington DC

Rice, R.C. (1983), 'The origins of basic economic ideas and their impact on "New Order" policies', *BIES* 19(2), pp. 60–82

——(1991), 'Environmental degradation, pollution, and the exploitation of Indonesia's fishery resources', in *Indonesia, Resources, Ecology, and Environment*, J. Hardjono (ed.), Oxford University Press, Singapore, pp. 154–76

Riggs, F.W. (1966), *Thailand: The Modernization of a Bureaucratic Polity*, East–West Center Press, Honolulu

Robinson, K. (1986), 'Stepchildren in their own land: class and identity in an Indonesian corporate town', *Mankind* 16(2), pp. 85–98

——(1986), *Stepchildren of Progress: The Political Economy of Development in an Indonesian Mining Town*, State University of New York Press, Albany

Robison, R. (1978), 'Towards a class analysis of the Indonesian military–bureaucratic state', *Indonesia* 25, pp. 17–40

——(1986), *Indonesia: The Rise of Capital*, Allen & Unwin, Sydney, for the Asian Studies Association of Australia

——(1989), 'Authoritarian states, capital-owning classes, and the politics of newly industrializing countries: the case of Indonesia', *World Politics* 41(1), pp. 52–74

Rodgers, S. (1986), 'Batak tape cassette kinship; constructing kinship through the Indonesian mass media', *American Ethnologist* 13(1), pp. 23–42

Roeder, O.G. (1969), *The Smiling General—President Soeharto of Indonesia*, Gunung Agung, Jakarta

Rogers, P. (1982), 'The domestic and foreign press in Indonesia: free but responsible?', Centre for the Study of Australia–Asia Relations, Research Paper no. 18, Griffith University, Brisbane

Rosendale, P. (1976), 'The equilibrium exchange rate: some considerations', *BIES* 12(1), pp. 93–102

——(1981), 'The balance of payments', in *The Indonesian Economy During the Soeharto Era*, A. Booth and P. McCawley (eds), Oxford University Press, Kuala Lumpur, pp. 162–80

Rosidi, A. (1985), *Anak Tanah Air*, PT Gramedia, Jakarta

Ross, J. and Poedjastoeti, S. (1983), 'Contraceptive use and program development: new information from Indonesia', *International Family Planning Perspectives* 9(3), pp. 68–77

Bibliography

RUDS (1989), *Natural Environment Study: Bandung Metropolitan Area*, Final Report, Review of Urban Development Strategy Programme, Bandung

Ruttan, V.W. (1990), 'The direction of agricultural development in Asia: into the 21st century', *Journal of Asian Economies* 1(2), pp. 189–203

Ruzicka, I. (1979), 'Rent appropriation in Indonesian logging: East Kalimantan 1972/3–1976/7', *BIES* 15(2), pp. 45–74

Sadli, M. (1963), 'Indonesia's hundred millions', *Far Eastern Economic Review* 42, pp. 21–3

——(1972), 'Foreign investment in developing countries: Indonesia', in *Direct Foreign Investment in Asia and the Pacific*, P. Drysdale (ed.), Australian National University Press, Canberra, pp. 201–25

——(1973), 'Indonesia's experience with the application of technology and its employment effects', *Ekonomi dan Keuangan Indonesia* 21(3), pp. 147–60

Sadli, M. et al. (1988), 'Private sector and public sector', in *Indonesian Economic Development: Issues and Analysis*, S. Ichimura (ed.), Japanese International Cooperation Agency, Tokyo, pp. 353–71

Said, S. (1990), 'Pemerintah mengacaukan appresiasi seni' (Government disrupts art appreciation), *Tempo* 29 December

Salim Said (1987), 'The political role of the Indonesian military: past, present and future', *Southeast Asian Journal of Social Science* 15(1), pp. 16–34

Saparin, Sumber (1977), *Tata Pemerintahan dan Administrasi Pemerintahan Desa* (The Rules of Village Government and Public Administration), Ghalia Indonesia, Jakarta

Sasongko, A.T. and Katjasungkana, N. (1991), 'Pasang surut rock Indonesia' (The rise and fall of Indonesian rock), *Prisma* 10, pp. 47–66

Sastrowardojo, S. (1970), *Daerah Perbatasan* (Border Area), Balai Pustaka, Jakarta

Schiller, J. (1986), 'State formation in New Order Indonesia: the powerhouse state in Jepara', PhD thesis, Monash University, Clayton

——(1990), 'State formation and rural transformation: adapting to the New Order in Jepara', in *State and Civil Society in Indonesia*, Arief Budiman (ed.), Monash University, Clayton, pp. 395–420

Schulte Nordholt, H. (1989), 'Village, state and ritual in south Bali: an historical perspective', Paper prepared for the workshop on Contesting Cultural Symbols in Southeast Asia, Research School of Pacific Studies, Australian National University, Canberra

Scitovsky, T. (1986), 'Economic development in Taiwan and South Korea 1965–1981', in *Models of Development: A Comparative Study of Economic Growth in South Korea and Taiwan*, L.J. Lau (ed.), ICS Press, San Francisco

Sen, K. (1981), 'Wajah wanita dalam filem Indonesia: beberapa catatan' (The representation of women in Indonesian film: some notes), *Prisma* 7, pp. 31–43

——(1987), 'Indonesian films, 1965–1982: perceptions of society and history', unpublished PhD thesis, Department of Politics, Monash University, Clayton

Shaw, G.K. (1980), 'Intergovernmental fiscal relations', in *The Indonesian Economy*, G.F. Papanek (ed.), Praeger, New York, pp. 278–94

Shaxson, T.F. (1991), 'National development policy vis-a-vis soil conservation programmes', Paper presented to the International Workshop on Conservation Policies for Sustainable Hillslope Farming, Solo, Indonesia, March

Siegel, J. (1986), *Solo in the New Order: Language and Hierarchy in an Indonesian City*, Princeton University Press, Princeton

Simatupang, I. (1969), *Ziarah* (The Pilgrim), Djambatan, Jakarta

——(1972), *Kering* (Drought), Gunung Agung, Jakarta

Sinaga, R.S. (1978), 'Implications of agricultural mechanisation for employment and income distribution', *BIES* 14(2), pp. 102–11

Singarimbun, M. (1970), 'Economic aspects of family planning', *BIES* 6(3), pp. 102–5

——(1990), 'Perubahan-perubahan sosial-ekonomi di Miri Sriharjo' (Socio-economic change in Miri Sriharjo), in *D.H. Penny—Kemiskinan: Peranan Sistem Pasar* (D.H. Penny—Poverty: The Role of the Market System), Mubyarto (ed.), Penerbit Universitas Indonesia, Jakarta, pp. 167–77

Sinukaban, N. (1991), 'Impact of erosion on socio-economic and conservation policy as affected by climatic changes', Paper presented to the International Workshop on Conservation Policies for Sustainable Hillslope Farming, Solo, Indonesia, March

Sita Aripurnomo (1990), 'Sosok perempuan dalam filem Indonesia' (The portrayal of women in Indonesian film), *Prisma* 5

Sjahrir (1987), *Kebijaksanaan Negara: Konsistensi dan Implementasi* (State Policy: Consistency and Implementation), LP3ES, Jakarta

Smith-Hefner, N. (1989), 'A social history of language change in highland East Java', *The Journal of Asian Studies* 48(2), pp. 257–71

Snodgrass, D.R. and Patten, R.H. (1991), 'Reform of rural credit in Indonesia: inducing bureaucracies to behave competitively', in *Reforming Economic Systems in Developing Countries*, D.H. Perkins and M. Roemer (eds), Harvard Studies in International Development, Harvard Institute for International Development, Boston, pp. 341–63

Soedarsono (1989), *Seni Pertunjukan Jawa Tradisional dan Pariwisata di DIY* (Traditional Javanese Performing Arts and Tourism in Jogyakarta), Departemen Pendidikan dan Kebudayaan Republik Indonesia, Jakarta

Soedjatmoko (1967), 'Indonesia: problems and opportunities', *Australian Outlook* 21(4), pp. 263–306

Soegiarto, A. (1986), 'The Indonesian marine environment: problems and prospects for national development', *Prisma* 39 (English edition), pp. 14–26

Soeharto (1970), 'Pidato Presiden Soeharto pada pelantikan Dewan Pembimbing Keluarga Berentjana Nasional pada tanggal 29 Djuni 1970' (Speech by President Soeharto at the inauguration of the National Family Planning Advisory Council on 29 June 1970), Badan Koordinasi Keluarga Berentjana Nasional, Jakarta

——(1984), *Saksi Sejarah: Mengikuti Perjuangan Dwitunggal.* (Witness to History: Participation in the Struggles of the Founding Fathers), Gunung Agung, Jakarta

——(1989), *Pikiran, Ucapan, dan Tindakan Saya: Otobiografi* (My Thoughts, Sayings, and Actions: An Autobiography), as related to G. Dwipayana and K.H. Ramadhan, PT Citra Lamtoro Gung Persada, Jakarta

Soehoed, A.R. (1967), 'Manufacturing in Indonesia', *BIES* 8, pp. 65–84

Soemarwoto, O. (1991), 'Human ecology in Indonesia: the search for sustainability in development', in *Indonesia: Resources, Ecology, and Environment*, J. Hardjono (ed.), Oxford University Press, Singapore, pp. 212–35

Soesastro, M.H. (1989), 'The political economy of deregulation in Indonesia', *Asian Survey* 29(9), pp. 853–68

Soesastro, M.H. et al. (1988), *Financing Public Sector Development Expenditure in Selected Countries: Indonesia*, Economics Office, Asian Development Bank, Manila

Southward, J. and Flanagan, P. (1983), *Indonesia: Law, Propaganda and Terror*, Zed Books, London

Sri Rahayu Prihatmi (1985), 'Fantasi dalam kedua kumpulan cerpen Danarto: dialogue antara dunia nyata dan tidak nyata' (Fantasy in the two short-story collections of Danarto: a dialogue between the real and the imaginary world), MA thesis, Asian Studies, Flinders University, Adelaide

Stoler, A. (1977), 'Rice harvesting in Kali Loro: a study of class and labor relations in rural Java', *American Ethnologist* 4(4), pp. 678–98

Streatfield, K. (1985), 'A comparison of census and family planning program data on contraceptive prevalence, Indonesia', *Studies in Family Planning* 16(6), pp. 342–9

——(1986), *Fertility Decline in a Traditional Society: The Case of Bali*, Indonesian Monograph Series no. 4, Department of Demography, Australian National University, Canberra

Sudarwohadi, S. (1987), 'Integrated biological and chemical control of cabbage moth', PhD thesis, Padjadjaran University, Bandung

Sukarndi (1992), 'Angka kelahiran di Indonesia: perkembangan selama dua dasa warsa terakhir' (Birth rates in Indonesia: developments in the last two decades), *Populasi* 2(3), pp. 24–38

Sullivan, J. (1986), 'Kampung and state: the role of government in the development of urban community in Yogyakarta', *Indonesia* 41, pp. 63–8

——(1990), 'Community and local government on Java: facts and fictions', unpublished paper, Centre for Southeast Asian Studies, Monash University, Clayton

——(1991), 'Inventing and imagining community: two modern ideologies', Working Paper no. 69, Centre for Southeast Asian Studies, Monash

Sullivan, N. (1983), 'Indonesian women in development: state theory and urban kampung practice', in *Women's Work and Women's Place*, L. Manderson (ed.), Australian National University, Canberra, pp. 147–71

——(1989), 'The hidden economy and kampung women', in *Creating Indonesian Cultures*, P. Alexander (ed.), Oceania Publications, Sydney, pp. 75–90

Sumantoro (1984), 'MNCs and the host country: the Indonesian case', Research Notes and Discussion Paper no. 45, Institute of Southeast Asian Studies, Singapore

Sumardjo, J. (1977), 'Indonesian popular novels', *Prisma* 7, pp. 44–53

——(1984), 'Beberapa kecenderungan sastra Indonesia mutakhir' (Some recent trends in Indonesian literature), Paper presented to a National Symposium on Modern Indonesian Literature at Gadjah Mada University, Yogyakarta, 26–27 October

Sumbung, P. (1989), 'Management information system: the Indonesian experience', in *Readings in Population Programme Management*, G. Giridhar, E. Sattar and J.S. Kang (eds), ICOMP, Kuala Lumpur, pp. 13–28

Sumitro Djojohadikusumo (1977), 'Indonesia towards the year 2000', in *Science, Resources and Development: Selected Essays*, LP3ES, Jakarta, pp. 95–128

Sundhaussen, U. (1978), 'The military: structures, procedures, and effects on Indonesian society', in L.W. Pye and K. D. Jackson (eds), *Political Power and Communications in Indonesia*, University of California Press, Berkeley, pp. 45–81

Sundrum, R.M. (1986), 'Indonesia's rapid economic growth', *BIES* 22(3), pp. 40–69

——(1988), 'Indonesia's slow economic growth 1981–86', *BIES* 24(1), pp. 37–72

Sunindyo, S. (1992), 'Gender discourse and resistance: the state's T.V. film production in Indonesia 1987–1988', in *Culture and Society in New Order Indonesia*, V. Hooker (ed.), Oxford University Press, Singapore

Suratman and Guinness, P. (1977), 'The changing focus of transmigration', *BIES* 13(2), pp. 78–101

Suryadinata, Leo (1978), *Pribumi Indonesians: The Chinese Minority and China*, Heinemann, Singapore

——(1986), *Pribumi Indonesians: The Chinese Minority and China*, 2nd edn, Heinemann Asia, Singapore

——(1988), 'Chinese economic elites in Indonesia: a preliminary study', in *Changing Identities of the Southeast Asian Chinese*, J. Cushman and Wang Gungwu (eds), Hong Kong University Press, Hong Kong

——(1989), *Military Ascendancy and Political Culture: A Study of Indonesia's Golkar*, Ohio University, Monographs in International Studies, Southeast Asia series no. 85, Athens, Ohio

Suryakusuma, J.I. (1991), 'Seksualitas dalam pengaturan negara' (Sexuality and state organisation), *Prisma* 20(7), pp. 70–83

Sutton, R.A. (1985a), 'Commercial cassette recordings of traditional music in Java: implications for performers and scholars', *The World of Music* 27(3), pp. 23–43

——(1985b), 'Musical pluralism in Java: three local traditions', *Ethnomusicology* 29(1), pp. 56–85

——(1988), 'East Javanese gamelan tradition', School of Music, Working Paper no. 18, University of Wisconsin, Madison,

Syamsuddin Haris (1990), 'PPP and politics under the New Order', *Prisma* 49, pp. 31–51

Sylado, R. (1977), 'Musik pop Indonesia: satu kebebalan Sang Mengapa' (Indonesian pop music: the triviality of 'Why, oh Why?'), *Prisma* 6, pp. 23–31

Tabor, S.R. (1992), 'Agriculture in transition', in *The Oil Boom and After: Indonesian Economic Policy and Performance in the Soeharto Era*, A. Booth (ed.), Oxford University Press, Singapore, pp. 161–203

Tamba, J.L. and Nishimura, H. (1988), 'Agricultural development', in *Indonesian Economic Development: Issues and Analysis*, S. Ichimura (ed.), Japanese International Cooperation Agency, Tokyo, pp. 62–78

Tan, Mely G. (1991), 'The social and cultural dimensions of the role of ethnic Chinese in Indonesian society', *Indonesia* (Special Issue on The Role of the Indonesian Chinese in Shaping Modern Indonesian Life), pp. 113–26

Tanter, R. and Young, K. (eds) (1990), 'The politics of middle class Indonesia',

Centre for Southeast Asian Studies, Monash Papers on Southeast Asia no. 19, Monash University, Clayton

Tarrant, J. et al. (1987), *Natural Resources and Environmental Management in Indonesia: An Overview*, USAID, Jakarta

Taylor, J.G. (1991), *Indonesia's Forgotten War*, Zed Press, London, pp. 327–50

Thee Kian Wie (1984), 'Japanese direct investment in Indonesian manufacturing', *BIES* 20(2), pp. 90–106

——(1988), *Industrialisasi Indonesia: Analisis dan Catatan Kritis* (Industrialisation in Indonesia: Analysis and Critical Notes), Pustaka Sinar Harapan, Jakarta

——(1990), 'Indonesia: technology transfer in the manufacturing industry', in *Technological Challenge in the Pacific*, H. Soesastro and M. Pangestu (eds), Allen & Unwin, Sydney, pp. 200–32

——(1991), 'The surge of Asian NIC investment into Indonesia', *BIES* 27(3), pp. 55–89

Thee Kian Wie and Yoshihara Kunio (1987), 'Foreign and domestic capital in Indonesian industrialization', *Southeast Asian Studies* 24(4), pp. 327–49

Tickell, P. (1976), 'Style and language in Arifin C. Noer's Kapai-Kapai', BA Honours thesis, Department of Indonesian and Malay, Monash University, Clayton

——(1986), 'Subversion or escapism: the fantastic in recent Indonesian fiction', *Review of Indonesian and Malayan Affairs* 20(1), pp. 50–67

Timmer, C.P. (1973), 'Choice of technique in rice milling in Java', *BIES* 9(2), pp. 57–76

——(1974), 'Reply' (to Collier et al., 1974), *BIES* 10(1), pp. 121–6

——(1975), 'The political economy of rice in Asia: Indonesia', *Food Research Institute Studies* 14(3), pp. 197–231

——(ed.) (1987), *The Corn Economy of Indonesia*, Cornell University Press, Ithaca

——(1989), 'Food price policy in Indonesia', in *Food Price Policy in Asia*, T. Sicular (ed.), Cornell University Press, Ithaca

——(1991), 'Food price stabilization: rationale, design, and implementation', in *Reforming Economic Systems in Developing Countries*, D.H. Perkins and M. Roemer (eds), Harvard Studies in International Development, Harvard Institute for International Development, Boston, pp. 219–48

Titus, M. (1978), 'Inter-regional migration in Indonesia as a reflection of social and economic activities', *Tijdschrift voor Economische en Sociale Geografie* 62(4), pp. 194–204

Tjondronegoro, S.M.P. (1991a), 'Probing into resettlement and relocation problems with varying degrees of administrative compulsion', Paper presented at the GOI–IBRD Seminar on Resettlement, Planning and Implementation, Jakarta, June

——(1991b), 'The utilization and management of land resources in Indonesia 1970–1990', in *Indonesia: Resources, Ecology, and Environment*, J. Hardjono (ed.), Oxford University Press, Singapore, pp. 17–35

Toeti Heraty (1974), *Sajak 33*, Jakarta

——(1989), 'Dalam bahasa, wanita pun tersudut' (In language, women too are marginalised), *Prisma* 1

Tomich, T.P. (1991), 'Smallholder rubber development in Indonesia', in *Reforming*

Economic Systems in Developing Countries, D.H. Perkins and M. Roemer (eds), Harvard Studies in International Development, Harvard Institute for International Development, Boston, pp. 249–70

Tsurumi, Y. (1980), 'Japanese investments in Indonesia: ownership, technology transfer, and political conflict, in *The Indonesian Economy*, G.F. Papanek (ed.), Praeger, New York, pp. 295–323

Umar Kayam (1975), *Sri Sumarah dan Bawuk* (Sri Sumarah and Bawuk), Pustaka Jaya, Jakarta

——(1981), *Seni, Tradisi, Masyarakat* (Art, Tradition, Society), Pustaka Jaya, Jakarta

United Nations (1989), *World Population Prospects 1988*, Department of International Economic and Social Affairs, United Nations, New York

——(1991), *World Population Prospects 1990*, Department of International Economic and Social Affairs, United Nations, New York

Uppal, J.S. (1986), *Taxation in Indonesia,* Gadjah Mada University Press, Yogyakarta

Uppal, J.S. and Budiono Sri Handoko (1986), 'Regional income disparities in Indonesia', *Ekonomi dan Keuangan Indonesia* 34(3), pp. 287–304

van Bruinessen, M. (1990), 'Indonesia's ulama and politics: caught between legitimising the status quo and searching for alternatives', *Prisma* 49, pp. 52–69

van Groenendael, V.M. Clara (1985), *The Dalang Behind the Wayang*, Foris Publications, Dordrecht, Holland; Cinnaminson, USA

van Langenberg, M. (1990), 'The New Order state: language, ideology, hegemony', in *State and Civil Society in Indonesia*, Arief Budiman (ed.), Centre for Southeast Asian Studies, Monash University, Clayton, pp. 121–49

van Leeuwen, R. (1975), 'Central government subsidies for regional development', *BIES* 11(1), pp. 66–75

Vannucci, M. (1988), 'The UNEP/UNESCO mangrove programme in Asia and the Pacific', *Ambio* 17(3), pp. 214–17

Vickers, A. (1989a), *Bali: A Paradise Created*, Penguin, Ringwood

——(1989b), 'Who authorizes Balinese culture?', Paper prepared for the workshop on Contesting Cultural Symbols in Southeast Asia, Research School of Pacific Studies, Australian National University, Canberra, November

Volkman, T. (1984), 'Great performances: Toraja cultural identity in the 1970s', *American Ethnologist* 11(1), pp. 152–69

——(1985), *Feast of Honour: Ritual and Change in the Toraja Highlands*, University of Illinois Press, Urbana and Chicago

Ward, K. (1974), 'The 1971 election in Indonesia: an East Java case study', Centre for Southeast Asian Studies, Monash Papers on Southeast Asia no. 2, Monash University, Clayton

Wardhana, Ali (1989), 'Structural adjustment in Indonesia: export and the "high cost" economy', *Indonesia Quarterly* 27(3), pp. 207–17

Warr, P. G. (1984), 'Exchange rate protection in Indonesia', *BIES* 20(2), pp. 53–89

——(1986), 'Indonesia's other Dutch Disease: economic effects of the petroleum boom', in J.P. Neary and S. van Wijnbergen (eds), *Natural Resources and the Macroeconomy*, Basil Blackwell, Oxford, pp. 288–320

Bibliography

——(1992), 'Exchange rate policy, petroleum prices, and the balance of payments, in A. Booth (ed.), *The Oil Boom and After: Indonesian Economic Policy and Performance in the Soeharto Era*, Oxford University Press, Singapore, pp. 132–58

Warren, C. (1986), 'Indonesian development policy and community organization in Bali', *Contemporary Southeast Asia* 8(3), pp. 213–30

——(1989), 'Balinese political culture and the rhetoric of national development', in *Creating Indonesian Culture*, P. Alexander (ed.), Oceania Publications, Sydney, pp. 39–54

Warwick, D.P. (1978), 'The integration of population policy into development planning: a progress report', Development Discussion Paper no. 49, Harvard Institute for International Development, Cambridge

——(1986), 'The Indonesian family planning program: government influence and client choice', *Population and Development Review* 12(3), pp. 453–90

Webb, A.J. et al. (eds) (1990), *Estimates of Producer and Consumer Subsidy Equivalents: Government Intervention in Agriculture 1982–87*, US Department of Agriculture, Statistical Bulletin 803, Washington DC

Weinstein, F.B. (1976), 'Multinational corporations and the Third World: the case of Japan and Southeast Asia', *International Organization* 30(3), pp. 373–404

Wells, L.T. Jr (1973), 'Economic man and engineering man: choice of technology in a low-wage country', *Public Policy* 21(3), pp. 319–42

Wertheim, W.F. (1977), 'From aliran towards class struggle in the countryside of Java', in *Friends, Followers and Factions*, S. Schmidt et al. (eds), University of California Press, Berkeley, pp. 458–67

White, B. (1983), ' "Agricultural involution" and its critics: twenty years after', *Bulletin of Concerned Asian Scholars* 15(2), pp. 18–31

——(1989), 'Java's green revolution in long-term perspective', *Prisma* 48, pp. 66–81

Whitten, A.J., Damanik, S.J., Anwar J. and Hisyam, N. (1984), *The Ecology of Sumatra*, second edn, Gadjah Mada University Press, Yogyakarta

Whitten, A.J., Mustafa, M. and Henderson, G.S. (1987), *The Ecology of Sulawesi*, Gadjah Mada University Press, Yogyakarta

Widarti, D. (1984), 'Hubungan antara sektor informal dan sektor service di kota' (Relationship between the informal sector and the service sector in urban areas), in *Angkatan Kerja di Indonesia, Partisipasi, Kesempatan dan Pengangguran* (The Indonesian Labour Force, Participation, Opportunities and Unemployment) C. Manning and Z. Bakir (eds), Population Studies Centre, Gadjah Mada University, Yogyakarta

Widodo, A. (1991), 'Panggung-Panggung negara: kesenian rakyat dan ritus-ritus hegemonisasi' (The state and the stage: popular art and rites of hegemonisation), Paper delivered at Satya Wacana University, Salatiga

Wirakartakusumah, M.D. (1989), 'Menjelang sensus penduduk 1990, pemanfaatan data bagi pemerintah dan swasta' (Approaching the 1990 population census, data, usefulness for government and the private sector), *Warta Demografi* 19(2) pp. 1–4

Wirosardjono, S. (1985), 'Pengertian, batasan dan masalah sektor informal' (The meaning, limits and problems of the informal sector), *Prisma* 3, pp. 3–10

Wolf, D. (1984), 'Making the bread and bringing it home: female factory workers and the family economy in rural Java', in *Women in the Urban and Industrial Workforce*, G.W. Jones (ed.), Australian National University, Canberra, pp. 215–31

——(1986), 'The rural development of modern manufacturing: a case-study from Central Java', in *Central Government and Local Development in Indonesia*, C. MacAndrews (ed.), Oxford University Press, Singapore, pp. 132–55

——(1990), 'Daughters, decisions and domination: an empirical and conceptual critique of household strategies', *Development and Change* 21(1), pp. 43–74

Woo, W.T. and Nasution, A. (1989), 'Indonesian economic policies and their relation to external debt management', in *Developing Country Debt and Economic Performance*, J.D. Sachs and S.M. Collins (eds), vol. 3, University of Chicago Press for the NBER, Chicago, pp. 17–149

World Bank (1980), *Indonesia: Appraisal of the Nucleus Estate and Smallholders IV Project*, Projects Department, East Asia and Pacific Regional Office, Washington DC

——(1981), *Indonesia: Selected Issues of Industrial Development and Trade Strategy, Annex 2—The Foreign Trade Regime*, Washington DC

——(1988), *Indonesia: The Transmigration Program in Perspective*, Washington DC

——(1989), *Renewable Resource Management in Agriculture*, Operations Evaluation Department, Washington DC

——(1990a), *Indonesia: Sustainable Development of Forests, Land, and Water*, Washington DC

——(1990b), *Indonesia: Poverty Assessment and Strategy Report*, Washington DC

Yampolsky, P. (1989), '*Hati Yang Luka*, an Indonesian hit', *Indonesia* 47, pp. 1–17

Yoshihara, K. (1988), *The Rise of Ersatz Capitalism in Southeast Asia*, Oxford University Press, Singapore

Young, K. (1986), 'Transformation or temporary respite? Agricultural growth, industrialisation and the modernisation of Java', *Review of Indonesian and Malayan Affairs* 22, pp. 114–32

——(1990), 'Middle bureaucrats, middle peasants, middle class? The extra-urban dimension', in R. Tanter and K. Young (eds), *The Politics of Middle Class Indonesia*, Centre for Southeast Asian Studies, Monash Papers on Southeast Asia no. 19, Monash University, Clayton, pp. 147–66

Zamakhasari Dhofier (1989), 'Pesantren and the Nahdatul Ulama in the New Order', Paper presented at a conference on Indonesia's New Order, Australian National University, Canberra, December

Zarsky, L. (1991), *Trade–Environment Linkages and Sustainable Development*, Nautilus Pacific Research, North Fitzroy

Zirfirdaus Adnan (1990), 'Islamic religion: Yes, Islamic (political) ideology: No! Islam and the state in Indonesia', in *State and Civil Society in Indonesia*, Arief Budiman (ed.), Centre for Southeast Asian Studies, Monash University, Clayton, pp. 441–7

Zumrotin K. Susilo (1989), 'The women's movement under the New Order', unpublished paper presented at a conference on Indonesia's New Order, Australian National University, Canberra, December

Author Index

Author Index

Subject Index

control over, 209; *see also* degradation (natural resources); forests; water resources
neighbourhoods, *see* local neighbourhoods
Netherlands, 50
New Order: origins of, xxiii, 10–11, 48; assessment of, xxii–xxiii, 44–8
newspapers, 220, 238, 241, 244, 245–6, 257–8, 266, 269, 272; *Bisnis Indonesia*, 257; *Jawa Pos*, 258, 266; *Kompas*, 222, 246, 257, 258, 266; *Media Indonesia*, 258; *Monitor*, 258; *Sinar Harapan, Suara Pembaruan*, 222, 257
Ngaju Dayak people, religion, 297
NGOs, 4, 9, 28, 299
NIEs, 82, 104–5, 115
Nigeria, 57–60, 116
Noer, Arifin C., 223, 225, 264
non-alignment, 42, 43, 44
North Sulawesi: economic structure and development, 109, 112; education, 161; family planning xxvi; fertility decline, 135–6; land degradation, 182; smallholder coconuts, 204
North Sumatra: economic structure and development, 109; fertility decline, xxxi; land degradation, 182; smallholder rubber, 205; *see also* Batak people
Northeast Asia, 164–5
NU, 18, 31–2, 298
nuclear power, 180, 200
Nusa Tenggara,

economic strucure and development, 108, 109, 112; drought, 180; *lamtoro* in, 213; land degradation, 205; natural resources, 179; poverty and underdevelopment, 108–9; *see also* East Nusa Tenggara; West Nusa Tenggara
nutrition levels, xxiv, 184

OECD countries, 118
oil and gas sector, 64, 68, 78, 80, 83, 108, 109, 112, 114; reserves, xxxii, 199
oil boom, xxviii, xxxi, 2, 6, 9, 14, 22, 43, 55, 63, 66, 68, 70, 76, 77, 80, 82, 87, 89–90, 93, 95, 96, 98, 100, 101, 102, 109, 112, 113, 120, 145, 156
oil revenues, xxvii, xxx, xxxi, 5, 11–12, 16, 17, 37, 38, 164, 239; declining, xxx, xxxi, 55, 56, 60, 63, 70, 76, 80, 87, 91, 93, 100, 101, 102, 104, 115, 185
Old Order, xxiv, xxix, 1, 5, 8, 10–11, 12, 45, 48, 50, 216, 222, 229, 235, 236, 239; *see also* Sukarno
Oman, 114
OPEC, 55, 57–60; production quotas, 61, 98
openness, xix, xxix

P4 program, 9, 15, 26, 52, 272
painting, *see* visual arts
Palapa satellite, 239, 258, 284
palawija cultivation, 75, 117, 277; expansion, 183–4, 191;

competition from sugar, 192
Palembang, pollution in, 206, 212
palm oil production, 72, 74, 75, 76, 204
Pamong praja, 20, 22
Pancasila, 15, 18, 23, 26–7, 31, 45, 50, 52, 271–2, 276, 295, 300, 302, 303, 304
Panggabean, Maraden, 48
Panglaykim, Dr J., 66
Paraguay, 114
'pariah capitalists' and 'pariah entrepreneurs', 33, 41, 53
Parisada Hindu Dharma, 296, 297, 298
parliament, *see* DPR
'patrimonialism', 6, 9, 14, 16, 45, 46
patron–client relations, 7, 41–2, 288
PDI, 12, 13
peanut cultivation, 75, 183
Pelni, 116
pepper cultivation, 203, 210
peranakan, 34
Pertamina, xxxi, 8, 14, 36, 37, 50, 63, 69, 70, 90, 100, 114, 116, 120
pest management, integrated, 191
pesticides, 190–1, 276, 277, 288; ban, 191; impact on aquaculture, 193; subsidies, 75, 97, 117, 190, 191
Petisi 50, 15–16, 25
petro-chemical industry, 83
petroleum, *see* oil and gas sector
petty manufacturing, *see* manufacturing
petty trading, *see* trading, small-scale
pharmaceutical industry, 83

Philippines, 33, 47, 57–60, 121, 140, 147, 174–5, 212, 250, 265
plantations, 72, 73, 74, 75, 76, 184–5, 203–4; nationalisation, 184–5; neglect, 184, 204; rehabilitation, 185, 204; squatters, 185; usage rights, 185
PKI, xxii, 3, 9, 10, 11, 31, 42, 47, 49, 50, 51, 52, 127, 220, 230
PLN, 116
plywood industry, 76, 81, 83, 104, 211
PNI, 8, 10, 49, 229, 230, 235
political parties, 4, 8, 9, 12–13, 20, 21, 23, 297; *see also* Golkar; NU; PDI; PKI; PNI; PPP
political prisoners, 247–8
political system (New Order): character, xix-xx, xxx, 2–3, 4–7; evolution of power structure, 7–19; institutions, xxviii-xxix, 19–23; origins, 10–14; narrowing of base, 14–17; Soeharto's control over, 17–18; *see also* armed forces; elections; ideology; Islam; political parties; Soeharto
political theory, 4–7
political system (New
pollution: chemical, 193, 194, 198; of fisheries, 193, 194, 215; industrial, 193, 194, 198, 199, 215; of rivers, 199, 206, 212, 215, 292; urban waste, 198, 199, 215; of water, 197–8
Ponorogo, 251
popular culture, *see* film;

music; literature; television
population: growth rate, xix, xxvi, xxxii, 123, 124, 125, 126, 128, 129, 131, 143; impact on environment and natural resources, xxxii, 180–1, 183, 189, 199, 200, 201; policy, 123, 124, 126–9, 130, 138, 144–5; projections, xxvi-xxvii, xxxii, 143–5; size, 124, 125, 143, 145
Population and Environment, Ministry of, 130, 198, 214
population mobility, increasing level of, xxvii, 30, 284–5, 290
Portuguese colonialism, 43–4, 298
poultry industry, 77
poverty, 105–7, 108–9; alleviation, xix, xxxi, 55, 56, 57, 67, 105, 106, 121; and film, 242; regional patterns, xxviii, 108–9, 112; in rural Java, 287–8; in transmigration settlements, 285
poverty lines, xix, 105, 107
PPP, 9, 12, 13, 15, 18, 31–2, 243, 298
Pramudya Ananta Tur, 219, 248, 260
presidency, xxix, 18, 19
press, xxix, xxx, xxxiii, 8, 12, 15, 16, 26, 28, 29, 36, 51–2, 218; *see also* newspapers; publishing industry
Pribumi and non-*Pribumi*, 33, 67, 69, 115
private enterprise, xxv, xxvi, xxxi, 2, 8, 9, 17, 18–19, 35, 36, 37, 38,

39–42, 47, 63, 83, 93; and arts sponsorship, xxvi, xxxiv, 245, 256–7; and the film industry, 240; and mass media, 244, 257–8, 263; political importance of, 40–2; status of, 39–40; *see also* capitalism; Chinese business; conglomerates
privatisation, 68–9
priyayi, 48, 49, 286
proletariat, development of, 290–1
prostitution, 283, 286
protectionism: in agriculture, 78, 118; in industry, 70, 80
provincial government, *see* regional government and administration
public administration (services), *see* services
publishing industry, 217, 221, 222, 238, 240–1, 257–8; Balai Pustaka, 222; Grafitipers, 222, 257, 258; Gramedia, 222, 246, 257, 258; Pustaka Jaya, 222; Sinar Kasih, 222; Surya Persindo, 258, 266; *see also* magazines; newspapers; press
pulp and paper industry, 81, 83, 211, 213
Puncak, 200

quarrying, environmental impact, 197

radio, xxxiv, 29, 217, 239, 241, 254–5, 257, 262, 263, 271; RRI and *wayang*, 231, 236; RRI and *kethoprak*, 233, 253
randai, 265

221, 244; and family
planning, 128–9
sago palm, 203
Sakernas, 149, 153
Salu Mambi people,
traditional religion of,
302
Samarinda, 210
sand, excavation of, 189,
194
Sani, Asrul, 223, 240
santri, 31, 32, 48, 52
Sapardi, Djoko Darmono,
223
Sardono W. Kusumo, 223
Sarwo Edhie, 25, 51
Sastra kontekstual, 224,
249
Sastrowardojo, Soebagio,
223, 224
sawah, see rice
'Sawito affair', 50
secondary food crops,
see palawija
security and intelligence,
13, 23–4, 26, 51
sedimentation, 180; in
Java, xxxiii, 183,
189–90; in other
islands, 201, 205–6,
212
Semarang: factory
employment of
women, 291; flooding,
200; pollution, 215;
wayang orang in, 233,
237, 253
Senayan sports stadium,
245
Senen, Gedung Kesenian,
245
services sector, xxviii,
60, 61, 62, 64, 65,
84–7, 105, 290, 293,
115; government,
xxviii, 84, 85, 92–3,
120; public
administration, 84, 85;
trade, 84, 85; see also
banking; labour force
share-cropping, 288
shipbuilding, 81

shifting cultivation,
xxxiii, 201, 202–3,
209, 268; government
policy on, 202; impact
on natural resources,
202; modified form of,
202–3; resettlement
programs, 202; and
tidal-rice cultivation;
traditional form of,
202–3
shrimp production, *see*
aquaculture
Siahaan, Semsar, 248
Simatupang, Iwan, 224
Singapore, 28, 43, 47,
105
Slamet Rahardjo, 266
slash and burn
cultivation, *see*
shifting cultivation
smallholder cultivation,
72, 73, 74, 75, 76, 77,
183, 203–5; expansion,
156, 160, 185, 201,
204, 205; impact of
markets upon, 203–4;
development projects,
205; nucleus estate
scheme, 156, 205
social control
mechanisms, xxiii,
xxxiii, 1, 9, 22, 25–9,
47, 52, 280
Social Welfare,
Department of, 261
social welfare policy, 123
Soedjono Humardhani, 25
Soeharto: xxix, 54, 75,
230–1; assessment of
his regime, xxii–xxiii,
1–4, 44–8; *Bapak
Pembangunan*, 269;
and 'the cooperative
principle', 27, 40;
economic policy, xxx,
35, 38, 40; family
business interests, 3, 4,
13, 18, 22, 34, 38, 39,
46, 47, 50, 51, 69, 71,
117; as 'father' of the
nation, 272; and

family planning, xxxi,
124, 127–8, 129, 132,
144, 231; and Islam,
xxx, xxxv, 31–2, 298;
and MPR–DPR,
19–20; personal
authority of, xxx, 4, 6,
8–9, 14, 16, 17–18,
45; personality of,
xxix, xxx, 45–6, 53;
place in New Order
power structure, 7–9;
relations with ABRI,
xxx, 4, 8, 18, 20,
24–5, 48, 51; role in
New Order origins,
10–12, 48, 49; student
demonstrations against,
14, 15
Soeharto, Dr R., 127
soil conservation, 181,
187, 188, 209
soil fertility, declining:
Java uplands, xxxiii,
184, 188; other
islands, 201, 205, 208;
in shifting cultivation,
202, 203
Solo: anti-Chinese riots
in, 287; *gamelan* in,
255; *kethoprak* in,
253, 256, 266; modern
theatre in, 249–50;
pop music in, 262;
regional arts centre,
222; *wayang orang* in,
233, 237, 238, 253
Soroako, impact of
mining, 292–3
South Kalimantan:
banjar sunatan ritual,
279; tidal-rice
cultivation, 208
South Korea, 3, 36, 47,
114, 118, 121, 174–5
South Sulawesi:
aquaculture, 192;
education, 161;
erosion, 206; mining,
292–3; regional
rebellion, 269; *see*